Snow from Broken Eyes

*Australisch-
Neuseeländische Studien
zur deutschen Sprache
und Literatur*

*Australian and
New Zealand Studies
in German Language
and Literature*

*Etudes parues en
Australie et Nouvelle-
Zélande en relation avec
la philologie allemande*

Vol. 20

*founded by
Gerhard Schulz
and John Asher †*

*edited by
Gerhard Schulz (Melbourne)*

Richard Millington

Snow from Broken Eyes

Cocaine in the Lives and Works of Three Expressionist Poets

PETER LANG
Bern · Berlin · Bruxelles · Frankfurt am Main · New York · Oxford · Wien

Bibliographic information published by die Deutsche Nationalbibliothek
Die Deutsche Nationalbibliothek lists this publication in the Deutsche Nationalbibliografie; detailed bibliographic data is available on the Internet at ‹http://dnb.d-nb.de›.

British Library Cataloguing-in-Publication Data: A catalogue record for this book is available from The British Library, Great Britain

Library of Congress Cataloging-in-Publication Data

Millington, Richard H.
Snow from broken eyes : cocaine in the lives and works of three expressionist poets / Richard Millington.
p. cm. – (Australisch-Neuseeländische Studien zur deutschen Sprache und Literatur ISSN 0171-6867 ; v. 20)
Includes bibliographical references and index.
ISBN 978-3-0343-1069-7
1. German poetry–20th century–History and criticism. 2. Cocaine abuse in literature. 3. Expressionism–Germany. 4. Benn, Gottfried, 1886-1956–Drug use. 5. Rheiner, Walter, 1895-1925–Drug use. 6. Trakl, Georg, 1887-1914–Drug use. 7. Poets, German–20th century. I. Title.
PT553.M55 2012
831'.912093556–dc23
2011042103

ISBN 978-3-0343-1069-7
ISSN 0171-6867

Hochfeldstrasse 32, CH-3012 Bern, Switzerland
info@peterlang.com, www.peterlang.com

Printed in Switzerland

Contents

For the listener, who listens in the snow,
And, nothing himself, beholds
Nothing that is not there and the nothing that is.
– Wallace Stevens, 'The Snow Man'

1 Introduction

1.1 'Snow from Broken Eyes'

The image 'snow from broken eyes' – 'Schnee aus brochenen [sic] Augen' in the original German (Trakl *SW* 2:283–286) – has been chosen as the title for the present study because it captures, with supreme concision, several essential facets of its principal object: the relationship between a set of literary texts composed by three Expressionist poets on the one hand, and the psychoactive drug cocaine on the other. The image is taken from the poem 'Rosiger Spiegel: ein häßliches Bild,' written by the Austrian poet Georg Trakl between December 1912 and February 1913 (the full text is quoted and discussed in 10.2). Although the austerity and subtlety of Trakl's poetic style sets it apart from the stridency typical of Expressionism, and although the poet himself had no serious association with the movement's various programmatic forms, his image of 'snow from broken eyes' is quintessentially Expressionist in its combination of the destructive and surreal, and displays his affinity with the artistic and literary movement that dominated the German cultural scene throughout the second decade of the 20th century.

For this study it is significant that Trakl's image – and the poem 'Rosiger Spiegel' as a whole – conveys a perspective of the world and the self distinct from the perspective of normal, sober consciousness, and consistent rather in several fundamental respects with the condition of intoxication, in particular as associated with the use and abuse of psychoactive substances. The most obvious parallel is the painful bodily destruction leading to death evoked in the collocation 'broken eyes,' in so far as physiological damage is one inevitable consequence of excessive or prolonged drug taking; the allusion to death is conveyed by means of play on the German phrase 'seine Augen brechen,' used to refer to the glazing over of eyes at the moment of death. Further, we might also note that these 'eyes' are unmodified by any possessive adjective or other determiner that would indicate their owner, and so appear strangely detached and autonomous, as body parts frequently do in the intoxicated consciousness of the drug user. Further, and perhaps most importantly, Trakl's image is imbued with the ontological amorphousness characteristic of the drugged perspective. The perception of snow emanating – or 'crying', which is the verb used in 'Rosiger Spiegel' – from eyes, whether broken or whole, alive or dead, fits most uneasily with the range of perceptions that can normally be made in the world outside this text. Is the reader, therefore, to understand this perception as imaginary, or perhaps hallucinatory? If so, we must then ask which elements – the snow, the eyes, their brokenness (or glazing), the 'crying' of the snow 'from' the eyes – are imaginary or hallucinatory, and which are real. But the poem offers no indications as to where this line should be drawn. The reader might be tempted to avoid this interpretative dilemma by adopting a different strategy and assuming that Trakl's image, in whole or in part, is not in fact an account of perceptual or imaginary experience, but a metaphorical expression of something else. Here, however, new difficulties arise, for the boundary between literal and metaphorical meaning is no more evident than that between perception and hallucination. A figurative interpretation of 'brochenen' as 'dead', for example, in no way precludes the literal interpretation 'broken'; it merely complicates the matter further by adding another layer of possible meaning,[1] while it is hardly clear what meaning could be attributed to any other metaphor that might be present. As a result, Trakl's image remains suspended between imaginary and real, literal and figurative dimensions, and appears loaded with possible meanings in all of them. It takes on the same quality of amplified semantic potential that objects, people, thoughts, and dreams typically assume in the intoxicated mind of the drug user. As Henri

1 Trakl's play on the literal and figurative dimensions of the phrase 'seine Augen brechen' has a precedent in the work of another renowned Expressionist, Georg Heym. The penultimate stanza of Heym's poem 'Umbra Vitae' (1911) reads:

> Wer stirbt, der setzt sich auf, sich zu erheben,
> Und eben hat er noch ein Wort gesprochen,
> Auf einmal ist er fort. Wo ist sein Leben?
> Und seine Augen sind wie Glas zerbrochen. (Pinthus 40)

Trakl's usage, in which neither meaning is fully activated or deactivated, is stylistically more radical than Heym's, in which the figurative meaning is activated unambiguously by the description of death that precedes it.

Michaux observed of one of his mescaline trips, 'everything tingles with possibilities' (Plant 146).

The various intoxicated features concentrated in this image may induce the suspicion that Trakl's 'snow' represents an allusion to cocaine, that is, an agent of intoxication. Clearly such a reference would have to be posited on a secondary and figurative level of meaning, for it is no more credible that cocaine should literally 'cry from broken eyes' than snow in its primary sense of 'flakes of ice crystals.' Yet even an indirect or enciphered reference of this sort would cohere with and reinforce the subtextual intoxication motif already identified. At this stage the reader might question the historical legitimacy of such a reading, for although the German *Schnee*, like its equivalents in English and many other languages, is today among the most widely used and recognizable of the numerous epithets for the white, crystalline powder of cocaine, this metaphorical association was surely less familiar, perhaps even unborn, when this poem was written. Indeed, Douglas Harper's *Online Etymology Dictionary* informs us that the first attested use of 'snow' for 'cocaine' dates from 1914, at least one year after the composition of 'Rosiger Spiegel.' This information, however, far from settling the question, makes it all the more intriguing, for when we consider the etymologists' warning that such dates must be taken as purely indicative (due to the impossibility of accounting for the vast quantity of unrecorded language use or the time that may have passed before a new word or meaning appears in written form), this dating demonstrates that 'snow' acquired its codified metaphorical association with cocaine in the same period in which Trakl was poetically active.[2] Of broader relevance here, this was also the high point of the Expressionist period, which coincided not only with the beginning of the First World War, the social and political upheavals resulting from which were partly foreshadowed in the works of Expressionism's

2 One of the few German dictionaries to comment on the etymology of *Schnee* as an epithet for cocaine is Heinz Küpper's *Wörterbuch der deutschen Umgangssprache* (1970). Küpper dates the emergence of this usage to post-World War One, when it became widespread. But this etymology is approximate, and Küpper's main concern is to underline that its origin is not more recent: 'Den heutigen Halbwüchsigen eine sehr geläufige Vokabel; aber nicht von ihnen aufgebracht und wahrscheinlich kurz nach 1918 in Berlin aufgekommen' (6:283). Note also that nasal inhalation is documented as having become a popular mode of administration of the drug in the years 1912–14 (Maier 64); the emergence of the epithet 'snow' would logically have coincided with the increased distribution of the drug in powder form resulting from this development.

early exponents, but also with the beginning of cocaine's first wave of large-scale popularity, which would peak a decade later in the hedonistic excesses of the 'Golden Twenties.' Furthermore, even if it were demonstrable that at the time of writing 'Rosiger Spiegel' Trakl himself could not have been aware of a possible cocaine connotation in this snow image, to exclude a reference to the drug on this basis alone would amount to an arbitrary and – for Trakl – un-poetic conflation of meaning with authorial intention. As we shall see in part 3, not only 'Rosiger Spiegel' but Trakl's poetry as a whole is particularly resistant to reductive interpretations of this or any other kind.

For now, suffice it to note that one of the chief reasons the image of 'snow from broken eyes' can be considered representative of the text–drug relationship under examination here is, curiously, that its reference to cocaine is essentially indeterminate and elusive. Elusiveness is a theme that will be met with repeatedly in this study, and as we shall have several occasions to observe, the uncertainty it produces often has the paradoxical effect of reinforcing the text–drug relationship by investing it with the force and fascination of mystery. Even in works that contain an unambiguous reference to the drug in the form of the word *Kokain* – these represent approximately half of those discussed – the same elusiveness invariably manifests itself in other aspects of the relationship, such as the drug's role in the syntactic, sonic and thematic structures of the text, or the link between the drug in the text and the drug experience of its writer, especially with regard to the confessional impulse that seems masked in certain works, such as Walter Rheiner's 1918 novella *Kokain*, while assuming a suspiciously exaggerated prominence in others, for example in Gottfried Benn's 1916 poem 'O Nacht.' Significantly, ambivalence, intangibility and elusiveness are features that permeate not only these texts, but also many if not most aspects of drug taking as a whole. This can in part be attributed to the illegality and stigma connected with the production, distribution, and consumption of so many psychoactive drugs, cocaine included. But this connection is preceded, both historically and causally, by a more fundamental link between drug use and transcendental experience that can never be fully assimilated to the conventional categories and codes of sober consciousness or rational thought. In written accounts of drug use, this transcendental aspect often finds expression in the disruption or subversion of these categories and codes, in what amounts to a form of *textual intoxication* that manifests itself, for example, in lexical idiosyncrasies, syntactic or semantic ambiguities, paradoxes, ellipses, or conceptual discontinuity. In certain texts, especially of the literary variety and including several of those that will be discussed in this study, such textual intoxication may represent the most solid link between the work and the writer's drug experience, particularly in the absence of direct references to drugs themselves; in this respect too, Trakl's 'snow from broken eyes' is illustrative. Crucially, however, for the reader it is impossible to determine whether such features result from the influence of an external agent, such as a psychoactive drug, or are cultivated by the writer as stylistic devices – or some combination of the two. For this reason we must be careful not to use the text as a basis for rash assumptions about the writer's methods or the influence of his drug use on his creativity. Here also, elusiveness remains the keynote.

Indeterminacies of this sort add complexity to our investigation and also broaden its relevance, for they extend its ramifications beyond the purely historical problem of establishing which Expressionist writers used cocaine and what literature they produced while using it, knowledge in itself of marginal value for enhancing our appreciation of the writers' works. We will be faced, rather, with a series of more fundamental questions concerning the 'multiform interpenetration' of text and world (Jakobson 320), the purpose and possibilities of poetic expression, and the place of Expressionism both as heir to the Romantic tradition and the first full-blown manifestation of literary Modernism. In particular, we will examine what the treatment of the drug and cocaine motifs in each work reveals about the text's aesthetic and communicative strategies, and how this treatment coheres with other aspects of the work – its themes, form, and style. A more specific consideration will be how each text manipulates, via enhancement or containment, the elusive qualities central to the experience of transcendence-through-intoxication. Where this is enhanced via a poetic defamiliarization of the linguistic code, as it is in most of these works, we shall assess to what extent the text itself suggests a correspondence between poetic language and drugged consciousness as parallel manifestations of the transcendental. This study will also investigate how a text–drug relationship can be manifested in a given work even in the absence of explicit references to psychoactive substances, and further, the possibility of relating our knowledge of a writer's drug use to a reading of his works without reducing the literary text to a form of encrypted autobiography. Finally, we are interested in placing our findings in a broader context, identifying patterns and developments in the œuvre of each writer, highlighting significant similarities and differences between the three poets under discussion, as well as between their works and the drug-associated literature of other periods, in particular distinguishing elements that perpetuate the literary concerns of the Expressionists' 19th-century predecessors from those that represent innovations in the literary elaboration of the drug theme.

Considering the centrality to our topic of such features as opacity, indeterminacy and mystification, it will remain imperative throughout to ascertain what can be said with certainty about the role of cocaine in the lives and works of our three poets, and what on the other hand results from implication, deduction, or speculation. This is not to say that only certainties are valuable to our analysis; on the contrary, particular attention will be dedicated to the exploration of aspects – of both text and biography – that appear ambiguous or puzzling, as it is usually here that the key to an enriched response to the work lies. This circumstance makes it doubly important not to confuse assumption with fact. As a general methodological guideline, therefore, we shall adopt the French sociologist Edgar Morin's dictum that 'one must learn to sail through an ocean of uncertainties from one archipelago of certainty to the next.'[3] A similar consideration underlies the overall organization of this study, which is divided into three parts, each dealing with the life and works of one poet: Benn, Rheiner and Trakl. This order is unchronological and only coincidentally alphabetical. Its procedural basis is a decreasing level of explicitness, and inversely an increasing level of uncertainty, in the references to cocaine in each writer's works: the word *Kokain* appears in all four works by Benn analyzed in part 1, in three of the six that make up Rheiner's 'master narrative of addiction' traced in part 2, and in none of the seven by Trakl quoted in full (or the numerous others quoted in part) in part 3. To extend Morin's metaphor, this approach will allow us to take our bearings in an archipelago of relative certainty before confronting the rigours of the open sea. The first chapter in each part will investigate the nature and extent of the writer's own drug use and evaluate possible relationships between these biographical factors and the writer's literary activity (the greater space given to Rheiner reflecting an assumption of lesser familiarity with both his biography and his work), while the subsequent chapters will be concerned with close textual analysis, addressing questions such as those outlined in

3 'Il faut apprendre à naviguer dans un océan d'incertitudes à travers des archipels de certitude.'

the previous paragraph. With Rheiner and Trakl, the biographical perspective provided in the opening chapter will similarly serve as a relatively secure departure point for the textual exploration that follows; with Benn it will confirm that the certainty his explicit cocaine references seem to offer is only relative, or to stretch Morin's metaphor even further, that the islands in Benn's archipelago are separated by treacherous waters.

The following three sections of this introductory chapter represent the preliminary stages for the exploration contained in the three main parts of this study. Our first concerns will be to sketch a brief history of the association between psychoactive drugs and creative writing, and to draw from this an overview of cocaine's literary role in the periods before, during and after the Expressionist era. This will be followed by a summary and assessment of the critical material relevant to the topic, including studies concerned directly with the three writers in question and those that approach the drug–literature relationship more generically. In the last section of this chapter, on the basis of the observations made in the preceding ones, we will expand on the methodological considerations already delineated and propose an analytical system adapted to the conditions and parameters of this study, one that accounts for the complex interweaving of certainties and uncertainties, affirmations, ambiguities and evasions with which a critical investigation into the text–drug relationship must come to terms.

1.2 Drugs, Cocaine: A Condensed Literary History

We preface this necessarily abbreviated historical account with two terminological clarifications. First, throughout this study the word 'drug' is used broadly and inclusively – alcohol, tobacco and caffeine are drugs – and is considered interchangeable with the terms 'psychoactive substance' and 'intoxicant'. The intricacies of questions such as 'what is a drug?' or, just as pertinently, 'how does a particular substance come to be considered a drug?' have been dealt with elsewhere and will not be reiterated here in detail. In one such discussion that has gained particular currency among scholars in literary and cultural studies, Jacques Derrida's 'The Rhetoric of Drugs' (1989), the philosopher (via his translator Michael Israel) states that 'one can, of course, refer to alcohol or tobacco as "drugs", but this will necessarily imply a sort of irony, as if in doing so one only marked a sort of rhetorical displacement' (22). The inclusiveness of the definition offered here, however, neither implies any 'sort of irony,' nor is it intended to 'mark a rhetorical displacement.' This contradiction serves as a useful reminder that the degree of inclusiveness of the term is a significant semantic variable (making this note of clarification necessary), and that cognate terms in other languages may have broader or narrower semantic fields. The equally broad pharmaceutical sense of the term 'drug' as a synonym for 'medicament', as it is used chiefly in American English, also has some bearing, especially in so far as the substances it denotes overlap with those of the first definition. Historically, the widespread pharmaceutical use of cocaine extended to the period with which we are concerned here, and both Benn and Trakl, in their respective capacities as medical doctor and pharmacist, must have been actively involved in its medical application. In this connection, it is worth underlining the fundamental ambivalence of the word 'drug' as denoting substances that can have either harmful or beneficial effects, and often both at once, depending on the frequency and size of the dosage, the psychological and physiological condition of the user, his social and physical environment, etc. This ambivalence is shared by the Latin *venenum* and the Greek *pharmakon*, the latter having become something of an academic buzzword since the implications of its use by Plato as a metaphor for writing were scrutinized by Derrida in 'La Pharmacie de Platon' (1972).

The second clarification concerns terms used to denote literary movements and epochs such as Romanticism, Realism, Modernism and Expressionism, all of which have received book-length analyses. In this study they, too, are used broadly, in accordance with the following considerations made by Martin Seymour-Smith in his *Guide to Modern World Literature*:

> Our understanding of literature does not benefit from attempts to narrow down the meaning of terms too precisely: the terms themselves lose their value. They are very useful, but become abstract when allowed to dominate individual achievement. Literature is generated by men and women, not by movements. (xii)

In this respect it is significant that the subtitle of this study identifies 'the lives and works of three Expressionist poets,' rather than Expressionism itself, as the object of our investigation.[4] It is certainly legitimate and useful, as well as conventional, to link Benn, Trakl and Rheiner with Expressionism, and via Expressionism with each other, but it must also be emphasized that the works of the first two always transcend the movement's programmatic interests, while Rheiner's assumption of a zealously and polemically Expressionist position, alien to his own temperament, renders much of his verse – for today's reader – trivial and dated. His most interesting works, on the other hand, including those examined in chapter 6, are also his least Expressionist (the story 'Der Tod des Schwärmers Gautier Fémin' presents itself as a song of 'welcome' to Expressionism, but intriguingly comes to undermine its own precepts; see 6.2). Trakl never actively subscribed to any Expressionist doctrine; Benn declared his allegiance to the movement only *post factum* in his essay 'Bekenntnis zum Expressionismus' (*GW* 3:802–818) of November 1933, written in response to the Nazis' proclamation of Expressionism's – and Benn's own – 'degeneracy'; Rheiner, by contrast, participated in the foundation of the 'Expressionistische Arbeitsgemeinschaft Dresden' in 1917 and a year later became editor of the Dresden-based Expressionist journal *Menschen*. These differences confirm that, as Seymour-Smith remarks, 'the more considerable the gifts of those poets or writers now usually called expressionist, the more isolated or remote from the movement they tended to be' (571). They also explain why the Expressionist ethos, the movement's favourite forms and motifs, its historical development and its reception, its various currents and their most prominent representatives will be afforded much greater consideration in part two than in either parts one or three. That said, let us begin our history.

All primitive peoples, Friedrich Nietzsche tells us in *Die Geburt der Tragödie* (1872), speak of narcotic potions in their hymns (3:24). This observation has set the tone for more recent statements on the nebulous origins of the association between intoxicants and literature, with the cultural historians of drugs fond of reminding us that this association is as old as literature itself (Kupfer *GG* 21, *kP* 12–15; Plant 96–98). Thanks not least to Nietzsche, the most celebrated of the numerous forms that the association took in antiquity was the cult of Dionysos, which combined the

4 'Poets' has been favoured over 'writers' because although all three also wrote in forms other than poetry, they all dedicated most energy – and attached most importance – to the lyric genre.

ecstatic worship of the Greek god of wine and madness with dramatic performance, culminating in the theatrical competitions that framed the Golden Age of Greek drama in the 5th century B.C. Nietzsche himself traces the Dionysian tradition to Asia Minor, 'bis hin zu Babylon und den orgiastischen Sakäen' (3:24), and more recent studies have confirmed his assertion that the entheogenic use of psychoactive substances, often involving forms of creative expression, was common to the earliest cultures of every continent (Kupfer *GG* 38–39). Of particular note is the shamanic practice, widespread in the traditional cultures of both northern Asia and the Americas, of narrating visions brought about by the ingestion of such naturally occurring hallucinogens as the fly agaric mushroom or peyote, the cactus from which mescaline is derived. Despite the differences in cultural context and mode of expression – shamanic narratives are predominantly oral rather than written – the basic communicative principle of articulating and interpreting drug-induced transcendental experience inherent in this practice is also the dominant impulse behind many of the works that can be posited in the modern canon of drug literature. This parallel is underlined by the substantial interest shown in shamanism by several of the 20th-century writers whose drug-related works are considered seminal. Although not popularized until the late 1960s in Carlos Castaneda's best-selling mock anthropology,[5] the roots of this interest stretch further back, via *The Yage Letters* (1963) of William Burroughs and Allen Ginsberg, to Antonin Artaud's 'Le Rite du Peyotl chez les Tarahumaras' (1943–44), purportedly based on the French playwright's Mexican journey of 1936, and to Benn's own essay 'Provoziertes Leben' (1943), the pseudo-science of which anticipated Castaneda's by 25 years.

The role of psychoactive drugs in European – later also North American – literature of the Christian era remained peripheral (but constant; Boon 6–7) until the turn of the 19th century, when the Romantic preoccupation with the mysteries of the unconscious mind and the power of the irrational placed alternative states of consciousness – madness, dreams, somnambulism, hypnotism, intoxication – at the centre of popular attention. From the historical point of view, the surge of literary interest in drug use that occurred during the Romantic period, embodied most completely in Thomas De Quincey's *Confessions of an English Opium Eater*

5 The first and most widely read of Castaneda's many books is *The Teachings of Don Juan. A Yaqui Way of Knowledge* (1968).

(1821), must be seen as the result of a confluence of developments in a variety of spheres, many of them non-literary. As Marcus Boon observes,

> the notion of a specifically Romantic or aesthetic attitude toward drugs masks a profound interdependence with the scientific practices and the marketplace of the day, as well as the fate of religion in the West. (6)

This is not the place to examine such relations in depth. Nonetheless, one particular historical change should be singled out as particularly relevant, namely that this period saw the definitive affirmation of the modern conception of art, imaginative literature included, as an autonomous field of cultural activity no longer subordinate to political, philosophical, or – crucially – religious systems, which it had always acknowledged as greater than itself. This development gave painters, musicians and writers unprecedented freedom to explore unconventional means of experiencing and expressing the transcendental, which was then, much more readily than today, equated with the divine, or conversely the demonic. Derrida, using a florid 'rhetoric' of his own, describes the consequences of this shift for the association between drugs and literature:

> When the sky of transcendence comes to be emptied, and not just of Gods, but of any Other, a fatal rhetoric fills the void, and this is the fetishism of drug addiction. Not religion as the opiate of the people, but drugs as the religion of the atheist poets – and of some others, more or less atheists, more or less poets. (*RD* 29)

A related and equally significant result of this cultural reconfiguration was the emergence of a new perception of the artist's status. Whereas previously poets, playwrights and novelists – like painters, sculptors and composers – had been seen in the first place as craftsmen, in the Romantic mindset they were ascribed mystical power and elevated to the status of prophets and visionaries. The poet in particular, like the shaman in primitive societies, became 'one who by use of his intuition may unravel the mysteries of the universe' (Seymour-Smith 424), although the utilitarian imperative of a rapidly developing capitalist economy meant that the poet, unlike the shaman, usually occupied a marginal social position. The notion of the artist as a 'genius', an exceptionally sensitive individual with privileged or even divine insight who is destined to be misunderstood by his contemporaries, was already inherent in the works of the *Sturm und Drang*, and so underlay Romantic thought and literature from the outset. Perhaps its most succinct and accomplished expression, wisely spiced with a dash of self-irony, can be found in three poems by Alexander Pushkin: 'Prorok' ('The Prophet'; 1826), 'Poet' and 'Arion' (both 1827). Not until decades later, however, did it find its most radical and subsequently most acclaimed formulation, which occurs in the *voyant* letters (1871) of Arthur Rimbaud, where the poet is characterized as 'le grand malade, le grand criminel, le grand maudit, – et le suprême Savant!' (*Oc* 270). The dating of Rimbaud's *voyant* letters is significant because it attests to the enduring nature of the shift that the Romantic perception of the creative artist came to represent.[6] Indeed, notwithstanding critical attempts to deconstruct the myth of the artist in the second half of the 20th century, the same view has persisted to the present day. Paradoxically, this has resulted in the idolization of the most prominent of those who would do away with it, notably Roland Barthes, who despite himself reserved a place in the pantheon of authors (or its academic adjunct, the pantheon of theorists) with his 1968 pronouncement of the 'death of the author.' Its currency during the period with which we are concerned here might be exemplified by Rheiner's Expressionist radicalization ('Ein Untermensch. Ein Übergott') of the Romantic archetype in 'Der Dichter in der Welt' (1919):

> – Der Dichter; was ist das? Ein steter Schmerz.
> Ach weniger als ihr alle ahnt. Und mehr!
> Ein Untermensch. Ein Übergott. Ein Zwischentier.
> Oh, Fackel unbekannten Brands! Ein Wolken-Winkel. (*M* 45)

Such 'inter-animal poets' figure repeatedly in Rheiner's works, with the protagonists of both the novella *Kokain* and the short story 'Die Erniedrigung' (see 6.3), for example, conforming to this type. The opening paragraph of the latter contains a further elaboration of this author's view of the poetic vocation as both gift and curse:

> Wer ist mehr berufen, die Mächte über sich zu fühlen, als der Dichter? Wer mehr berufen, alle Schauerlichkeit ihrer hallenden Grotten auszutrinken, als er, der Berufene kat' exochän, der Bejaher, der ewig Kämpfende am Ölberge, der da spricht: Ist es nicht möglich, daß dieser Kelch von mir gehe, ich trinke ihn denn; so geschehe dein Wille! … Er lebt auf allen Inseln; er stürzt in jede Stadt; erfrorner Sperling,

6 As a further sign of its persistence in the late 19th century despite shifting literary fashions, one might refer to its successful parody by the Naturalist Arno Holz in his poem 'Ihr Dach stieß fast bis an die Sterne' of 1885.

schwebt er auf jeden Park hernieder; und jede Nacht ist ihm feindlich! – Nur wer dienet, mag befehlen! … So dient er, der Prinz, und über Nacht und Finsternis wird er König, triumphaler Rufer und Herrscher des Lichts! (*M* 100)

In both these texts the poet's role is conceptualised as a divine calling (aptronymically underlined in 'Die Erniedrigung' by the protagonist's improbable surname 'Sternraffer'), or better an imposition from God, a burden to be borne, lending him special insight into the mechanics of the human soul but at the same time creating an unbridgeable gap between him and his fellow men and condemning him to a short, miserable life on the fringes of society.

Introducing the visionary theme in the first of his *voyant* letters, Rimbaud wrote:

Now I am going in for debauchery. Why? I want to be a poet, and I am working to make myself a visionary: you won't possibly understand, and I hardly know how to explain it to you. To arrive at the unknown through the disordering of all the senses, that's the point.[7] (*Oc* 270)

In his introduction to the 1907 edition of Rimbaud's work in Karl Klammer's German translation (identified as one of Trakl's major sources, *SW* 1:16), Stefan Zweig specifies 'Wein, Gifte, Abenteuer' as three elements of the French poet's visionary 'debauchery' (Springer *N* 29). We need hardly reiterate the potential attraction of psychoactive substances as an aid to the 'disordering of all the senses,' as a means of 'arriving at the unknown,' or from a more detached perspective, as a 'prop' to literature's 'new-found independence' (Boon 6), and the Romantics had in fact assigned them this role long before Rimbaud famously asserted the poet's visionary calling in 1871. In 1844, for example, the poet's penchant for agents of intoxication as keys to the 'life of the Universe' had been highlighted by Ralph Waldo Emerson, himself a firm advocate of unmediated experience of the divine, in terms that prefigure Nietzsche's characterization of 'Dionysian' ecstasy in *Die Geburt der Tragödie*:

It is a secret which every intellectual man quickly learns, that, beyond the energy of his possessed and conscious intellect, he is capable of a new energy (as of an intellect

7 'Maintenant, je m'encrapule le plus possible. Pourquoi? Je veux être poète, et je travaille à me rendre voyant: vous ne comprendrez pas du tout, et je ne saurais presque vous expliquer. Il s'agit d'arriver à l'inconnu par le dérèglement de tous les sens.'

> doubled on itself), by abandonment to the nature of things; that, beside his privacy of power as an individual man, there is a great public power, on which he can draw, by unlocking, at all risks, his human doors, and suffering the ethereal tides to roll and circulate through him [Nietzsche would write of 'the shattering of the *principium individuationis*' (3:24)]: then he is caught up into the life of the Universe, his speech is thunder, his thought is law, and his words are universally intelligible as the plants and animals. The poet knows that he speaks adequately, then, only when he speaks somewhat wildly, or, 'with the flower of the mind'; not with the intellect, used as an organ, but with the intellect released from all service, and suffered to take its direction from its celestial life; or, as the ancients were wont to express themselves, not with intellect alone, but with the intellect inebriated by nectar. [...] This is the reason why bards love wine, mead, narcotics, coffee, tea, opium, the fumes of sandal-wood and tobacco, or whatever other species of animal exhilaration. (274–275)

The opening paragraph of 'Die Erniedrigung,' written over 80 years later, follows an equivalent trajectory, positing an almost natural connection between the poet's painful predicament and his recourse to drug use: 'So dient er, der Prinz, und über Nacht und Finsternis wird er König, triumphaler Rufer und Herrscher des Lichts! – So fiel er in (trostlose) Wüste orientalischen Giftes' (*M* 100).

Two 'species of animal exhilaration' are most strongly linked with the literature of the Romantic period. The first is opium, which in the form of laudanum, a tincture of 90% alcohol, was in widespread use during the same period, and remained so until the beginning of the 20th century, as a universal analgesic with a status equivalent to that of aspirin today (Kupfer *GG* 434). The second is hashish, which achieved particular prominence in France through the activities of the *Club des Hachichins*, a group of avant-garde artists and intellectuals of the early 1840s whose meetings consisted in communal drug experiments and were attended by writers such as Honoré de Balzac, Charles Baudelaire and Gustave Flaubert, even if not all participated actively in its goings-on. In the Romantic imagination, the appeal of both these intoxicants was immeasurably enhanced by their association with the distant and exotic lands where they were produced, and with hashish in particular by the greatly exaggerated perception of the drug's importance to Islamic culture, a view based on its role in the tales of the *Thousand and One Nights* and the legend of the Old Man of the Mountain, founder of the hashish-imbibing Assassins, first recounted to a European readership by Marco Polo. The list of writers who can be linked to either or both of these substances – by medicinal use, inquisitive dabbling, full-blown addiction, as well as literary treatment – features many of the most familiar names of 19th century literature, as the drug historians have thoroughly documented (Boon 27–46, 132–144; Castoldi 18–85; Kupfer *GG* 75–214, *kP* 25–53; Plant 9–47). Apart from De Quincey's sensational *Confessions*, which effectively gave rise to the concept of recreational drug use and not only inspired a host of imitations and parodies, but was also connected to an increase in opium-related deaths (Boon 41), the most influential 19th-century work dedicated to the drug question was written by one of De Quincey's many admirers, Baudelaire, and bore the title *Les Paradis artificiels* (1860). Only the first part of the three into which *Les Paradis artificiels* is divided – containing Baudelaire's reflections on hashish – is entirely original; the second and third in fact comprise a free translation of De Quincey's *Confessions* interspersed with Baudelaire's own commentary. Both De Quincey and Baudelaire offer profoundly ambivalent evaluations of the drug experiences they examine. Both dwell on the detrimental effects of drug use, yet their fascination with the intoxication produced by these substances is evident not least in the space devoted to the description of the states of mind and perceptions they induce. Moreover, although Baudelaire expressly and repeatedly denies the efficacy of hashish as a creative tool, the title he gives the first part of his study – 'Le Poëme du Haschisch' – stands in ironic contrast with his own conclusions.

Reflecting on the importance of De Quincey's autobiography and Baudelaire's monograph to the subsequent development of drug literature, Alberto Castoldi characterizes them as 'precise archetypes' for an 'encoded literary tradition' that has tinged subsequent treatments of the theme – whatever the individual author's intentions – with the preconceptions underlying these earlier works (104). Although this observation is certainly valid for many texts, including those Castoldi cites in support of his argument, it is also true that De Quincey's *Confessions* and Baudelaire's *Paradis artificiels* have determined the criteria for the critical reception of drug literature as much as, if not more than, they have influenced its production. In particular, the fact that De Quincey, and Baudelaire following him, bases his drug-discourse on personal experience that precedes the act of writing – and that he is at pains to illuminate in its full complexity – has seemingly led many to the false assumption that all literary drug-discourse is primarily autobiographical or confessional in nature, or rather that it should be read as such even when the work under discussion offers no apparent stimulus for such an interpretation (one work that does offer such stimulus is Rheiner's *Kokain*; see 6.3). Indeed, in the course of this investigation we shall have cause to mention several previous studies that, explicitly or implicitly taking De Quincey's autobiographical concerns as an analytical model, overlook the innovative or noteworthy aspects of a given text's handling of the drug theme (Castoldi's own comments on the role of cocaine in Trakl's poetry are illustrative; see 10.1), or where autobiographical criteria prove difficult to apply, fail to find any foothold for further enquiry (for example, Boon on Trakl; see 8.1).

For these reasons it is important to call attention to a second, no less fruitful branch of drug literature that is certainly as relevant to the present study as that which originates with the *Confessions of an English Opium Eater* and *Les Paradis artificiels*. This second branch comprises literary works not in the first place *about* drugs or drug experience, but containing references or – sometimes very subtle – allusions to psychoactive substances or their effects that may at first appear incidental, but that on reflection may be read as indications of a deeper, unspoken connection between text and intoxicant. Pre-eminent works belonging to and shaping this tradition include: Samuel Taylor Coleridge's poem 'Kubla Khan' (composed in 1797 but first published in 1816); the *Hymnen an die Nacht* (1799–1800) of Novalis (Friedrich von Hardenberg); various narratives of E. T. A. Hoffmann – especially the tale *Der goldene Topf* (1814), the novel *Die Elixiere des Teufels* (1816) and the collection *Die Serapions-Brüder* (1819–21); numerous stories by Edgar Allan Poe, including 'Ligeia' (1838), 'The Fall of the House of Usher' (1839) and 'A Tale of the Ragged Mountains' (1850), as well as Poe's poems 'The Sleeper' (1831), 'The City in the Sea' (1831), 'Dream-Land' (1844), and 'The Bells' (1849); Alexandre Dumas's novel *Le Comte de Monte-Cristo* (1844–45); several of Baudelaire's poems in *Les Fleurs du Mal* (1857–61), as well as his prose poems in *Le Spleen de Paris* (1869);[8] and finally, various works by Rimbaud, notably the long poem 'Le Bateau ivre' (1871) and the prose poem 'Matinée d'ivresse' (published in *Les Illuminations* of 1886 but written in 1872). In many of these texts – firstly and most famously in Coleridge's prose introduction to 'Kubla Khan' (compare 2.2) – the reference or allusion in question suggests a role for the intoxicant in the very composition of the work, or in shaping the expression of the narrative

---

8 Jean Pierrot identifies drug motifs in the following works by Baudelaire: 'Le Poison,' 'Le Voyage,' 'Alchimie de la douleur,' 'Horreur sympathique,' 'Rêve parisien,' 'Un hémisphère dans une chevelure,' 'Les Projets,' 'L'Invitation au voyage' and 'La Chambre double' (243; cf. Boon 308).

or lyric voice, as if the text were somehow manipulated, distorted or even dictated by the drug itself at the author's expense. Taking the dictation motif to an extreme, William Burroughs claims in the introduction to his 1959 novel *Naked Lunch*, one of the most heavily drugged literary texts of all time, to have no recollection of actually writing the book (Boon 35). In view of the reader's evident powerlessness to verify such statements, drug references of the kind contained in the works listed above are best treated primarily as literary devices that perpetuate the Romantic mystery-cult of the author while mischievously forestalling and subverting the enthusiasm for biographical interpretation that has arisen from it.

All the 19th-century works mentioned in the previous paragraph had been written, and Romanticism itself had long given way to other artistic currents that had variously advanced or reacted against each of its principles, before cocaine first came to popular attention in the 1880s, when it also made its literary debut. However, the nature of the more recent relationship between cocaine and literature cannot be grasped without reference to the historical developments already outlined, for although cocaine – a drug pharmacologically quite distinct from either opium or hashish, the two archetypally Romantic intoxicants – has since marked out its own territory in the field of imaginative literature, this territory is located *within* the larger and ever-expanding domain of drug literature, blending at certain points indistinguishably into the territory of other psychoactive substances, and its essential conditions were to a large extent predetermined by the circumstances described above. In effect, at the end of the 19th century cocaine was assimilated into the group of psychoactive substances that in 1844 Emerson had characterized as objects of the 'bard's love' (275). Whereas Emerson named 'wine, mead, narcotics, coffee, tea, opium, the fumes of sandal-wood and tobacco' as the pre-eminent 'species of animal exhilaration' (ibid.), cocaine is one significant addition featured in an equivalent list made in the early 20th century and used as the title of a study by the dramatist, novelist, painter and regular drug-user Stanisław Ignacy Witkiewicz, one of the leading figures of Polish Modernism: *Nikotyna, Alkohol, Kokaina, Peyotl, Morfina, Eter* (1932). The fall of Rheiner's poet-protagonist in 'Die Erniedrigung' 'into Oriental poison' (*M* 100) illustrates the extent to which cocaine as a literary phenomenon came to share the symbolism already attendant upon opium and hashish: in the story it becomes clear that the only 'poison' to which this phrase can refer is cocaine, so that from the purely geographical point of view, its description as 'Oriental' is paradoxical, as we shall now see (Benn makes equivalent use of a geographical misattribution of cocaine in *Karandasch*; see 4.3).

The cocaine alkaloid was first isolated from the leaves of the coca bush, *Erythroxylon coca*, by Albert Niemann, a chemist at Göttingen University, in 1859. For thousands of years before that, the same leaves had been chewed for both ritual and practical purposes by the native populations of the Andes, where the plant is endemic and 'revered as a source of physical energy and divine nourishment' (Plant 58). In 'Provoziertes Leben' Benn himself provides a summary – a montage of characteristically clipped observations – of coca's role in pre-Hispanic America:

> Die Königin der Inkas nannte sich nach der wunderbaren Pflanze Erythroxylon coca: Mama Cuca; den Götzenbildern wird als Zeichen ihrer Göttlichkeit die eine Backe mit Cocablättern gefüllt; überall stehen die flaschenförmigen Kürbisse, in denen das Blatt, gemischt mit Kalk und Pflanzenasche, als fertiger Bissen verwahrt wird, die Spitze der langen Nadel wird mit dem Mund angefeuchtet, mit der man sie einnimmt. Die Wirkung eines Cocabissens dauert vierzig Minuten = drei Kilometer auf ebenem Terrain, zwei Kilometer beim Bergsteigen, das ist der Maßstab des Dosierens. (*GW* 3:895)

The plant's use in religious ceremonies was prohibited in the 16th century by the Spanish colonists, who nonetheless understood and soon set about exploiting the potential economic value of the leaves as a means of increasing the productivity of their workers, 'notably to invigorate slave labourers in the mines of Peru' (Boon 177). Unlike many other vegetable products of American derivation – tobacco, coffee, potatoes, tomatoes – coca leaves had little influence outside their area of cultivation until Niemann's isolation of their most active alkaloid, apparently because they 'do not travel very well' (Plant 60). Nonetheless, travellers' accounts of the plant's properties generated a certain mystique about coca that was bolstered, as had already occurred with both opium and hashish, by a new set of exotic associations. In his late essay 'The Turning Point of My Life' (1910), Mark Twain (Samuel Langhorne Clemens) reflects on his impressions of reading one such account as a young man:

> Among the books that interested me in those days was one about the Amazon. The traveler told an alluring tale of his long voyage up the great river from Para to the sources of the Madeira, through the heart of an enchanted land, a land wastefully rich in tropical wonders, a romantic land where all the birds and flowers and animals were of the museum varieties, and where the alligator and the crocodile and the monkey

> seemed as much at home as if they were in the Zoo. Also, he told an astonishing tale about COCA, a vegetable product of miraculous powers, asserting that it was so nourishing and so strength-giving that the native of the mountains of the Madeira region would tramp up hill and down all day on a pinch of powdered coca and require no other sustenance.
> I was fired with a longing to ascend the Amazon. Also with a longing to open up a trade in coca with all the world. (147)

In the decades following Niemann's discovery, cocaine became the key ingredient in 'endless syrups, pastilles, wines and elixirs' (Plant 61). Commercially, the most successful European cocaine concoction was Vin Mariani, the brainchild of the Corsican chemist Angelo Mariani, which was first produced in 1863 and subsequently used and endorsed by a host of celebrities from political, religious and artistic fields, including writers such as Victor Hugo, Jules Verne, Henrik Ibsen, and Emile Zola. Although Vin Mariani did not survive the increasingly restrictive legislation regulating the distribution and sale of cocaine that followed in the early 20th century once the alkaloid's dangers had become evident, the manufacturers of one of its American counterparts circumvented this same legal reaction by gradually replacing cocaine with another, more reputable stimulant: caffeine. This was Coca-Cola, which first went on sale in 1886 (its cocaine content had disappeared entirely by 1904), and which was made following a recipe developed by John Pemberton, a doctor and morphine addict who believed – wrongly – that cocaine could free him of his morphine addiction: 'It supplies the place of that drug, and the patient who will use it as a means of cure may deliver himself from the pernicious habit without inconvenience or pain' (cited by Plant 68).

The idea that cocaine could be used pharmacologically in the treatment of morphine addiction enjoyed a certain vogue in the period of Pemberton's development of the Coca-Cola formula. Its persistent influence can be seen as late as 1927 in Mikhail Bulgakov's story 'Morfij' – set in 1917–18 and based on Bulgakov's experience of the Revolutionary period – in which a young doctor posted to a remote Russian province repeats Pemberton's substitution, only to conclude that cocaine itself is the 'foulest and most devious poison' (164).[9] One of the earliest and most zealous proponents of the substitution theory was Sigmund Freud, who advises cocaine therapy for morphine addicts in 'Über Coca' (1884), the first of

---

9 ‹Сквернейший и коварнейший яд.›

several adulatory articles he would write about the drug during the mid-1880s. Freud's misjudgement of cocaine's medicinal value would have fatal consequences: after he recommended the drug to his friend Ernst von Fleischl to relieve the latter's morphine addiction, Fleischl soon became a cocaine addict – one of the first – and eventually died of cocaine poisoning in 1891 (Plant 72–75; Castoldi 151–152). Other applications Freud proposes for cocaine in 'Über Coca' include the treatment of such wide-ranging conditions as alcoholism, asthma, digestive disorders and wasting diseases; he also extols its usefulness as a mental stimulant, an aphrodisiac and an anaesthetic. However, much to his later chagrin, he failed to realize the full significance of his observations of the drug's anaesthetic properties, and it was another doctor experimenting with cocaine, the eye specialist Carl Köller, who was credited with the discovery of its function as the first local anaesthetic. In this capacity the drug had its most profound and enduring impact on medical practice. Indeed, a significant consideration for the present study is that cocaine continued to be used as an anaesthetic even after its other medical applications had been abandoned due to the undesirable side-effects of repeated use. In the literature of Expressionism, a reflection of this continuing application can be found in Georg Heym's short story 'Jonathan' (1913), which is set a Hamburg hospital:

> Überall wurde getröstet, beruhigt, eingeschläfert, überall machte man Morphium- und Kokaininjektionen, das Chaos zu besänftigen, überall wurde dementiert, an allen Betten wurden beruhigende Bulletins ausgegeben. (2:47)

Cocaine's on-going medical favour explains its widespread availability before and especially during the First World War, when all three writers under discussion in this study are known to have used it, even if it was the drug's psychoactive rather than local-anaesthetic qualities that attracted non-medicinal users.

Predictably, it was as a mental stimulant, another of the functions identified in Freud's study, that cocaine made its first literary appearance and came to be associated with one of the most popular and influential literary characters of all time: Sherlock Holmes (although this association is generally censored out of cinema and television adaptations). References to Holmes's cocaine habit can be found in various stories spanning the years 1886–1896, from 'A Scandal in Bohemia' to 'The Adventure of the Missing Three-Quarter,' and a familiar, De Quincey-like pattern can be traced in the detective's attitude to the drug, which shifts from initial enthusiasm to final malediction and – happily – 'cure' (Castoldi 152–153). The most protracted treatment of the theme occurs in 'The Sign of Four' (1888), in which Dr Watson, after silently observing his friend's drug injections 'three times a day for many months' (Doyle 89), finds the courage to speak out and warn Holmes of the risks of substance abuse.

> He smiled at my vehemence. 'Perhaps you are right, Watson,' he said. 'I suppose that its influence is physically a bad one. I find it, however, so transcendently stimulating and clarifying to the mind that its secondary action is a matter of small moment' [...] 'My mind,' he said, 'rebels at stagnation. Give me problems, give me work, give me the most abstruse cryptograms, or the most intricate analysis, and I am in my own proper atmosphere. I can dispense with artificial stimulants. But I abhor the dull routine of existence. I crave for mental exaltation.' (Doyle 89–90)

Cocaine as a means of escape from 'the dull routine of existence' is a motif that we shall meet again in this study, in particular in relation to Benn's cocaine poems (see 3.1–3.3). As far as their cocaine references are concerned, the *Sherlock Holmes* stories can clearly be placed in the second of the two literary traditions arising from the Romantic elaboration of the drug theme outlined above, where passing, indirect or seemingly marginal references may be read as hints of a deeper connection between drug and text. Various *Holmes* commentators have followed these hints in an attempt to illuminate the connection, in effect treating the stories' cocaine references as precisely the kind of obscure but meaningful clues that the detective himself uses to unravel so many crimes. Boon, for example, not only observes that for Holmes 'cocaine provides a double for the stimulation of solving a crime,' but also asserts that 'Holmes's sensitivity to signs and traces' – in other words, his most important professional attribute – 'could be linked' to his cocaine use (181).

Another archetypal literary work of the same period, Robert Louis Stevenson's *The Strange Case of Dr Jekyll and Mr Hyde* (1886), can be seen as a further manifestation of the same tradition. Indeed, despite the central, obvious and undeniable role played by psychoactive drugs in the transformation of Jekyll into Hyde, Stevenson's tale gives the elusiveness theme a new twist, and it is revealing that although the work has recently been described as a 'great 19th-century cocaine book' (Boon 181–182), it was enjoyed and discussed by generations of readers before anyone even suggested that cocaine might be involved (Schultz 90–94; cf. Ashley 40,

Boon 321). The fact is that Henry Jekyll, in his tantalizingly incomplete 'Full Statement of the Case' that constitutes the last part of the story, never reveals the ingredients of his magic potion; instead he merely refers cryptically to 'a particular salt which I knew, from my experiments, to be the last ingredient required' (57). This reference corresponds with, but does not expand on, several earlier mentions of a 'white salt' (45, 50). To be sure, Jekyll's potion, like Jekyll himself and his evil surrogate Hyde, is a fictional creation and its 'last ingredient' cannot be directly equated with any particular drug, but it is also true that the potion's effects correspond most closely with those that would typically follow a heavy dose of the 1880s wonder-drug – a very 'particular salt' – cocaine:

> I felt younger, lighter, happier in body; within I was conscious of a heady recklessness, a current of disordered sensual images running like a mill race in my fancy, a solution of the bonds of obligation, an unknown but not an innocent freedom of the soul. (57)

Indeed, the central themes of *The Strange Case* – metamorphosis, the displacement of self, the drug-induced revelation of the essential multiplicity or disjointedness of the psyche – recur in several later literary works with a more certain connection with cocaine, for example in the novels *Cocaina* (1921) by Pitigrilli (Dino Segre) and *Roman s kokainom* (*Novel with Cocaine*, 1934) by M. Ageev (Mark Levi), and as we shall see, these themes are also important in the writings of Benn, Trakl and Rheiner. Predictably, the link established between Stevenson's story and cocaine has led to conjecture about a possible role for the drug in the production of the text, and the fact that Stevenson first drafted his tale during a period of ill health – when he may well have been inclined to use a cure-all such as cocaine, as it was then considered – has served to fuel the speculation (Ashley 40; Boon 182; Plant 65–66; Schultz 90–94). Furthermore, it was perhaps inevitable, in view of the literary drug mythology we have inherited from the Romantics, that once the whiff of a cocaine connection had been detected, this would take on a life of its own, and that theory would sooner or later come to be presented, sensationally, as fact, as for example in Sadie Plant's *Writing on Drugs*:

> Robert Louis Stevenson wrote *The Strange Case* during six days and nights of a cocaine high. In spite – or perhaps because – of his poor state of health, he shut himself away and reappeared with the story complete. [...] The potion used by Jekyll is a telling caricature of Stevenson's drug. (65–66)

Plant's account might be considered an inadvertent confirmation of Robert Mighall's observation that the story, at the core of which lie 'silences, evasions, suppressions [...], lives and grows in the imaginations of those who read and reread it over a hundred years after Dr Jekyll first concocted his potion' (Stevenson xxx).

Both the *Sherlock Holmes* stories and *The Strange Case of Dr Jekyll and Mr Hyde* were written during the second of the four distinct phases into which Dominique Antonin roughly but usefully divides the moral history of coca and cocaine:

> Coca consumption in pre-Columbian America gave rise to celebrations; the cocaine obsession of the first experimenters was born of scientific enthusiasm; the popular cocainism of the mad years reflected the frenetic artistic activity of the period. Today's *cocaine mania* is more symptomatic of a great emptiness, and sometimes of great suffering.[10] (220)

The third phase, which she characterizes as 'mad years' of 'frenetic artistic activity,' reached its climax in the 1920s, when cocaine became a so-called 'champagne drug,' associated with fashionable social circles and the artistic avant-garde, and was consumed in large quantities in the cafés, dance halls and brothels of major European cities. Although in many countries the sale and even possession of the drug became illegal during this decade (the International Opium Convention of 1912, ratified by the German parliament in late 1920, was expanded in 1925 to regulate the trade in coca and cocaine, as well; Maier 241–246), it remained easy to come by because of an active black market that was only sporadically policed.[11] Two novels portraying cocaine use in the urban high society of this period are Pitigrilli's *Cocaina* and Aleister Crowley's *Diary of a Drug Fiend* (1922), both of which achieved considerable popularity upon first publication. A commercially

10 'La consommation de coca dans l'Amérique précolombienne donnait lieu à des fêtes, la cocaïnomanie des premiers expérimentateurs relevait de l'enthousiasme scientifique, le cocaïnisme populaire des années folles reflétait la frénésie artistique de l'époque. La *cocaïnomania* d'aujourd'hui est plus symptomatique d'un grand manque, et parfois d'une grande souffrance.'

11 As Carl Zuckmayer recounts in his autobiography *Als wär's ein Stück von mir*, in one curious incident predating the success of his 1925 play *Der fröhliche Weinberg*, the impecunious young author unwittingly found himself peddling cocaine on the streets of Berlin. He soon began to suspect that he was being observed by an undercover policeman, but fortunately was 'rescued' by a Polish prostitute (349–354).

less successful but no less accomplished depiction of an equivalent milieu, noteworthy in the present context not least because of its Viennese setting, is Max Pulver's *Himmelpfortgasse* (1927), marketed – perhaps too simplistically for its own good – by Kurt Wolff as 'Roman der Laster unserer Zeit.'[12] Two other novels of the 1920s that feature the same drug, although less prominently, and that can perhaps be considered more representative products of the 'frenetic artistic activity' Antonin mentions, are Jean Cocteau's *Le Grand Ecart* (1923) and Hermann Hesse's *Der Steppenwolf* (1927).[13]

An earlier literary work to highlight the role of cocaine in the colourful night-life of the big city was Rheiner's story 'Der Tod des Schwärmers Gautier Fémin' (see 6.2), written on the Eastern Front in 1915 but set in Paris of the immediate prewar period, where Rheiner had spent several months of 1912. These dates are important because they confirm that the cocaine vogue of the 1920s – when in certain cafés taking a pinch of cocaine from a snuffbox was considered 'hardly different' from ordering a glass of cognac (Röbel 152) – in fact had its roots firmly planted in the previous decade. As Hans Maier reports (62), cocaine use had already become common in the Bohemian cultural scene of major urban centres in the pre-War years; this observation is borne out, for example, by Johannes R. Becher's characterization of the favourite rendezvous of the early Munich Expressionists in his poem 'Café Stefanie 1912':

> Am Tisch nebenan spielte Mühsam Schach,
> Und Frank saß einem Geldmann auf der Lauer.
> (Vielleicht saß der indes im Café Bauer?)
> Ein Denker hielt mit Kokain sich wach.[14] (Raabe 84)

---

12 A brief but intriguing reference to the illicit cocaine trade in Imperial (as opposed to Republican) Vienna can be found in Joseph Roth's novel *Die Geschichte von der 1002. Nacht* (1939), in which the journalist Bernhard Lazik is revealed as a dealer (2:1109).

13 The literature of this decade, with a strong emphasis on that from the German-speaking world, is especially well represented in Alfred Springer's anthology *Kokain: Mythos und Realität.*

14 Curious here is that the cocaine user remains anonymous, while the other café customers are named: the chess player 'Mühsam' (Erich Mühsam) and the indigent 'Frank' (Leonhard Frank). This is perhaps a strategy for protecting Becher's 'thinker' from the stigma that had become attached to cocaine use by the early 20th century, a stigma that fellow-Expressionist Benn would demonstratively embrace in his own cocaine poems (see 3.1–3.4).

The extension of the drug's popularity beyond artistic circles came about with the unprecedented diffusion arising from the mass-production of pharmaceuticals during the First World War ('damals war in Europa die deutsche chemische Industrie die Hauptproduzentin,' Maier 66). In his 1926 monograph *Der Kokainismus*, Maier describes the conditions of the immediate post-War period that provided the means and motive for the rapid growth in the drug's popularity in German-speaking Europe:

> In Deutschland und Österreich war es die Revolutionszeit von 1918/19, die in doppelter Richtung der Ausbreitung des Kokainschnupfens Vorschub leistete. Einesteils schuf die neurotisch-psychopathische Stimmung, die ganze Bevölkerungsklassen, besonders der Großstädte, ergriff, den Boden und das Bedürfnis nach narkotischen Mitteln, wie auch damals trotz der äußeren Not der Alkoholkonsum wieder sehr stark zunahm; andernteils kamen durch die ungeregelte Auflösung der Truppenbestände und des Heeresmaterials große Mengen von Arzneistoffen, und besonders auch Alkoloide, unter die Bevölkerung, und es bildete sich ein unkontrollierter Handel mit diesen Stoffen heraus. (69)

We might also mention here that two later works dealing with cocaine abuse in Russia, namely Bulgakov's 'Morfij' and Ageev's *Roman s kokainom*, are both set in the revolutionary year 1917.

The diffusion of the drug during the First World War, in particular its increased availability outside major cities, is also significant for the link between cocaine and Expressionism, and when we consider the three poets with whom this study is primarily concerned, the geographical diversity of their cocaine experiences is itself indicative of the scale of this diffusion. Trakl is reported to have taken 'sehr viel Kokain zu sich' (*HkA* 2:730) during the brief period he spent on active duty as a medical assistant in Galicia, near what is now the border between Poland and the Ukraine, following his enlistment in August 1914, and died of a cocaine overdose in a military hospital in Kraków in November of the same year (see 7.1). Benn, a doctor specializing in skin and venereal diseases, dabbled with the drug in 1916 while stationed in a hospital for prostitutes in Brussels (see 2.2; the occupied Belgian capital was frequented by German soldiers on leave from the front, so the health of Brussels prostitutes was considered a question of national security).[15] Rheiner is known to have taken cocaine during his first visit to Berlin in summer 1914 in an unsuccessful attempt to

15 Werner Rübe writes: 'Die Heeresleitung war ernstlich besorgt, die Syphilis und Gonorrhoe begannen die Kampfkraft der Truppe zu beeinträchtigen' (*RiH* 156–57).

avoid conscription by simulating an addictive illness, and the real addiction that he subsequently developed accompanied him through several years on the Eastern Front, a period of detoxification treatment in Cologne, and finally back to Berlin where he moved in June 1917 following his dismissal from the army (see 5.1). The role of cocaine in the lives and works of these three writers will be discussed in detail in the chapters that follow. However, several points about Modernism in general and Expressionism in particular are worth highlighting beforehand.

With the advent of Modernism the association between drugs – or better, intoxication – and literature became at once more profound and more subtle. In a fundamental and far-reaching manner, the Modernist aesthetic assimilated the Romantic fascination with abnormal states of consciousness into its own procedures, so that even representations of normal consciousness – for example, as a deliberately inarticulate 'stream' – were constructed to reveal the amorphous, fluid, indeed irrational basis of so-called rational thought. In its reaction to the Realism that had dominated literary practice in the second half of the 19th century and that had implied a secular, sober, middle-class (even in the depiction of other social groups) conception of the 'real' related to philosophical trends such as empiricism, pragmatism and utilitarianism, the Modernist aesthetic emphasized aspects of experience that undermined this conception, contrasting it with one that tended variously towards the mythical, ecstatic, cosmic, primitive or politically subversive. In its formal aspects Modernism distanced itself from Realist aspirations to mimesis, objectivity and lucidity, and frequently spurned or distorted established narrative conventions, such as causality or chronology, and stylistic ones, such as syntactic or semantic transparency.

In its disruption of the norms governing the referential and representational use of language, Modernist literature aligned itself with intoxication against 'bourgeois' sobriety. In his 'Bekenntnis zum Expressionismus,' Benn tellingly describes the Modernist method as a 'certain kind of internal intoxication' (*GW* 3:807), and André Breton's description of the drug-like character of his fledgling movement in his 1924 *Manifeste du surréalisme* further underlines the same parallel (Kupfer *GG* 225–226). Thus, although no work of the early 20th century dealing primarily and explicitly with drugs or drug users can lay claim to the same position of influence in the Modernist canon that De Quincey's *Confessions* occupies in the Romantic one, drug experience can be considered a deep-rooted – if usually intangible – subtext in many of the most radically Modernist literary texts. In the history of the drug–literature relationship, the Modernist subtextualization of the drug theme may be considered a further, decisive development in the Romantic tradition of mystification-via-elusiveness already described. Nowhere is the subtextual importance of drug experience to Modernist literature more evident than in Trakl's poetry; indeed, in chapter 9 it will be argued that his poetry's most distinctive stylistic features constitute elements of a system of 'poetics of intoxication,' which contributes in large part to the distinctive tone of Trakl's mature verse (see 9.1). Important subtextual references to drug experience will also be identified in individual works by Benn (see 4.1) and Rheiner (see 6.1 and 6.4).

If Modernism as a whole displays a cognitive and linguistic affinity with the experience of intoxication, then Expressionism, its 'first, [...] most violent and explicit' manifestation (Seymour-Smith 571), can be said to display the same affinity with the experience of cocaine intoxication, as Alfred Springer observes:

> Schlagworte, mit denen die Wirkung des Kokain zusammenfassend beschrieben wurden, waren immer wieder: Weltumarmungsgefühl, Simultaneität des Erlebens, gesteigerte Empfindsamkeit, angeregte, beschleunigte Gedankentätigkeit und Fantasietätigkeit, erhöhte Suggestibilität und Autosuggestibilität, Größenideen. Viele dieser Merkmale finden sich in der frühexpressionistischen Dichtung wieder, die aus den verschiedenen Café Größenwahn hervorging. (*N* 28–29 & *KMR* 43)

This correlation is striking and suggests potentially productive avenues of investigation for literary scholars, yet caution must be exercised in their pursuit. In particular, it would be misleading to infer that the Expressionist aesthetic was shaped to any significant degree by the cognitive and emotive characteristics of cocaine intoxication as experienced by certain of its most influential practitioners. To do so would merely perpetuate a form of hermeneutic mystification described by Félix Guattari:

> One of the formative elements of the myth of hard drugs lies in the idea that they inspire a specific and novel kind of production. There would thus be a culture linked to drugs – a theme exploited particularly by the 'Beat Generation.' [...] Certain drug environments develop certain cultures, but one cannot infer from this that drugs create a specific mode of expression. (202)

Indeed, considering both the strength of the affinity Springer identifies and the popularity of cocaine in artistic circles dating to the first decade of the 20th century (Maier 62), one might well expect the drug to appear more frequently than it does in the literature of the Expressionist epoch. If we consider, for example, the literary works featuring cocaine that Springer cites in his study of 'Narkotomanie in der Boheme des Deutschen Expressionismus,' we find that although their authors all had close associations with Expressionism, most of the works were in fact written well after the epoch itself had ended: Franz Werfel's *Barbara oder die Frömmigkeit* (1929), Johannes R. Becher's *Abschied* (1940), Leonhard Frank's *Links, wo das Herz ist* (1952) and Franz Jung's *Der Weg nach unten* (1961; Jung's *Sophie: Der Kreuzweg der Demut* of 1916 is the sole exception).

Furthermore, it should be underlined that cocaine was certainly not the only drug used or written about by the Expressionists, and that it would be mistaken to attribute to it – by literary historical analogy – the same self-evident primacy among intoxicants that opium and later hashish had had for the Romantics. The opiates especially, as well as retaining an important role in pharmacology (the use of the opium-derivative and powerful analgesic morphine became standard medical practice in the late 19th century following the invention of the hypodermic syringe), continued to attract many new users among the artistically inclined. Indeed, the parallels Springer notes between cocaine intoxication and the Expressionist world-view ought to be balanced by the observation, extrapolated from the same scholar's findings, that addiction to morphine, rather than cocaine, was if anything the more common affliction among the movement's devotees. For writers of the Modernist period, the opiates were made all the more appealing by their now-legendary associations with the Romantic yearning for transcendence, thanks to which they came complete with their own ready-made symbolism, in particular in the form of poppy imagery. Benn would suggestively describe this flower, in a 1916 story, as 'groß und sagenhaft' (5:1232; see also 4.1). The poppy motif is also important in the poetry of Trakl (see 9.2), who reportedly began using opium as a boy (see 7.1), while Rheiner was a morphine addict for the last six years of his life and in 1925 died of an overdose of that drug (see 5.1). In addition, in his works Benn mentions an eclectic range of psychoactive substances: cocaine, caffeine and curare in his *Pameelen* plays (see 4.1–4.3); opium, absinthe, ether, hashish and alcohol in his *Genie* essays (see 2.1–2.2); and betel, tea, mescaline and pervitin in 'Provoziertes Leben' (see 2.1–2.2). Trakl's drug *use* was similarly multifarious (see 7.1) – in contrast to his writing on the subject. To examine the role of cocaine in the lives and works of these writers without consideration of their wider interest in intoxicants and intoxication would misrepresent their perception of the drug's status as one of a group of agents of – in Benn's terminology – 'bionegative' transcendence. This is particularly relevant with regard to Trakl, the only one of the three who never names cocaine directly in his works. In fact, in order to undertake an informed analysis of possible cocaine allusions in Trakl's poetry (see 10.1–10.2), it will first be necessary to consider how his poetic style and lexicon treat the experience of intoxication in general, as well as several other individual psychoactive substances (see 9.1–9.2). It is nonetheless clear that cocaine merits particular attention in relation to these three Expressionist poets because of its unusually prominent and unifying role, the precise nature of which – or natures, as this was by no means fixed – will emerge in the course of this study.

In view of these considerations, we must be wary of overstating the connection between Expressionism and cocaine and thereby contributing to a myth that does more to obscure than to reveal the true nature of the object of our study. It is therefore prudent to specify that the analyses of specific text–drug relationships contained in the chapters that follow are presented not as case studies representing broader trends within Expressionism, but rather as objectifications of certain possibilities arising from the confluence of the various literary, pharmacological and sociocultural developments outlined here. The fact that these possibilities were realized when others were not, and moreover that they were realized in the particular ways that we shall undertake to describe, cannot itself be considered an inevitable consequence of these developments themselves (one can admire the audacity of Osip Brik's ultra-deterministic statement, 'had Pushkin not existed *Evgeny Onegin* would all the same have been written' (90), but this does not make it any more plausible). To account for these particularities, rather, close attention must be paid to the characteristics and circumstances of the individual writers and works in question.

1.3 Secondary Literature Review

The scholarly and critical works relevant to our investigation can be classified in three groups. The first consists of works that deal directly and in depth with one or more of the poets under discussion; the second of those that approach the relationship between drugs and literature from a historical perspective; while the third collects studies that fit in neither of the first two categories, but that nonetheless have conceptual or methodological pertinence to this study.

The first group may be further divided into two sub-groups. We can distinguish studies that give particular weight to the writer's drug use or the drug theme in his works, or that propose some connection between the two, from those that mention such questions only in passing or not at all. The second of these sub-groups is by far the larger, and it is striking that the Expressionists' drug use has attracted far less critical attention than that of the Romantics, Symbolists, or the Beat Generation (which should not be taken as a sign of lesser relative importance). Only in relation to Benn can we talk of an enduring critical discourse addressing the text–drug relationship. Benn studies that are primarily concerned with this aspect of his life and work include Kurt Rothmann's 'Zu Gottfried Benns Drogenlyrik' (1967), Günther Witschel's *Rausch und Rauschgift bei Baudelaire, Huxley, Burroughs und Benn* (1968), Klaus Modick's 'Formenpräger der weißen Spur' (1975), Angelika Arend's 'Der Dichter braucht die Droge nicht' (1987), Konstantin Bendix's *Rauschformen und Formenrausch* (1988), Werner Rübe's 'Im Irrgarten der Alkaloide' (1993), and Daniel Ketteler's 'Drogengebrauch im Dienste der Neurologie?' (2005). Studies concerned in the first place with other questions that nonetheless include substantial comment on the role of drugs in Benn's works, in particular his cocaine poems (*GW* 1:52–54) of the Brussels period that is our chief interest here, include Albrecht Schöne's 'Überdauernde Temporalstruktur' (1958),[16] Bodo Heimann's 'Ich-Zerfall als Thema und Stil' (1964), Theo Meyer's *Kunstproblematik und Wortkombinatorik bei Gottfried Benn* (1971), Johannes Østbø's *Expressionismus und Montage* (1981), Jürgen Haupt's *Natur und Lyrik* (1983), and Oskar Sahlberg's 'Gottfried Benns Ekstasen' (1988).

One of the main issues considered by these scholars, particularly by the authors of the first set of studies listed, is the connection between Benn's use of drugs – whether in his life, works, or both – and his 'reality-smashing' (*GW* 4:1076) theory of artistic creativity that is a dominant theme in many of his works, in his poetry and imaginative prose as well as his

16 The 1968 edition of Schöne's *Säkularisation als sprachbildende Kraft* listed in the bibliography and cited in this and the following chapters is a second, revised and expanded version of the 1958 edition.

essays. A recurrent characteristic and, as we shall argue in chapter 2, a recurrent weakness of a significant number of these critical works, including those by Heimann, Rothmann, Witschel, Modick, Bendix and Ketteler, is their tendency to accept Benn's theorizing at face value and as constituting a coherent philosophical system, and their consequent failure to weigh his often extravagant theoretical and biographical pronouncements against his proclivity for posturing, concealment and mystification (one concomitant of this deference to Benn's rhetoric is a fondness for imitation of his style). In relation to Benn's treatment of the drug theme, as Arend observes, such a lack of 'Sorgfalt und Umsicht in der Interpretation' may tempt the critic to reduce 'die poetisch angedeuteten Vorgänge zu einem einfachen poetologischen Rezept' (104–105), in other words, to take Benn's works as a stylized but sincere account of their own genesis. Arend's veiled accusation of 'poetological' reductionism is directed primarily towards Modick, and secondarily towards Rothmann and Witschel, but the same criticism could also be made of Bendix's *Rauschformen und Formenrausch*, which was published one year after Arend's article. Interestingly, the interpretative disorientation that has developed in the analysis of Benn's personal and literary drug use was shrewdly anticipated by Schöne, who warns against reading the 'vom eigenen Gestaltungswillen überformte fiktive Gestalt des Dichters' (226) as an unmediated textual embodiment of the writer's own consciousness and convictions:

> Der objektive Dokumentationswert seiner Lebensbeschreibung, die man bruchstückweise aus Essays und Gedichten herauslösen und zusammensetzen mag, bleibt für den Historiker weithin ebenso unbestimmbar wie dem Geisteswissenschaftler die direkte Aufschlußkraft der eigenen naturwissenschaftlichen und kulturphilosophischen Aufsätze Benns für seine Dichtung sein muß. Beides bringt in Gefahr, *an der Hand des Autors in die Irre zu gehen*, sofern man es anders versteht, denn als Versuchsfelder, Steinbrüche, Vorhöfe des dichterischen Werkes. (ibid.; italics added)

More recently, Arend's 'Der Dichter braucht die Droge nicht' stands out as a renewed call for exegetic prudence in view of Benn's obvious delight in exaggeration and obfuscation. But as will become evident in 2.2, Arend's own evaluation in fact errs in the opposite direction towards an over-hasty, critically convenient dismissal of Benn's drug motifs – her stated intention is 'ein [Mißverständnis] aus dem Weg zu räumen' (102) – and ultimately comes little closer than Modick's to capturing the complexity and ambivalence of Benn's literary practice.

Both Sahlberg's and Rübe's studies might also be faulted for their biographically reductive intentions, although their readings are oriented towards psychopathological rather than poetological decipherment. In Benn criticism generally, in contrast to that concerned with Trakl, the 'wild' psychoanalytical approach (cf. Felman 149–159; see 3.4) that treats the literary work as a symptom of the writer's mental disturbance has been applied only sparingly, although Sahlberg in particular, whose arguments are outlined in 3.4, seems intent on making up the shortfall single-handed. As we shall see in our discussion of the poem 'Kokain', Sahlberg certainly succeeds in out-Benning Benn in sheer outrageousness, although this success tends to distract from what is not only original but also valuable in his commentary (Arend admits to reading Sahlberg 'mit Erstaunen'; 113). To a lesser degree the same is true of Rübe's analysis, which nonetheless appears positively subdued and cautious by comparison with Sahlberg's. Rübe's perception of the 'Wahlverwandschaft' between Benn's 'konstitutioneller Grundstimmung' and the consciousness of the drug user will be developed in our analysis (148; see 2.2).

Meyer's *Kunstproblematik und Wortkombinatorik*, Østbø's *Expressionismus und Montage* and Haupt's *Natur und Lyrik* contain general Benn studies that include commentaries on one or both of the cocaine poems (see 3.1–3.4). Both Modick and, following him, Bendix note that studies of this type have traditionally made short shrift of – 'weggeblendet oder banalisiert,' as Modick puts it (49; cf. Bendix 150) – Benn's interest in psychoactive substances. The attention paid to the cocaine poems in the works of Meyer, Østbø and Haupt perhaps indicates an increasing open-mindedness towards the drug question in the mainstream of Benn scholarship, although even here it is clear that ingrained misapprehensions persist. Thus, both Meyer and Haupt emphasize the 'artificial' nature of cocaine (Meyer *KW* 267–268, Haupt 360; see 3.2), overlooking the drug's vegetable derivation that Benn himself highlights, for example, in the short play *Karandasch* (see 4.3); while Østbø's 'astonishment' at the formal regularity of Benn's depiction of cocaine-induced euphoria in the poem 'O Nacht' suggests a failure to grasp the long-standing association between poetic expression and intoxication (91; see 1.2). Truly 'astonishing' is perhaps Østbø's abbreviation of the same poem from 29 to 21 lines; he describes the fifth of its seven stanzas as the 'last' (ibid.) and leaves the sixth and seventh without comment despite their unquestionable thematic importance (as these are printed overleaf in some editions, for example the 1960 *Gesammelte Werke* referred to in this study, the suspicion arises that Østbø neglected to turn the page).

Quite a different picture is presented by the canon of scholarly works examining the life and poetry of Trakl. Although it would be difficult to find another creative writer of any epoch or nationality who surpasses this poet in the scope, intensity and relentlessness of his drug consumption, this aspect of his life, and more importantly its possible relationship to his writing, has received very little attention from critics. This neglect is perhaps best understood as a consequence of the lack of ready-made interpretive tools that might both prompt and facilitate an investigation of this type in relation to a set of texts in which the drug theme is not as conspicuous as in, for example, Benn's works (even when, as with Benn, this conspicuousness is potentially deceptive). Prior to the chapter on Trakl in Eve Sattler's very recent *Vergiftete Sensationen: Soziale und kulturelle Dimensionen des Rausches im literarischen Expressionismus 1910–1914* (2010), the only major study to affirm and elaborate – albeit briefly – a direct relationship between Trakl's poetry and his drug use is Clemens Heselhaus's 'Das metaphorische Gedicht von Georg Trakl' (1962). However, as Heselhaus sees this relationship as important primarily in relation to Trakl's method of composition (229), he risks stumbling into the same poetological reductionism against which Arend warns Benn's readers (105). Perceiving this danger, he is forced to retreat from his bold initial affirmation – 'Mit Trakls Werk tritt die Wirksamkeit der Drogen […] in die Dichtung ein' (229) – with the truism that 'die eigentliche Bedeutung Trakls' lies in his use of words, not of drugs (229–230). In fact the exploration of the drug–text relationship becomes a relatively low priority in Heselhaus's readings of individual Trakl poems, even if he continues to sense that more could be said on the matter: 'wenn es nicht mißverständlich wäre, würde ich von Drogentraum-Gedichten sprechen' (240; see 8.1).

Sattler's chapter on Trakl is one of three case studies – the other two deal with Emmy Hennings and Johannes R. Becher – intended to illustrate the main points that emerge from her more general examination of the 'social and cultural dimensions of drug consumption' by the early Expressionists. Considering the sociological nature of her approach, it is perhaps not surprising that her discusion of Trakl, like that of the other two writers, is more concerned with the role of drugs in the poet's biography than in his works. However, in her attempt to relate the biographical data she presents to Trakl's lyric production, Sattler, unlike Heselhaus, shows no hesitation in reducing the essence of this relationship to a poetological formula, in effect repeating in isolation for Trakl the hermeneutic over-simplification we have already observed *en masse* in connection with Benn: 'Eine Vielzahl der Gedichte Trakls erscheint [...] als Verarbeitung seiner nächtlichen, berauschten Sinneswahrnehmungen, allerdings in der nüchternen Nachbearbeitung' (247). While Sattler's brief comments on the poetry itself usefully draw attention to the importance of its numerous references to both wine and opium (248–249), her reflections on the prominence of colour in Trakl's verse are curiously open-ended and do not lead to any conclusions about the significance of this feature for the relationship between drug and text (249–250).

By contrast with the relative scarcity of drug-oriented Trakl studies, the abundance of ready-made interpretative tools that literary criticism has appropriated, with increasing voracity, from the fields of psychology and especially psychoanalysis has resulted in a veritable flood of critical works that read Trakl's poetry primarily with reference to the poet's real or presumed mental and emotional instabilities. The magnitude of this flood is such that the psychopathological current has, over the last 50 years, become dominant in Trakl scholarship. In addition to works that openly adopt a diagnostic approach, notable among which are Theodor Spoerri's *Georg Trakl* (1954), Heinrich Goldmann's *Katabasis* (1957), Gunilla Bergsten's 'Georg Trakls traumatischer Kode' (1971), Maire Kurrik's *Georg Trakl* (1974), and Francis Michael Sharp's *The Poet's Madness* (1981), the influence of this psychopathological orientation is also manifested more or less directly in many other studies. It is apparent, for example, in the readiness – which must appear extraordinary to any reader uninitiated in Trakl criticism – with which so many commentators negate the referentiality or meaningfulness of Trakl's language, or the coherence and integrity of his poetic utterances, negations originally presented by the poet's critics-cum-psychiatrists as both symptoms and proofs of his 'madness'. General studies with a marked bias to semiotic negativity include Eckhard Philipp's *Die Funktion des Wortes in den Gedichten Georg Trakls* (1971), Hans Esselborn's *Georg Trakl* (1974), and Eric Williams's *The Mirror and the Word* (1993). In *Das Gedicht als Sühne* (1985), Gunther Kleefeld immediately identifies the principal methodological shortcoming of the psychopathological tradition in Trakl interpretation: 'Verwischt wurde die entscheidende Differenz zwischen Krankheitssymptom und Kunstprodukt' (4). However, Kleefeld's own reading of Trakl's poetry as an artistic embodiment of Freud's theory of the unconscious tends to blur another 'entscheidende Differenz,' that between 'Kunstprodukt' and scientific (or as some would have it, pseudo-scientific) theory. Moreover, despite the objection noted, Kleefeld himself continues to interpret the 'sprachliche Verhältnisse' of Trakl's poetry in the first place as symptomatic of the poet's 'psychische Verhältnisse,' and in this respect it changes little that he sees Trakl's poetic sublimation of Oedipal guilt as representative of a 'central problem of human culture' rather than as a purely personal concern (389–390). In general, the direction taken by Trakl scholarship under the influence of psychoanalytical theory – the potential usefulness of which to the study of literature is not in question – illustrates how interpretative tools, applied with laudable enthusiasm but without due care, may come to subjugate the purpose for which they are adopted, or in other words, how the methodology of an investigation may come to distort or displace its object.

The fullest recognition of – and most substantial reaction to – the distortions and displacements perpetrated by this branch of Trakl criticism can be found in Hildegard Steinkamp's *Die Gedichte Georg Trakls* (1988), which may be credited with redirecting attention towards what Heselhaus had, in quite a different context, pinpointed as 'die eigentliche Bedeutung Trakls' (229–230): his use of words. Indeed, although Steinkamp displays no particular interest in the poet's drug use and generally attributes minimal importance to biographical factors, the Trakl discussion contained in part 3 of the present study will to a significant extent draw and build on, and in certain ways revise, her judicious analysis of Trakl's 'landscape code' (see 7.2–9.1). This certainly represents a more workable model for understanding and examining Trakl's linguistic art than the chronic aphasia characteristic of schizophrenia presented as an interpretative paradigm by various critics of the psychopathological school. In her treatment of Trakl's poetry as poetry, to state the matter in the simplest possible terms, Steinkamp applauds the work of various predecessors – a minority among Trakl scholars, as she repeatedly underlines – whose studies manifest the same determination to illuminate the intrinsic if idiosyncratic coherence linking the phonetic, morpho-syntactic and semantic elements of the poems analyzed, and so set out to describe the features that make Trakl's verse both recognizable as poetry and an original contribution to this genre. In addition to Heselhaus's 'Das Metaphorische Gedicht,' other important precedents she acknowledges include Karl-Ludwig Schneider's *Der bildhafte Ausdruck in den Dichtungen Georg Heyms, Georg Trakls und Ernst Stadlers* (1954),

Klaus Simon's *Traum und Orpheus* (1955), and the various Trakl studies of Steinkamp's own mentor Hans Georg Kemper, notably his *Georg Trakls Entwürfe* (1970). Our own investigation of Trakl's poetry will seek to complement the text-analytical orientation of these studies with a parallel – but *not* subordinating – consideration of the role drugs and intoxication played in Trakl's life, and in this latter respect another important point of reference will be Hans Weichselbaum's excellent 1994 biography *Georg Trakl* (see especially 7.1).

Another scholar to earn special mention is Martin Seymour-Smith, whose erudite and extraordinarily comprehensive *Guide to Modern World Literature* (all references are to the revised 1985 edition) contains discerning and useful observations on both Benn and Trakl, and more generally exemplifies a balanced and pragmatic approach to literary analysis (see, for example, his comments on the use of critical terminology quoted in 1.2). His remarks exhibit a rigour of critical judgement that more specialist commentators would do well to emulate.

The critical literature concerned with Rheiner is easily summarized because its scope is so limited. Walter Huder (1977) and Thomas Rietzschel (1985 and 1986) accompany their collections of Rheiner's writings with essays of their own, offering a biographical and historical perspective on this lesser-known poet and his work, while his most recent editor Michael Grimm (2008) gives generous space to biographical material, including transcripts of documents and a memoir by the poet's wife. Collectively, these studies provide the foundation for our own biographical account in 5.1. In addition, two short articles appeared in the 1990s that remind us of Rheiner's status as a 'forgotten Expressionist': Michael Kohtes's 'Der Dichter auf der Nadel' (1992) and Norbert Weiß's 'Die große Krankheit' (1995). The first published monograph to deal with Rheiner's work in detail is Jeanine Atai's *Kokainliteratur in der Zwischenkriegszeit* (2008), in which elements of *Kokain*, in fact written during World War One, are compared to equivalent ones in both Danish author Otto Rung's 1923 novella with the same title (a work with the distinction of having suffered critical neglect even greater than that of its German namesake) and Pitigrilli's *Cocaina*. Atai's choice of terms of comparison confirms the trend in Rheiner reception, embodied in Grimm's edition published in the same year, towards raising his 1918 novella and with it the poet's biography to canonical status at the expense of his other prose works and poetry (see

5.1–5.2), while overlooking both his indebtedness to existing literary models and his place in Expressionism (see 5.1–6.4).

The second main group of critical texts germane to our topic comprises studies that investigate the relationship between literature and psychoactive substances from a historical perspective. The last two decades have seen the publication of numerous book-length works that adopt a broad, survey-type approach to this subject matter, in part at least in response to a growing interest in it from the wider reading public.[17] These include Alberto Castoldi's *Il testo drogato* (1994), Alexander Kupfer's *Die künstlichen Paradiese* and *Göttliche Gifte* (both 1996), Sadie Plant's *Writing on Drugs* (1999) and Marcus Boon's *The Road of Excess* (2002), all of which have already been referred to in 1.2. Also worthy of mention here are Alfred Springer's *Kokain: Mythos und Realität* (1989), and Dominique Antonin's *Un peu d'encre sur la neige* (1997), two anthologies of cocaine-related excerpts from literary works both containing substantial critical commentaries that in fundamental respects, including the texts discussed, resemble the cocaine chapters contained in the other books listed. Judging by the number of new publications in the field, this heightened interest in the historical development of drug literature is nowhere stronger than in the German-speaking world. In addition to Springer's and Kupfer's books, special volumes of both *Kritische Ausgabe* (2005) and *Amsterdamer Beiträge zur neueren Germanistik* (2008) have been dedicated to this subject, as well as several monographs, notably two concerned with the previously neglected question of drugs in German literature since the Second World War: Martin Tauss's *Rausch, Kultur, Geschichte* (2005) and Stephan Resch's *Provoziertes Schreiben* (2007). Atai's *Kokainliteratur in der Zwischenkriegszeit* and Sattler's *Vergiftete Sensationen* also belong to this trend and can thus be said to straddle our first and second groups of secondary literature.

Despite this wave of publications, it would be a mistake to describe the critical interest in the association between drugs and imaginative literature as recent in origin, and in this respect it is difficult to credit Boon's immodest claim that his book describes, 'for the first time, the history of the connection between writers and drugs' (6). Not only do all these works in fact draw on earlier studies, but Boon's draws heavily on

17 Kupfer, for example, describes his aim 'alle zu erörternden Zusammenhänge so darzustellen, daß sie nicht nur einem engen Kreis von Experten, sondern auch und vor allem einem allgemeinen interessierten Leserkreis zugänglich sind' (*kP* 8).

those of Springer, Castoldi, Kupfer and Plant as well. Seminal among earlier studies are Jean-Louis Brau's *Histoire de la drogue* (1968), Alethea Hayter's *Opium and the Romantic Imagination* (1968), the essays collected in *Intoxication and Literature* (a special 1974 issue of *Yale French Studies*), Arnould de Liedekerke's *La Belle Epoque de l'opium* (1984), and with particular reference to cocaine, Richard Ashley's *Cocaine: Its History, Uses and Effects* and George Andrews and David Solomon's *The Coca Leaf and Cocaine Papers* (both 1975). Attention should also be called to Benn's *Genie* essays of the early 1930s as an early manifestation of critical interest in the drug question. These cite numerous writer–drug associations as examples of Benn's 'bionegative' theory of artistic production (see 2.2), even though the connections are stated in strictly minimalist form: '*Opium:* De Quincey, Coleridge, Poe. *Absinth:* Musset, Wilde. *Äther:* Maupassant (außer Alkohol und Opium), Jean Lorrain. *Haschisch:* Baudelaire, Gautier [etc.]' (*GW* 3:647). A recent and expanded version of Benn's observations, although not presented as such, can be found in Philip Sandblom's *Creativity and Disease* (1992), which includes a chapter on the 'Artificial stimulation of creativity' (45–59). Predating even the *Genie* essays, Hans Maier's *Kokainismus* (1926) is in the first place a clinical treatise on the physiological and psychological damage caused by cocaine abuse, but also contains a detailed account of the drug's history, which the author himself recognizes as holding 'general cultural interest' (v). Although this is not directly concerned with cocaine's role in literature, Maier's chapters on the development of coca and cocaine use are perhaps the most valuable source of all as far as the historical background to our study is concerned, and the meticulousness of his history remains unsurpassed.

Another distinctive strand of academic interest in drug literature, emphasizing the drug-like nature of the literary text itself over and above any depictions of drug use it or its author's biography might contain, can be traced to Derrida's 'La Pharmacie de Platon' (1972, see 1.2). Derrida's influence is unmistakable, for example, in Avital Ronell's *Crack Wars: Literature, Addiction, Mania* (1992) – which offers a reading against-the-grain of Gustave Flaubert's *Madame Bovary* as a novel 'about bad drugs' and 'about thinking we have properly understood them' (61) – and in the volume of essays edited by Anna Alexander and Mark S. Roberts entitled *High Addiction: Reflections on Addiction and Modernity* (2003). As in the tradition of Benn-reverent scholarship described above, one distinguishing trait of scholars working in Derrida's wake is their habit of mimicking their master's rhetorical style, the density and opacity of which means that their arguments often appear arcane. On the other hand, their view of literary texts as ambivalent and volatile, potentially even dangerous entities serves as a valuable corrective to the tendency apparent in the historical surveys to treat them as inert documents that do little more than reflect attitudes, beliefs and behaviours (whether orthodox or rebellious) of individuals or groups in certain historical periods. The prospect Derrida offers of the '*pharmakon* writing' (see 1.2) is illustrative of both these characteristics – the stylistic and the conceptual – of the tradition that his own writing has spawned: 'We will watch it infinitely promise itself and endlessly vanish through concealed doorways that shine like mirrors and open into a labyrinth' (*PP* 128).

The value of diachronic studies such as those by Castoldi, Kupfer, Plant and Boon as reference works can hardly be overstated, as they are based on wide-ranging and complementary bibliographical research that in its entirety achieves encyclopaedic proportions. Yet their usefulness as methodological guides for exploring the more complex and obscure aspects of the drug–literature relationship is disappointingly limited, for to varying degrees they all manifest what we can identify as the three major, characteristic and related shortcomings of the critical treatment this relationship has received. First, their approach is predominantly anecdotal rather than analytical, which is understandable in view of the wealth of inviting anecdotal material, much of it potentially sensational, that can be collected under the drugs-in-literature rubric, and with these studies in particular it is doubly understandable because of their popular orientation. Second and more important, they tend to reduce or even ignore, in a manner that is often arbitrary and indiscriminate, the important distinctions between biography and literary text, creative method and rhetorical effect, fact and conjecture, in order to iron over apparent inconsistencies or fill in epistemological gaps rather than, as would be more in keeping with the mission of the literary scholar, evaluate their significance. Plant's choice of title, *Writing on Drugs* (echoed in Boon's choice of subtitle: *A History of Writers on Drugs*), is illustrative of this tendency to wilful conflation: it may be understood as either writing under the influence of drugs or writing about drugs, and the 'clever' ambiguity of this formulation establishes a certain, decidedly misleading identity of the two, which by no means presuppose one another (see 1.4). The predilection for reading all literary drug texts as De Quincey-like confession or Baudelaire-like reportage, already touched on in 1.2, is a further, prevalent manifestation of the same tendency to homogenize textual and non-textual events. Such reduction of textual analysis to a search for traces of the author's drug use – *Spurensuche* is a favourite term in the German-language studies – suggests uncritical adherence to the Romantic author cult (see 1.2) and embodies an attitude that Brik, one of this cult's most outspoken opponents, characterizes in a memorable hyperbole as 'maniacal':

> If the poetic work is understood as a 'human document,' as a diary entry, then it is interesting to the author, to his wife, his relatives, friends, and to maniacs such as those passionately seeking the answer to the question 'did Pushkin smoke?' – and to no one else. (90)

A more tempered view, formulated in accordance with Boris Tomashevsky's theory of 'literary biography' outlined below (see 1.4), might allow a place for the identification of traces as one strategy in a broader-based approach, but would also have to account for the possibility that such traces can be deceptive and might even be deliberately so, as well as recognizing that the search for them cannot be treated as an interpretive end in itself.

Readings of the 'did Pushkin smoke?'-variety are also symptomatic of the third major shortcoming of this line of literary criticism, namely the imposition of often ill-fitting interpretative models on individual texts or on bodies of work by individual writers, a form of what Seymour-Smith describes as the domination of critical terminology over individual achievement (xii; see 1.2). To a certain extent this tendency, too, is understandable, considering the vast range and variety of texts that the historical surveyors undertake to combine in succinct and meaningful patterns. As a pertinent example we might name Castoldi's and Boon's classification of Trakl as, in the first place, 'a writer we can link directly to cocaine' (Boon 185), a perspective which does not even attempt to do justice to Trakl's literary achievement and that also vastly over-simplifies his relationship to drugs (see 7.1). Resch's contradictory positioning of Trakl's poetry in a tradition of literature displaying 'Opiatspuren' (60) demonstrates the arbitrary and imprecise nature of such classifications.

To his credit, Kupfer largely avoids such misrepresentations by emphasizing, in addition to the class of substance administered or written about, the fundamental importance to any drug experience of cognitive, emotive, conceptual, and ideological variables on the one hand, and environmental, historical and cultural contingencies on the other, considerations encapsulated in the terms *set* and *setting* respectively (*GG* 437, *kP* 243–244). Kupfer's threefold analytical model is borrowed from Norman E. Zinberg's clinical study of heroin addiction *Drug, Set and Setting: The Basis for Controlled Intoxicant Use* (1984). In contrast to one based purely on neurochemical effects, this model can, for example, account for the fact that a user in search of contact with the divine will probably experience intoxication as a form of religious insight whether he drinks wine, as during Communion, takes opium, like 'der einsam Sinnende' in Trakl's 'Träumerei am Abend' (*SW* 1:558–562; see 9.2), or cocaine, like the lyric subject in Benn's 'O Nacht' (*GW* 1:53–54; see 3.1–3.3), whereas users with different expectations will experience intoxication brought about by the same drugs in a completely different way. Following Kupfer's lead, several other scholars, including Tauss, Resch and Atai, have also adopted the drug–set–setting model as an analytical framework. Its application to the study of literature, however, is not unproblematic, for although its distinctions provide a basis for more nuanced understandings of particular instances of drug use, they are not in themselves sufficient to account for the complexities of relationships between drugs and literary texts, in which a host of other variables deriving from the literary nature of the object of study come into play. When dealing with drug use of the literary variety, it is far from obvious, for example, where this 'use' is to be located in the communicative pathway between writer and reader, how many 'users' we have to consider – the writer, the narrator, a character or characters, the reader (as consumer of the *pharmakon*), perhaps even the text itself (Castoldi's 'il testo drogato') – and whether the 'drug' can be said to exist in a real, imaginary or symbolic dimension, or in some combination thereof (these variables are discussed in more depth in 1.4). Because of this insufficiency, the unreflected appropriation of Zinberg's analytical categories ultimately compounds the tendency evident in the historical surveys to treat the history of drug literature as an appendage to the pharmacological and social history of drug use, while downplaying its embedment in the history of literature as a whole.

A further point of interest concerning this second main group of critical works is that they give relatively little weight to the Expressionist period and hence to the three poets discussed here. Between them, the recent volumes of *Kritische Ausgabe* and *Amsterdamer Beiträge zur neueren Ger-*

manistik dedicated to drug literature contain only one essay concerned with an Expressionist writer: Ketteler's piece on Benn's cocaine poems cited above. In the monographs, Benn comes off best once again, obtaining two paragraphs from Castoldi (160–161), seven pages from Kupfer (*GG* 231–238), three pages plus a chapter heading – 'Induced Life'– from Boon (190–192), and four pages from Resch (263–266), who also uses a paraphrase of the same coinage as the title for his entire study: 'Provoziertes Leben' becomes *Provoziertes Schreiben.* Interestingly, Castoldi, Kupfer and Boon all quote either 'O Nacht' or 'Kokain' (*GW* 1:52; see 3.3–3.4) in full, each in a different language; little, however, is to be gained from their commentaries. Castoldi's observations are limited to bibliographical description. Kupfer neatly restates earlier critics' positions, including those of Arend and Rübe (see above). Boon's emphasis on the 'racial', even 'fascist' concerns he sees in 'Provoziertes Leben' – which Benn in fact wrote despite the Nazi ban on his literary activity (see 2.2) – is misleading, while his denial of a 'spiritual dimension' in Benn's writing suggests a failure to see beyond the writer's calculated coolness and what Schöne has perspicaciously described as the 'überformte fiktive Gestalt des Dichters' (226). Resch, whose interest in Benn is primarily as background to the literature of the post-War period, notes the abundance of existing scholarship dealing with this writer's personal and literary use of drugs, and limits himself to sketching a few essential motifs. For Trakl the same critics reserve, in quantitative terms, about half the attention they pay to Benn. But here, importantly, several original and, for our purposes, potentially fruitful channels of investigation into the relationship between Trakl's poetry and drug use can be found, which is all the more remarkable in view of the dearth of such channels offered by specialist Trakl criticism. Of particular note are Castoldi's – very brief – comments on Trakl's poetic use of black–white contrasts (160) and snow imagery (ibid.), and Kupfer's remarks on the prevalence of colour in Trakl's lyrics (*GG* 230–231). In truth, both Castoldi and Kupfer direct their readings towards biographical decipherment, but their observations may also be taken as starting points for less reductive lines of enquiry (see 9.1–10.2). Finally, the three and a half pages that Resch devotes to Rheiner (266–270) seem like a veritable avalanche in view of the scant attention paid to him in previous studies; the poet and his novella *Kokain* had been mentioned in passing – and then not again – by Kupfer and Boon, although the former had also offered a full-page reprint of Conrad Felixmüller's painting 'Der Tod des Dichters Walter Rheiner'

(*GG* 223; see 5.1), a gesture replicated by Resch, who squeezes the image into half a page (267).

The three key works excluded from this summary of the literary historians' interest in Benn, Trakl and Rheiner are Atai's *Kokainliteratur in der Zwischenkriegszeit*, Sattler's *Vergiftete Sensationen* and Springer's *Kokain: Mythos und Realität*. Atai's book has already been discussed in relation to works of specialist Rheiner criticism, and the salient features of Sattler's Trakl study have already been noted in our summary of previous scholarship on that poet. However, the fact that the latter is only part of a much broader investigation of drug use in literary Expressionism sets Sattler's book apart, and for this reason it warrants particular attention. As far as Springer's annotated anthology is concerned, this by contrast gives no more space to Expressionism than the other works already described, covering the entire epoch in only six pages (43–48); although brief, this treatment appears decisive in having shaped the coverage given by later scholars, especially in its quotation of Benn's 'Kokain', Trakl's 'Der Schlaf' (*SW* 4i:13–24; see 9.2) and its reproduction of Felixmüller's Rheiner portrait, works that have continued to reappear in more recent studies. More importantly, however, Springer justifies his omission of an 'ausführliche Darstellung des Kokain- und Drogengebrauchs im Expressionistischen Jahrzehnt' (13) by noting that he has already provided such an account in his essay 'Narkotomanie in der Boheme des Deutschen Expressionismus' (1979). In its focus on the role of drug use in Expressionism, this essay (already cited in 1.2 above) can be seen alongside Sattler's book as exceptional among the works of this second group in its degree of pertinence to our own study. Springer approaches his task of assessing the significance of drug use for the Bohemian subculture of the Expressionist epoch via detailed consideration of the lives, addictions and influence of two of its prominent representatives: the psychiatrist and psychoanalyst Otto Gross and the poet Johannes R. Becher. He follows this with a wide-ranging report on drug use and abuse among creative and performing artists of the period, each case dealt with in terms that are only marginally less minimalist than those employed by Benn in his *Genie* essays. Collectively, these 'Einzelschicksale' are intended to illustrate Springer's main point: 'daß die allgemeine Stimmung die Droge als integrales Element der literarischen Subkultur anzusehen schien; darüber hinaus auch Drogenkonsumation als allgemeines Recht anerkannte' (31). Benn, Trakl and Rheiner are all mentioned, but even here they occupy no more than a few lines each. Considering this fact in combination with the observation made above that Springer's cocaine references are taken from texts written *about* rather than *during* the epoch in question (see 1.2), the present study clearly complements his work much more than it overlaps with it.

To a large extent, Sattler's *Vergiftete Sensationen* builds on and refines the approach adopted by Springer in his essay. Gross and Becher occupy similarly prominent positions in her work as in Springer's, but more importantly, her overall aim is broadly similar to his in that she is primarily concerned with identifying and describing the specific social conditions, attitudes and values that made drug use an integral part of the 'Expressionist counter-culture' (108) of the immediate pre-War years. As a foundation for this analysis, she dedicates considerable space to a discussion of various sociological terms and to their application in characterizing the society of late Wilhelmine Germany. A further parallel to Springer's 'Narkotomanie' is that Benn and Rheiner are both mentioned in passing, but neither is given extended treatment. By contrast, Trakl, as already discussed, figures as one of three case studies, although when we consider the specific arguments that these studies are meant to illustrate, his inclusion may seem surprising and unfortunate, and if anything it reveals – against the author's own intentions – the limitations of the analytical framework employed:

> Den expressionistischen Autoren dient er [der Rauschmittelkonsum] als wirksames Instrument des sozialen Rückzugs und des demonstrativen Protestes gegen die kulturellen Axiome der wilhelminischen Gesellschaft und die Maßstäbe der protestantischen Ethik, denen sich vor allem das kulturdominante Bildungsbürgertum auf seinem Weg in eine moderne Industriegesellschaft ergibt. (161)

Trakl's singular unsuitability for illustrating these points has a twofold basis. For one thing, it is hardly plausible to interpret his drug use as a form of protest against a society of which he was never part, for he lived, wrote and took drugs not in Wilhelmine Germany, but in a quite separate and in important respects very different state, late-Habsburg Austria; his only extended period of immersion in Wilhelmine society was a two-week visit to Berlin in March 1914, only eight months before his death. Similarly, it makes little sense to see his 'protest' as directed at anything that might be called the 'protestant ethic,' for although he indeed came from a protestant family, this was part of a small denominational minority in his native Salzburg, where the dominant religious orientation was in fact overwhelmingly Roman Catholic, as Weichselbaum underlines: 'Der Katholizismus war herrschende Religion, 98% der [Salzburger] Bevölkerung bekannten sich zu ihm oder waren zumindest katholisch getauft' (19). For Sattler's purposes, Benn, as the son of a protestant priest from Prignitz in the heart of Prussia, would surely have fitted more neatly with the thrust of her argument, whereas Trakl's case in fact serves to demonstrate that the Expressionist rebellion – in so far as he can be associated with it – reached beyond the parameters within which she positions it.

The third category of secondary literature drawn on in the present study might best be labelled 'miscellaneous literary scholarship,' as the unifying quality of the works it contains is that they belong to neither of the two groups already described. The necessity for such a category derives from the realization that rigorous analysis of texts in the field of drug literature depends on consideration of their embedment in the wider field of literature in general, a realization which, as already indicated, is less self-evident than might be assumed. The relevance of the works in this group to the topic under discussion is perhaps less obvious, but their importance to our analysis of a given text or texts, in particular as interpretative analogies or precedents, may in fact be more decisive than that of other studies that deal explicitly with the same object. Three examples suggest themselves by their prominence: Shoshana Felman's reflections on the potentialities and limits of relating psychoanalytical theory to literature, contained in 'Henry James: Madness and the Risks of Practice' (1985), will act as an important direction marker in our reading of Benn's poem 'Kokain' (see 3.4), which to a significant extent invites psychoanalytical interpretation; Johann Wolfgang von Goethe's remarks on the possibility of a therapeutic relationship between writer and text, made in *Dichtung und Wahrheit* (1811–33) in relation to his own novel *Die Leiden des jungen Werthers* (1774), offer a propitious model for understanding the lightly veiled autobiographical references in Rheiner's novella *Kokain* (see 6.3); while Roman Jakobson's comments on the 'metonymical expression' (307) of the lyric ego in the poetry of Boris Pasternak, found in his article 'Randbemerkungen zur Prosa des Dichters Pasternak' (1935),[18] can be applied almost verbatim to the poetry of Trakl, where they constitute an alternative and antithetical interpretative position

18 The titles and dates of Jakobson's studies named in the main text refer to their first publication or, where this is anterior, first delivery. All citations, by contrast, are taken from the English versions collected in *Language and Literature*, and all page numbers refer to this edition.

to that sustained by the poet's psychic disintegrationalists (see 9.1). In addition to this specific parallel, we should also stress that Jakobson's theoretical concepts, along with those of his Formalist colleague Tomashevsky, have a more fundamental importance to the approach adopted in this study, as shall now be explained in 1.4.

1.4 Reading Cocaine: Some Methodological Considerations

We have already mentioned that the approach adopted in this study will be based on Edgar Morin's principle of using certainties as reference points to explore uncertainties, which necessarily implies recognizing and maintaining the distinction between the two (see 1.1). Moreover, we have also noted that many previous studies addressing the relationship between drugs and literature have adopted a different approach, one that blurs this distinction by superimposing certainty upon uncertainty or presenting speculation as established truth, inevitably resulting in over-simplification or other forms of misrepresentation (see 1.3). Especially but not exclusively, this problem concerns the distinction between the writer's biography and his literary works, where a mixture of certainties and uncertainties may often be found in both areas, as well as in the many and varied links between them. By way of illustration, we offer two simplistic examples in which the potential for misreading is most evident. First, the fact that a text

(a) exhibits 'symptoms' of intoxication,
(b) portrays drug use, whether in the first or third person, or
(c) mentions or alludes to a drug, whether once or repeatedly,

does not necessarily mean that its author was a user of that drug or that he composed the text under its influence; conversely, the knowledge that a writer used a particular drug in a particular period does not necessarily mean that his literary works of the same period describe that use, whether directly or in enciphered form. In both these examples, what is certain may be used as a springboard for a closer examination of what is uncertain, but care must be taken not to confuse the two by an arbitrary transposition of epistemological category.

Schools of thought that claim the author is dead or irrelevant avoid possible confusion between the text and the biography of its writer by disregarding the latter altogether. This theoretical position might at first appear to offer a tidy solution to the problem, but in truth it is an over-reaction to it that does little to reduce the risk of interpretive distortion. The idea that the author's situation should be of no interest to the reader – whether the specific type of reader known as the literary critic or of any other kind – betrays a fundamental misconception of the institution of literature in its modern form and in particular the normative modes of production and reception of literary texts as they have developed over the last centuries. These developments, which are closely related to the shift in the perception of the poet's role discussed in 1.2 above, are described with particular cogency by Tomashevsky in his 1923 essay 'Literatura i biografiya' ('Literature and Biography'), which sets out to 'consider how the poet's biography operates in the reader's consciousness' (47). This essay contains several insights that can help us to negotiate the difficulties associated with the biographical question that arises in the study of drug literature; for this reason we shall now undertake to summarize its main points.

Tomashevsky dates the cultivation of 'subjectivism in the artistic process' (48) to the 18th century and associates it in particular with the figures of Voltaire and Jean-Jacques Rousseau, who were 'not only writers but also public figures' (ibid.) and whose works, even during their own lifetimes, became inseparably linked in their readers' minds with their personalities. The decisive step towards what we can today recognize as distinctively modern literary practice came when the two writers began to exploit this link for the purpose of self-stylization:

> The knowledge that their biographies were a constant background for their works compelled Voltaire and Rousseau to dramatize certain epic motifs in their own lives and, furthermore, to create for themselves an artificial legendary biography composed of intentionally selected real and imaginary events. (49)

Following their lead, the Romantics found an even more radical application for the same strategy:

> A biography of a Romantic poet was more than a biography of an author and public figure. The Romantic poet *was* his own hero. His *life* was poetry, and soon there developed a canonical set of actions to be carried out by the poet. [...] The author

> becomes a witness to and living participant in his novels, a living hero. A double transformation takes place: heroes are taken for living personages, and poets become living heroes – their biographies become poems. (49–50, italics in the original)

The Romantic period thus represents a first peak in the history of what we might call the 'biographical aesthetic.' Tomashevsky notes an ebb that occurred in the mid-19th century when 'the poet-hero was replaced by the professional poet, the businessman-journalist' (52), and writers withdrew to the anonymity of their desks. However, the decisive shift brought about by the Romantics and their immediate predecessors could no longer be undone; even when most writers had abandoned Romantic pretensions to heroism, the obsession with authorial biography remained ingrained in the reception of their works, so that certain scholars set themselves the task of inventing biographies for these writers and projecting their literary works onto them, attempts that 'consistently ended in farce' (ibid.). With the advent of what we have called literary Modernism (Tomashevsky, who takes most of his examples from Russian literature, uses different terminology), writers developed a new fondness for manipulating their own biographical images, and writing in 1923, Tomashevsky records that this trend 'has continued to grow to the present day' (53). A characteristic of this new peak was the diversification of forms this manipulation took: Tomashevsky's list ranges from 'petty naughtiness' (ibid.) to a literature of 'intimate conversations and confidential confessions' (54), and from the 'biographical lyricism' of the Russian Symbolists (ibid.) to the 'demonstrative declarations delivered in a monumental style' of the Futurists who superseded them (ibid.).

On the basis of these historical observations, Tomashevsky makes two fundamental theoretical distinctions. The first concerns the divergence of 'literary' from 'actual' biographies, the latter consisting in the writer's curriculum vitae, the former in the 'ideal biographical legend' that he shapes in collaboration with his readers and critics, playing on the conventional expectations and assumptions resulting from the historical developments described, and that – crucially for scholars of his works – 'the poet considers as a premise to his creations' (52). The second is the distinction between 'writers with biographies and writers without biographies' (55), where the biography in question is of the 'literary' variety (of 'writers without biographies,' Tomashevsky specifies that obviously 'these authors do have *actual* biographies,' 53). The works of writers of the latter type, dominant prior to Romanticism and then again in the mid-19th century, can be considered 'self-contained units. There are no biographical features shedding light on the meaning of their works' (52). Scholars must take both these distinctions into account in decisions regarding the extent and manner of integration of biographical knowledge into the study of particular literary works; one consequence of failure to do so, Tomashevsky warns in conclusion, would be the reduction of literary scholarship to the composition of 'satires or denunciations on the alive or the dead' (55).

How do Tomashevsky's findings relate specifically to the study of drug literature? Three points warrant attention. First, the blurring of boundaries between art and life, between text and non-text, which we have identified as a characteristic weakness of scholarship concerned with drug literature, is now revealed as an essentially literary phenomenon. The tendency to biographical conflation is already present in the object of study, and the willingness of certain literary scholars to perpetuate or exaggerate it thus appears to signal ensnarement in literature's mechanisms of self-mystification; we might say that consciously or unconsciously, such scholars are playing the literary game rather than attempting to describe its rules.[19] Without question, the confused relationship between literature and life that has predominated since the Romantic period complicates the task of literary analysis. Tomashevsky writes, for example, that 'it is sometimes difficult to decide whether literature recreates phenomena from life or whether the opposite is in fact the case: that the phenomena of life are the result of the penetration of literary clichés into reality' (51). However, suspension of the distinction between the two, which would amount to a kind of anti-analysis, cannot be considered an adequate scholarly response to this difficulty.

Second and on the other hand, we find confirmation in 'Literatura i biografiya' that consideration of the writer's drug use, in so far as we are dealing with a 'writer with a biography' in which drugs figure, is not only legitimate but necessary for the understanding of his works, for 'in the works themselves the juxtaposition of the texts and the author's biography

---

19 It may well be illusory, as the post-structuralists insist, to think that one can ever put oneself outside the game, but such an objection makes little difference. An essential distinction remains between players who take the rules as given and have internalized them to the point where they show no awareness of them, and those who recognize them as constructed and, to the extent allowed by their status as players, undertake to examine and question them.

plays a structural role' (55). The three writers under investigation in the present study all fall into this category: their respective œuvres are linked not only by drug references, but also by a tendency towards subjectiveness, even if this takes a noticeably different form in each. In Benn's, we encounter a mixture of 'demonstrative declarations,' some of them mutually contradictory, and self-conscious intellectualism; in Rheiner's, revolutionary posturing alternates with pained expressions of existential angst that is frequently attributed to a figure identified as 'the poet'; in Trakl's, the masking – or better, metonymical displacement – of subjectivity casts the author in an enigmatic shroud and thus serves to stimulate the reader's curiosity about his identity, as it did most famously with Rainer Maria Rilke, who responded to his reading of *Sebastian im Traum* with the question: 'wer mag er gewesen sein?' (letter to Ludwig von Ficker, 15.2.1915; Rilke *B* 37). In these subjective contexts, the three poets' drug references, like many other elements, clearly play on their 'potential [non-textual] reality' (Tomashevsky 55).

The third point, which might be considered a synthesis of the first two, concerns the vigilance required in distinguishing between 'literary' and 'actual' biographies, between the image of the author that is projected or implied by his works – as well as in their reception – and the documented facts that make up his curriculum vitae. This call for vigilance echoes Schöne's warning of the hazard for Benn scholars represented by the 'vom eigenen Gestaltungswillen überformte fiktive Gestalt des Dichters' (226; see 1.3), but gives it general relevance: the same considerations apply to all 'writers with biographies,' even when the fictionality of the poet's image is less apparent than in Benn's works. In regard to this third point, the approach adopted in the present study diverges in one respect from that advocated by Tomashevsky, who argues that only knowledge of the literary biography is required 'to reconstruct the psychological milieu surrounding a literary work' (52), whereas 'actual biographies of private individuals' hold no substantial interest for literary scholars (53). The underlying assumption here, by contrast, is that the identification of points of similarity and difference between the two can be instrumental in recognizing and understanding the author's strategies of self-stylization operative in a given text. For example, the hyperbole in Benn's claim that all the literature he produced between 1912 and 1922 was written in 1916 (*GW* 8:1873; see 2.2), the year of his so-called 'episode with cocaine,' only becomes visible when we bring our knowledge of his actual biography to bear.

An approach to textual analysis that affirms the pertinence of biographical data has a distinct but complementary theoretical basis in the recognition of literary expression as a *linguistic* practice. Recognition of the literary text as a verbal act necessarily implies acknowledgement of the addresser, meaning the speaker or writer, as one of its six indispensable elements as identified by Jakobson in his seminal 1958 lecture 'Linguistics and Poetics' (66). Such a perspective is also useful in so far as it underlines that the writer is only one among several elements, that the relationship between author and literary work is not unmediated or transparent, and that an approach to the text that concentrates on biographical considerations to the exclusion of others cannot but lead to a blinkered perspective. At the same time, it would be delusive to suggest that the author can simply be deleted from the basic formula of the communicative act: 'The ADDRESSER sends a MESSAGE to the ADDRESSEE' (Jakobson 66). According to this view, the existence of the *literary text as message* is itself sufficient to imply the existence of an *author as addresser* (whether alive or dead, singular or plural), even if the text in question contains no reference to its own authorship of the type that could be considered to constitute, in Tomashevsky's terms, a literary biography. This implication is in turn sufficient to legitimize scholarly attention to the author as a constitutive element of the larger semiotic system within which the text operates.

Jakobson's own literary studies, which variously anticipate, accompany or grow from his theoretical analyses of language and its operations, represent a further valuable source of guidelines, which can be integrated with those we have already drawn from Tomashevsky's work, for dealing with the biographical question that arises in the study of drug literature. Readers with a second-hand familiarity of Jakobson's concepts and procedures may be surprised that the co-founder of both the Moscow and Prague schools of Formalism could provide guidelines for a meaningful examination of the relationship between a literary work and its writer's circumstances. However, as early as 1933 in his lecture 'Co je poezie?' ('What is Poetry?'), the scholar himself offered a terse and properly indignant response to the widespread 'one-dimensional' view of his approach as overly technical, abstract and unfeeling, a view which, incidentally, has been endorsed and perpetuated more recently in Trakl scholarship by Sharp (*PM* 193) and Williams (122; see 7.2), both of whom make objections of the sort Jakobson describes here:

> It has been quite fashionable in critical circles to profess certain doubts about what is called the Formalist study of literature. The school, say its detractors, fails to grasp the relationship of art to real life; it calls for an 'art for art's sake' approach; it is following in the footsteps of Kantian aesthetics. Critics with objections in this vein are so completely one-sided in their radicalism that, forgetting the existence of a third dimension, they view everything on a single plane. Neither Tynjanov nor Mukařovský nor Šklovskij nor I have ever proclaimed the self-sufficiency of art. What we have been trying to show is that art is an integral part of the social structure, a component that interacts with all the others and is itself mutable since both the domain of art and its relationship to the other constituents of the social structure are in constant dialectical flux. What we stand for is not the separatism of art but the autonomy of the aesthetic function. (377–378)

In fact many of Jakobson's studies call attention to the relationship between writer and text, which elsewhere in 'Co je poezie?' he aptly characterizes as a 'dialectical alliance with constant shifts' (371), and yet others take this relationship as their principal object and examine it in depth. One such is the article 'Socha v symbolice Puškinově' (1937; 'The Statue in Pushkin's Poetic Mythology'), which is introduced with a set of general methodological reflections of absolute relevance to our own study:

> We must not, of course, succumb to either vulgar *biographism*, which takes a literary work for a reproduction of the situation from which it originated and infers an unknown situation from a work, or to vulgar *antibiographism*, which dogmatically denies any connection between the work and the situation. The analysis of poetic language can profit greatly from the important information provided by contemporary linguistics about the multiform interpenetration of the word and the situation, about their mutual tension and mutual influence. We do not wish mechanically to derive a work from a situation, but at the same time, in analyzing a poetic work, we should not overlook significant repeated correspondences between a situation and the work, especially a regular connection between certain common characteristics of a poet's several works and a common place or common dates; nor should we overlook the biographical preconditions of their origin if they are the same. The situation is a component of speech; the poetic function transforms it like every other component of speech, sometimes emphasizing it as an efficient formal device, sometimes, on the contrary, subduing it, but whether a work includes the situation positively or negatively, the work is never indifferent to it. (320)

Here, then, we have a clear summary of the dangers, but also of the possibilities and indeed the value, of integrating biographical data into the reading of a literary work. Two principles Jakobson registers appear especially important for the evaluation of text–drug relationships. The first is the need for a balanced view that, to paraphrase Matthew, renders unto the biography the things that are the biography's, and unto the text the things that are the text's, if the critic is to avoid veering off towards either of the two extremes named at the beginning of this passage. Of the two, 'vulgar biographism' is undoubtedly the more immediate danger, although an extreme reaction in the opposite direction, one that either states or implies that the work is indeed 'indifferent' to the situation, is also conceivable. The second important principle is recognition of the multiform and bidirectional relationship between these two entities; their influence and tension are 'mutual'. Thus, we should immediately be put on guard by critics who tell us their aim is to investigate 'the influence of the author's drug use on his writing' (*literarische Verarbeitung der eigenen Drogenerfahrung* is another favourite phrase among the German-language scholars), for such a statement of intent, by placing the author's situation and his works in a hierarchical, unidirectional relationship, already implies a serious oversimplification of the matter in hand. But what, we might ask in reply, about the influence of his literary activity on his drug use? Or what, regardless of whether something as clear-cut yet evasive as 'influence' can be identified, about other possible forms of 'interpenetration of the word and the situation'?

It has been noted above that the complex web of certainties and uncertainties that confronts the critic investigating the association between literature and psychoactive substances concerns the distinction between biography and work 'especially but not exclusively,' and the methodological considerations made thusfar all relate to this particular aspect. To give a more complete picture of the possible complications involved – and as will become apparent in the chapters that follow, these are not only possible but very real – it is necessary to expand our theoretical model to include all the constitutive elements of the semiotic system within which the literary work operates, which on the most basic level are the same as those of any speech act.[20] Once again we refer to Jakobson's 'Linguistics and Poetics' for a succinct description and diagrammatic representation (also reproduced in many textbooks of linguistics) of these elements:

20 The idea that the criteria used in the analysis of other verbal operations cannot or should not be applied to the study of literature is pure mystification. The non-specificity of the addressee, for example, is by no means peculiar to literature (it is also a feature of journalism, or for that matter, bank notes).

The ADDRESSER sends a MESSAGE to the ADDRESSEE. To be operative the message requires a CONTEXT referred to (the 'referent' in another, somewhat ambiguous, nomenclature), graspable by the addressee, and either verbal or capable of being verbalized; a CODE fully, or at least partially, common to the addresser and addressee (or in other words, to the encoder and decoder of the message); and, finally, a CONTACT, a physical channel and psychological connection between the addresser and the addressee, enabling both of them to enter and stay in communication. All these factors inalienably involved in verbal communication may be schematized as follows:

	CONTEXT		
ADDRESSER	MESSAGE	ADDRESSEE	
	CONTACT		
	CODE		(66)

When examining a text in view of its known or possible relationships to another entity – whether cocaine, cabbages or kings – certain basic considerations should be made that allow us both to describe those relationships in their full complexity and to capture their specific nuances, considerations deriving from a conception of the text itself, the 'message' in Jakobson's model, as part of a larger system that by its very nature must comprise other components as well. We should ask, first, where in Jakobson's schema representing this system, in which element or combination of elements, the entity can be located; second, in what form it is manifested in that location; and third, how this manifestation may affect our perception of other elements and of the dynamic interplay of all elements that determines the text's overall function and character. In the analysis of literary texts, furthermore, the multiplication and ambiguity of individual elements, qualities intrinsically associated with the literary use of language, must also be taken into account.

Clearly, we must distinguish between the author as primary addresser, the narrator or lyric subject as secondary addresser, and other characters to whom speech acts contained in the text may be attributed, who effectively become tertiary addressers. Thus, in Benn's poems 'O Nacht' and 'Kokain', which not only describe cocaine intoxication, but date from their author's 'episode' with the drug (see 2.1–2.2), both the primary and secondary addressers can be identified with certainty as cocaine users. However, in line with Tomashevsky's theory of multiple biographies, it would be careless to construe a straightforward identification between the two on this basis without deeper consideration of the problematic relationship between

Benn and his often deceptively candid literary persona. By contrast, in Trakl's poems 'Klage' and 'Grodek' (see 8.1–8.2), written in the first months of the First World War when the poet is known to have taken 'sehr viel Kokain zu sich' (*HkA* 2:730; see 7.1), only the primary addresser can be described with certainty as a cocaine user. Still, important textual factors indicate that the voice of the lyric subject or secondary addresser embodies a consciousness displaying significant and specific parallels with the consciousness of the drug user. Foremost among these factors are the stylistic idiosyncrasies arising from Trakl's skilful manipulation – really a controlled 'disordering' in the manner of Rimbaud (see 1.2), although linguistic rather than sensory – of the interplay between message, context, contact and code (see 9.1).

Similar distinctions can also be made in relation to the addressee, where the reader or primary addressee may be supplemented by a secondary addressee, such as a fictitious character to whom a certain utterance is directed, or in apostrophe – a rhetorical device most common in poetry – an imaginary or absent person or personification. In Benn's 'Kokain', the position of secondary addressee is occupied by the drug itself in the opening stanza, and by the intoxication it produces in the final lines, in a clear example of what Jakobson defines as the 'magic, incantatory' verbal function (68). A further example of this function can be found in Rheiner's poem 'Komm, holder Schnee!' (172; see 6.4), although here the possible cocaine reference is metaphoric and therefore ambiguous. On the other hand, a study that located cocaine in the primary addressee, in other words, a study of 'reading on cocaine,' would be fraught with obvious legal difficulties, whatever insights it may yield.

Even if we do not treat the reader's neurochemical state as an object of investigation, however, the importance of the reader's role as 'decoder of the message' remains fundamental to our evaluation of the drug's place in other parts of the schema; in this sense the present study might be characterized as an exercise not in 'reading *on* cocaine,' but simply in 'reading cocaine.' Where the drug can be located in a given element only with a degree of uncertainty, as in 'Komm, holder Schnee!', the individual reader's attention to certain textual features and readiness to interpret them as cocaine references may be decisive to the overall reading effect and so to any subsequent interpretation of the literary work (nowhere is this clearer, perhaps, than in the cocaine-oriented readings of Stevenson's *The Strange Case of Dr Jekyll and Mr Hyde* discussed in 1.2). In literature, as in all forms of communication in which the text is somehow recorded or fixed, the 'reification' of the message, its transformation into 'an enduring thing' (Jakobson 86), permits a potentially unlimited variety of *reading instances*, each at a different distance in space and time from the original act of encoding, and each shaped by the individual addressee's expectations, beliefs, and knowledge of the code. It is evident, then, that the variables encapsulated in the terms *set* and *setting* (see 1.3) are just as determinant in the practice of reading as they are in the practice of drug taking.

At the same time, it is likely that the reader's response to a literary work will be influenced, whether directly or indirectly, consciously or unconsciously, by previous reading instances which have themselves become reified as its 'reception' and which as such become decisive factors in shaping the set and setting for new readers. As already noted (see 1.2), once a link to drugs in a particular work has been hypothesized, the association tends to become self-perpetuating and rapidly comes to be taken – or at least presented – as self-evident. Similarly, the potential for intervention of other actors, such as editors, publishers, critics or translators, who may manipulate the message before it reaches its addressee, must also be accounted for, and it is conceivable that cocaine might be introduced into the communicative pathway not by the author or reader, but by these third parties. A pertinent example is the decision made by Rheiner's editors to apply the title of his novella *Kokain* to several collections of his works (see 5.1–5.2); for a reader in otherwise equivalent conditions, a particular Rheiner poem contained in a collection with that title might prompt a quite different response from the same poem in, say, an anthology of Expressionist verse. It goes without saying that the present study could itself contribute to precisely the same kind of manipulation of the reader's perceptions of the texts it quotes and investigates; awareness of this possibility adds an ethical dimension to the need already identified for systematic analysis involving careful distinction between certainties and uncertainties.

The occurrence of the word *Kokain* in the message indicates that the drug necessarily features in the referent context as well, whereas an indirect reference to it – which may or may not be taken as such by the reader – necessarily makes its role in the context ambiguous. Indirect references may be of various types. Benn's play *Karandasch* alone contains several (see 4.1–4.3): in addition to one direct reference, here we find a metaphorical reference in the phrase 'kleine schimmernde Kristalle' (*GW* 6:1531), a metonymical reference in the main character's sore throat, and a stylistic reference – also metonymical in nature – in the play's frenzied dialogue. As explained in 1.1, any radical stylistic abnormality, meaning any obvious distortion or subversion of the linguistic code, may invite interpretation as an indirect reference to drug use. Such subversion may also result in partial or total incomprehension, that is, a partial or total loss of psychological contact between addresser and addressee, and so may cause the reader to question the extent to which the code itself can be considered common or the writer's use of it communicative. The notion that in his poetry Trakl unfetters words from their meanings, sustained for example by Philipp (137), is illustrative as an extreme denial of communicative efficacy (see 7.2); we should also note that there is no empirical justification for the extremity of such a claim. In the analysis of the interplay between message, code and contact, it must be remembered that in literature, and especially in Modernist literature (see 1.2), the balance between these factors – a balance for which language users normally strive and which renders the interplay between these components inconspicuous in most verbal operations – is often disturbed for aesthetic ends.

Whatever the nature of the cocaine reference contained in the message, if the drug's role in the context is to be accurately assessed, this must also be seen in relation to the total context, a perspective that opens up several further lines of critical investigation. A clear priority is to determine whether cocaine is a central or peripheral element in a particular work, which may depend on whether references to it are isolated or repeated. For example, a crucial distinction between Rheiner's story 'Der Tod des Schwärmers Gautier Fémin' and his later novella *Kokain*, both of which include direct references to cocaine, is that the drug is a secondary element in the former but, as the title suggests, a primary one in the latter. When confronted with an indirect reference, on the other hand, we ought to ask to what extent this may be activated or supported by analogous references in the same text. This will be a chief concern in our discussion of possible cocaine allusions in Trakl's poetry, in which the drug is never mentioned by name (see 10.1–10.2). Whether cocaine is central or peripheral, explicit or disguised, the thematic connection between the drug and other elements of the context will be a fundamental consideration in respect to all the works examined. An equally significant and perhaps less obvious question regards the overall degree of semantic clarity in the context, given that a high or low degree of clarity may suggest an implicit affirmation of sobriety or intoxication respectively, regardless of the actual subject matter or attitudes expressed in a work. The question of clarity is closely related to the one of style mentioned in the previous paragraph, and in particular to the relative hierarchical positions of the referential and poetic functions in an individual text. In Jakobson's most concise definition of these terms, the referential function involves 'orientation toward the context' (66), and the poetic function a contrasting 'focus on the message for its own sake' (69). Ambiguity in the context is, he explains, an inevitable consequence of 'the supremacy of the poetic function over the referential function,' and therefore a 'corollary feature of poetry' (85–86). It can be argued, therefore, that poetry always manifests a degree of *textual intoxication* in the sense described in 1.1, although this characteristic may be augmented or moderated by the individual poet, and may vary noticeably between poetic schools and genres (generally it is much more prominent in the lyric, with its emotive emphasis, than the epic, in which the narrative function is determinant). In fact, the same quality may be just as evident in poetic prose, that is, in prose that displays a strong tendency to poeticity, 'when words and their composition, their meaning, their external and inner form, acquire a weight and value of their own instead of referring indifferently to reality' (Jakobson 378). That poetic prose lends itself to the representation of intoxicated consciousness is exemplified by Benn's short stories and plays of the Expressionist period (see 4.1).

By now it should be clear that 'reading cocaine' is a multi-faceted undertaking, and that failure to appreciate the extent of its multi-facetedness may easily transform reading into misreading. It should also be clear, however, that because of this same multi-facetedness, it may give rise to interesting and unusual perspectives on the different aspects of a literary work or body of works, the interrelations between these aspects, and between textual and non-textual elements. It remains, then, to apply the theoretical considerations outlined here to the practical analysis of the poems, stories and plays that present themselves as most relevant to our topic.

Part One: Gottfried Benn

Welches war der Weg der Menschheit gewesen bis hierher? Sie hatte Ordnung herstellen wollen in etwas, das hätte Spiel bleiben sollen. Aber schließlich war es doch Spiel geblieben, denn nichts war wirklich.

– Benn, 'Der Geburtstag' (GW 5:1227–1228)

2 The Toxicology of Genius

2.1 Disentangling Benn

Among the European writers who sniffed, injected and imbibed cocaine during the first decades of the twentieth century, Gottfried Benn (1886–1956) occupies a singular position. He is the only one to have both treated the drug directly as a literary object – it appears in two of his poems and two of his plays – *and* to have explored, in a more theoretical (but no less exalted) manner, the relationship between artistic production and drug-taking, and more broadly between creative 'genius' and abnormal physiological and psychological states. Yet the importance of cocaine, and drugs in general, in Benn's works is far from self-evident, and an even denser haze enshrouds the purely biographical matter of his personal experience with psychoactive substances. That he took cocaine is undisputed, although how much and how often remains a matter of conjecture. Benn's correspondence offers conflicting accounts of his drug usage. Schöne has isolated two seemingly contradictory passages (247; cf. Witschel 72–73, Bendix 17):

> Wenn ich das Zeitliche segne, was wohl bald der Fall ist bei meiner exzessiven Art zu leben (mit Drogen, Zigaretten, Koffein, Pyramidon à la carte und in Mengen),[21] weniger romantisch ausgedrückt: 'die Kartoffeln von unten besehe' – wäre es mir ein angenehmer Gedanke, Sie unter den Erinnerern und Betreuern meiner literarischen Dinge zu wissen. (To Frank Maraun, 30. 7. 1946; Benn *AB* 102)

> Darf ich bei dieser Gelegenheit erwähnen, daß ich selber Drogen weder nehme noch genommen habe (außer einer kurzen Episode mit Kokain im 1. Weltkrieg); es wird das oft von mir angenommen und behauptet, zu Unrecht, außer Café und Zigaretten brauche ich keine Stimulantien. (To Ernst Jünger, 19. 11. 1951; Benn *AB* 220)

One of the few things we can say with certainty about Benn's personal drug history (providing we disregard his caffeine and nicotine consumption, as

21 Pyramidon: 'A white crystalline solid used as an anti-pyretic and analgesic' (*OED*).

he does himself in the second passage) is that he never became an addict. Despite the concerns he expresses in the first letter, he never suffered any serious ill effects as a result of his 'excesses'. As a medical doctor, a profession he practised for over 40 of his 70 years, he certainly had easy access to drugs of all descriptions, but also the knowledge – and on a more personal level the restraint – to regulate dosage and avoid dependency. Whatever the precise reasons, the fact is that he did not have a 'drug problem,' and this helps to explain the scarcity of documentary evidence concerning his drug use (it was simply not something he needed to talk about) and in itself is enough to distinguish him from the majority of his intoxicated literary contemporaries. Trakl's 'brief episode with cocaine in the First World War' ended, in catastrophic contrast to Benn's, in his untimely death.

Yet the drug theme *is* a recurring one in Benn's writings, and the drugs he makes reference to are many and varied (see 1.2). It first occurs in one of his earliest prose pieces, 'Heinrich Mann. Ein Untergang' (1913), in which we encounter a sentence that immediately draws on the Romantic tradition of drug-related mystique: 'Und er sagte, er wüßte nichts von einem Gifte, das er täglich zu sich nähme' (*GW* 5:1182). From there, the theme can be traced through the poems, stories and plays contemporaneous with their author's 'brief episode with cocaine,' as well as various poems of the 1920s, notably the *Betäubung* cycle, to the essays of his middle and late periods, most obviously 'Provoziertes Leben' (1943), a polemic against the stigmatisation and illegality of psychoactive drugs in the modern era reminiscent of those written by Benn's French contemporary Arthur Artaud. The drug theme was, without question, one that interested Benn, but one that he consistently dealt with at second remove, so to speak, so that to draw conclusions about Benn's experience on the basis of his literary work would amount to a highly problematic reading-back of literature on to life.

In this respect his *Rönne* stories (1915–16), for example, differ fundamentally from the two works which Bendix uses as a frame of reference for his study, the most voluminous to date, of the influence of drugs on Benn's prose: Baudelaire's *Paradis artificiels* (1860) and Aldous Huxley's *Doors of Perception* (1954), both of which describe the author's personal experiences and impressions (Baudelaire, as well as describing his own, describes De Quincey's; see 1.2). The failure to consider this distinction is one of the chief shortcomings of Bendix's study, most of which is devoted to finding parallels between the three works, conscientiously detecting *symptoms* of drug taking in *Rönne*, comparing the relevant passages to excerpts from the other two works, and in the process superimposing the premises and objectives of Baudelaire's and Huxley's texts on to Benn's. Important question suggest themselves but remain unexplored. To what extent can these symptoms be taken as hard evidence? Why, if the *Rönne* stories are about a man on drugs, are drugs themselves not more prominent, not more explicit, in the stories? And what, if anything, does this tell us about the author, his experience and his attitudes, or the relationship between writer and text, life and fiction, neurochemistry and literature? Bendix's final, hopeful verdict on the *Rönne* stories is that in them Benn arrives at 'Schlußfolgerungen von universaler Bedeutung,' and that 'man darf den Beitrag des Rauschgiftes dazu nicht übersehen' (81). To claim that these stories provide anything as definitive and categorical as conclusions is itself surely indicative of a basic misreading. In the stories' own terms, such an interpretation can be considered symptomatic of a mode of cognition Benn labels 'der psychische Komplex,' described in 'Die Insel' (1916) as the desire 'das Ungeklärte zu entwirren, das Zweifelhafte sicherzustellen' (*GW* 5:1214). It is precisely such a reduction to easy comprehensibility, such a rendering-harmless, that these stories do everything possible to resist.

This deliberate elusiveness is a recurrent problem critics face in defining – disentangling, taking possession of – the role and importance of drugs in Benn's writings, and is reflected in the divergent critical response to this aspect of his work. Modick, in his essay 'Benns Konzeption des produktiven Rausches,' writes that 'Substanzen wie Kokain, Haschisch, Meskalin sind für ihn von primärer Wichtigkeit' (49), and describes the 'quasi Treibsatz-Funktion von Drogenerfahrungen für Benns Werk' (50). Further, he perceptively identifies an intimate link between drugs and Benn's other major themes, a point that can be related to the Modernist subtextualization of the drug theme described in the introductory chapter (see 1.2):

> Gedichte wie 'Kokain', 'O Nacht' und 'Betäubung', der Essay 'Provoziertes Leben' und die szenischen Gespräche 'Drei Alte Männer,' Arbeiten, die unmittelbar den Zusammenhang zwischen psychoaktiven Wirkungen aufs Bewußtsein und poetischer Produktion thematisieren, stellen im Gesamtwerk Benns die Spitze jenes Eisbergs dar, dessen Masse ein aus den Begriffen Rausch, Traum, Vision, etc. zusammengesetzer Bedeutungskomplex bildet. (49)

Arend responds to Modick in an indignant article entitled 'Der Dichter braucht die Droge nicht.' She sees Benn's drug references in the context of his self-appointed role of *provocateur* (102). Thus, they amount to nothing more than an attempt to shock, or at least unsettle his bourgeois readership ('disillusion' is the word Benn himself chose; *BaO* 91), and their function is comparable in this respect to that of the carnival of horrors depicted in the *Morgue* cycle (1912). She dismisses interpretations such as Modick's as a misunderstanding (ibid.), and emphasizes, quite rightly, that Benn's theory of poetry set out in his enormously influential lecture 'Probleme der Lyrik' (1951) makes no mention of artificially induced stimulation – or narcosis – in the creative process, even in the section dealing with the necessary psychological dissociation that precedes poetic inspiration, evoked in characteristically Bennian terms such as 'südliche Komplexe' and 'Wirklichkeitszertrümmerung' (110). There is no correlation, Arend argues, between Benn's *Schaffensrausch* and the intoxication brought about by psychoactive drugs. The assumption of such a correlation amounts to a 'janusköpfiger Irrtum' that underlies this entire branch of Benn scholarship (103).

Among critics of an era in which psychoactive substances have themselves become an object of violent, often ill-considered polemics, the hint of a connection between drugs and literature has always tended to elicit extreme critical responses such as Modick's and Arend's: maximum affirmation on the one hand; total repudiation on the other. It is normally true that the subtler the hint, the greater the potential for wild interpretation. What is surprising, and in its way illuminating, is that these polarized positions have been adopted by critics reading – of all people – Benn, who in the course of his literary career produced a wealth of apparent self-explication, as well as an essay, 'Provoziertes Leben,' which dwells at length on the (pre-)history, effects and potential applications of psychoactive substances. We can perhaps best account for this anomaly by reference to another, more detached reaction that Benn's theoretical writings have generated, namely the suggestion that they set out 'to conceal as much as to reveal,' and that never, 'although appearances may suggest the contrary, [does Benn] adequately explain his poetic impulse' (Seymour-Smith 585). This idea was first expressed as early as 1958 by Schöne, one of Benn's most astute critics:

> Eine überzeugende philosophische und anthropologische Grundlegung seiner Dichtung ist Benn hier keineswegs gelungen [...] Ohne unmittelbare theoretische Auf-

> schlußkraft für Benns Lyrik erweisen […] sich [die Essays] eher als eine 'Verhüllung' der wirklichen Zusammenhänge. (239)

According to this view, furthermore, there is a palpable tension between the persona Benn projects in his often 'brilliant, disgusting or shocking public performance' (Seymour-Smith 585), manifested in the strident cynicism and stylistic contortions of much of his poetry, and the underlying motivation of his imaginative writing, the urge to articulate the 'disturbances of an intelligent modern sensibility' (ibid.). As Schöne puts it, 'nicht der Zynismus und die Blasphemie ist der eigentliche Ausdruck der "fiktiven Gestalt" [Benns], sondern der Verzweiflungsschrei' (232).

Reformulating the Modick–Arend debate in the light of such remarks, we might say that, for the latter, Benn's drug allusions represent a purely performative ingredient, or rhetorical device, in his poetry and fiction, whereas for the former they come closer to revealing something fundamental about the nature of his poetic impulse. It is doubtful whether a definitive resolution to this dispute can ever be reached, no matter how forthright and determined the critics would like to be in pinning Benn down. As Felman has shown in exemplary fashion in her review of critical reactions to Henry James's *The Turn of the Screw*, the ambiguity of literary texts will always expose the prejudices and conceptual inadequacies underlying attempts at rigid interpretation of them. 'The story *won't* tell, […] not in any literal, vulgar way,' as the narrator warns his listeners in the prologue to James's tale (3; cf. Felman 152). The relevance of Felman's insight to the analysis of Benn's writings – and their unspoken agenda of concealment – becomes all the more apparent when we consider Benn's own notion of 'poetic' thought, characterized in his 1930 essay 'Zur Problematik des Dichterischen' as 'in gewisser Weise festgelegt, aber immer ambivalent, a priori, aber immer zweideutig' (*GW* 3:639). In the discussion of Benn's works that follows in chapters 3 and 4, our task, then, will not be to exercise the 'psychic complex' (*GW* 5:1214) in order to arrive at a neat summary of Benn's methods or message – not, that is, to 'disentangle' Benn – but to observe and evaluate his entanglements, in other words to explore, via a reading of the poems and plays that mention cocaine and a consideration of their place within his œuvre, the mechanics of evasiveness, fluidity and tension at work within these texts themselves. It is the consistent exploitation of these qualities for literary effect, although following an idiosyncratic procedure quite unlike anyone else's, that places Benn among the seminal figures of literary Modernism. But before embarking on this investigation, another aspect of Benn's biography demands our attention.

2.2 Artificially Inspired? Brussels, 1916

One curious fact which makes the mystery of Benn's drug use all the more compelling is that the 'episode with cocaine in the First World War' he mentions in his letter to Jünger coincided with a more general, for him unprecedented sense of well-being and a surge of creative energy which resulted in a period of prolific output in a range of forms and genres. Modick, without any hesitation, describes these circumstances as 'unmittelbar verknüpft' (50).[22] Although Benn reminisced about his so-called 'Brussels spring' on numerous later occasions, he never made the connection explicit. But it is intriguing to note that he indulged in speculation of a drug–creativity link in relation to other artists. In his essay 'Genie und Gesundheit' (1930) he affirms the biological – specifically bodily, predominantly pathological – basis of creative 'genius', and gives a long list, modified and expanded in 'Das Genieproblem' (also 1930), of artistic luminaries classified according to their preferred poison (opium, absinthe, ether, hashish, alcohol), their particular psychological disturbance, or sexual abnormality. Together, these essays represent the first appearance of Benn's theory of the 'bionegative' tendency represented by creative artists within society: '[die kulturelle Gemeinschaft] bildet neben der Gesundheit und auf ihre Kosten die moderne Mythologie aus Rausch und Untergang und nennt es Genie' (*GW* 3:682). Towards the end of 'Genie und Gesundheit,' Benn notes the 'fieberhaft gesteigerte Produktivität' of Nietzsche, Guy de Maupassant, Vincent van Gogh and Robert Schumann in the years immediately preceding the outbreak of mental illness and states that this is 'nicht anders auslegbar, als daß hier die Toxinwirkung einen positiven biologischen Reiz zur Produktionsauslösung gewann' (*GW* 3:651). In these examples he is dealing with substances that arise from organic,

22 Schöne is more restrained in his assessment: 'Manches scheint darauf hinzuweisen, daß der eigene Umgang mit Drogen, insonderheit für das "Durchbruchserlebnis" des Brüsseler Frühjahrs von 1916, eine wesentliche Bedeutung gehabt hat' (247).

unassisted changes in body chemistry, but significantly, these essays do not distinguish between conditions that result from internal bodily processes and those brought about by the administration of drugs: for the purposes of genius, the difference is inconsequential. 'Genie ist Krankheit, Genie ist Entartung, davon muß man sich, glaube ich, für überzeugt erklären' (*GW* 3:678). Whatever their source, the 'positive biological stimulus to production' of toxins is constant. In 'Provoziertes Leben' he goes so far as to describe alkaloids – such as cocaine – as necessary nourishment for the 'potent' brain (a passage almost identical to the following also occurs in Benn's 1948 dramatic dialogue 'Drei Alte Männer;' 6:1580):

> Potente Gehirne aber stärken sich nicht durch Milch, sondern durch Alkaloide. Ein so kleines Organ von dieser Verletzlichkeit, das es fertigbrachte, die Pyramiden und die Gammastrahlen, die Löwen und die Eisberge nicht nur anzugehen, sondern sie zu erzeugen und zu denken, kann man nicht wie ein Vergißmeinnicht mit Grundwasser begießen, Abgestandenes findet es schon genug. (*GW* 3:903)

Arend is correct to question the sincerity of such statements and consequently their value as interpretive tools for illuminating Benn's work. To take them as convincing evidence that Benn used drugs to stimulate his own poetic production would be as critically naïve as to accept at face value Coleridge's tale of opiate dreams and the 'man from Porlock' as a strictly factual and unadorned history of the composition of 'Kubla Khan.' Benn, who openly admits that as far as he is concerned 'Stil ist der Wahrheit überlegen' (*GW* 3:854), is clearly an heir to the same Romantic tradition that the Coleridge of 'Kubla Khan' has come to embody (see 2.1). It is a tradition that elevates the cult of the writer and the mystery of inspiration to pre-eminent, almost sacred positions in the field of literature, and for which irony, incongruity and dissimulation are important tools that guarantee the continued sanctity of the muse. For both Coleridge and Benn psychoactive drugs represent – among other things – a means of generating and sustaining a sense of ambiguity and mystery around the connections between life and work. On the other hand, Arend's unqualified scepticism is not an entirely satisfactory critical response either, for surely it is misguided to dismiss lines such as those from 'Provoziertes Leben' cited above as mere provocation, given that Benn wrote them in 1943, at the height of the Second World War, five years after he had been placed under a *Schreibverbot* and when, as far as he knew, he had little prospect of ever publishing anything again. The fact is that in 1943 Benn had no self-satisfied bourgeois readership to provoke, so there must have been more to his interest in drugs than simply provocation, even if for his readers this 'more' must remain suspended between the 'fixity and ambivalence' of his literary expression (*GW* 3:639). The connection between neurochemical disturbance and artistic creativity was a matter that Benn, in his own convoluted and self-contradictory way, treated very seriously.

But to what extent does this support a connection between his own cocaine experience and literary prolificacy during the First World War? Certainly it would be rash, simply on the basis of the circumstantial evidence, to dismiss such a link, but it is equally precipitate to make it without considering other important factors which contributed to Benn's accelerated literary production of that time, factors suggested by his own descriptions of the period. The following is taken from the epilogue to his *Gesammelte Schriften* of 1922:

> was ich an Literatur verfaßte, schrieb ich, mit Ausnahme der 'Morgue', die 1912 bei A. R. Meyer erschien, im Frühjahr 1916 in Brüssel. Ich war Arzt an einem Prostituiertenkrankenhaus, ein ganz isolierter Posten, lebte in einem konfiszierten Haus, elf Zimmer, allein mit meinem Burschen, hatte wenig Dienst, durfte in Zivil gehen, war mit nichts behaftet, hing an keinem, verstand die Sprache kaum; strich durch die Straßen, fremdes Volk; eigentümlicher Frühling, drei Monate ganz ohne Vergleich, was war die Kanonade von der Yser, ohne die kein Tag verging, das Leben schwang in einer Sphäre von Schweigen und Verlorenheit, ich lebte am Rande, wo das Dasein fällt und das Ich beginnt. Ich denke oft an diese Wochen zurück; sie waren das Leben, sie werden nicht wiederkommen, alles andere war Bruch. (*GW* 8:1873–1874)

Isolation, detachment, routine, serenity, independence: these were the catalysts of Benn's creativity, and in the later period of his life he came to celebrate them, notably in *Statische Gedichte* (1948; see especially the poem of the same name, *GW* 1:236) and 'Probleme der Lyrik,' as the necessary conditions of all true poetry: 'Er arbeitet allein, der Lyriker arbeitet besonders allein' (*GW* 4:1081).

The ethical implications of social detachment in the name of art are problematic, here manifested disturbingly in Benn's apparent indifference to the carnage on the frontline only a few miles away ('was war die Kanonade von der Yser, ohne die kein Tag verging').[23] Much discussion has been devoted to the political obtuseness that grew from this attitude and that,

23 Even Benn's advocacy of moral aloofness, however, must be considered equivocal. It cannot be overlooked that, in his day job, he continued to heal the sick.

combined with Benn's stubborn irrationalism, ultimately led him to be taken in by the Nazis in 1933. His fervent if short-lived support for Adolf Hitler's 'Ästhetisierung der Politik,' to use Walter Benjamin's celebrated formulation (168), was largely a bloody-minded reaction to the call for radical engagement, or 'Politisierung der Kunst,' made by the leftist literati who attacked him in the late twenties and early thirties, luring him down, if only briefly, from his ivory tower. The processes at work here have been described by Günter Grass, who quite possibly had Benn in mind when he commented that 'Die Verweigerung des Umgangs mit der politischen, das heißt der sozialen Wirklichkeit, ist gleichwohl eine politische Entscheidung. Der Ausstieg verhärtet sich zur politischen Position' (64).[24] Klaus Mann expressed similar sentiments in a desperate appeal he wrote to Benn in 1933, warning him of the danger of trying to defend a politically disinterested attitude when confronted with an ideology such as National Socialism (Mann's letter is cited in Benn's autobiographical reflections collected in 'Doppelleben'; *GW* 1940–44), to which Benn replied publicly – and dismissively – in his 'Antwort an die literarischen Emigranten' (1933).

Noteworthy here is that Benn's exalted sense of isolation during the 'Brussels spring' that he describes in the passage from the 1922 epilogue cited above, although not necessarily attributable to his apparently limited if contemporaneous drug experience, is consistent with one of the states of mind that drug use typically brings about: an indifference to all external matters that do not impinge immediately on the consciousness of the user. Alexander Trocchi offers an eloquent description of this perspective: 'That is one of the virtues of the drug, that it empties such questions of all anguish, transports them to another region, a painless theoretical region, surprising, fertile, and unmoral. One is no longer grotesquely involved in becoming. One simply is. I remember saying to Sebastian, before he returned to Europe with his new wife, that it was imperative to know what it was to be a vegetable, as well' (cited in Plant 162–163). Trocchi's 'vegetable imperative' is reminiscent of Benn's regressive desire to become 'Ein Klümpchen Schleim in einem warmen Moor'(*GW* 1:25), formulated in what is perhaps his most frequently quoted poem, 'Gesänge' of 1913. But 'Gesänge' cannot be described as a drugged poem, just as Benn's apolitical aesthetics cannot be described as drugged indifference.

24 In the same interview Grass mentions Benn directly, noting that he signed letters with 'Heil Hitler' (64).

What is beginning to emerge here is that not only does Benn's fiction, as Bendix has shown, exhibit symptoms associated with the use of psychoactive substances, but that his opinions, attitudes and aspirations often did as well, and that he developed and maintained these independently of any contact he had with such substances. As Rübe perceptively remarks, 'wegen dieser autochthonen Gegebenheiten kann Benn auch ohne Halluzinogene sein *toxisches Weltbild* ein Leben lang durchhalten' (*IdA* 149). This circumstance makes determining the role of drugs in Benn's life and work that much more difficult. We might say that Benn had an intellectual affinity with drugs that overshadows and disguises any real, physical contact he had with them. It is significant that under the influence of cocaine, Benn did not experience revelations of previously unimagined realms of delight or evil, as De Quincey had more than a century earlier when he tried opium for the first time, or as Huxley would on mescaline forty years later, nor was there any major shift in his outlook or poetic method that arose from his encounter with the drug. Rather, the literary products of the 'Brussels spring' represent a consolidation and intensification of themes and techniques that he had been developing for some years and that continued to evolve long after the 'episode' was behind him. Moreover, it should be noted that Benn's claim that all the literature he produced between 1912 and 1922 was written in the spring of 1916 is exaggerated, as a quick glance at his list of publications will show.[25] Even the first two stories of the *Rönne* cycle, considered the central and most representative work of the Brussels period, were published a year earlier in 1915.

But what of the other circumstances that contributed to Benn's intensified literary production of those spring months? It is revealing to relate Benn's description of his Brussels lifestyle to his endorsement, in 'Genie und Gesundheit,' of Ernst Kretschmer's observation that 'ein kräftiges Stück Gesundheit und Spießbürgertum gehöre zum ganz großen Genie meist mit hinzu' (*GW* 3:648). It is precisely such factors as routine and serenity, as well as 'Fleiß, [...] Stetigkeit, ruhige Geschlossenheit und frische Natürlichkeit' (*GW* 3:649) that he seems to consider both 'bourgeois' characteristics and vital to poetic production. Do these bourgeois tendencies somehow reduce or contradict the importance of the 'positive biological stimulus to production' (*GW* 3:651) of toxins? Arend

25 Schöne comments, 'noch die bibliographischen Angaben müssen sich dem Verlangen nach Kompromierung, Steigerung, Überhöhung fügen' (239).

thinks so, and in 'Probleme der Lyrik' at least, Benn seems to as well: 'Die großen Dichter der letzten hundert Jahre stammen aus bürgerlichen Schichten, [...] keiner war süchtig, kriminell oder endete durch Selbstmord' (*GW* 4:1082). The last part of this statement is clearly untrue. Benn himself had provided more than sufficient evidence to the contrary in his earlier essays, and in 'Probleme der Lyrik' he is immediately forced to qualify this statement through the exception of the *poètes maudits*. What underlies Benn's and Arend's arguments here is the misconception that drug taking and mental illness are fundamentally incompatible with such 'bourgeois' qualities as diligence, self-discipline, application and routine. In 'Genie und Gesundheit' Benn had more perspicaciously concluded that for the great creative artists of the modern era they often go hand in hand. Trakl, a great poet and addict who ended in suicide, always referred to the process of writing as 'work', surely the most sacred of bourgeois values.[26] In summary, then, the other circumstances described by Benn himself as the conditions of his creative inspiration by no means preclude a role for cocaine, but this remains at best one factor among several that contributed to the singularity of his spring in Brussels, 1916.

As far as the role of drugs in Benn's literary activity is concerned, what we are left with, then, is a number of coincidences and possibilities on which the critic can base nothing more solid than impassioned conjecture. In a roundabout way, Benn has in effect constructed his own version of Coleridge's story of the 'man from Porlock,' submerging the question of his own poetic method in a murky pool of hints, red herrings and contradictions. As Tomashevsky notes of Pushkin (50), the core of Benn's biographical legend is the unknown, and obligingly, his critics have gone into battle with one another to fill this gap, each grasping at the textual extracts that lend weight to one side in the drugs-and-inspiration debate, and ignoring or belittling those that would support the opposite view. What unites the opposing positions is the unspoken intention to make Benn, in one way or another, consistent with himself, an enterprise that is inevitably frustrated by the poet's cultivated enthusiasm for disrupting such attempts to set his lands in order (see the lines from 'Der Geburtstag' that we have chosen as our motto for part one). Ultimately one must defer to the mys-

26 See Trakl's letters to Karl von Kalmár of August/September 1905 and May 1906, and his letters to Erhard Buschbeck of June/July and late July 1910 (*HkA* 1:469, 1:471, 1:476, 1:479; cf. Weichselbaum 45).

tery that Benn, aided by his more unsuspecting critics, has 'woven thrice' – to borrow Coleridge's phrase from 'Kubla Khan' – around his own poetic persona.

A more practical approach to evaluating the literary significance of Benn's 'brief episode with cocaine' is suggested by a statement we find in the preface to a late (1952) edition of his early poetry and drama: 'Im allgemeinen weiß ich nicht, was ich schreibe, was ich vorhabe und wie etwas in mir entsteht, damals wie heute, ich weiß nur, wann das Einzelne fertig ist' (*GW* 7:1866). The only way to progress beyond Benn's biographical smokescreen, it would seem, is to adopt an attitude similar to the one the poet himself manifests here, that is, to take the individual works themselves, rather than the circumstances of their composition or the pursuit of the 'true' opinions or intentions of their author, as the central object of study. For the purposes of the present discussion, this allows us to consider the works in which cocaine appears as a textual 'episode with cocaine' in its own right, more tangible in its characteristics and scope than its supposed biographical counterpart. Such an approach acknowledges, as Benn does implictly in his 1952 preface, that works of literature must have some relationship with the situation of their author – in Jakobson's words, 'that the situation is a component of speech' (320; see 1.4) – but that this relationship is not entirely knowable; indeed in Benn's case, thanks to his mystifications, it is less knowable than in many others.

This distinction between 'biographical' and 'textual' episodes defines our task more clearly, but hardly simplifies it. If, as in the next chapter, we consider just the two works that together constitute the central component in Benn's textual episode, the Brussels-era poems 'O Nacht' and 'Kokain', we find that between them they amount to just 45 lines of verse, yet these lines have a thematic density that belies their small number, and in themselves they present substantial obstacles to interpretation, obstacles which, as we shall have occasion to note, have caused their share of stumbling among previous exegetes. To do justice to these works, therefore, and to avoid getting caught in their snares, we shall adopt a wide-ranging approach to their analysis that not only draws on numerous other works by Benn and other writers, but that progressively integrates several considerations of more general relevance to Benn scholarship into our discussion:

- their author's attack on the psychological norms of modern civilization and his surprisingly forward-looking insights into language (3.1),

- his notion of poetry as the key to trascending the prisonhouse of history (3.2),
- the unresolved tension between the poetic and poetological elements in his writing (3.3),
- and the correspondences between his pet ideas and the theories of Freudian and Lacanian psychoanalysis (3.4).

Just as a nuanced assessment of Benn's biographical episode requires consideration of numerous factors relating to both his time in Brussels and the attitudes and beliefs he developed and held over a much longer period, so too a nuanced assessment of his textual episode calls for its careful contextualization in relation to these broader thematic concerns. As it happens, the oscillation between the general and the particular (*hin und her*) that is characteristic of this approach itself manifests a certain affinity with Benn's thinking (see 3.2), but this should not distract from the basic contrast between the goal we have set ourselves of casting Benn's intricacies into greater relief and the poet's own fondness for dissolution and amorphousness that is articulated as forcefully in these poems as anywhere else in his œuvre.

3 Benn's Cocaine Poems

3.1 Depersonalization and the Blueness of Poetry

In 1799–1800 Novalis wrote a series of *Hymnen an die Nacht*, in which the speaker celebrates the infinite nocturnal mysteries as they are revealed to him in a state of half spontaneous, half artificially provoked intoxication: 'Heiliger Schlaf [...] Sie [die Thoren] fühlen dich nicht in der goldenen Flut der Trauben – in des Mandelbaums Wunderöl,[27] und dem braunen Safte des Mohns' (1:133/35). In 1916 Benn wrote his own hymn to the night, in which his lyric subject also turns to a plant-based intoxicant – cocaine – to achieve mystical insight. 'O Nacht' first appeared in *Die Aktion VI*, 39/40 (30. 9. 1916).

O Nacht –:

O Nacht! Ich nahm schon Kokain,
und Blutverteilung ist im Gange,
das Haar wird grau, die Jahre fliehn,
ich muß, ich muß im Überschwange
noch einmal vorm Vergängnis blühn.

O Nacht! Ich will ja nicht so viel,
ein kleines Stück Zusammenballung,
ein Abendnebel, eine Wallung
von Raumverdrang, von Ichgefühl.

Tastkörperchen, Rotzellensaum,
ein Hin und Her und mit Gerüchen,
zerfetzt von Worte-Wolkenbrüchen –:
zu tief im Hirn, zu schmal im Traum.

---

27 N.B.: 'the almond tree's / Wondrous oil' refers to bitter almond oil, or *Bittermandelöl*, made from the stones of various fruits, such as apricots or plums, as well as almonds. It has analgesic properties.

Die Steine flügeln an die Erde,
nach kleinen Schatten schnappt der Fisch,
nur tückisch durch das Ding-Gewerde
taumelt der Schädel-Flederwisch.

O Nacht! Ich mag dich kaum bemühn!
Ein kleines Stück nur, eine Spange
von Ichgefühl – im Überschwange
noch einmal vorm Vergängnis blühn!

O Nacht, o leih mir Stirn und Haar,
verfließ dich um das Tag-verblühte;
sei, die mich aus der Nervenmythe
zu Kelch und Krone heimgebar.

O still! Ich spüre kleines Rammeln:
Es sternt mich an – es ist kein Spott –:
Gesicht, ich: mich, einsamen Gott,
sich groß um einen Donner sammeln. (*GW* 1:53–54)

Seen alongside Novalis's hymn, Benn's poem testifies to both the perpetuation of the Romantic emphasis on irrationality, subjectivity and transcendental aspiration in poetry of the early 20th century, and the radical shift in modes of cognition and expression that distinguishes literary Modernism from the movements that preceded it. The radicalness of this shift brings the applicability of inherited genre classifications into question, and critics have adopted the term 'Scheinhymnen', coined by Theo Meyer (*GBE* 397), to describe this and the other poems which Benn published in *Die Aktion* in 1915–16 (they were included six months later in the collection *Fleisch*). These include 'Ikarus' (*GW* 1:47–47), 'Kretische Vase' (*GW* 1:48), 'Karyatide' (*GW* 1:45), and 'Aufblick' (*GW* 1:49), as well as 'O Nacht.' Meyer's point is that these poems, although filled with emphatic apostrophes and imperatives, invoke a purely rhetorical lyric object, and in essence amount to solipsistic monologues concerned more seriously with the subject than the object, the addresser rather than the addressee. This trait was recognized also by one of Benn's Expressionist colleagues, Carl Einstein, who in 1927 described these poems as 'Hymnen vom Selbst' (369–372). In 'Probleme der Lyrik' Benn himself proclaims that 'ein Gedicht ist immer die Frage nach dem Ich' (*GW* 4:1066). This is certainly evident in 'O Nacht,' where the speaker states his objective of achieving 'eine Wallung' or 'eine Spange' of 'Ichgefühl' (ll. 8–9, 19–20) and of blossoming 'noch einmal vorm Vergängnis' (ll. 5, 21), rather than confronting the awesome secrets of 'holy, inexpressible, mysterious night,' which was the end proposed by Novalis. Indeed, the question arises of just how seriously, at this stage in his life, Benn took the idea of night as a sanctum of transcendental experience.[28] In 'O Nacht' there is little to suggest that it was any more than a ready-made Romantic leitmotif that he adopted as a convenient vehicle for his own poetic probings into the irrational. This distinction between Novalis's hymn and Benn's 'mock hymn' is ultimately one of emphasis, as the nocturnal experience glorified in 'Hymnen an die Nacht' is no less subjective than the 'Ichgefühl' sought in 'O Nacht.' But it is precisely this difference in emphasis that is indicative of Benn's distinctly modern concern with the fragility and mutability of subjectivity. In the 1922 epilogue Benn describes the course his thinking had taken in the previous decade:

> ich vertiefte mich in die Schilderungen des Zustandes, der als Depersonalisation oder als Entfremdung der Wahrnehmungswelt bezeichnet wird, ich begann, das Ich zu erkennen als ein Gebilde, das mit einer Gewalt, gegen die die Schwerkraft der Hauch einer Schneeflocke war, zu einem Zustande strebte, in dem nichts mehr von dem, was die moderne Kultur als Geistesgabe bezeichnete, eine Rolle spielte, sondern in dem alles, was die Zivilisation unter Führung der Schulmedizin anrüchig gemacht hatte als Nervenschwäche, Ermüdbarkeit, Psychasthenie, die tiefe, schrankenlose, mythenalte Fremdheit zugab zwischen dem Menschen und der Welt. (*GW* 8:1875)

Benn's enquiry into the 'disreputable' – a term we may translate as 'abject' in today's theoretical parlance – side of human psychology and the instability of the 'geologically' constructed ego grew into one of his major preoccupations and came to play a central role in both his literary and later his theoretical writings. Essentially, he reacted against the rational, categorizing or scientific mode of thought, for which he found various names (in 'Die Insel' it was 'der psychische Komplex'; see 2.1), and the superficial ego-construct that exercises it, in favour of what he considered a 'prelogical' visionary state modelled on the 'mystical participation' of ancient and primitive societies. In the modern world, by contrast, it is the rational that is privileged, and 'das Rauschhafte, das Ermüdbare, das schwer Bewegbare'

28 It was different later – see, for example, the poems 'Nacht' of 1923 (*GW* 1:84–85) and 'Dunkler' of 1925 (*GW* 1:116–117).

(*GW*, 8:1902) breaks through only in exceptional moments of heightened sensory stimulation – 'in Gerüchen / vom Strand,' for example, in the 1927 poem 'Regressiv' (*GW* 1:131) – or when the structure of the ego collapses, as with Rönne, 'der eine kontinuierliche Psychologie nicht mehr in sich trägt' (*GW* 8:1902). Benn asserts the possibility for such 'eruptions of the abject,' to continue our translation, in his 1930 essay 'Der Aufbau der Persönlichkeit':

> Wir tragen die frühen Völker in unserer Seele, und wenn die späte Ratio sich lockert, in Traum und Rausch, steigen sie empor mit ihren Riten, ihrer prälogischen Geistesart und vergeben eine Stunde der mystischen Partizipation. (*GW* 3:661)

In another essay of the same year, 'Zur Problematik des Dichterischen,' Benn argues that the prelogical state – although repressed by modern society, classified in terms of various psychiatric disorders, and so divested of its spiritual value – is intimately connected to the act of poetic expression: 'Das archaisch erweiterte, hyperämisch sich entladende Ich, dem scheint das Dichterische ganz verbunden' (*GW* 3:643).[29] Certainly, one of the major currents in his poetry of the two decades preceding the publication of 'Zur Problematik des Dichterischen' is the exploration of such alternative (for Benn 'primary') states of consciousness. It is an exploration that moved in various, sometimes contradictory, directions: from the biological regression of 'Gesänge' (*GW* 1:25) to the bacchanalian revelry of 'Kretische Vase' (*GW* 1:48), or the tropical fertility of the 1922 poem 'Palau' (*GW* 1:62–63). Recurring motifs include the South, the Mediterranean, the exotic, the sea and islands, rich animal and vegetable life, as well as sexual energy, fertility and procreation. These combine in the development of an idiosyncratic vocabulary made up of what Benn calls 'Chiffren', or at other times 'Südwörter'. Such words are meaningful, the poet would have us believe, but not in the sense that they mechanically generate determinate meaning; they are widely evocative rather than narrowly referential, sensual rather than abstract; they tend to set off chains of ecstatic associations; they incorporate, for Benn, the mystery of the visionary state. His meditation on the word *Blau*, from 'Epilog und lyrisches Ich' (1928),[30] is

29 N.B.: 'Hyperaemia: an excessive accumulation of blood in a particular part, arising either from increased flow through the arteries [...] or obstruction in a vein' (*OED*).

30 This is an expanded version of the 1922 epilogue. In 'Probleme der Lyrik' Benn claims to have written this passage in 1923 (*GW* 4:1075).

illustrative of this conviction and features some of his favourite terminology with its distinctive mixture of medical, scientific and exotic influences:

> Da wäre vielleicht eine Befreundung für Blau, welch Glück, welch reines Erlebnis! Man denke alle die leeren entkräfteten Bespielungen, die suggestionslosen Präambeln für dies einzige Kolorit, nun kann man ja den Himmel von Sansibar über den Blüten der Bougainville und das Meer der Syrten in sein Herz beschwören, man denke dies ewige und schöne Wort! Nicht umsonst sage ich Blau. Es ist das Südwort schlechthin, der Exponent des 'ligurischen Komplexes,' von enormem 'Wallungswert', das Hauptmittel zur 'Zusammenhangsdurchstoßung', nach der die Selbstentzündung beginnt, das 'tödliche Fanal', auf das sie zuströmen die fernen Reiche, um sich einzufügen in die Ordnung jener 'fahlen Hyperämie.' (*GW* 8:1879)

Fundamentally, Benn conceives his poetic ciphers as the embodiment of the prelogical in language. All but the most uncritical of Benn devotees will admit that the success of the literary enterprise he bases on this conception is at best inconsistent. Yet, even if his terminology is often eccentric and his thinking remains anchored in a quintessentially Romantic mysticism, in his reflections on the workings of language and its relationship to consciousness, Benn anticipates several of the most influential 20th-century developments in psycholinguistic theory, in particular those associated with the poststructuralist school that emerged in France in the 1960s and 70s, and whose most important exponents were Derrida (see 1.1–1.3), the psychoanalyst Jacques Lacan, and the feminist critic Julia Kristeva (Benn's intimations of this school's principles are illustrated in a table on the following page). This affinity with the *Zeitgeist*, even if it surprised him,[31] helps to explain the enormous appeal of Benn's poetics of encipherment in the post-war period when he and his works were finally restored to respectability. When we translate these ideas to a reading of Benn's lyrics, and especially to an examination of his poetic style, we see that many of his poems function first and foremost as linguistic performances, attempts to enact 'mystical participation' and manifest the prelogical 'depersonalization' of consciousness in textual form. Benn's endorsement of Stéphane Mallarmé's maxim that 'a poem arises not from feelings, but from words,'

31 The following passage appears in 'Doppelleben' (1950): 'Ich schließe daraus mit Überraschung, daß die inneren Strömungen, denen ich Ausdruck zu geben versuche, innerhalb der europäischen Literatur weit allgemeiner verbreitet sind, als obenhin angenommen wird' (*GW* 8:2023).

Some principles of the poststructuralist view of language[32]	**Intimations of these principles in Benn's works**[33]
1) That the relationship between words and concepts, signifiers and signifieds, is unstable and fluid; that therefore any kind of precision or enclosure in language is illusory.	'Worte schlagen mehr an als die Nachricht und den Inhalt, sie sind einerseits Geist, aber haben andererseits das Wesenhafte und Zweideutige der Dinge der Natur.' (*GW* 4:1075) 'Wer glaubt, daß man mit Worten lügen könne, könnte meinen, daß es hier geschähe.' (*GW* 5:1185)
2) That language is intimately tied up with the unconscious.	'Das Wort ist der Phallus des Geistes, zentral verwurzelt.' (*GW* 4:1074)
3) That in any discourse what is excluded or repressed is always present as a constitutive limit or an 'unspeakable' subtext.	'Gespräche, Diskussionen – es ist alles nur Sesselgemurmel, nichtswürdiges Verwölben privater Reizzustände, in der Tiefe ist ruhelos das Andere, das uns machte, das wir aber nicht sehen.' (*GW* 4:1093)
4) That unconscious meaning emerges where coherence seems to break down.	'Wenn der logische Oberbau sich löst, die Rinde, müde des Ansturms der vormondalten Bestände, die ewig umkämpfte Grenze des Bewußtseins öffnet, ist es, daß das Alte, das Unbewußte, erscheint in der magischen

32 It should be emphasized that the intention here is not to provide a systematic summary of the poststructuralist view of language, which is complex and heterogeneous, but merely to sketch several main ideas anticipated in Benn's poetic theory and practice.

33 These range from almost direct theoretical correspondences (point 2), to passages from literary works that foreground the theoretical ideas presented (point 5, example 2). Although the proposition here is that significant parallels are evident, the statements on the left are not given as paraphrases or explanations of these passages. The purpose, rather, is to illustrate how Benn's writings anticipate certain ideas about language that have since gained wider currency. It must be remembered that despite the parallels highlighted here, Benn's views on related matters may contrast diametrically with those of Derrida, Lacan and Kristeva. Consider, for example, Lacan's rejection, as explained by his commentator Madan Sarup, of the link between the unconscious mind and the Romantic models used to portray it, including those most dear to Benn: 'Lacan conceives the unconscious as a "language which escapes the subject in its operation and in its effects." For Lacan the unconscious is a self and not a series of disorganised drives. *He repudiates any conception of the unconscious as linked with the instinctual, the archaic or the regressive, as the place of the divinities of night.* In his view the key to understanding the unconscious is to realise that it is structured logically' (Sarup 75, italics added).

	Ichumwandlung und Identifizierung, im frühen Erlebnis des Überall und des Ewigseins.' (*GW* 3:661)
5) That the mechanisms of condensation and displacement are constantly at work in language, as in dreams, in the dual (vertical and horizontal) axes of metaphor and metonymy.	'Schwer erklärbare Macht des Wortes, das löst und fügt.' (*GW* 4:1077) 'Noch hingegeben der Befriedigung, so ausgiebig zu assoziieren, stieß er auf ein Glasschild mit der Aufschrift: Cigarette Maita, beleuchtet von einem Sonnenstrahl. Und nun vollzog sich über Maita – Malta – Strände – leuchtend – Fähre – Hafen – Muschelfresser – Verkommenheiten – der helle klingende Ton einer leisen Zersplitterung, und Rönne schwankte in einem Glück.' (*GW* 5:1222)
6) That poetic qualities such as rhythm, euphony and repetition call up an earlier, prelinguistic form of subjectivity and constitute a counter-weight (the *semiotic*) to rational, linear discourse (the *symbolic*).	'Regressionstendenzen mit Hilfe des Worts' (*GW* 8:1880). 'Transzendente Realität der Strophe voll von Untergang und voll von Wiederkehr' (*GW* 4:1077).

contained in 'Probleme der Lyrik' (*GW* 4:1073), should not be taken as a negation of content, message or intent, but as a recognition, to put it in poststructuralist terms, of the primacy of the signifier, its irreducible 'excess' in relation to the signified. Simply, the idea that words rigidly stand in for thought or feeling is fallacious, '*weil alles kürzer ist als das Wort und die Lippe, die es sagen will, weil alles über seinen Rand zerbricht, zu tief geschwellt von der Vermischung*' (*GW* 5:1250–1251; italics in the original). For Benn it is the poetic word, the word freed from the constraints of rigid representation to which 'civilized' logic would subject it, the signifier whose 'excess' is celebrated rather than suppressed, that offers the surest means of attaining, albeit temporarily, the 'prelogical disposition' he believes – rightly or wrongly – was enjoyed by our distant ancestors.

3.2 Gods in the Last Line

'O Nacht' presents one such poetic attempt to revisit the 'mystical participation' of ancient and primitive people, this time with the aid of cocaine. It has been asked how such an 'artificial' or 'civilization-bound' substance as cocaine could be useful for such purposes (Meyer *KW* 267–268, Haupt 360; see 1.3). But such an objection holds little water when we consider that

(a) cocaine is not in fact artificial, but comes from the coca plant,
(b) the leaves of this plant have been chewed and worshipped as *Mama Coca* by the indigenous people of South America for hundreds, if not thousands of years, and
(c) Benn was very well aware of these facts (as can be seen from the *Mama Cuca* passage in 'Provoziertes Leben,' *GW* 3:895; see 1.2).

Further and more important, if one of the characteristic themes of Benn's would-be voyages into prerational consciousness is regression towards a vegetable state, it is suggestive that his lyric subject uses a botanical term, 'blühen' (ll. 5, 21), to describe his desired destination in this poem. It seems that in consuming cocaine, a plant derivative, his objective is to assume some of the qualities of the plant it comes from; once again an analogy might be drawn with Trocchi's 'vegetable imperative' (see 2.2).

The position of cocaine in the text is another significant factor. Although the poem as a whole is structured on rhythmic repetition, it contains only one reference to cocaine, in the first line of the first stanza, which after the exultant 'O Nacht!' displays a contrasting emotional detachment that would be more characteristic of a medical report: 'Ich nahm schon Kokain' (l. 1). The point here is that even if what follows presupposes and results from taking cocaine, it is what follows – intoxication – and not the act of drug taking itself that is the crux. The poem is ostensibly a hymn to the night, not to the drug, whose role is best described as that of a catalyst, to put it in chemical terms, or a premise, if we put it in literary ones. But even though cocaine does not appear again, its effects remain conspicuous. These effects can be observed on several levels: body, mind, language and myth are all as 'entangled' in the poem as in Benn's mythopoeic theory outlined in 3.1. The first of these effects appears in line 2, 'und Blutverteilung ist im Gange,' which uses the same mock-medical tone of line 1 to refer to the physiological processes activated by the drug. The bodily and perceptual alterations resulting from the speaker's cocaine use are taken up again in the third stanza. Although the vocabulary here still has a distinctly medical or pseudo-medical flavour, the tone is notably less matter-of-fact than in the opening lines. As the drug kicks in, the poet's language is gradually becoming charged with poetic, 'southern' force. The first two lines of this stanza evoke heightened sensory awareness, comprising increased sensitivity to touch, smell and movement, the last indicated by the formulation 'ein Hin und Her' (l. 11). This expression was one Benn employed frequently during his early period, and as the following passage from the 1922 epilogue suggests, the movement implied is not just physical, but in an 'enciphered' sense more broadly ontological – between stasis and motion, order and spontaneity, the particular and the universal, boundaries and boundlessness:

> Ich blicke über die Straße, ein Herr stäubt sich den Rock ab, es stäuben sich aber in diesem Augenblick viele Herren den Rock ab, wohin man blickt, immer dies Simultane, hin und her zwischen der Stabilisation und dem Fraglos-Weiten, zwischen Begriff und Absolutem hin und her. (*GW* 1876–1877)

The second half of stanza three explicitly links these bodily processes to language, which itself assumes physical, even violent characteristics ('zerfetzt von Worte-Wolkenbrüchen,' l. 12). Loquacity is one of cocaine's most characteristic effects and was commented on as early as 1886 by Freud, one of the drug's first enthusiasts (see 1.2), who also hinted that under its influence language seems to escape the control of the speaker or writer. In a long and rambling letter of early Februrary to his fiancée Martha Bernays, Freud interrupted his ruminations to note, 'Das bißchen Cocain, was ich genommen habe, macht mich geschwätzig, Weibchen' (*B* 207). The letter then sets off on further digressive musings before concluding, 'Solche dumme Geständnisse mache ich Dir, mein süßer Schatz, und eigentlich ganz ohne Anlaß, wenn es nicht das Cocain ist, was mich zum Reden treibt' (*B* 209). Both these drug-related effects, that is, an increase in quantity and corresponding decrease in the controllability of language, might be read into Benn's 'Worte-Wolkenbrüchen'.

But we must also consider a larger context here, one that encompasses and transcends the drug's influence on the linguistic faculty, namely Benn's conception of the poetic quality of words, their hidden powers and deep, subsemantic reverberations, as outlined in 3.1. This was one of his most intense and enduring interests, and although his own poetic diction was methodically trimmed down over the years, his ideas about language and poetry display a notable consistency throughout his career. His 'Flimmerhaar' metaphor represents perhaps the clearest manifestation of this consistency. This was originally presented in 1928 in 'Epilog und lyrisches Ich' as a form of anatomy of Benn's own early-period lyric subject; he reaffirmed its validity, quoting himself verbatim and at length, in 1951 in 'Probleme der Lyrik.'[34] As this passage shows, for Benn one of the principal traits of poetic language is its timelessness, specifically that it dissolves the temporal and conceptual framework – in other words, history – that divides the modern, Western subject from the 'mystical participation' of our primitive forebears.

> Worte, Worte – Substantive! Sie brauchen nur die Schwingen zu öffnen und Jahrtausende entfallen ihrem Flug [...] Botanisches und Geographisches, Völker und Länder, alle die historisch und systematisch so verlorenen Welten hier ihre Blüte, hier ihr Traum. (*GW* 4:1077, 8:1879–1880)

This notion of historical dissolution via poetry suggests one reading of what are perhaps the most difficult images in 'O Nacht,' those that open the fourth, central stanza: 'Die Steine flügeln an die Erde, / nach kleinen Schatten schnappt der Fisch' (ll. 14–15). The cloudbursts of words in stanza three would seem to have conjured up this elemental vision of falling stones and primitive animal life, the latter represented here by the fish with its purely instinctual, *prelogical* response (snapping) to environmental stimuli (small shadows). It is an 'organic' reaction equivalent to the one Rönne observes in 'Die Insel': 'jawohl, auf Reize antwortet hier Organisches' (*GW* 5:1210). In the third stanza's images of flying stones and snapping fish, then, we seem to have the first flash of the 'mystical participation' the poet longs for, the first sign that the 'flowering of lost worlds' is at hand.

The conviction that this flowering represents a return to a previous, uncorrupted state of affairs is the basis for Benn's cherished notion of transcendence via *regression*. Schöne, in his insightful analysis of Benn's 'Überdauernde Temporalstruktur,' describes how this view links the poet – despite himself – to the Christian concept of history he inherited as a child (his father was a parish priest).

> Gegen Benns erklärte Absicht überdauern in der temporalen Struktur seiner Dichtung jene vorgeprägten Zeitvorstellungen des Christentums, die das gegenwärtig-irdische

34 In 'Probleme der Lyrik' this extended metaphor occurs at the beginning of the passage Benn dates to 1923 (*GW* 4:1075; see note 29).

Dasein zwischen das Paradies der Schöpfungsfrühe und jene neue Erde stellten, welche aus dem apokalyptischen Untergang steigt. (264)

Schöne identifies three key temporal adverbs that recur throughout Benn's work: 'schon', 'noch einmal' and 'erst wenn.' When considered together in an overview of his lyric œuvre, it becomes evident that each is connected to one aspect of the temporal structure underlying Benn's thought; they act, so to speak, as 'adverbial ciphers.' The first two, 'schon' (l. 1) and 'noch einmal' (ll. 5, 21), are both prominent in 'O Nacht.' Schöne argues that the first of these occurs repeatedly in those privileged moments when some kind of visionary or transcendental experience seems about to break into the speaker's mundane, devitalized existence (248), which in itself holds only the uninviting prospect of relentless and meaningless decline towards decay and death (in 'O Nacht' this prospect is encapsulated in line 3: 'Das Haar wird grau, die Jahre fliehen'). 'Schon', therefore, stands at the threshold of 'mystical participation.' 'Noch einmal,' on the other hand, represents a looking-back from the iniquity of the present towards the lost paradise of the past (255); at the same time it is always associated with impending doom, nowhere more clearly than in 'O Nacht': 'noch einmal vorm Vergängnis blühen' (ll. 5, 21). Benn himself explicitly evoked the link between the lost harmony of prehistory and the approaching cataclysm in 'Zur Problematik des Dichterischen': 'o schöner Tag der Reue der Natur [...] o Heimkehr der Schöpfung' (*GW* 3:642–643). Similarly, the image of falling stones in the third stanza of 'O Nacht' can be seen as suspended between the Creation and the Apocalypse; the creative energy of the former and the destructive energy of the latter become indistinguishable. By the same token, the snapping fish of the next line is not only *pre-* but also *post-logical*;[35] it offers a glimpse of both what was and what is to come. However, at this stage the vision remains no more than a glimpse. Despite the cocaine in his bloodstream and the words cascading through his mind, the speaker is still restrained by his over-developed cerebrum, as the concluding lines of both stanzas three and four suggest:

zu tief im Hirn, zu schmal im Traum (l. 13);

35 Curiously, Ödön von Horvath, in his 1937 novel *Jugend ohne Gott*, would use precisely the image of the fish to condemn the immorality, irrationalism ('post-logic') and facelessness of the Nazi era. He described it as 'die Zeit der Fische.'

nur tückisch durch das Ding-Gewerde
taumelt der Schädel-Flederwisch (ll. 16–17).

Consequently, in the fifth and sixth stanzas he renews his appeal to the night, echoing and elaborating the supplications of stanzas one and two. Here, too, the transcendence he longs for is entwined with the notion of return and homecoming, even rebirth (re-Creation): 'sei, die mich aus der Nervenmythe / zu Kelch und Krone heimgebar' (ll. 24–25).

The emphasis on body imagery seen in stanzas one and three is echoed in line 22: 'O Nacht, o leih mir Stirn und Haar.' By this point, however, the clinical, descriptive precision of the poem's opening, traces of which are still detectable in stanza three, has entirely given way to an exalted, symbolic, 'southern' lyricism. As Benn uses them, formulations such as 'Stirn und Haar' or 'Kelch und Krone' resist determinate interpretation. They become what he describes in 'Probleme der Lyrik' as 'seltsam beladene Worte' (*GW* 4:1082), in that they suggest myriad directions of meaning simultaneously. They may be read as allusions to rejuvenation, wisdom, nobility, mythology, festivity, flowering (if we take 'Kelch und Krone' as botanical terms, not unreasonable in the context of the poem),[36] etc. These all co-exist in enciphered suspension, evocable in the subjunctive – 'man denke' – in the same way as the sky above Zanzibar and the blossoms of the bougainvillaea that Benn associates with the colour blue (*GW* 8:1879; see 3.1).[37] 'O Nacht' is constructed so that expressions like 'Stirn und Haar' result as semantically underdetermined, their meaning incomplete and open to various completions of limited but equal validity (the concept of semantic underdetermination is discussed in more detail in 9.1). Simply, they appear not to 'make sense' to the same extent as more narrowly referential terms such as 'Blutverteilung' and 'Rotzellensaum' that occur nearer the beginning, even though it is the latter, considered in isolation, that seem to be more sophisticated and difficult words. Thus, we can detect a shift through the poem not only from one *sphere* of meaning to

---

36 The *Kelch–Krone* collocation also occurs in the Rönne story 'Der Geburtstag,' published the same year as 'O Nacht.' Here their potential botanical meaning is foregrounded, for the context is a garden love scene involving Rönne and Edmée: 'Im Garten wurde Vermischung [...] Kronen lösten sich weich, Kelche sanken ein, der Park ging unter im Blute des Entformten' (*GW* 5:1227).

37 N.B.: The blossoms of the bougainvillaea are in fact a brilliant red or magenta purple. For Benn the contrast presumably reinforces the brightness of the blue sky.

another, from the physiological-perceptual to the mystical-sensual, but also from one *mode* of meaning to another, a progressive loosening of the signifier, so to speak, a change that accompanies and offsets the rhythmic constancy and anaphoric repetitions that carry the poem forward.

This semantic shift may usefully be characterized in relation to Jakobson's distinction, presented in 'Linguistics and Poetics,' between 'the two basic modes of arrangement used in verbal behaviour, *selection* and *combination*,' where 'the selection [for example, of one word over another] is produced on the basis of equivalence, similarity and dissimilarity, synonymy and antinomy, while the combination [of different words in an utterance], the build-up of the sequence, is based on contiguity' (71). This configuration of modes, selection by equivalence and combination by contiguity, which is dominant in most language use, produces an utterance that the addressee will normally recognize as prosaic. On the other hand, '*the poetic function*,' as Jakobson italicizes, '*projects the principle of equivalence from the axis of selection to the axis of combination.* Equivalence is promoted to the constitutive device of the sequence' (ibid.). The sequential equivalences characteristic of poetry may be of various types; in fact they are more likely to be formal – syntactic, metric or phonetic – than semantic, although any obvious formal equivalence, such as rhyme, also implies a semantic association. An obvious example of combination by phonetic association is the 'Maita–Malta' sequence Rönne formulates in 'Der Geburtstag' (*GW* 5:1222; see also point 5 in the table in 3.1). Further examples of the same mechanism can be observed in 'O Nacht,' only here its operation is more subtle and complex. The phrase 'Stirn und Haar,' considered from this perspective, becomes a nodal point for several distinct but interweaving phonetic and lexical patterns that run right through the poem, as illustrated in the diagram on the following page. These echoings suggest even more slants of potential meaning which complement and enrich those already mentioned that stem from a conceptual interpretation of this image; 'St*irn* und *H*aar' could be seen, for example, as the disintegration of '*H-irn*'. This reading would certainly confirm that the appeal 'o leih mir Stirn und Haar' is consistent with the poet's prelogical aspirations.

The shift in modes of signification we have observed in 'O Nacht' can therefore be attributed to a progressive reconfiguration in the text's 'modes of arrangement,' in particular from a more prosaic model to a more poetic one. It should be noted that this progression is not a movement from one

- und -		*H-, H-r, Haar*
'Hin **und** Her' (l. 11) 'Kelch **und** Krone' (l. 25)	'**Stirn und Haar**' (l. 22)	'**Haar**' (l. 3) '**H**in und **Her**' (l. 11) '**Hir**n' (l. 13)

S- (Sch-), S-n (Sch-n)	*St- and St-n*	*St-rn and –irn*
'**schon**' (l. 1) 'Über**schw**ange' (ll. 4, 20) '…**Schatten schn**appt der **Fisch**' (l. 15) 'tück**isch**' (l. 16) '**Sch**ädel-Flederw**isch**' (l.17) '**Spang**e' (l. 18); '**sp**üre' (l. 26) '**Sp**ott' (l. 27)	'**St**ück' (ll. 7 and 18) '**Stein**e' (l. 14) '**st**ill' (l. 26)	'**sternt**' (l. 27) '**Hirn**' (l. 13)

extreme to another (undeniably, the first stanza also has important poetic features), but rather a shift in the balance, an increasing orientation towards the poetic function at the expense of referential clarity. Adapting Benn's terminology, we might describe this process as a 'southern-ization', which consists not only in poeticization but also in erotic energization. This development reaches a climax (the sexual connotation is appropriate) in the final stanza, where the grammatical coherence becomes extremely tenuous. Verbs become nouns ('Ich spüre kleines Rammeln'; l. 26) and vice-versa ('Es sternt mich an'; l. 27); line 28 presents a composite subject and object, each consisting of noun and pronoun in apposition, but is conspicuously verbless ('Gesicht, ich: mich, einsamen Gott'); line 29, by contrast, offers a predicate without a subject, but syntactically it fails to cohere with line 28 because of the end position of the verb, which suggests that it is part of a subordinate clause, and the excess of object complements ('mich, einsamen Gott' in line 28, 'sich' in line 29); finally, the punctuation throughout is eccentric. Literally, the four lines and 25 words of this stanza are held together more by rhyme than reason. The last two lines in particular appear to embody the 'Zusammenhangsdurchstoßung' (*GW* 8:1879) towards which the rest of the poem has been building. In this moment when logical coherence breaks down, what emerges? 'Gesicht, ich: mich, einsamen Gott' – here, finally, it would seem, we have the realization of 'Ichgefühl', a subject–object synthesis that is all ego, without even the hint of contamination that a finite, transitive verb might imply, in so far as such verbs admit a universe of relationships between different and distinct entities. Such an outcome may come across less as 'mystical participation' than as 'mystical isolation' or solipsism.[38] However, the distinction is of little consequence for Benn's mythopoeic purposes. Indeed, there is no essential contradiction between a poem like 'Palau', where – superficially, grammatically – the ego is entirely absent, and line 28 of 'O Nacht,' where it is entirely present. Whether it is the universe that dissolves into the ego (as in 'O Nacht') or the ego that dissolves into the universe (as in 'Kokain', see 3.3–3.4), the effect is substantially the same. Important in either situation is what Nietzsche characterizes as '[das] Zerbrechen des principii individuationis' (3:24; see 1.2) and its attendant dissolution of subject–object relations, as these, for Benn, represent one consequence of the compartmentalization that the historically recent ego-construct has imposed on the human perception of the world.[39]

This desire for subject–object dissolution, which Nietzsche likewise posits as the main aim of drug taking (ibid.), can be considered a further point of intersection between Benn's poetics and the characteristics of a 'drugged' perspective. For this reason, the last stanza of 'O Nacht' fits easily into a reading of the poem as an accumulation and intensification of the effects resulting from the cocaine administration announced in line 1. Benn's 'Gesicht, ich: mich, einsamen Gott' is comparable, in a broad literary context, to a veritable multitude of distorted, doubled and dis-

38 'Solipsistic' is a word that critics have used repeatedly to describe Benn's poetry of this period (Dierick 3–28).

39 A further parallel with Lacanian psychoanalysis is apparent here. For Lacan, the subject depends for its existence on the 'mis-recognition' of its own unity, which originates in the mis-recognition of the unity of an object, specifically the image of him- or herself that an infant sees in the mirror. The role of the ego is to maintain, narcissistically and through mis-recognition, the illusion of a unified subject that exists and functions in a world of objects.

sociated subjects that have populated drug literature ever since the first Romantic encounters with opium and hashish. One archetypal example is Baudelaire's pipe from *Les Paradis artificiels*: 'You are sitting smoking; you think you are sitting in your pipe and that your pipe is smoking you; you are exhaling yourself in the form of blue-tinged clouds' (*Pa* 365).[40] The thematic resemblance ('ich: mich' – 'you [...] yourself') is striking, but so too is the fundamental difference between the two poets' treatments of equivalent themes. Whereas Baudelaire *reports on* the distortions in subjecthood that occur in intoxication from a detached perspective, Benn *exults in* them from within. For Benn, moreover, the diffusion ('Kokain') or compression ('O Nacht') of selfhood is more than just a happy consequence of experimentation with psychoactive agents; it is the consciously sought end – 'ich muß' (l. 4), 'ich will' (l. 6) – of a process in which the drug is a vehicle chosen specifically for its capacity to take his speaker to the desired destination, and arrival at this destination is proclaimed as an event of religious consequence: 'sich groß um einen Donner sammeln' (l. 29). His choice of cocaine over the numerous other 'medicines' he must have had at his disposal is not incidental: whereas opium and its derivatives are famous for sending users to sleep, cocaine, one of the strongest stimulants, has quite the opposite effect. Benn's aim here is to overcome conventional, rational modes of thought not through a suppression of consciousness, as has been maintained, but through its amplification and transfiguration.[41] The role of language in this process is pivotal: in 'O Nacht' these changes are not represented or reflected in language so much as they *occur* in language. Or rather, one of the fundamental aspects of the transformation consists precisely in the shift away from representational and narrative discourse towards a form of poetic expression that foregrounds and glorifies what Benn calls 'das Wesenhafte und Zweideutige' (*GW* 4:1075; see point 1 in

40 'Vous êtes assis et vous fumez; vous croyez être dans votre pipe, et c'est vous que votre pipe fume, c'est vous qui vous exhalez sous la forme de nuages bleuâtres.' Tr. Plant (43).

41 Dieter Lieuwerscheidt's contention that the goal in 'O Nacht' is to switch off the central nervous system (Dierick 19) does not cohere with the physiological effects of the drug featured in the poem. This error can perhaps be explained as a projection of the slimy yearnings expressed in 'Gesänge' onto Benn's work as a whole. In general, Benn was less concerned with overcoming consciousness per se than overcoming the particular, artificial, modern form of consciousness that he saw as a barrier to 'primary' experience.

the table in 3.1) of words. If 'O Nacht' opens as a kind of *Erlebnislyrik*, it ends as something else altogether, something more like *Erlebnis in Lyrik*. It seems probable, therefore, that Benn had this poem in mind when he noted, in 'Epilog und lyrisches Ich,' 'Götter im zweiten Vers etwas anderes wie Götter im letzten Vers – ein neues ICH, das die Götter erlebt' (*GW* 8:1877).

3.3 Poetological Interference, or the Will to Explanation

Benn's second cocaine poem, this one a hymn to the drug itself, was first published in the *Fleisch* collection in March 1917. This collection also included 'O Nacht,' which had originally appeared six months earlier in *Die Aktion*.

Kokain

Den Ich-Zerfall, den süßen, tiefersehnten,
den gibst du mir: schon ist die Kehle rauh,
schon ist der fremde Klang an unerwähnten
Gebilden meines Ichs am Unterbau.

Nicht mehr am Schwerte, das der Mutter Scheide
entsprang, um da und dort ein Werk zu tun,
und stählern schlägt –: gesunken in die Heide,
wo Hügel kaum enthüllter Formen ruhn!

Ein laues Glatt, ein kleines Etwas, Eben –
und nun entsteigt für Hauche eines Wehns
das Ur, geballt, Nicht-seine beben
Hirnschauer mürbesten Vorübergehens.

Zersprengtes Ich – o aufgetrunkene Schwäre –
verwehte Fieber – süß zerborstene Wehr –:
verströme, o verströme du – gebäre
Blutbäuchig das Entformte her. (*GW* 1:52)

‘O Nacht’ and ‘Kokain’ are clearly variations on a theme. Both present, and seek to embody in language, an experience of cocaine-induced intoxication that transports the speaker towards a state that Benn equated with original cosmic unity. The apparent contradiction between the ‘Ichgefühl’ of ‘O Nacht’ (l. 9) and the ‘Ich-Zerfall’ of ‘Kokain’ (l. 1) is superficial and masks an essential identity in thematic substance. As can be seen from the critical response it has generated, however, Benn’s erratic terminology remains potentially misleading. For example, Heimann’s ‘Ich-Zerfall als Thema und Stil’ attempts to define separate directions of metamorphosis in Benn’s poetic subjectivity along lines corresponding to a neat *Ichgefühl–Ich-Zerfall* distinction, but ends up as something of a wild goose chase, or better, a wild *ghost* chase, for as Benn writes in the introduction to his short play *Der Vermessungsdirigent* (see 4.2), ‘Das Ich ist ein Phantom. Kein Wort gibt es, das seine Existenz verbürgte, keine Prüfung und keine Grenze’ (*GW* 6:1499). At the beginning of his essay, Heimann characterizes the two directions as ‘Selbstpreisgabe an die Faszination des Nichts’ and ‘Selbstpreisgabe an die Faszination des Seins’ (384), but is later forced to conclude, when confronted with the entangled reality of Benn’s writings, that the two directions are not so distinct after all: ‘Die Formel “Leere des All” bestätigt die Bedenken gegen eine allzu grundsätzliche Trennung der beiden eingangs dargelegten Zerfallsrichtungen’ (393). In a comparison of ‘O Nacht’ and ‘Kokain’, it is more pragmatic to consider ‘Ichgefühl’ and ‘Ich-Zerfall’ as variant poetic renderings of the same subject–object dissolution described in 3.2 rather than opposite poles within an orderly metaphysical system, which it would be mistaken to attribute to Benn in any case.

In addition to their thematic similarities, the two poems share patterns of sound (‘sch’ and ‘h’; in ‘Kokain’ see particularly the second stanza) and imagery (body parts and physiological processes, including birth). Another feature they have in common is an increasing degree of linguistic deviance that operates on various levels (lexical, morphosyntactic, semantic) and that, as we have seen in ‘O Nacht,’ textually enacts the central theme of the transfiguration of consciousness. Furthermore, the adverbial ciphers that delineate the temporal structure of Benn’s post-Christian worldview, as described by Schöne (see 3.2), are as prominent in ‘Kokain’ as in ‘O Nacht.’ *Schon*, which marks an imminent return to ‘mystical participation,’ occurs twice in the first stanza (ll. 2–3). ‘Nicht mehr’ (l. 5), although not among the three recurrent adverbial phrases singled out by Schöne, has a similar function; in effect, it is an inversion of *schon*, a form of good riddance to the sordidness of day-to-day existence.

Despite these similarities between the two poems, significant differences are also evident, a consideration of which will reveal that 'O Nacht' is not only longer but poetically the more sophisticated of the two.[42] The most obvious difference is in the titles, which is pertinent because in both poems the title also introduces the addressee. Whereas 'Kokain' apostrophizes the drug directly, 'O Nacht' places it at second remove. The evocation of night not only brings a whole series of literary associations into play, of which Novalis's famous hymns are but one example, it also serves to generate an elementary narrative context, which these associations then help to 'fill out.' Østbø, for example, notes the Faustian overtones of the poem's opening (89). This narrative context, in turn, highlights other features in the poem that seem either to fit uneasily into the context, or at times to escape it altogether (flying rocks, snapping fish, chalices and crowns), or to subvert the very idea of the poem as a narrative, that is, as the representation of an external situation distinct from its articulation in language. The effect is comparable to that which Rönne perceives in his own consciousness in 'Die Insel': 'in mir durchwächst sich Wirkliches und Traum' (*GW* 5:1215). To be sure, 'Kokain' also goes some way towards creating the same sort of tensions. The last two and a half lines of the first stanza, with the repetition of the adverb 'schon' and the description of the physical sensations resulting from the administration of the drug, give the poem a sense of immediacy and reveal that it, like 'O Nacht,' is the 'story' of an intoxication (a story which in the course of the poem will transform itself into an act of intoxication), rather than a treatise on the drug, a poetic equivalent of Baudelaire's *Paradis artificiels*. 'O Nacht,' by contrast, from the very beginning leaves no room for such doubts.

A comparison of the two poems' first lines underlines the difference already implicit in the titles. In 'O Nacht' the first line may be considered striking for what Arend (see 2.1) would see as its provocative affront to

42 We may speculate that it was for this reason, rather than because of earlier composition, that Benn chose to publish 'O Nacht' separately in *Die Aktion* in September 1916. Indeed, if the order of composition does not necessarily coincide with the order of first publication, then 'O Nacht' might be seen as a reworking and refinement of 'Kokain'. Such a reading is supported by Benn's own arrangement of these poems: in his *Gesammelte Gedichte* of 1956, used as a model for *GW*, he placed 'Kokain' immediately before 'O Nacht' (*GW* 8:2244).

bourgeois respectability, its 'demonstrative delcaration' (Tomashevsky 54) that the lyric subject is not only a 'drug fiend,' but not even remotely ashamed of being one. From the narratological point of view, however, it is less striking for what it says than what it leaves out, or better, *defers*. From here, the poem could go anywhere, or at least in any one of a number of directions. For example, it is quite conceivable, if we consider just the opening stanza, that the drug experience in question could turn out to be a big disappointment, something equivalent to Rimbaud's impressions of the effects of hashish as he described them to Paul Verlaine: 'Well, nothing really … some white moons, some black moons that follow each other' (from an anecdote recounted by Ernest Delahaye; cited in Castoldi 76). Indeed, in 'O Nacht' the risk of disappointment remains very real until the last stanza; only then can the lyric subject be sure that his intoxication is more substantial than Rimbaud's vision of black and white moons: 'es ist kein Spott' (l. 27). In 'Kokain', on the other hand, the success of the operation is guaranteed in the first line and a half: 'Den Ich-Zerfall, den süßen, tiefersehnten, / den gibst du mir' (ll. 1–2). But the reticence of the first line of 'O Nacht' does more than simply produce suspense through the deferral of a happy ending; in a broader sense it is indicative of how the poem relates to its subject matter, and consequently of how it can be read. 'O Nacht' requires the reader to piece together the poem's thematic complexity progressively and retrospectively (3.2 is one attempt to do just that), not to give the work a conceptual coherence to match its evident coherence of form, but to grasp the implications of the tension between its unwavering formal regularity and its increasing conceptual fragmentation. In 'Kokain', by contrast, the poem's main theme is trumpeted at the beginning of line 1, and for the reader all that remains is to see how the poem will achieve the goal it sets itself: 'Ich-Zerfall'. One consequence of this explicitness is that critics have elevated the first line of 'Kokain' to 'eine Schlüsselformel, die über der ganzen Lebensproblematik des frühen Benn stehen könnte' (Meyer *KW* 267),[43] without however considering what its thematic transparency might mean for the poem itself, or indeed what this might reveal about the less obvious but no less fundamental aspects of Benn's 'Lebensproblematik'.

---

43 Consider also the importance given to the same line in the title of Heimann's article referred to above: 'Ich-Zerfall als Thema und Stil.'

In 'Kokain' we can detect signs of a subtle but far-reaching tendency to abstraction, which paradoxically co-exists in many of Benn's works alongside expressions of an almost moral imperative to eliminate all abstraction. This contradiction is the inevitable result of combining the aim to transcend rationality through poetry with the aim to explain, in the same poetry, the how and why of this transcendence. It is by the same principle that Benn can employ ciphers for poetic effect one moment, and the next tell us that he is doing so, how they work, and what sort of thing it is that they encipher, as he does most famously in the poem 'Ein Wort' of 1941: 'Ein Wort, ein Satz –: aus Chiffren steigen / erkanntes Leben, jäher Sinn' (*GW* 1:208). In an important sense, Benn's lyric œuvre is the site of an unresolved conflict, or better a delicate *im*balance, between poetry as language that foregrounds its 'essential and ambiguous' nature (*GW* 4:1075), and poetry as a meta-language that explains its own 'essence and ambiguity,' in doing so subverting it. Thus, often the reader may detect an incongruity between 'the means used and the effects aimed at' (Jakobson 64). Tracing the dynamics of this imbalance through the course of Benn's literary career, we find that it arose in the post-*Morgue* period when he moved from simply unmasking the corruption of the world-to-be-transcended, in which task poems such as 'Schöne Jugend' (*GW* 1:8) and 'Mann und Frau gehn durch die Krebsbaracke' (*GW* 1:14–15) had been extraordinarily and shockingly successful, to proposing various alternatives or means of escape, including – briefly – cocaine intoxication. Thus, its emergence coincided with his first substantial compositions in prose, a suggestive expansion of his repertoire beyond lyric poetry, and in the 1920s and early 30s he turned to a new prose genre, the essay, that gave him even greater scope than fiction to map out his attitudes, procedures and objectives, or rather semi-fictitious confabulations that he could present as such. The poetic qualities of Benn's prose works, which not only feature much of the vocabulary characteristic of his verse, but on occasion even fall into regular rhyme and metre, confirm the inextricability of the two levels of discourse. In his post-*Morgue* poetry the influence of the 'will to explanation' varies in intensity from one poem to the next. In 'Kokain' it is less extreme than in 'Ein Wort,' but more evident than in 'O Nacht,' which can be numbered among those poems in which, happily, the poetic triumphs over the poetological. Beyond the differences in the titles and first lines already discussed, several other points can be identified in the two cocaine poems where partial correspondences disguise significant variations in the degree of abstraction. The 'Abendnebel' (l. 8) of 'O Nacht' *implies* the 'kaum enthüllte Formen' (l. 8) of 'Kokain'. Similarly, whereas in 'Kokain' we find the abstraction 'das Ur, geballt' (l. 11), in 'O Nacht' we encounter rocks winging towards the earth (l. 14) and fish snapping at shadows (l. 15). In 'Kokain', the ephemerality of this primeval vision is stated explicitly ('entsteigt für Hauche eines Wehns,' l. 10); in 'O Nacht' suddenly the vision is there, and then just as suddenly it is gone. Finally, the crucial last stage of intoxication, the dissolution of subject–object boundaries, is announced in 'Kokain' by the phrase 'zersprengtes Ich' (l. 13); its occurrence in 'O Nacht' is conveyed primarily in the striking syntactic peculiarity of the formulation 'Gesicht, ich: mich, einsamen Gott' (l. 28; see 3.2). From this comparison, 'Kokain' emerges almost as a poetological commentary on the poetry of 'O Nacht.'

3.4 The Second Regression

It should be emphasised that the tendency to abstraction observable in 'Kokain' is no more than that, a tendency that becomes conspicuous by comparison with its absence in 'O Nacht.' At the same time, as if to illustrate the ambivalence at the heart of Benn's poetics, the poem moves just as forcefully in the opposite direction, towards a linguistic *concretion* as it strives, in the ways described above for 'O Nacht' (see 3.2), to become a textual enactment of its own themes. Before it finally arrives at 'das Entformte' (l. 16), the poem engages in some serious *Entformung* of its own, and the linguistic contortions this process yields are no less remarkable in 'Kokain' than in its sister poem. Most notable of these is the transformation, in the final two lines, of the *ich* into a *du* as the lyric subject assails his own intoxicated – 'exploded' – consciousness with imperatives. However, as the *du*-position is already occupied by cocaine, this may be read as an implicit fusion of subject-man and object-drug that constitutes another original take on Baudelaire's pipe. Else Buddeberg remarks, rather enigmatically, 'es ist äußerst aufschlußreich, daß das Ich sich zum erstenmal im Kokain-Genuß "Du" nennt' (23).

What is perhaps truly 'revealing' in the final stanza of 'Kokain', in that it highlights an aspect of the *Ich-Zerfall* theme that is not given such prominence elsewhere, is the apposition of 'zersprengtes Ich' with three other noun phrases: 'o aufgetrunkene Schwäre – / verwehte Fieber – süß zerborstene Wehr' (ll. 13–14). Each of these noun phrases contains an attributive adjective, formed from the past participle of a prefixed verb, denoting some kind of destruction or finality: '*zer*sprengtes', '*auf*getrunkene', '*ver*wehte', '*zer*borstene'. This morphological and semantic equivalence in the adjectives further emphasizes the equivalence of the nouns themselves, already established by their placement in apposition: 'Ich', 'Schwäre', 'Fieber', and 'Wehr'. What, then, are we to make of this equivalence that the text makes such efforts to underline? What does it reveal about the *ich* that we find 'exploded' at the pinnacle of the lyric subject's cocaine intoxication? The association of 'Ich' with 'Schwäre' and 'Fieber' suggests that the ego-construct, the seat of subjectivity and the apparent if illusory centre of consciousness, is not only physiologically determined, an idea Benn would elaborate in his essays of the early 1930s (especially 'Der Aufbau der Persönlichkeit'), but inherently pathological. This view is clearly an extension of Benn's reaction against the rational and positivist – in the most literal sense ego-centric – thought that he considered the root problem of the modern condition. At the same time it represents an inversion of the categories that this mode of thought has imposed on the understanding of human psychology by equating the 'abnormal' with disease and so securing its own privileged, 'healthy' status. To paraphrase Benn's 1922 epilogue, if civilization, under the direction of school medicine, has rendered certain 'primitive' states of mind disreputable by giving them such labels as neurasthenia, fatigability, or psychasthenia (*GW* 8:1875), then Benn is determined to turn such evaluations upside down by disputing the sanity of 'civilized' reason, or more specifically, as in 'Kokain', the health of the ego on which this reason depends. If we add the fourth element of Benn's equation, 'Wehr', to this mix, it becomes evident that the hegemony of reason is not only unnatural, a corruption of the primary, organic state, but also unstable and constantly under threat from the forces it has relegated to the periphery of human experience. Here, once again, Benn anticipates the psychoanalytic concept of the 'eruption of the abject' (see 3.1).

Indeed, the presentation of the ego as a defence mechanism links Benn's poem to one of the central tenets of psychoanalysis. According to Freud, the ego protects the subject against the animal drives of the id by banishing them to the unconscious; for Lacan, the ego consists in the continual mis-recognition of the de-centred subject that can never be identical with itself (see note 38). Both these models offer potentially fruitful avenues for exploring the ramifications of Benn's *Ich–Wehr* juxtaposition. In the former, Benn's *Ich-Zerfall* could be considered a 'laying-bare' of the id, or perhaps better, a reversal of the process of normal psychic development that Freud summarized, in his 1933 introductory lectures on psychoanalysis, in the axiom, 'wo Es war, soll Ich werden' However, a simple switching of *Es* and *Ich* in this axiom may capture the regression, but not the dissolution that is equally crucial to *Ich-Zerfall*, an experience that involves regression beyond the 'mere' liberation of the id. A more authentically Bennian rendering might read, 'wo Ich war, wo Du warst, wo Es war, da soll das Entformte werden.'[44] Expressed in Lacanian terms, the explosion of the ego might represent a form of release from misrecognition, the suspension of the illusion that the subject is identical with itself, and in its place a momentous *recognition* that it is an open structure, ultimately identical with everything and anything, a recognition that Benn characterizes in 'Der Aufbau der Persönlichkeit' as '[das] frühe Erlebnis des Überall und des Ewigseins' (*GW* 3:661; see point 4 on the table in 3.1).

To clarify and develop this last point, let us turn to another source of fertile intertextual resonance for Benn's depictions of 'disreputable' mental states, namely Michaux's writings on his mescaline experiments. Michaux, like Benn (although ostensibly for scientific rather than mystical ends), was set on re-evaluating these states and debunking the prejudices commonly associated with them, and turned to psychoactive substances as a passport to direct experience of 'the dementias, the backwardnesses, the deliriums, the ecstasies and agonies, the breakdowns in mental skills which are really suited to "reveal" us to ourselves' (6).[45] The following passage is taken from his *Les Grandes Epreuves de l'esprit et les innombrables petites* (1966):

---

44 Such a transformation, if sustained, would involve disastrous consequences on the social level, for Freud maintains that the repression of drives, the subjugation of id to ego, occurs precisely in order to facilitate the successful social integration of the individual. Benn's 'Hymnen vom Selbst' (Einstein 369–372), however, do not concern themselves with such problems; on the contrary, they are distinctly anti-social. In the Rönne stories, by contrast, Benn addresses the repercussions for human interaction of the 'sweet shattering' of the individual ego.

45 N.B.: The wish to 'explore madness from the inside' has long been one of the primary motivations given by writers using drugs, and in its earlier manifestations is linked especially with the works of Jacques Moreau de Tours, the instigator of the *Club des Haschischins*, who claimed to have discovered 'in hashish, or rather in its actions on the

> In a way, this [the schizophrenic sense of limitlessness] is something of a regression. The child at its earliest age identified hand, head, breast, the mother and himself in a spherical, spherifying, global impression, with no beginning or end. Only sleep, recurring often, returned to surround them, but is sleep a boundary?
> What a strange planet each of us has been. Man is a child who has spent a lifetime confining, limiting, testing himself, seeing himself as limited, accepting himself as limited. As an adult he has succeeded, almost succeeded.
> Whatever he says or does, Infinity is something every man responds to, something fundamental. It reminds him of something. This is where he comes from.
> This is why Infinity, taught to the child somewhat later, but still in his early years, 'takes' so well. He offers little resistance to the infinite god inculcated in him in most civilizations at a time when he was virtually defenseless; a belief, which henceforth becomes second nature, is taken for granted, self-evident, a conviction for which he will do battle if need be.
> Yet the schizophrenic rarely regains his religion, and almost never in distressed states. Religion was also a kind of localization, a one-way street, a dam to keep Infinity blocked up, in its place.[46] (118–119)

In relation to the observations made above on the last stanza of 'Kokain', this passage highlights the connection between Benn's dam-busting regression towards 'das Entformte' (which in essence corresponds with Michaux's 'Infinity'), a regression experienced as religious euphoria in poetry, and the psychosexual development of human subjects (the first infantile stage of which is a presubjective autoeroticism akin to Michaux's 'spherifying, global impression, with no beginning or end') that is the domain of psychoanalysis. However, there remains the crucial distinction that Benn's perspective is resolutely historical or anthropological, rather than personal or psycho-biographical like that of psychoanalysis. For Benn, the modern subject is the product of an evolutionary process, and the study of this subject takes the form of a 'Geologie des Ich' ('Grundriß einer Geologie des Ich' is the subtitle of 'Der Aufbau der Persönlichkeit'; *GW* 3:652). From his perspective, we are psychologically tied to the earlier representatives of our species, a tie that Rönne perceives intuitively in 'Die Insel': 'Er fühlte sich seiner Entwicklung verpflichtet und die ging auf Jahrtausende

---

moral faculties, a powerful and unique means of exploring mental pathologies' (4; cited in Castoldi 65).

46 In 'Der Mann Moses und die monotheistische Religion' (1939) Freud makes a similar connection between the cognitive scope of the infant and 'adult' religion (although mescaline played no part in his insight): 'Kindliche Gefühlsregungen sind in ganz anderem Ausmaß als die Erwachsener intensiv und unausschöpfbar tief, nur die religiöse Ekstase kann das wiederbringen' (*GW* 16:242).

zurück' (*GW* 5:1212). Significantly, the regression Benn describes is not pre-Oedipal but prelogical, and denotes a return to a mythical prehistoric moment represented most famously by 'unsere Ururahnen' of the early poem 'Gesänge' (*GW* 1:25), rather than a previous stage in the life of the individual.

But is it really so clear-cut? Could prelogical not also mean pre-Oedipal, or even prenatal, as well as precivilized and premodern? If precivilized is *all* it means, the reader is obliged to reduce the birth imagery of poems like 'O Nacht' and 'Kokain' to mere metaphors for Creation or apocalyptic re-Creation. But could there not be a literal, physical birth that plays a role here? And if Benn's regression is directed exclusively towards human prehistory and not individual prehistory, what are we to make of his often explicit references to parent–child relationships, such as that in the second stanza of 'Kokain': 'Nicht mehr am Schwerte, das der Mutter Scheide / entsprang' (ll. 5–6)?[47] The answer to such questions can only be that in much of Benn's work these two perspectives, the macro- and microcosmic, co-exist, overlap and even merge. Thus, the *Schwert–Scheide–Mutter* pun can be seen as an artful entanglement of a suggestively mythological cipher (*Schwert–Scheide)*, implying a historical frame of reference, and an allusion to the physical act of birth (*Mutter–Scheide)*, the point of departure of each individual life. Indeed, in Benn's works the reader may encounter several such superimpositions, where prenatal or birth imagery occurs in connection with temporal regression of historical proportions. The most concise example is probably the coinage 'Schöpfungsschoß' from 'Palau' (*GW* 1:62). Another can be found in 'Epilog und lyrisches Ich': 'Ach immer wieder in diese Glut, in die Grade der *plazentaren* Räume, in die Vorstufe der Meere des Urgesichts: Regressionstendenzen, Zerlösung des Ich!' (*GW* 8:1880, italics added). But perhaps the most telling example occurs in the following lines of poetry-in-prose from 'Zur Problematik des Dichterischen,' which in the 1951 version included in *Essays* reads, 'Ekstase, süße, die ihm die Ferne bringt; Stimme, ganz dunkle, die von der *Frühe* singt' (*GW* 3:641, italics added). In its two 1930 editions, in *Die Neue Rundschau* XLI and *Fazit der Perspektiven*, the final clause reads, 'die von den *Müttern* singt' (*GW* 8:2165, italics added). The historical *Frühe* and the biological *Mütter* are, if not interchangeable, at least somehow homologous

47 Here Benn is punning on the double sense of 'Scheide', which means both the 'sheath' or 'scabbard' of a sword, as well as 'vagina'.

in Benn's thinking. We must also mention that in 1933, during his ill-fated flirtation with Nazism, Benn's use of birth imagery in connection with large-scale socio-historical movements would take on decidedly sinister overtones, demonstrating just how easily his defiantly apolitical irrationalism could transform itself into fascist propaganda. In his open letter to Klaus Mann of May 1933, entitled 'Antwort an die literarischen Emigranten,' Benn describes 'einen neuen menschlichen Typ' emerging 'aus dem unerschöpflichen Schoß der Rasse' (*GW* 7:1697), and goes on to summarize the point the 'emigrants', who stubbornly cling to democratic ideals, fail to grasp in respect to the rise of National Socialism: 'es handelt sich gar nicht um Regierungsformen, sondern um eine neue Vision von der Geburt des Menschen, vielleicht um eine alte, vielleicht um die letzte großartige Konzeption der weißen Rasse' (*GW* 7:1699).

In the critical analysis of Benn's works, the concentration on either of these two frameworks of regression to the exclusion of the other would amount to a distortion of the essential thematic ambivalence generated by their superimposition in his writings. In this respect most critics have tended to err in favour of the macrocosmic or anthropological perspective (a term we use loosely to encompass an array of themes and images spanning the fields of religion, antiquity, mythology, botany and zoology), at the expense of the microcosmic or individual perspective more immediately compatible with psychoanalysis. This tendency is understandable, as it is the former perspective to which Benn himself, generally speaking, seems to have attached most weight. To illustrate this point one need only consider that in 'Gesänge', the poem that set the tone for both Benn's and his critics' subsequent treatments of the regression theme, he did not write 'O daß wir noch Föten wären' or anything to that effect, but 'O daß wir unsere Ururahnen wären' (*GW* 1:25). Benn would reformulate the idea of radical genealogical regression a year later in his play *Ithaka* (1914): 'Aber wegen meiner hätten wir Quallen bleiben können' (*GW* 6:1475).

One critic, Oskar Sahlberg, has inverted this thematic hierarchy, regarding a literal return to the womb as the fundamental theme and Benn's primitivistic, exotic and mythological imagery as metaphorical expressions of it. Sahlberg's reversal derives largely from his reading of Benn's 'geological' notion, laid down in 'Der Aufbau der Persönlichkeit,' that human anatomy, particularly the anatomy of the brain, mirrors human evolution, consisting of more primitive and more evolved elements (*GBE* 127–128).

In particular, Benn distinguishes the 'Großhirn', the seat of rational thought, which he describes as the 'entwicklungsgeschichtlich jüngste Teil der menschlichen Nervenorganisation,' from the 'Stammhirn', one of the 'biologisch älteren Teilen des Gehirns' and the storehouse of 'Urmythen' and 'Urtrieben' (*GW* 3:656). It follows that the biological regression of the individual, which consists in the repression or switching-off of the 'younger' neurological components with the ultimate goal of returning to the prelogical, 'spherifying' (Michaux 118) condition enjoyed before birth, is *experienced* as historical regression or the return to a previous stage in the evolutionary development of our species because only the more 'ancient' parts of the brain remain in operation. Therefore, Sahlberg's premise is that even when a poem seems to present only the anthropological perspective, the real problem is always re-birth. In his essay 'Gottfried Benns Ekstasen' (1988), 'Kokain' is one of the poems to which Sahlberg gives most prominence because of its relatively high concentration of birth imagery: 'Auf den Ich-Zerfall folgt die Phantasie, etwas zu gebären' (*GBE* 123).

Unfortunately, the originality of Sahlberg's position is compromised by his crude methods. He provides a 'vulgar Freudian' interpretation *par excellence*, that is, a reading that attempts to psychoanalyze the author, treating the text as a symptom and positing the diagnosis of the writer's psychological make-up as the final goal of the hermeneutic process. As he sees it, Benn's poetic images 'seem, and probably are, modelled on the free associations that emerge from the psychoanalyst's couch' (*JL* 155). This view leads Sahlberg into increasingly tenuous speculation about Benn's private life that often drifts into the preposterous. From a few short textual excerpts combined with scraps of biography, he deduces that Benn's thematic preoccupations were the result of a trauma suffered at birth (*GBE* 125), that he was subject to epileptic fits (*GBE* 126), that he was beaten as a child (*GBE* 130), and that his relationship to Hitler was one of 'therapeutic transference' (*GBE* 131)! Sahlberg's work is thus a rich source of examples for the critical vice that Jakobson describes as inferring 'an unknown situation from a work' (320; see 1.4).

It is precisely this kind of slapdash application of his insights that Freud rejects in his 1910 article 'Über "Wilde" Psychoanalyse.' Here he stresses the importance of tact, a central concern not only of analytical practice (where it is necessary in order not to terrify the patient), but of analytical theory as well, for, as he puts it, one is 'niemals imstande [...] alles zu erraten' (*GW* 8:124). Even if we disregard the improbability of

Sahlberg's conclusions, the fact that these arise from an attempt 'alles zu erraten,' to piece together a coherent 'whole truth' from Benn's deliberately evasive writings, is itself a misrepresentation of both Benn's poetics and Freud's analytics, in other words, of both the purported object and methodology of his study. A more faithful psychoanalytical reading, one that accepts and affirms the complexity of Benn's literary enterprise rather than seeking to boil it down to globules of definitive meaning, may arise from a consideration of his cultivated stylistic ambiguity and thematic ambivalence, such as that suggested by the *Schwert–Scheide–Mutter* motif of 'Kokain', in relation to arguments such as the following, which Felman develops from her reading of 'Über "Wilde" Psychoanalyse':

> If, far from implying the simplicity of a self-present literal meaning, sexuality points rather to a multiplicity of conflicting forces, to the complexity of its own divisiveness and contradictions, its meaning can by no means be univocal or unified, but must necessarily be *ambiguous*. It is thus not rhetoric which disguises and hides sex; sexuality *is* rhetoric, since it essentially consists of ambiguity: it is the coexistence of dynamically antagonistic meanings. Sexuality is the *division and divisiveness of meaning*; it is meaning *as* division, meaning *as* conflict. (158)

From this point of view, the question of how best to interpret Benn's regression theme, of where to locate and fix its parameters, is supplanted by the recognition that its parameters are fluid and permeable. The essence of Benn's poetic 'ecstasies', it must be remembered, is 'am Grunde nur Strömendes hin und her, eine Ambivalenz, Bilden und Entformen, Stundengötter, die auflösen und gestalten' (*GW* 4:1001). This is the answer the poet himself gives to the question 'was erleben wir nun in diesen Räuschen?,' posed in his 1932 'Akademie-Rede' (ibid.). A similar indeterminateness and indeterminability of *Rauscherleben* is conveyed in line 9 of 'Kokain', most evidently in the phrase 'ein kleines Etwas.' For the early Benn, the 'rhetoric' or 'sexuality' of poetry, to modify Felman's formula, consists less in 'meaning as division' than in 'meaning as fluidity,' meaning that allows for divisiveness, but also for a new synthesis that in turn will be divided or dissolve in an endless flux: 'hin und her, […] Bilden und Entformen' (ibid.).[48] Regardless of this qualification, the conception of meaning as instability and potential self-contradiction, common to Benn

48 After the Second World War, Benn would 'regress' to a view of art, poetry in particular, as a still point in a turning world ('Die Kunst ist statisch,' *GW* 8:2022).

and Felman, is the crucial point that Sahlberg's diagnoses spectacularly fail to accommodate.

How, then, might Benn's primordial-cum-prenatal yearnings, realized through the transfiguration of the ego, be usefully related to the terms of psychoanalytic discourse, with which they manifest obvious affiliation? One way forward is suggested by Sahlberg himself. Interpreting Benn's 'Kalk und Stein' (*GW* 3:896) image from 'Provoziertes Leben' as 'the beginnings of death' and 'a return to the inorganic,' he notes parenthetically that 'Freud's "death drive" strives for a return to the material state' (*JL* 152). Freud developed the concept of the 'death drive' in his 1920 'Jenseits des Lustprinzips' (1920). Its elaboration was based on his observations of various forms of repetition compulsion, a pattern of behaviour that did not fit with his earlier idea that the avoidance of unpleasure, or pain, was the overriding instinct of the human organism, because the patterns repeated, or experiences relived, were often extremely traumatic, even self-destructive. This led him to the idea that there was another set of impulses acting as a powerful counterweight to those that had previously prompted him to formulate the 'pleasure principle,' and the objective of this other set was, quite simply, the '*Wiederherstellung eines früheren Zustandes*' (*GW* 13:38; italics in the original). He explained apparently self-destructive or masochistic behaviour as expressions of the desire for disturbance inherent in all living systems, even the most life-affirming, and envisaged death as the ultimate restoration of matter to its primal, inorganic condition:

> Wenn wir es als ausnahmslose Erfahrung annehmen dürfen, daß alles Lebende aus *inneren* Gründen stirbt, ins Anorganische zurückkehrt, so können wir nur sagen: *Das Ziel alles Lebens ist der Tod*, und zurückgreifend: *Das Leblose war früher da als das Lebende.* (*GW* 13:40; italics in the original)

The idea is the same as that which Benn expressed, just two years after the publication of 'Jenseits des Lustprinzips,' in 'Palau': 'was sich noch hält und steht, / will auch Zermalmung' (*GW* 1:62). According to Freud, the original loss that triggers the mechanics of the death drive is the infant's separation from the mother, a separation that begins with birth and ends with weaning. Thus, the inexorable movement towards death is prompted by the unconscious wish to reinstate the 'spherifying' (Michaux 118) symbiosis of the mother–child relationship.

Benn's treatment of the birth–death theme exhibits certain significant parallels with Freud's ideas, nowhere more evidently, perhaps, than in 'Palau': 'alle Tode der Welt / sind Fähren und Furten, / und von Fremdem umstellt / auch deine Geburten' (*GW* 1:62). In 'Kokain' the birth–death link is not stated so directly, although even here the association of birth with destruction and injury is striking. It is most evident in the final stanza, particularly in the formulation 'gebäre / blutbäuchig' (ll. 15–16). But in the second stanza, too, there is another, less visible but more profound expression of the birth–death connection. Here, it would seem, death is implicit in birth, for life outside the womb is condemned from the beginning to eventual annihilation; it will end as soon as the sword that emerged from the mother's sheath 'stählern schlägt' (l. 7), and the most we can aspire to in the meantime is 'da und dort ein Werk zu tun' (l. 6). The futility of postnatal existence is contrasted in the final line and a half of this stanza to the transcendence of 'Ich-Zerfall': 'gesunken in die Heide, / wo Hügel kaum enthüllter Formen ruhn!' (ll. 7–8). Although there is no explicit reference to death here, its presence is enciphered in several different ways. Firstly, 'gesunken', the past participle of one of Benn's favourite verbs of the *Rönne* period, denotes downward movement and therefore decline, and the formulation 'gesunken in die Heide' suggests not only communion with nature but also burial. This connotation is reinforced in the following line by the verb 'ruhn', which means 'rest' in its general sense but also more specifically 'lie or be buried' in such set phrases as *hier ruht* or *ruhe in Frieden.* Further, the conjunction of 'Heide' and 'Hügel' could be read as an evocation of prehistoric grave mounds, or barrows as archaeologists call them, such as are found on some German heaths. The German equivalent of 'barrow' is *Hügel.*[49] Such an association (which is certainly less oblique than that between the word *blau* and the skies of Zanzibar in Benn's model cipher, *GW* 8:1879; see 3.1) links death to historical regression and so heralds the restoration of 'an earlier state of things' on both the micro- and macrocosmic levels. Thus, the 'Hügel' of 'Kokain' become both prehistoric graves and the womb of Mother Earth.

Here, then, we have a definite parallel between Benn's art and Freud's theory: in Benn's poetry in general, and in 'Kokain' in particular, death is represented as a kind of re-birth or birth in reverse, in the same way as, according to Freud's 'Jenseits des Lustprinzips,' it is apprehended instinc-

---

49 This reading of Benn's 'Hügel' image was suggested by Peter Russell.

tively and unconsciously by each human subject. In the poem in question cocaine provides one means of realizing, in advance, this conception of death, of satisfying or placating, for the duration of the intoxication, the impulses that Freud described as constituting the death drive. Ironically, it is a form of death that results from an overflowing of life, as it is the drug's vitalizing qualities that cause the ego – and the linguistic code in which it exists and functions – to distort and then to 'explode'. Death through an excess of life is in a sense characteristic of cocaine, which is potentially lethal because taken in excess it causes the central nervous system to overload; death may occur through seizure, heart attack, or spontaneous cardiac arrest. The dose that gives the lyric subject a sore throat in line 2 of 'Kokain' is presumably smaller. The most serious of its physiological effects seem to be the brain-shudders, 'Hirnschauer' (l. 12), that immediately precede the 'explosion' of his ego.[50] The latter event, in turn, is in effect a happy premonition of death, or 'death substitute,' in that it consists in the temporary restoration of 'das Ur' (l. 11), the '*Wiederherstellung eines früheren Zustandes*' (Freud *GW* 13:38), the 'spherifying, global impression, with no beginning or end' of earliest human experience (Michaux 118), and despite the blood and destruction that follow in the final stanza, death, unlike birth, is never invoked directly. It remains, rather, a lightly veiled subtext.

Benn's vision of death as re-birth can be seen, in the dualistic framework of his regressionism, as the microcosmic equivalent of his macrocosmic vision of the impending Apocalypse as a 'Heimkehr der Schöpfung' (*GW* 3:643), already mentioned in connection with 'O Nacht' (see 3.2). At this point Benn's and Freud's concepts may appear to diverge. However, it should be noted that within both these frameworks, as well as in the murky middle ground where they enmesh, Benn's formula is always consistent with that which Freud posits, in 'Jenseits des Lustprinzips,' as the archetypal Ur-narrative that acts as a model for even the longest and most complex fictional narratives. Freud derived this theory from the so-called *fort-da* game he had seen his grandson playing and that he considered an enactment of the child's coming-to-terms with the absence of his mother and the first premonition of his own mortality that this absence

50 In his translation of 'Kokain', Boon renders Benn's neologism 'Hirnschauer' as 'brain-spectators' (190)! Presumably he reads it not as a reference to the intoxicated instability of the lyric subject's own psychological condition, as here, but as an animate noun referring to his sober contemporaries still trapped in the prisonhouse of rational thought and so excluded from his experience of 'das Ur.'

implied (*GW* 13:11–15). The model is essentially this: something is lost, then it is regained. An equilibrium is disturbed, and after a period of yearning, suffering and adventure that may vary in duration and intensity from one narrative to the next, it is reinstated. Both death as re-birth and Apocalypse as re-Creation conform to this pattern, and indeed, Freud's narrative model is clearly embedded in Benn's poetic practice, as both 'O Nacht' and 'Kokain' progress from yearning and suffering towards the reinstatement – or re-enactment – of a lost equilibrium. It follows that despite the contortions in their narrative *medium*, that is, in their language, the two poems are in fact highly conventional in their narrative *structure*. The basic pattern is the same as that which can be identified in countless sagas, fairytales, detective stories and realist novels. Even the idiosyncrasy of Benn's poetic lexicon can be considered consistent with Freud's model. With his eccentric style, Benn's stated intention is to revive the primitive condition of 'mystical participation' (*GW* 3:661), in other words, to reinstate what has been lost, to restore to the *da*-position something that has too long been *fort*.

It is remarkable, in fact, that both 'O Nacht' and 'Kokain' conform so precisely and succinctly with Freud's *fort-da* formula. Their manifestation of it is unusually spare, trimmed of the intrigues and deferments that normally serve to fill out a narrative, the human interaction and drama that normally give it substance. From this perspective, it is tempting to characterize Benn's approach as a regression in literary method, regression towards the earliest forms of Greek drama that emerged from the intoxicated celebration of Dionysus (see 1.2) and that initially, like 'O Nacht' and 'Kokain', featured just one character. Further, once we have recognized the *fort-da* model as a unifying structure in Benn's twofold framework of regression, his adverbial ciphers, identified by Schöne as signposts within an 'Überdauernde Temporalstruktur' (see 3.2), do more than just testify to the influence of the poet's Christian heritage. 'Schon', 'noch einmal,' 'erst wenn' and 'nicht mehr' become, rather, minimalist conjunctions in a bare-boned Ur-narrative. Significantly, in the two poems under discussion cocaine also functions as a form of narrative shortcut. Its chief virtue, as specified in 'Kokain', is that it takes the speaker directly to his destination: 'Den Ich-Zerfall, den süßen, tiefersehnten, / den gibst du mir' (ll. 1–2). To draw an analogy with other, archetypal *fort-da* narratives, it is as if cocaine could have led Lancelot straight to the Holy Grail or blown Homer's hero all the way from Troy back to Ithaca in the first sixteen lines of the *Odyssey*. A cocaine epic, for Benn, would be unwritable. Gilles Deleuze and Félix Guattari have noted that 'all drugs fundamentally concern speeds, and modifications of speed' (282). If, as Springer remarks, 'angeregte, beschleunigte Gedankentätigkeit und Fantasietätigkeit' (*N* 28–29 & *KMR* 43; see 1.2) is a common characteristic of cocaine intoxication and the Expressionist aesthetic, then nowhere in the Expressionist canon is this link exploited to greater effect than in 'O Nacht' and 'Kokain'. Moreover, the speed factor links these poems to Benn's two plays of the Brussels period featuring the same drug, as shall be made clear in the following chapter.

4 Benn's Cocaine Plays

4.1 The Strange Case of Doctors Rönne and Pameelen

In the numerous works produced in the burst of creative energy the young Dr. Benn experienced while stationed in the occupied Belgian capital, the word *Kokain* appears four times: in the poems 'O Nacht' and 'Kokain', and once each in the two short plays that feature Dr Jef van Pameelen as their protagonist: *Der Vermessungsdirigent*, first published in Berlin in 1919, but containing the note 'Brüssel, März 1916' (*GW* 8:2213), and *Karandasch,* first published in *Die Weißen Blätter* IV, 5, 1917. Even if the role of the drug in these two plays is clearly given less weight relative to the whole when compared to its prominence in the two poems discussed in the previous chapter, it is surprising, considering the explicit presence not only of cocaine but of a number of other psychoactive substances as well, that Benn's 'drug critics' have shown little interest in them. One explanation for this circumstance might be that Benn's early plays were for many years considered the least successful of his literary creations (Dierick 50), and hence in studies of his Brussels-period works they were usually passed over in favour of the better-known poetry and fiction. Recently, however, there has been a revival of interest in these plays and a re-evaluation of their place in Benn's œuvre. But the role of cocaine, its relationships to the themes and style of these plays, and the similarities and differences between its role here and its role in the two cocaine poems are all questions that remain unexplored. Our purpose in this chapter, therefore, is to open up new lines of investigation into these two plays by proposing a reading of them as elements of Benn's textual 'episode with cocaine' (*AB* 220; see 2.1).

One of the main points of interest that has emerged in the reassessment of *Der Vermessungsdirigent* and *Karandasch* is Pameelen's role as a counterbalance to Rönne, another young doctor and the protagonist of the cycle of five stories of 1915–16 that begins with 'Gehirne' and ends with 'Der Geburtstag' (e.g. Balser 55; Dickhoff 144; Kügler 80; Meister 49; Rumold 63; Wodtke 323–325). The doppelgänger-like relationship between the two characters was first suggested by Benn himself in a 1934 retrospective of his early period: 'Neben Rönne tritt Pameelen, ebenfalls Brüssel 1916' (*GW* 8:1904). While Rönne is passive, reserved and quiescent, Pameelen is active, confrontational and even violent (in Act 2 of *Der Vermessungsdirigent* he commits infanticide).[51] To employ a rough literary typology, we might call Pameelen the Mr Hyde to Rönne's Dr Jekyll. Certainly, Rönne's aspiration to social integration and respectability and Pameelen's contrasting disregard, even disdain for these same values fit neatly into a Jekyll-and-Hyde paradigm. While in the story 'Die Eroberung,' Rönne pleads, 'Nehmt mich auf in die Gemeinschaft!' (*GW* 5:1193), in *Karandasch* Pameelen establishes a revolutionary 'Geheimbund' (*GW* 6:1529f). In the context of Benn's 'episode with cocaine' the Jekyll-and-Hyde analogy is doubly suggestive, for in Stevenson's tale the respectable doctor's transformation into a hedonistic murderer is brought about by the 'drinking-off' of a potion, the last ingredient of which is a 'particular salt' that, although unnamed, bears a distinct resemblance in its form and effects to cocaine (57; see 1.2). Can a similar neurochemical modification be used to account for the Rönne–Pameelen opposition? Admittedly this hypothesis is problematic when applied to the differences in personality between the two characters. The *Rönne* stories never explicitly describe their protagonist as a drug taker, and although Pameelen is shown taking cocaine in *Karandasch*, in *Der Vermessungsdirigent* the drug user is another character altogether. However, the drug model is more useful for characterizing the different tones of the texts in which Rönne and Pameelen appear. The languor and introspection of the Rönne stories has, if anything, more of a narcotic flavour to it, in contrast to the self-confidence, restlessness, and almost manic loquacity of Pameelen and his fellow dramatis personae, qualities more reminiscent of the effects of stimulants.

The divergent patterns of imagery that inform the stories and plays tend to bear out this drug-based distinction in textual mood. The stories of the *Rönne* cycle abound with plants and flowers. One that recurs several times and that in a sense frames the whole cycle, appearing on both the first page of 'Gehirne' and the last page of 'Der Geburtstag,' is *der Mohn*, since

51 The Rönne who appears in Benn's earliest play *Ithaka* (1914) is quite different from the character of the same name featured in the stories, and is in fact more like a prototype of Pameelen. His similarity to the later character adds further weight to the notion of a genealogical and conceptual link between them.

the time of Novalis (see 3.1) a loaded word in literary contexts and difficult to dissociate from the opiate drugs. Not that Benn is at all interested in such a dissociation; on the contrary, in 'Der Geburtstag' the poppy's literary heritage is underlined in the description of the flower as 'groß und sagenhaft' (*GW* 5:1232). Bendix has noted that another of Benn's favourite flowers, *die Anemone*, phonetically encloses the word *Mohn* (41). One might similarly argue that his daphnes, violets, crocuses and narcissi can also be associated with the poppy by common semantic category, and so reinforce the same motif. That for Benn the word *Blume* in itself connotes intoxication is most strongly implied by a statement from his essay 'Das moderne Ich,' written just a few years later in 1920: 'es sind Felder über der Erde, die tragen nichts als Blumen des Rauschs' (*GW* 3:584). The idea that the recurrent poppy and more generally floral references of the *Rönne* cycle allude to opiate drugs is supported by their proximity to images of languor, drowsiness and sleep, another of the leitmotifs in these stories. For an example of this second pattern, we might consider the following sentence from 'Die Insel,' which also contains the strongest hint of the entire cycle that Rönne may indeed be a drug user: 'Plötzlich fühlte er sich tief ermüdet und ein Gift in seinen Gliedern'(*GW* 5:1218). To reconnect with the floral pattern, Rönne immediately approaches a window to look out over his garden and its 'white blossom.'

In the *Pameelen* plays the predominant drug is cocaine, which is supplemented by another stimulant: caffeine. The role of the drug is perceptible not only on the two occasions on which cocaine is named directly, but also in the more numerous oblique references to it. These include sniffing, sore throats and – less obliquely – snuffboxes containing 'kleine flimmernde Kristalle' (*GW* 6:1531). Another recurrent image that can be linked to this pattern is that of *Firnenschnee*, given that the word *Schnee* is commonly used to denote cocaine in its crystallized form (see 1.1). In the play *Der Vermessungsdirigent* it becomes clear that this word has very different symbolic overtones for Pameelen (see 4.2), and so it would certainly be mistaken to interpret it exclusively as a metaphor for the drug. At the same time it would be equally mistaken to disregard this as one of its enciphered connotations simply because it has others that one of the two texts does more to accentuate. As Pameelen is at pains to explain in *Karandasch*, such semantic rigidity, which he sees as a distinguishing trait of the bourgeois mentality, degrades the richness and expressiveness of language and needs to be combatted. It is therefore legitimate to see exchanges such as the following as consistent with the 'cocaine flavour' of the *Pameelen* plays not only because of their euphoric tone and staccato rhythm, but also because of their more specific symbolic implications:

> Pameelen: Ein Widerstand!!
> Sternheim: Ideenkampf.
> Pameelen: Lokalgeruch.
> Sternheim: Mit großer Zeit!
> Pameelen: Und Ewigkeit!
> Sternheim: Und Firnenschnee!
> Pameelen: Und Karandasch! (*GW* 6:1540)

In these ways the *Rönne* stories and the *Pameelen* plays themselves hint at associations between certain psychoactive drugs and their own textual tonalities, without however coming clean in the same way as the two cocaine poems and stating the matter unequivocally. But this inherent equivocacy does not make a drug-oriented reading any less valid. For Benn, it is precisely in fluidity of impression and semantic openness that the essential and natural quality of literary – as opposed to 'logical' – language lies (see 3.1). In any case, the important point is that the alternative genre of the Pameelen plays provides Benn with an alternative mood – whether or not one chooses to define it in relation to psychoactive drugs – for broadening his exploration of the same themes that dominate his other works of the 'Brussels spring': the *Fleisch* collection and the *Rönne* cycle. This mood is reflected, furthermore, in the grotesque and absurdist characteristics of these works, qualities more pronounced here than anywhere else in Benn's œuvre. These can in part be attributed to the influence of dramatist Carl Sternheim on Benn's theatrical experiments of this period, as Rainer Rumold has documented (63). Sternheim was one of Benn's closest friends in Brussels. As can be seen in the passage quoted above, he even makes a cameo appearance as a character in *Karandasch*, declaiming his aggressive ideas on how theatre should work.

The thematic likeness of the *Pameelen* plays and the *Rönne* stories highlights the difference in the protagonists' responses to similar problems: the perplexities that energize Pameelen are largely the same as those that paralyze Rönne. Both find themselves confronted with the inadequacy and fragility of rational, positivist thought and the various conceptual and behavioural systems (linguistic, psychological, social and sexual) that modern society has constructed upon it. It would clearly be incorrect to attribute the difference in their responses solely or even primarily to the different categories of psychoactive drugs that, as argued here, can be associated with the texts. At the very beginning of 'Gehirne', it is suggested that the protagonist's lethargy and detachment are symptoms of a psychological trauma, a form of nervous exhaustion resulting from his previous employment in a 'pathological institute.' The brief description of Rönne's last position brings to mind the ghastly scenes portrayed so dispassionately in the *Morgue* collection:

> Er hatte die letzten Monate tatenlos verbracht; er war zwei Jahre lang an einem pathologischen Institut angestellt gewesen, das bedeutet, es waren ungefähr zweitausend Leichen ohne Besinnen durch seine Hände gegangen, und das hatte ihn in einer merkwürdigen und ungeklärten Weise erschöpft. (*GW* 5:1185)

More simply, one must also consider that Rönne, either by nature or inexperience, is to all appearances the more ingenuous of the two, and for *this* reason more easily and consistently overwhelmed by his on-going confrontation with the limits of reason and the absurdity of convention. The following description of his submissiveness in the face of mystery, taken from 'Die Eroberung,' is representative:

> Er stand demütig vor dem Unbegreiflichen, aller Rätsel wurde auch er nicht Herr; das Mythische ragte in sein Leben hinein, die guten und die bösen Dinge, die Träne und das Blut. (*GW* 5:1197)

Pameelen, on the other hand, whether sober or intoxicated, absolutely refuses to stand 'humbly before the incomprehensible,' or before anything else for that matter. Rather, he either tackles *das Unbegreifliche* head-on (in *Der Vermessungsdirigent*) or embraces it ecstatically (in *Karandasch*). In the latter case, to underline further his distinction from Rönne, he projects himself into the realm of the 'mystic' rather than vice-versa, presenting cocaine as one of several potential instruments that may facilitate such a projection: 'Husten, Onanie, Kokain, alles was den Unterbau etwas lockert, muß gesetzlich eingeführt werden (*schnupft*)' (*GW* 6:1529).

The point of the suggestion that the Rönne–Pameelen dichotomy corresponds in some way with a narcotic–stimulant opposition – specifically an opiate–cocaine opposition – is not, therefore, that the two characters' diverse attitudes are the result of their taking different psychoactive substances, and even less that their author used different psychoactive substances as creative tools to stimulate his various compositions. Rather, within each of the texts the use of imagery associated more or less directly with particular drugs and their effects, combined with more or less direct statements regarding the characters' own use of them, contributes to what, following Trocchi, we might call a certain 'coherence of posture' in the text itself (cited in Plant 132). Incoherence in just about everything else is, according to the same passage from Trocchi, a characteristic feature of drugged writing: 'I am of course incapable of sustaining a simple narrative...with no fixed valid categories...not so much line of thought as an area of experience...the immediate broth; I am left with a coherence of posture' (ibid). Benn's stories and plays, with their fragmented plots and unrelenting stylistic idiosyncrasies, can be seen as an artistic employment of the same kind of reduction to mere 'coherence of posture.' To offer too much coherence would, in their own terms, be to subscribe to the unhealthy illusion of logical causality, to 'live linearly' in the sense indicated by the motto to the first edition of *Karandasch*: 'Ein Mungo, wer noch linear lebt' (*GW* 8:2214). Thus Rönne need not necessarily take narcotics, or be portrayed as taking them, for their effects to be considered coherent with his character or for narcotic imagery to be coherent with the tone of the *Rönne* cycle as a whole. One might even say that for Benn's purposes, the vaguer the suggestions that his protagonist is on drugs, the better. In a similar way, allusions to cocaine can be considered posturally coherent with the *Pameelen* plays. *Karandasch* is sub-titled 'Rapides Drama' (*GW* 6:1527), so references to 'fast' drugs like cocaine and caffeine (see 3.4) can only enhance this quality.

It should be noted that, despite the fundamental differences between the two characters, Rönne's and Pameelen's reactions to the crises they face have certain significant features in common. Both turn to a characteristically Bennian brand of poetic mysticism that connects them with a 'prelogical', therefore precrisis world, although as neither in fact writes poetry, it is more accurate to describe their mysticism as *semiotic* in the Kristevan sense (see point 6 in the table in 3.1) rather than strictly poetic. The lost world they revive in this way, as elsewhere in Benn's works, has both natural (especially botanical) and historical-mythological (especially ancient) characteristics, which are reflected in the settings of both the *Rönne* stories and the *Pameelen* plays. Whereas Rönne's preferred refuge is the garden, in the final scene of *Karandasch* Pameelen, ostensibly in search of an escaped patient, rushes into a museum. Here, surrounded by the relics of lost civilizations, he breaks into a sustained exclamatory euphoria, interrupted only by the hackneyed, 'logical' protestations of the museum attendant: 'An diesem Ort muß Ruhe herrschen!' (*GW* 6:1554). For these reasons and within these limits the Rönne-Pameelen parallel noted by numerous critics can be considered legitimate. But whereas the idea that Rönne's perturbations stem from drug use is one that has been put forward notwithstanding the absence of direct drug references in the text (Bendix 23–84), the role of drugs in the Pameelen plays has long been overlooked.

4.2 Picasso's Drugged Exhaustion

In *Der Vermessungsdirigent*, subtitled 'Erkenntnistheoretisches Drama' (*GW* 6:1498), it is Picasso rather than Pameelen with whom drugs are associated. To what extent the character Picasso can be identified with the historical figure of the same name is, as one might expect with Benn, gloriously ambiguous. In the list of characters Pameelen is 'Jef van Pameelen, ein Arzt'; Picasso is simply 'Picasso' (*GW* 6:1500). In any case it is apparent that Benn is not in the least interested in drawing a portrait of the artist, let alone a realistic one; rather it is the name itself, with its associations of a revolutionary artistic perspective, that is important to him for reasons that should become clear in this discussion. Within the play Picasso acts as Pameelen's alter ego, as is made most evident in the third scene of act 1. Here Pameelen's father takes Picasso for his son, an error that Picasso, preoccupied with weightier metaphysical matters, feels no great compulsion to rectify: 'Daß zwischen uns Relationen bestehen, bestreite ich nicht; aber nur als Sonderfall eines Systems von Relationen zwischen weit allgemeineren Begriffen und Beziehungen' (*GW* 6:1513). Pameelen's father, having been reduced to tears by Picasso's tirade against the pettiness of bourgeois life and the baseness of logical thought, realizes his mistake only at the end of the scene when his son finally appears. The final lines read as follows:

> Der alte Pameelen: Wie? Ihr seht ja beide ganz gleich aus?
> Pameelen: Ja, wir sind prinzipiell archimedische Punkte –
> Picasso: Bezugsgebiete völlig gleichen Ranges –

Pameelen: Koordinatensysteme –
Der alte Pameelen: Ach so! (*GW* 6:1516)

Once a certain congruence between the two figures has been established, the next question is what to make of their diverse responses to the 'epistemological' dilemma that sets the drama in motion. In this connection Ulrich Meister argues that the new visual perspective that Picasso seeks and eventually achieves represents one way out of Pameelen's cognitive crisis (52–53). Certainly Pameelen's own response, that of turning 'der Trieb nach Definition [...] gegen das sogenannte eigene Ich' (*GW* 6:1498), as Benn puts it in his introductory 'Zusammenfassung', ends in failure. In the play's opening scene, labelled 'Vorspiel' and set in the most characteristic of Benn's Brussels-era locations, a hospital for prostitutes, Pameelen praises '[den] Wahrheitsdrang, der in uns schwachen Menschen ruht und uns höher und höher treibt bis in das Firnenlicht, bis in das große Leuchten'(*GW* 6:1502). Following this urge, Pameelen does indeed arrive at the heights he dreams of. His seemingly figurative aspiration to altitude is materialized in the physical setting of the play, the second and third acts taking place in a hut high in the mountains with snow all around. In this way the play's snow imagery is linked with Pameelen's quest for the ultimate definition of his own ego, a definition that continues to elude him even in his mountain hut and in place of which he finds only sterility, premature aging and an early death (although Benn would duly resurrect him in time for *Karandasch*). In what amounts to an act of irrepressible proto-deconstructionism, the egocentricity of Pameelen's 'logische Funktion des Urteils und des Vergleichens' (*GW* 6:1498) irrevocably collapses upon itself.

In response to Pameelen's mania for absolute self-knowledge, and specifically to his stated objective of making the human subject 'weiß [...] wie diese Marmorstufe hier: so hingebreitet, so wirklich, so erkenntlich' (*GW* 6:1522), Picasso half-mockingly calls him 'alter Vermessungsdirigent.' As already indicated, Picasso's own reaction to the failings of normative, institutionalized modes of thought is fundamentally different and consists in the attempt to escape their pathological, creatively repressive influence and find a workable alternative. In the first scene of act 1, with the idea that the alternative he seeks might be found in a psychoactive substance, he consults Pameelen for medical assistance. It is here we find cocaine, which appears in a guise very different from that in the two poems, for on this occasion it is presented as an already-tested solution that has proved inadequate over time:

> Picasso: Ich bin so krank.
> Pameelen: Sie wollen mich konsultieren wegen …?
> Picasso: … der Gehirnebene. Wenn dies *(mit der Hand)* die allgemeine staatlich-logisch fixierte Ebene ist, bitte ich eine Drehung erwirken zu wollen, um eine Kleinigkeit, vielleicht um fünf Grad. Nur daß das Reizpotential eben überschritten ist. Kokain habe ich genommen, bis mir die Schenkel zitterten; Koffein, daß mich das Herz an die Pariete warf, bitte etwas dauerhaft Wirksameres, vielleicht Curare? (*GW* 6:1505)

In the end Picasso achieves his permanent cerebral-visual 'rotation' not through drugs, but through the transplantation of a 'Tierauge' (*GW* 6:1509), an operation that has the comical side-effect of causing him to neigh. Even so, it is important to note that the unsuitability of drugs for Picasso's purposes is a consequence not of their inefficacy, but of the limited duration of their effects. In this sense they represent a partial failure – but equally a partial success – as a way out of his quandary. We can infer that his first experience of cocaine was similarly enthusiastic to that of Benn's cocaine poems, but that with increasing use the side-effects became more and more pronounced – to the extent that, as he puts it here, his 'thighs trembled.'[52] In this scene Picasso has not yet given up on drugs; rather he suggests that the answer to his problem may lie in rejecting two stimulants (cocaine and caffeine) in favour of a narcotic (curare). In other words, in his quest for longer-lasting intoxication his plan is turn from 'fast' drugs to a 'slow' one.

The direct link made in Scene 1 of *Der Vermessungsdirigent* between psychoactive substances and an artist like Picasso prefigures Benn's idea that certain toxins may have a 'positiven biologischen Reiz zur Produktionsauslösung' (*GW* 3:651), a notion that he would formulate as part of his 'bionegative' theory of artistic creativity in the *Genie* essays of the early 1930s (see 2.2). Significantly, then, Picasso's 'episode with cocaine' (and caffeine) demonstrates that this idea had already germinated long before Benn wrote the *Genie* essays, and indeed that its roots can be traced as far back as the period of Benn's own 'episode with cocaine in the First World War' (*AB* 220). It could be argued that the same idea is implicit in the two

---

52 As a user develops physical tolerance of a drug, the dosage must be increased to achieve the same level of intoxication, thus increasing the intensity of the side-effects to potentially dangerous levels.

cocaine poems, as in themselves they represent two artistic productions stimulated by taking the drug – at least their speaker is stimulated by taking the drug; the stimulation of their author remains less certain. But in *Der Vermessungsdirigent* it is the play itself that explicitly presents us with a genius in the throes of a creative – and sexual – crisis: 'Picasso: Meine Potenz ist gering, meine Zeugungsfähigkeit erloschen' (*GW* 6:1505). And the character himself sees a neurochemical modification brought about by the administration of certain drugs as a potential solution. Whether or not it is a theory that Benn subscribed to wholeheartedly or – as Modick would have it (50; see 2.1) – put into practice himself, it is evidently one that he enjoyed toying with in his writing, and thus it has become established as an element of his 'biographical legend' (Tomashevsky 52; see 1.4), if not a fact of his actual biography.

Meister asserts that Picasso's liberating 'five-degree' adjustment of his visual perspective, a solution appropriate to his own preferred media of creative expression, points the way to a linguistic solution as well (53). The latter, not surprisingly, coincides in significant ways with Benn's own notion of the nature and value of poetic language that he would formulate most completely in the 'Worte, Worte – Substantive!'-passage from 'Epilog und lyrisches Ich' (see 3.1). From one point of view this condensed poetic credo can be considered a résumé of the various statements on the subject we find interspersed among the works of his early period. In *Der Vermessungsdirigent* Picasso addresses the issue most directly. When he reappears in act 2 following his 'transplant', he makes the following observation to Pameelen:

> Pameelen, ich muß es Ihnen gestehen, ich habe plötzlich eine so große Liebe zu den Ausrufungssätzen bekommen. Sie schließlich sind doch primitiv, spargelförmig, unassoziiert. (*GW* 6:1522)

Curiously, of all the characters in the play it is Pameelen, *der Vermessungsdirigent* himself, who makes the most use of 'primitive, asparagus-shaped, unassociated' exclamations. In his rigorous deconstruction of logic he refuses to make, as he says, any 'Konzession an die Syntax!' (*GW* 6:1523). His lengthy monologues of the final act are the most vociferous of all. As his quest for the ultimate definition of his own ego leads him further and further into the black hole that, as he discovers, lies at the centre of rational thought, his mode of expression increasingly comes to resemble a raw form of the poetic-mystic alternative that he nonetheless tragically fails to grasp. At least in this particular play he fails to grasp it. In *Karandasch* he will reappear as both an avid proselytizer for the cult of 'die uralten Worte' (*GW* 6:1534) and an enthusiastic user of cocaine. 'Der alte Vermessungsdirigent' would seem to have learned his lesson.

4.3 The Etymology of a Magic Formula

In 'Probleme der Lyrik' Benn advises his listeners to accept the essential and mysterious power of the poetic word as an irreducible, irrational component of language:

> Wir werden uns damit abfinden müssen, daß Worte eine latente Existenz besitzen, die auf entsprechend Eingestellte als Zauber wirkt und sie befähigt, diesen Zauber weiterzugeben. Dies scheint mir das letzte Mysterium zu sein, vor dem unser immer waches, durchanalysiertes, nur von gelegentlichen Trancen durchbrochenes Bewußtsein seine Grenze fühlt. (*GW* 1077–1078)

The word Benn chose as the title for the second of the *Pameelen* plays, *Karandasch*, would appear to be endowed with particularly strong magical powers. In act 1, scene 2 of the play Pameelen explains the word's meaning and function. It is, he says, 'die große Eidesformel' (*GW* 6:1534) he habitually uses to evoke a prehistoric and preconceptual mode of linguistic expression that he contrasts with the vacuity of 'alle Vokabeln, in die das Bürgerhirn seine Seele sabberte, jahrtausendelang.' Rumold claims that Benn took the word from the name of the Swiss pen and pencil manufacturer Caran d'Ache, of which *Karandasch* is the *Eindeutschung* (63). However, this derivation is clearly anachronistic: the complany website informs us that Caran d'Ache, which continues to manufacture pens and pencils to this day, was founded only in 1924, that is, seven years after the original publication of Benn's play in *Die Weißen Blätter*. Where, then, does Benn's *Urwort* come from? And what meanings, if any, can be associated with this 'ancient' signifier that Pameelen treats as a kind of antisignifier, proffering as its definition 'als ob Worte Sinn hätten?'

Two possible and related sources present themselves for Benn's title. The first, which is incidentally also the source for the name of the Swiss pen and pencil manufacturer to which Rumold refers, is the nom de plume of the famous French caricaturist of the Belle Epoque, Emmanuel Poiré (1859–1909), who signed his drawings 'Caran d'Ache.' This possibility becomes all the more plausible when we consider that Benn, living in Brussels, may well have had the opportunity to encounter the works of famous French caricaturists. The second possible explanation is that Benn's source was the same as Poiré's. Poiré, the grandson of an officer in Napoleon's Grande Armée, was born in Moscow, and once he had established himself in France chose a disguised French transliteration of a word from his native Slavic tongue as his nom de plume. His choice fell upon not just any word, but one that was intimately connected to his trade: in Russian *karandash* means pencil. The idea that the title of Benn's play is a direct borrowing from the Russian is supported by the fact that *Karandasch* is an exact German transliteration of the original Cyrillic. One factor that speaks against such a theory is Benn's lack of Russian. So perhaps the most likely scenario involves a combination of these two possible derivations: it is conceivable that Benn may have learnt the story of Poiré's pen name (or better, pencil name) and gone back to the latter's own source for his title.

Whatever the course of events, one thing is certain: either directly or indirectly, Pameelen's 'great oath' derives from the Russian word for pencil. In this light, its definition 'als ob Worte Sinn hätten' is not as semantically nihilistic as it might at first seem, but is closely – etymologically – linked to written and more generally graphic expression. Consequently, we might say that *Karandasch* is not so much an antisignifier as an ultrasignifier. It represents a recognition of the limits of signification, but it does not attempt to nullify language or advocate silence; rather it affirms the validity of expression that acknowledges and seeks to transcend these limits. It is noteworthy that what prompts Pameelen's lengthy *Karandasch* speech at the end of act 1, scene 2 is another character's urge to express not *das Nichts*, but 'ein echtes Etwas':

> Renz: Aber ich habe etwas. Nehmen wir an, ich hätte etwas, das meine Ansicht wäre, das ich verteidigen könnte, etwas mit Schwurfinger, Physiognomie, kurz ein echtes Etwas.
>
> Pameelen: Dann sagen Sie Karandasch. (*GW* 6:1533–1534)

As in the poem 'Kokain' (see 3.4), a nominalized form of the pronoun *etwas* is used to convey the essential indeterminateness and indeterminability of experience that escapes the confines of respectable bourgeois life and the conventionally accepted limits of signification that imprison it in what Pameelen calls 'die Schachtel':

> das ist die Schachtel: die Worte sind geordnet: unter jedem steht ein kleiner Mann. Nachts schläft kleiner Mann bei kleiner Frau, fortzupflanzen, anzuschließen, Wort zu füllen mit neuem Mund. (*GW* 6:1534)

The etymology of Benn's magical, *Schachtel*-exploding word has one further twist, one that brings new implications for the peculiar nature of its magic. *Karandasch* is indeed a Russian word, but it is not based on Slavic or even Indo-European roots. It is in fact a borrowing from a more exotic source, the Turkic branch of the Altaic family of languages, where **karadaš* or *karataš*, depending on the individual language, means black stone or schist (Vasmer 256). In this respect it is comparable to the Spanish and Italian words for pencil, *làpiz* and *lapis* respectively, both of which derive from the Latin *lapis –ĭdis*, which means stone. With this even older source in mind we can see that *Karandasch*, the most representative of Pameelen's 'ancient words,' connotes not just written expression, but also – in consequence of its *Ursinn* – the inorganic geological material that Benn so often associates with his primordial vision of 'mystische Partizipation' (*GW* 3:661). The most direct expression of this association occurs in 'Provoziertes Leben,' in which Benn lists 'Stein, Vers, Flötenlied' as 'Bilder des großen Urtraums' (*GW* 3:905). Also, we have already seen that in 'O Nacht' one manifestation of the speaker's increasingly intense cocaine intoxication is a vision of flying stones (see 3.2). It is evident, then, that even if Pameelen presents *Karandasch* as a kind of nonsense or antisense word, it is one that, considering its long and involved history, is heavily loaded with enciphered connotations pertinent to the thematic complex of the play and is by no means as arbitrary as Rumold's erroneous etymology would suggest.

In *Karandasch* the role of cocaine is closely linked to the play's dominant linguistic theme. As indicated in 4.1, in this play Pameelen sees the drug as one of several tools that can be used to loosen the foundations that hold up the 'geschlossene Persönlichkeit' (*GW* 6:1529) of the bourgeois subject, embodied in act 1, scene 1 in the figure of the *Chefarzt*. In reaction to the *Chefarzt*'s grotesque pomposity, Pameelen urges his two companions,

Renz and Plenz, to join him in a revolutionary 'Geheimbund', the activity of which will leave the bourgeois citizen 'erschüttert' (*GW* 6:1530). Comically, the first and only action of their 'secret society' – Renz and Plenz do not reappear after act 1 – consists in the three of them taking cocaine together. That the drug they use is cocaine is not stated directly, but a high concentration of indirect references leaves little room for doubt. The first clue is in the context: Pameelen has only just advocated cocaine's legal 'introduction' (*GW* 6:1529). Second, the description of the substance, abbreviated as it is, corresponds closely with the most recognizable qualities of cocaine: 'small shimmering crystals' administered nasally and deriving from a 'delicate inconspicuous shrub.' The one detail that does not fit is its geographical origin. The coca plant is endemic to the Andean rainforests, but Benn's Levant may be taken as a metaphor for any distant, ancient and exotic place (see 1.2). Finally, and most convincingly, its subsequent effects – both physical and psychological – are consistent with the characteristic symptoms of cocaine intoxication: irritation of the throat, a feeling of general well-being tending towards euphoria, and an exaggerated sense of self-confidence and self-importance. We can conclude that at the very least Pameelen's drug is a cocaine-like substance that is essentially indistinguishable from the original.

> Pameelen *(mit Schnupfdose)*: und diese kleinen flimmernden Kristalle *(reicht herum)*, diese feine levantische Kraut *(alles schnupft)*, diese zarte unscheinbare Staude … *(flüsternd)* nehmen Sie, seien Sie von der rauhen Kehle …, wenn so der Atem darüberstreicht und es herkommt als eine fremde Stimme …, wenn Sie sinken: Stück um Stück …
> Renz: Wie ist mir …?
> Plenz: Taumel …
> Renz: Glücksgefühl.
> Plenz: Und wenn diese Schweine sterben, sagen sie, sie haben auch gelebt –
> Renz: Aber wir …
> Pameelen: … unter Schauern des Zerfalls, unter den Strömen des Vergehens …
> Plenz: Die neuen Typen.
> Pameelen: Der Chefarzt: da: klein, kleiner, am kleinsten … er schwankt, fort … Buchstaben …
> Renz: … Vier …
> Pameelen: Ein Hauptwort … und Pfeiffer: auch ein Hauptwort … mit Untergruppen.
> Plenz: Aber wir …
> Renz: … Die neuen Typen …
> Plenz: … Die neuen Schweine …
> Renz: … Der gelockerte Unterbau …
> Pameelen: … Ich glatte ein …

Renz: … Er glattet …
Pameelen: … Das Ur …
Plenz: … Die ….??
Pameelen: Das …!!!
Plenz: Prophete!
Renz: Jeremias!!
Pameelen: Amen!!!! – (*GW* 6:1531–1532)

This passage has several features – structural, lexical and more broadly thematic – that link it to the two cocaine poems 'O Nacht' and 'Kokain', thus adding further weight to our assumption that the crystallized herb in Pameelen's snuffbox is indeed the coca plant. These correspondences are significant also because they call attention to a distinctive and unifying quality of Benn's literary 'episode with cocaine,' namely that he seems, consciously or otherwise, to have developed a textual formula for portraying – or better enacting – cocaine intoxication, a formula that he could adapt to suit the particular needs of a given context. Thus, the obvious differences between this passage and the two poems can be attributed to its position in *Karandasch*: it is in prose rather than verse; it involves several characters and is informed with socially aggressive attitudes; and it features the grotesque humour that is characteristic of both *Pameelen* plays. On the other hand, important points of similarity include, first, the overall development of the scene, which moves from the taking of the drug to a description of the sensations it produces ('Taumel' and 'Glücksgefühl'). This brings a growing sense of a qualitative transformation in subjecthood ('die neuen Typen' and 'der gelockerte Unterbau'), and this new subjecthood is contrasted ('Aber wir…') with the squalor of everyday, bourgeois existence ('diese Schweine'). This in turn leads to the impression of having obtained access to an original, long-lost mode of being ('das Ur'), which in the final stage of the process causes the characters involved to erupt in a kind of religious euphoria ('Prophete! […] Jeremias!! […] Amen!!!! –'). Equivalent progressions can be found in the two poems, as explained in the previous chapter. The structural parallels between the poem 'Kokain' and the cocaine-taking scene in *Karandasch* are such that several key words and phrases indicating stages in the progression of the scene occur in both texts. These close or exact lexical correspondences represent the second major similarity between the play and the poems, and are summarized in the following table:

Karandasch	'Kokain'
'von der rauhen Kehle'	'schon ist die Kehle rauh' (l. 2)
'eine fremde Stimme'	'der fremde Klang' (l. 3)
'wenn Sie sinken'	'gesunken in die Heide' (l. 7)
'unter Schauern des Zerfalls'	'Ich-Zerfall' (l. 1) / 'Hirnschauer' (l. 12)
'Der gelockerte Unterbau'	' am Unterbau' (l. 4)
'Ich glatte ein' / 'Er glattet'	'Ein laues Glatt' (l. 9)
'Das Ur'	'das Ur' (l. 11)

In act 1, scene 3 Pameelen will repeat one of these cocaine phrases, as we might call them, describing himself as 'mit meistens rauher Kehle' (*GW* 6:1536) and so circuitously suggesting that he is a more than occasional user of the drug. Finally, a parallel that can be noted between this passage and the poem 'O Nacht,' in which the speaker describes himself as 'zerfetzt von Worte-Wolkenbrüchen' (*GW* 1:53; see 3.2), is an explicit concern with the effect of cocaine intoxication on the linguistic faculty, or rather the subject's perception of the nature and potentialities of the linguistic faculty. Implicitly this concern is deeply rooted in both the poems. In *Karandasch* this aspect is given particular emphasis as the *Chefarzt* and his assistant are reduced from human beings to 'Hauptwörter'. It is in this linguistic aspect that Pameelen's passion for cocaine ties in with the central theme of the play, formulated in the first sentence of the introductory 'Zusammenfassung' as follows: 'Pameelen betrachtet das sogenannte geistige Dasein unter dem Gesichtspunkt seiner sprachlichen Komponente' (*GW* 6:1527).

In the scene that immediately follows the 'secret society's' communal cocaine experiment Renz discovers his 'echtes Etwas' and touches on 'das große Problem der Schachtel' (*GW* 6:1533). That his lingering intoxication has some part in the discovery can be inferred not only from the placement in sequence of the two scenes, but also from his opening words, which echo those he had uttered in his first reaction to taking the drug: 'Wie ist mir …?' (*GW* 6:1533). His second question offers a partial response to the first and broaches the theme of poetic expression that dominates the rest of the scene: 'Mir ist so dichterisch …?' The word that Pameelen will offer him in order to articulate his extraordinary new state of mind is *Karandasch*, the 'nonsense' word that, etymologically speaking, connotes stone, a material that predates and transcends human history, and at the same time hints at graphic or written expression – artistic expression –as a way out of the prison-like *Schachtel* that the stale and impoverished norms of 'bourgeois' signification represent.

Clearly, in *Karandasch* as in the two cocaine poems, the administration of cocaine serves as a catalyst for the exploration of other issues with which the text is more concerned than the details of drug-taking itself. These details are dealt with quickly and in a few stylized brushstrokes that reveal far more about the possibilities and ambiguities of language – and of cocaine as a *textual* phenomenon – than they do about the practice of drug use, or indeed about the author's 'true' opinion of the merits or otherwise of such practice. In this last regard it is worth considering that both Modick and Arend, whose disagreement over Benn's estimation of drugs as stimulants to literary production has been outlined in 2.1, would find grist to their respective mills in *Karandasch*, a work to which neither makes reference. Modick might emphasize that Renz's 'poetic' disposition seems to arise directly out of his experience of cocaine. Arend, on the other hand, might find that in none of Benn's other works are drugs so obviously used as an instrument for provoking bourgeois sensibilities as in this play. These observations are both accurate as far as they go. It is when they are interpreted above all as evidence of the author's views and methods that problems arise. As we have seen, Benn's employment of cocaine as a textual device has stylistic and thematic implications that are many and varied. If there is one unifying thread, it is that these different aspects all in some way contribute to the process of mystification that Benn considers the essential function of literary discourse. His critics would do well to consider this last circumstance before engaging so confidently in the difficult task of demystifying and disentangling him. Benn will not be unmasked so easily.

Part Two: Walter Rheiner

In the darkness of my room there sounded a prolonged howl, and only a moment later did I realize that I was the one howling and that the hand covering my mouth was my own.

– *M. Ageev,* Roman s kokainom[53]

53 ‹Во мраке моей комнаты возник протяжный вой, и только спустя мгновение я понял, что вою-то это я сам, и что моя же рука зажимает мне рот.› (Ageev 155)

5 A Portrait of the Artist as a Drug Addict

5.1 Under the Influence: Cocaine, Morphine, Expressionism

When Expressionism became openly political and programmatic in about 1914, the number of poets who became associated with the movement grew to such proportions that, in the words of Seymour-Smith, 'only a directory – and that in small type – could deal with them all' (579). As early as 1919, Kurt Pinthus predicted in the preface to the first edition of his Expressionist anthology *Menschheitsdämmerung* that the work of most of these poets would soon fade from public and critical consciousness: 'Von den vielen, vielen Dichtungen dieser Generation werden fast alle mit den verebbenden Stürmen ihrer Epoche untergegangen sein' (31). Pinthus was no mere observer of this literary-historical development, but one of the main actors behind it, for as Sharp explains, exclusion from his epoch-defining anthology has itself been a major factor behind the neglect of several noteworthy poets associated with Expressionism, especially those of the so-called second generation born after 1891 that remains unrepresented even in later editions (*M* 144ff). Walter Rheiner (1895–1925; 'Rheiner' was a pseudonym – his real name was Schnorrenberg) is one poet whose work seemed, for many years after the passing of the Expressionist era, destined to share this collective oblivion.[54] But in 1969, with the opening of the Walter-Rheiner-Archiv at the *Akademie der Künste* in Berlin, a gradual rehabilitation began that has continued to gain momentum ever since, culminating in 2008 in the fourth book publication of Rheiner's work in just over 30 years.

This recent quantitative shift in Rheiner reception, that is, the increased availability of his work and the growth of his readership, is reflective of a

54 Huder evidently considers Rheiner's omission from *Menschheitsdämmerung* a mistake on Pinthus's part: 'Kurt Pinthus schrieb wohl dann und wann über Rheiner's Produktion, vergaß aber, wenigstens eines seiner Gedichte in die epochale Expressionisten-Anthologie *Menschheitsdämmerung* (1920) aufzunehmen' (77). It is somewhat ironic, then, that Huder's edition (*KNP*) does not contain any of Rheiner's poetry either.

qualitative one concerning the perception of his place in literary history. Whereas as late as 1992 Michael Kohtes could still talk of Rheiner as a 'vergessener Expressionist' (Kohtes 119), in the foreword to his 2008 selection of the writer's works, Michael Grimm introduces him as the author of a 'Meilenstein der Drogenliteratur', a work 'aktueller denn je' 90 years after its first publication (*K* 10). Notable here is not only the remarkable growth in significance attributed to Rheiner's writings, but also that this elevation seems to have gone hand in hand with a shift in the focus of critical attention from his involvement with and contribution to Expressionism (which extended beyond his own writing to various forms of collaboration with other representatives of that movement) to his choice of drug addiction as the subject matter for certain of his literary works and, concomitantly and no less importantly, the decisive and devastating role that drug abuse played in his own life. A parallel development is the increased importance attached to Rheiner's short prose, especially the novella *Kokain* (1918) that Grimm singles out as a 'milestone of drug literature,' relative to his poetry, even though the latter accounts for by far the largest part of his literary output.

These changes in the critical perception of Rheiner were foreshadowed in the first of the four collections of his works published since the establishment of his archive in 1969, a collection of four prose pieces that appeared in Leipzig in 1977 with an afterword by the then longstanding director of the Berlin *Akademie der Künste* Walter Huder. *Kokain* is not only the first of the four texts reproduced in this edition – arranged, curiously, in reverse chronological order – but it also takes pride of place in the title of the collection: *Kokain: Eine Novelle und andere Prosa.* The three stories 'Die Erniedrigung,' 'Der Tod des Schwärmers Gautier Fémin' and 'Mirameée', on the other hand, are relegated collectively to the status of 'other prose,' and the poetry is neglected altogether. The narrow scope of this edition suggests that it may have been intended as a foray to 'test the waters' for a larger publication, for within a decade its limitations were compensated for by two further volumes, both edited by Thomas Rietzschel, which together represent the first and only comprehensive collection of Rheiner's literary works and correspondence: *Kokain: Lyrik, Prosa,*

Briefe (1985) and *Ich bin ein Mensch – ich fürchte mich* (1986).[55] Rietzschel takes a more systematic approach to the task of presenting Rheiner's work to a latter-day readership, with both books featuring poetry and prose in discrete, chronologically arranged sections (*KLPB* includes a third section of the writer's correspondence). Nonetheless, the privileged status of *Kokain* within Rheiner's œuvre is maintained through Rietzschel's recycling of this title for the first and larger of his two editions. The tendency to canonization of Rheiner's novella, and to consideration of his other works and biography purely in relation, indeed almost as appendages to it, has found its fullest expression in Grimm's 2008 edition, entitled simply *Kokain*. This includes *Kokain*, 'Die Erniedrigung,' four poems (interspersed between the other texts), most of the letters from *KLPB* plus some previously unpublished correspondence between Rheiner's mother Ernestine Schnorrenberg and estranged wife Amalie Friederike Schnorrenberg (*née* Olle, later St. Saveur, known affectionately by Rheiner as 'Fo'),[56] as well as documents from the couple's divorce proceedings of early 1925, and introductory and biographical notes by St. Saveur. In total, this selection and its arrangement have the effect of blending Rheiner's prose, poetry, correspondence and even the legal documentation of his life into a single, remarkably smooth narrative, in which drug abuse functions as the central, unifying theme. The book ends with three excerpts from historical sources concerning cocaine production, distribution and abuse respectively at the turn of the 20th century, none of which mentions Rheiner or appears to bear any relation to him other than via the common denominator of cocaine use. These serve as confirmation of the editor's intention to portray the writer first and foremost through the lens of a cultural history of drugs, within which he can be attributed the status of an important contributor.[57] For Grimm, Rheiner's roles as poet and adherent of Expressionism are evidently sec-

55 Rietzschel confirms that these two volumes, despite their different publishers, were intended to complement one another: 'auch diese Werkauswahl will unser Band [*KLPB*] komplettieren' (*M* 110).

56 Hereafter referred to as Fo in her role as Rheiner's (ex-)wife and as St. Saveur as his biographer, a usage that conforms to her own: in her biography St. Saveur refers to herself in the third person as Fo.

57 This tendentious approach is consistent with the overall editorial strategy of Tatto's Taipan Classic series, whose motto is 'Autoren erzählen von Sex, Drogen und Gewalt' (*K* 150). The insertion of Rheiner's poem 'Die Prostituierte' between *Kokain* and 'Die Erniedrigung' appears to serve little purpose beyond catering to the first of the publisher's broader interests.

ondary considerations.[58] Considering these four collections of Rheiner's work together, then, Huder's 'Nachwort', St. Saveur's biographical notes and the court documents published in Grimm's edition represent valuable supplementary material for scholars, but Rietzschel's two editions clearly provide the best primary reference for readers who wish to gain a fuller appreciation of Rheiner's work and its development, and thus to assess whether the recent favour for *Kokain*, and more generally his prose over his poetry, is an objective reflection of the relative strengths and weaknesses of his œuvre, or rather of the saleability of the novella's drug theme.

As far as the poetry is concerned, what emerges from the extensive reading that Rietzschel's collections allow is that Rheiner, in contrast to many of the others whose names would appear in Seymour-Smith's hypothetical small-type directory of Expressionism, was unquestionably blessed with a natural lyrical gift. This is consistent with the impression that Rheiner is said to have made on his peers in Berlin during his first trip to that city in 1914, as reported by St. Saveur:

> Inzwischen waren seine Freunde nach Berlin verzogen, von wo sie begeisterte Briefe über das literarische Leben dieser Stadt schrieben. Er folgte ihnen und dort entdeckte man zum ersten Mal seine Begabung als Dichter. Viele Jahre später erzählte sein Freund Franz Knickenberg, einer der belesensten Menschen, wie der gesamte Freundeskreis damals plötzlich von dem Bewusstsein ergriffen wurde, dass hier kein Kaufmann, sondern ein Dichter war, dem die Sprache bis zum höchsten Einfühlungsvermögen zu Diensten war. (133)

Perhaps the most striking feature of Rheiner's lyric œuvre is his capacity to produce accomplished verse in the quite distinct styles of various better known contemporaries. In the context of mid to late-phase Expressionism, Rheiner's heavy use of poetic models is nothing exceptional, as the movement's fashionability led to the widespread appropriation of its most celebrated works as prototypes or templates by younger converts. As Pinthus notes in his 1959 preface to *Menschheitsdämmerung*,

58 This perhaps goes some way to explaining why in St. Saveur's introduction to 'Kokain', her dating of the birth of Expressionism to the years immediately *following* World War One has been neither corrected nor annotated (13).

Auch der Expressionismus um 1920 hatte viele Nachahmer erzeugt. Man spaßte damals: es wird viel gebechert, gewerfelt und gezecht; so könnte man heute sagen: es wird viel getraklt, gebennt und gegollt.[59] (15)

Rheiner's own hymn to Expressionism of 1919 thus stands as a very early example of Benn-imitation, with its chains of neologistic noun phrases, its chopped diction and its exhortation to destruction as the precondition for new, poetic creation:

Expressionismus

Zerhau das Wort, die Form, den Ton. Begriff!
Ob allen Trümmern wogend, Ätherschiff!

Stürz nieder in die Schlucht! Zerbrich den Bau.
Schlepp Brocken an, kristallisch und genau.

Zerspreng den Unsinn! Hau den Knoten durch!
Aus Fetzen bilde trunken Menschen-Burg!

Bedenke nicht das Was und nicht das Wie.
Der Kosmos weiß nicht seine Harmonie.

O Menschgewimmel, Fetzen Fleisch und Blut,
Schutt-Stadt und Pflanz-Gerüst und Lava-Glut!

O Tier-Maschine! Seele breiter Fluß!
Aus Blitzen alle Nahrung kommen muß.

Pan-Teufel-Gott und Dämon-Engel-Tod.
In tieferen Fernen rauschest du, Idiot!

Aus Erde, Wasser, Luft und Feuer spie
dich Menschen übermenschliche Symphonie.

Ja –: Flamme, Geist und Mord und ewiges Licht,
entsteht dein Bild, dein Lied, dein Bau, – Gedicht! (*M* 50–51)

---

59 Pinthus's neologistic past participles are formed from the surnames of Expressionist poets Johannes R. Becher, Franz Werfel, Paul Zech and Iwan Goll, as well as Trakl and Benn.

What seems to set Rheiner apart among the crowd of late-Expressionist imitators is both the fluency – apparent in 'Expressionismus' – and the stylistic range of his imitations. His poetic œuvre covers the gamut of Expressionism's lyric register from the messianic idealism of Werfel and Becher to the dark, eschatological visions characteristic of Trakl and Heym. As Pinthus's remarks suggest, the former mode was the more influential among contemporary readers, whereas the latter produced work that has proved more resonant with later generations (Trakl's influence on poets of the post-World War Two generation is nowhere more evident than in the little known but recently translated poetry of the young Thomas Bernhard, which dates to the very period in which Pinthus made this observation). The enduring critical favour for 'dark' Expressionism is one likely reason for both Huder's and Rietzschel's efforts to emphasise Rheiner's alignment with this mode over his no less sincere rearticulations of the 'light', humanistic variety associated with Werfel and Becher.[60] In any case, Rheiner's occasional adoption, against the prevailing trend, of a recognizably Traklesque style confirms that he was, not least, a sensitive and receptive *reader* of poetry. The poem 'Trauer' illustrates as well as any Rheiner's effort to assimilate Trakl's themes and methods:

Trauer

Die Straße seufzt. Schattende Winde hocken
Nieder auf Plätzen. Bronzene Plätze weinen
Über den Abend hin, der aus blauer Ferne gleitet.
Wolke schmilzt in der Frauen sterbenden Locken.
Leise wankt das verhangene Haus. Aus dem reinen
Äther sinkt ein zerfallender Mond herab. Und breiter
Dampft der Atem der Stadt. Es tropft
Nacht, ein fremdes Meer, das an die Fenster klopft.

60 It is difficult not to read Huder's assessment as a generous overstatement of Rheiner's achievement: 'Daneben gelangen Rheiner gelegentlich Verse und Prosatexte, die an Georg Trakls späte Produktion heranreichen' (82). Rietzschel is also generous, if less ambitious, in his attempt to position Rheiner closer to Trakl on a hypothetical Trakl-Becher axis: 'Rheiner steht dem Salzburger Melancholiker, der, keine 30 Jahre alt, an einer Kokainvergiftung starb, als jener das Gift gerade entdeckte, in der Tat besonders nahe, jedenfalls näher als etwa dem rebellischen, dem ungestüm auftrumpfenden Becher, in dessen Umkreis ihn noch Oskar Loerke wähnte' (297).

Wir sind begraben. Schwarz und mit Erde gefüllt
Starrt unser Mund. Das Haar, Traube
Bitteren Trankes voll, ist verwelkt und tot.
Schon nahet die letzte Stunde, die uns in Kälte hüllt.
Wir hören den Klang der Gestirne nicht mehr. Blinde wir, Taube.
Wir fühlen das Blut nicht mehr. Verblaßt ist sein Rot.
Niedergestürzt, zersprungene Säulen, über Trümmern liegen
Trümmer wir selbst im Feld. Doch über uns hin zahllose Schwärme schreiender
Vögel fliegen… (*M* 34)

In addition to more or less direct borrowings from particular poems (see especially 'De Profundis'; *SW* 2:111–123, and 'Untergang'; *SW* 3:361–370), several generic stylisitic qualities of 'Trauer' attest to Trakl's influence. The eschatological imagery, the animation and collapse of landscape features (especially celestial bodies), the perception of body parts in decay and in isolation from one another, the paradoxical collocation of adjectives and nouns, the piling-up of images whose relationship to one another is seldom made explicit syntactically, the prominence of colour, the progression from evening to night – these features of 'Trauer' are all characteristic of Trakl's poetry (as such we shall have occasion to comment on them further in part 3). Ultimately, however, 'Trauer', like Rheiner's other compositions in a recognizably Traklesque style, fails to recreate either the tautness or terseness of the mature verse of his role model. In 'Trauer', this failing is reflected in the unclear and inconsistent positioning of the lyric perspective within the apocalyptic space the poem evokes, whereas clarity and consistency in this regard have been identified as key, if less striking characteristics of Trakl's mature style (see Steinkamp, who attributes to Trakl 'Kohärenz durch eine homogene räumliche Perspektivierung'; 120–121). In this respect the lyric perspective in 'Trauer' might in fact be classified as a Heym-like element within what is otherwise a Trakl-like poem, in so far as in Heym's poetry, as James Rolleston remarks, 'the plural self [*wir*] speaks from a perspective both inside and outside the events,' thus generating 'a rigid duality of horror and detachment' (164). This point is worth underlining, as although previous commentators have not attached particular weight to this association (Rietzschel mentions Heym's name only in passing; 297), Heym's influence is probably the most pervasive of all when Rheiner's work is viewed in total, especially when the prose is considered as well, as in the discussion that follows (see 5.2 & 6.3).

At the other end of the Expressionist spectrum, Rheiner's chiming-in in the chorus of Werfel-inspired 'O Mensch!' poets (cf. Sharp *M* 148) can be illustrated by reference to 'Näher, mein Bruder, zu dir!' from the cycle *Das schmerzliche Meer* (1918):

Näher, mein Bruder, zu dir!
(1918)

I
In blauen Schlaf unendlich hingeglitten,
dehnt sich der Seele wunderbares Land.
Ein Stern und Engel, leuchtest du inmitten,
mein Mitmensch! ferne mir und unbekannt.

Ich kenn dich nicht. Und doch steht deine Schöne
in meiner Träume Gärten unerhört.
Aus Firmamenten klingst du Sphärentöne.
Dein Aug ist Flamme, die sich nie verzehrt.

Da unser Arm die Sonne aufwärts führte,
stand ich mit dir im Kreise voller Licht;
da unser Glaube Meer und Berge kürte,
waren wir Gott, an dem die Welt ausbricht!

Wir flogen Adler über unsre Wälder;
wir schwammen Fisch in der erlauchten See;
unschuldig Tier wir sprangen durch die Felder;
vom Himmel fielen wir, musikner Schnee.

– Nun bist du fort, und ich bin fort: ein anderer.
Ich geh durch Straßen in der Stadt Berlin.
New York grüßt dich vielleicht als seinen Wanderer.
… Am Himmel aber unsere Wolken ziehn!

Ich grüße dich, mein Mitmensch, in der Ferne.
Vertraue mir! Ich denke deiner gern!
Am Morgen grüßen hell mich deine Sterne,
an deinem Abend dich mein erster Stern!

II
Klingt nicht das Wort, als wir einander lebten,
das gute Wort, mein Bruder, ewig in den Sternen?

O lausch den guten Worten, die verschwebten!
O hör sie klingen in des Himmels Fernen!

Der Göttermund, der warme Menschenmund,
er sprach es aus, *und dein Herz war getroffen!*
Der Erde gold'ne Türen waren offen.
Die Lüfte schwangen, und der Tag war bunt.

Da schlug die dunkle Seele Augen auf.
Blut floß von Hand in Hand, leise Musik.
Aus toter Stadt, die uns umdräuend schwieg,
sprang unser Weh, ach! unser Glück herauf!

O lausch den Worten, die uns je erblühten!
O höre sie! Sie sind uns immer nah.
Und rufst du sie, so ist uns Meer und Süden
und Stern und Wald und Liebe ewig da! (*KLPB* 77–78)

The defining gesture of this poem, the melodramatic and idealistic invocation of a fraternity strong enough to overcome all barriers, whether physical, political, cultural or historical, is entirely typical of messianic Expressionism, which became the dominant strand within the movement towards the end of the First World War. Werfel's 'An den Leser,' which opens the final section of *Menschheitsdämmerung*, entitled 'Liebe den Menschen,' is one of the best known examples of this type. In it, the lyric subject claims solidarity with representatives of diverse social and ethnic groups ('ich habe alle Schicksale durchgemacht') before issuing an invitation to the reader to join the brotherhood of man, for which the poet serves as self-appointed spokesman and incarnation: 'O, könnte es einmal geschehen / Daß wir uns, Bruder, in die Arme fallen' (279). These lines that would not be out of place in 'Näher, mein Bruder, zu dir!'

Rheiner appears to have embraced the humanistic idealism of messianic Expressionism not only poetically, but also poetologically. His most elaborate reformulation of Werfel's *Mensch*-credo can be found in the draft of a letter to Heinar Schilling, fellow poet and publisher of the Dresden-based Expressionist journal *Menschen* (!), which Rheiner edited from January to March 1919 (*KLPB* 269). The draft in Rheiner's notebook, dated October 1919, begins with the following, distinctly condescending reflections on Schilling's own lyric production:

> Je mehr ich mich, anfangs in Stunden der Beschäftigungslosigkeit u. lange Weile [sic], später mit einer wirklichen interessierten geistigen Hingabe mit Ihren Versen beschäftigt habe, desto mehr habe ich erkannt, was Ihnen fehlt, um wahrhaft Dichter, das heißt nämlich: wahrhaft Mensch sein zu können. Der Dichter ist der Gestalter des Menschlichen (u. damit d. Geistlichen). Und die Voraussetzung zum Dichter ist der Mensch, dem nichts Menschliches fremd ist. Voraussetzung ist der Mensch, der den Sprung in das Chaos, den Sprung aus sich, aus seiner Haut hinaus, den Sprung aus der Welt wagt. Und das haben Sie, Schilling, bisher noch nie getan.[61] (*KLPB* 245)

The poetry that arose from such urges to 'give form to the human' has not aged well; as early as 1959 Walter Sokel remarked that messianic Expressionism had given birth to 'some of the worst rhetorical excesses of the movement' (*WiE* 163).[62] One of its most vocal proponents, on the other hand, was Pinthus, who in the same year, in the preface to the third edition of *Menschheitsdämmerung*, could still write: 'Die Humanitäts-Melodie kann als das messianische Hauptmotiv des Expressionismus bezeichnet werden' (14). These words reconfirm the predilection for the utopian yearnings of Werfel, Becher *et al.* that Pinthus had expressed in his original 1919 preface. In a passage that can be read almost as a gloss on 'Näher, mein Bruder, zu dir!', he had pinpointed the quality he considered the greatest virtue of Expressionist poetry:

> daß sie mit glühendem Finger, mit weckender Stimme immer wieder auf den Menschen selbst wies, daß sie die verlorengegangenene Bindung der Menschen untereinander, miteinander, das Verknüpftsein des einzelnen mit dem Unendlichen – zur Verwirklichung anfeuernd – in der Sphäre des Geistes wiederschuf. (29)

Pinthus goes on to identify the specific lexical consequences of the messianic agenda: 'Demgemäß ist es natürlich, daß dies die Worte sind, die sich am meisten in ihr finden: Mensch, Welt, Bruder, Gott' (ibid.). This observation provides a convenient quantitative measure for assessing Rheiner's adherence to the messianic code in 'Näher, mein Bruder, zu dir!': all four key words have occurred by the end of just the third quatrain, and

---

61 If it were not for the earnestness of his exposition, one might well suspect an element of self-parody, bordering on the grotesque, in Rheiner's *Mensch*-rhetoric. Consider that here the former editor of *Menschen* (Rheiner) is chastising the publisher of *Menschen* (Schilling), who in 1918 had published two cycles entitled *Du Bruder Mensch* and *Mensch, Mond, Sterne*, for not being *Mensch* enough!

62 More recent scholarship has underpinned Sokel's judgement. Cf. Vietta and Kemper (22), Korte (229), Paulsen (70), and Sharp (*M* 141).

eight occurrences can be counted in the poem as a whole. A comparison with 'Trauer', which scores zero on the same scale, underlines the thematic and stylistic distance between the poems.

Despite its sentimentality, high-flown rhetoric and overworked imagery, 'Näher, mein Bruder, zu dir!' is, to be fair, less marred by 'abstract verbiage, tastelessness, and grotesque hyperbole' (Sokel *WiE* 163) than many other works of messianic Expressionism. Rheiner's underlying lyricism is evident even here, and although it is hardly strong enough to redeem the poem, it does raise the question as to what the poet might have produced had he been less in thrall to prevailing Expressionist models. Even Rietzschel's collections provide no more than glimpses of an answer to this question; they make it clear, rather, that Rheiner's talent never matured into sustained literary accomplishment, at least in the genre in which he had made the greatest personal and professional investment: the lyric. The question of Rheiner's potential and accomplishment in various genres is dealt with directly in an exchange of letters between the poet and his wife of late 1920, signalling the beginning of a crisis in their marriage that would ultimately lead to their divorce of 1925.

> Rheiner: Ich bin stolz auf das Gedicht. Es macht mich glücklich und reich. Es zeigt mir nebenbei, daß ich die anderen alle doch schließlich in die Ecke hauen werde, – lyrisch… – aber dramatisch, – episch?? – Wir werden sehen. Ich traue mir viel zu und verlange viel von mir. In den nächsten Tagen beginnt entweder das Drama oder der Roman. O, ich freue mich auf die Arbeit! (Letter of 1.8.1920; *KLPB* 252)

> Fo: Sieh mal, Du schreibst, du habest während 6jährigen Bürodienstes Zeit gefunden 4 große und 'wichtige' (darüber ließe ich andere entscheiden) 'Werke' geschaffen. Ich wäre gleicher Meinung, wenn es sich dabei um ein philosophisches Werk oder einen Roman wie z.B. die Buddenbrooks von Mann handelte. Aber Gedichte, und wenn sie noch so groß wären, die geben nicht den Beweis für einen tüchtigen und soliden Arbeiter. […] Ich liebe Deine Gedichte wie Dich selbst, es ist mir aber rätselhaft, wie Du als Mann soviel Befriedigung dabei finden kannst, da, wo es sich um wirkliche, literarische Arbeit handelt, hast Du bisher nichts geleistet. (Letter of 4.10.1920; *KLPB* 253–254)

The poet's self-confidence soon slips into a cockiness that seems intended to convince himself as much as his wife. Her rebuttal is most forceful, her brutal frankness the product of repeated disappointments over the preceding years (her admonition that he has failed to produce a work at the level of Thomas Mann's *Buddenbrooks* suggests, however, that her own expectations may have been unreasonably high).

So why did Rheiner's lyric potential remain unfulfilled? It would appear to have been stifled by a combination of factors, including the First World War (during which he fought on the Eastern Front), drug addiction, extreme poverty, and social marginalization. Unlike Trakl, whose poetry became more profound the more his life deteriorated towards total derangement (see 7.1), evidently Rheiner did not benefit creatively from the bohemian lifestyle to which he was so fatally attracted, and in the last five years of his short life, reduced to increasingly desperate circumstances and increasingly isolated from his family, friends and society at large, he produced just a handful of poems. But perhaps the most influential factor in his creative decline was, ironically, the very exposure to and assimilation of Expressionist techniques and procedures described above in relation to 'Trauer' and 'Näher, mein Bruder, zu dir!' In the foreword to *Der bunte Tag*, the 1919 collection of early poems written between 1912 and 1914, Rheiner describes his own poetic development as leading 'vom naiven, unbeholfenen, naturalistisch-impressionistischen Gedicht zur bewußt sprachrevolutionären radikal expressionistischen Symphonie' (*KLPB* 8). The result was that in the latter years his own poetic voice – which was essentially delicate and personal as the early lyrics testify, and in many respects more reminiscent of Rilke than of Heym, Trakl, Werfel or any other Expressionists – only occasionally sounded through the rhetorical clamour of his 'Expressionist symphony.'[63] Rheiner's failure to fulfil his literary promise is

63 The Rilkean quality of the early poetry and its fading in the later work is noted also by Huder in his analysis of Rheiner's celestial imagery: 'Anfangs waren die Bilder der Gestirne noch stark von Rilkescher Manier bestimmt. Doch sehr bald durchpulste sie ein dynamischer und revolutionärer Elan, bis sie zuletzt wie Produkte einer monomanischen Wut, ja Verzweiflung ihres Autors sich auftürmten. [...] Damit hatte auch Rheiner die Hochform des expressionistischen Revolutions-Stils und dessen Thematik erreicht' (82). However, Rilkean overtones occasionally sound through the later poetry as well. The poem 'Die Anrufung des Engels' of 1918 (*KLPB* 79) reads, for example, like a hybrid of Rilke and – once again – Heym, especially 'Der Gott der Stadt,' a poem that reverberates repeatedly in Rheiner's œuvre. It begins with the appeal 'Höre mich!', a singular foreshadowing of the opening of the first of Rilke's *Duineser Elegien*, which although written in 1912, would not be published until 1923: 'Wer, wenn ich schriee, hörte mich denn aus der Engel / Ordnungnen?' (441; angels, it should be noted, also feature in Rilke's earlier cycles *Das Buch der Bilder* of 1902/06 and *Neue Gedichte* of 1907). Curiously, Resch argues that the angel in 'Die Anrufung

illustrative of a general observation on Expressionism made by Ladislao Mittner: 'Expressionism was in the first place a style of art and also a style of life, that is to say a technique and a programme, to which ultimately only minor poets adhered in full' (16).[64]

With hindsight it is apparent that Rheiner's adherence to Expressionism was too committed and self-effacing (paradoxically, considering that the principal tenet of Expressionism was the projection of subjective consciousness into the external world) not only for the good of his poetry, but also for his own well-being: his financial security, family life, and physical health. Within just a few years of his first contact with the Berlin Expressionists in 1914, Rheiner's attitudes and circumstances came to embody the Expressionist stereotype of the *poeta dolorosus*, a term Sokel borrows from Hanns Johst's 1917 play *Der Einsame: Ein Menschenuntergang* to characterise

> a type of writer, artist or intellectual who, in many variations, appears throughout Expressionist literature. Hermann Hesse in his semi-Expressionist novel has called his embodiment of this type *Steppenwolf*, the wolf of the steppes, an outcast from the sheltering warmth of society, roaming the barren wastes of his loneliness. Sensitive, gifted, creative, the Expressionist hero is superior to the self-satisfied majority. But his superiority is the bane of his life, the stigma which singles him out from among men; his superiority casts him into outer darkness. His nature is unique; his words find no echo. (*WiE* 55)

Had he been familiar with it, Sokel might well have cited Rheiner's 'Der Dichter in der Welt' (*M* 45, see 1.2) as an exemplary articulation of this view. Despite his middle-class background and the three years of commercial training and experience garnered pre-War with employers in his native Cologne, as well as in Liège, Paris and London, Rheiner, true to his poetic calling as he understood it, proved unwilling and eventually unable to function within mainstream society following his suspension from the army and return to Berlin in 1917: 'Mit der Übersiedlung in die Hauptstadt verfiel

---

des Engels' can be read as a straight metaphorical substitute for cocaine: 'Rheiner war sich der Schwierigkeit bewusst, die Gesamtheit der Drogenerfahrung verbal adäquat zu übermitteln. Im Gedicht "Anrufung des Engels," welches etwa zur gleichen Zeit wie die Novelle *Kokain* entstand, wird dies deutlich' (269; compare footnote 73).

64 'L'espressionismo fu in primo luogo uno stile d'arte e anche uno stile di vita, una tecnica cioè e un programma, cui in fondo soltanto poeti minori aderirono pienamente.'

Rheiner endgültig dem Lebensstil der Boheme' (Rietzschel 293). To begin with, this rejection of middle-class respectability in favour of late-night *Kaffeehauskultur* appeared, in literary terms, to bear fruit, with a raft of publications in 1918–19 and seemingly good prospects for establishing himself as an important figure in the cultural scene of post-War Germany. St. Saveur recalls: 'Mit einem Schlag waren sie [Rheiner and Fo] – oder so schien es ihnen – in den Mittelpunkt alles geistigen Geschehens geraten. Es war eine glückliche Zeit' (135). From late 1919 onwards, however, as Rheiner's personal situation began to deteriorate quickly, his creative energy dried up. One of Fo's letters written during the incipient crisis in their marriage of October 1920 contains this remonstrance:

> Aber gewiß hast Du Deine Pflichten vernachlässigt, hast statt zu arbeiten od. Stellung zu suchen, bis 11 Uhr im Bett gelegen mit der Entschuldigung, Deine entweder nährende oder schwangere Frau (mit Unterernährung) 'täte das auch.' Von Mf. [Morphium] ganz zu schweigen. (*KLPB* 262)

In her testimony in the divorce proceedings of 1925, Rheiner's mother-in-law Karoline Olle confirmed her daughter's view while explaining the need for the financial support she had offered the young couple following their marriage in February 1918:

> Zuerst hatte der Beklagte in Berlin eine sehr gute Stellung von Juli – November 1918 als Korrespondent bei einer großen Firma. Nachdem das erste Kind geboren war, hat er diese Stellung ohne jeden Grund dran aufgegeben. Er hatte seine Stellung so nachlässig ausgefüllt, dass seine Firma die erste Gelegenheit benutzte, um ihn abzubauen. Schuld ist meines Erachtens die Arbeitsscheu des Beklagten, der seine ganze Zeit im Kaffeehaus zubrachte. Ferner ist der Beklagte Morphinist, was ihn auch zu einer ernsten Arbeit untauglich macht. (*K* 112)

It is telling in this connection that in the continuation of the 1919 letter he drafted to Schilling, Rheiner had installed the bourgeois citizen as the diametric opposite of the true *Mensch*, and diagnosed Schilling's own bourgeois condition as the major obstacle to poetic 'greatness', as well as to friendship with Rheiner himself:

> Der Bourgeois, jenes hassenswerteste aller Wesen auf Erden, ist so stark in Ihnen, daß Ihr besseres, Ihr höheres, Ihr intelligentes Ich ihn bejaht, daß er Ihre Wesenheit unterjocht; und hier liegt das namenlos Traurige, welches mir immer wieder verwehrt, Ihr Freund zu sein, und welches Ihnen den Weg zur Größe, das heißt eben zur

> Unbedingtheit, versperrt. Warum halten Sie nicht einmal in einem einzigen entschiedenen Augenblick aus und erschlagen endgültig den Bourgeois in Ihnen. Wenn irgend etwas, so ist er es, der verdient, daß er zugrunde geht! (*KLPB* 245)

Rheiner's failure to break out of his downward spiral through several – perhaps belated – attempts to find gainful employment, attested to by three application letters from 1920–22 reproduced in *KLPB* (265–274), appears to have heightened his contempt for the middle-class and paved the way towards his martyrdom for the Expressionist rebellion (Sokel describes the 'martyr complex' as 'vital to an understanding [...] of Expressionism as a whole'; *WiE* 60). In a letter to his mother of 3 June 1925, written just 9 days before a fatal morphine overdose, Rheiner wrote, 'Aber ich weiß, daß in erster Linie die heutige menschliche Gesellschaft, in ihrer europäisch-bürgerlichen Form, das wirklich Minderwertige ist' (*KLPB* 282).

The fact that Rheiner's mother is the addressee of this remark is worthy of note, for the poet's difficult relationship with his family, especially his overbearing and reportedly penny-pinching mother (St. Saveur 129), who had been widowed in 1911, is a further feature that he shares with the Expressionist archetype. Sokel sees a close connection between the poet's dysfunctional family relations and his refusal to play by the rules of bourgeois-capitalist society: 'It is in his family that the poet meets for the first time and most starkly those forces of bourgeois society which will hound him all his life and finally crucify him' (*WiE* 56). Parental disdain for the poet's choice of occupation is typical. St. Saveur reports that neither Rheiner's mother nor sister showed much sympathy for his literary aspirations: 'Die Mutter im Besonderen hatte gehofft, dass er seine Intelligenz mehr lukrativen Bestrebungen widmen [...] würde' (*K* 137). Nonetheless, in Rheiner's case the familial attachment evidently ran deep, as suggested by his final letter to his mother, in which he addresses her repeatedly as 'meine liebe gute Mutter' (*KLPB* 278–282). Indeed, without the refuge and care provided by his mother and to a lesser extent also his sister, at considerable personal cost, during the most difficult years of his addiction in the early 1920s, his end would almost certainly have come much sooner. In a letter to the estranged Fo of September 1924, his mother wrote, 'Was ich mit ihm [...] durchgelitten habe – dies zu beschreiben geht auf keine Kuhhaut' (*K* 108). It is hardly surprising, therefore, that feelings of guilt and shame should have deeply coloured Rheiner's attitude to his mother and sister. Significantly, the most explicitly autobiographical features of the prose works 'Die Erniedrigung' and *Kokain* (both 1918) involve expressions of precisely such emotions towards mother and sister figures on the part of the stories' drug addict-protagonists (see 5.2 & 6.3).

Considered alongside his violent rejection of middle-class values, his difficult familial relations and his faith in his own poetic vocation, Rheiner's drug use can be seen as a further prop reinforcing his role as poet-outcast in rebellion against the bourgeois establishment. A parallel can be drawn with the main character in Johst's *Der Einsame*, the nineteenth-century poet and prototypical *poeta dolorosus* Christian Dietrich Grabbe, who relies on intoxicants to transcend the baseness and philistinism of his environment: 'An die Arbeit!!! Daß ich die Wirklichkeit vergesse und meiner Wahrheit wieder teilhaftig bin – und lebe! Schnaps! Schnaps! Schnaps! Oh, dreimal-heiliges Dämonium!' (55, cf. Sokel *WiE* 57).[65] Like Johst's Grabbe, Rheiner did not baulk at stealing from his own family members in order to finance his habit; St. Saveur describes a 'particularly sad incident' in which he even inveigled the Berlin children's home where his second child Johannes was being cared for into giving him the money she had sent from Cologne to cover his son's expenses for three months, at which point she was sent a second bill for the same amount (*K* 129–130). However, the meagre resources of his already impoverished family were obviously insufficient for Rheiner's purposes. St. Saveur records that at the time of his committal for detoxification in September 1924, Rheiner had more than 50 theft and fraud charges pending, and he was saved from prosecution only by legal incapacitation (*K* 142–143). In what could be read as a perverse homage to the leading dramatist of Expressionism, Georg Kaiser, whose trial for the theft of his landlord's rugs had generated headlines in Germany in February 1921 (Sokel *WiE* 65–66), the items Rheiner had stolen and subsequently pawned included his landlady's silver (*K* 142).

In these important and ultimately decisive respects, then, the two sides of Rheiner's life and work as *poeta dolorosus* became, to all appearances, entwined and mutually perpetuating. In his final years he essentially lived out the role he had written for himself as 'Der düstere Dichter' (albeit without writing much poetry), a title given to a pair of poems in his final

65 In *Kokain*, written a year after Johst's *Der Einsame*, Rheiner uses the same holy-demonic oxymoron to describe a different intoxicant: 'Heiliges Gift! Heiliges Gift! – Das fühlte Tobias und sah den Dämon, der ihm ebenso vertraut wie schrecklich war, weit über dem nächtigen Himmel stehen' (*KLPB* 205).

published cycle *Des Herzens Sturz und Erhebung* (1920). The second features lines that prefigure his own demise and lay the blame for it, before the fact, at the feet of the bourgeois society addressed here as 'ihr':

> Ich bin der Fremdling, den ihr alle hasset;
> – o fremd euch allen, die mich bös umdräuen.
> Ich bin der lange Mord, den ihr geschehen lasset;
> den eure frechen Fratzen niemals scheuen. (*KLPB* 164)

In this way Rheiner's case illustrates perfectly the difficulty identified by Tomashevsky of determining, in the Romantic and post-Romantic eras, 'whether literature recreates phenomena from life or whether [...] the phenomena of life are the result of the penetration of literary clichés into reality' (51; see 1.4). Considering that the clichés in question are those of literary Expressionism, it is sadly fitting that Rheiner's personal and literary decline largely mirrored that of the movement to which he had dedicated himself. 1925 is generally recognized as the year in which Expressionism, its original vitality long since extinguished, gave way to *Die neue Sachlichkeit* as the dominant literary and artistic movement in the Weimar Republic. In April of the same year Rheiner was released from the Bonn *Heil- und Pflege-anstalt* after seven months' detoxification treatment (Rietzschel 302). Shortly afterwards he returned to Berlin, the city whose vibrancy and flair had originally inspired his enthusiasm for Expressionism and its bohemian trappings during his first visit in 1914, and where he had experienced the most prolific period of his literary career in the eighteen months before his move to Dresden in December 1918 (ibid. 299). In the spring of 1925, however, he found the German capital 'erbarmungslos und erbärmlich' (*KLPB* 280), and his circumstances soon became more desperate than ever. Penniless and unable to find work or even regular accommodation, he died on 12 June of a morphine overdose at the age of just 30. 'Die Welt,' as Rietzschel notes, 'nahm kaum Notiz' (285).

Although by the time of his death Rheiner and his works had already faded into one of the more obscure corners of literary history, a list of his friends, associates and admirers from his most productive years includes several of the most prominent names in German cultural life of the early 20th century. St. Saveur writes, for instance, of the hospitality frequently extended to Rheiner by the painter Ludwig Meidner (135–136), whose 'Apokalyptische Landschaften' represent a likely source for the ruined cityscape in the final chapter of 'Die Erniedrigung' (see 6.3). A cameo mention of the 'Maler Ludwig M.' in *Kokain* (*KLPB* 215) can perhaps be read as an expression of the poet's gratitude. On the literary front, one result of Rheiner's first encounter with the Berlin Expressionists in 1914 was a close acquaintance with. Becher (*KLPB* 289), who continued to admire Rheiner's poetry as late as 1920 despite a rupture between the two caused by the publication in 1918 of an uncomplimentary article by Rheiner about the future (1954–58) East German Minister of Culture. In a letter to Rheiner of May 1920, Becher wrote:

> Trotz der ehrlichen Wut, die einmal wegen Ihres unehrlichen Angriffes gegen mich, ich gegen Sie hatte, hat es mich in den letzten Zeiten oft empört, daß man Sie von Verlagen aus zurückwies, die darnach den gemeinsten Schund reproduzierten. (Becher 219)

Rietzschel identifies several other notable contemporaries who recognized Rheiner's talent, including Theodor Däubler (Rietzschel 285), Oskar Loerke (ibid. 295–296) and Iwan Goll (ibid. 287). The last of these, who in a 1918 letter to Rheiner praised 'die warme Quelle Ihrer besternten Sprache' (ibid. 287), became the godfather to Rheiner's second child, born in 1920. Loerke, in a review of the collection *Das tönende Herz* (1918) in *Die neue Rundschau*, perceptively identified both Rheiner's underlying lyricism and its stylistic (Expressionist) distortion in all too many poems. While acknowledging the presence of 'wohlgebildete Gedichte,' in which Rheiner expresses himself 'ohne die kunstfertige Zauberei allein mit seinem tönenden Herzen,' Loerke notes that 'ein oft sehr zartes, dennoch seiner selbst gewisses Gefühl weiß bei Rheiner keinen anderen Weg in die Welt, als sich an nervös wilden, umherschießenden und -tastenden Assoziationen hinaustragen zu lassen' (cited in ibid. 295–296).

Creatively, Rheiner's most important relationship was his collaboration with the painter and illustrator Conrad Felixmüller, founder of the 1919 Dresden Secession. It was on Felixmüller's invitation that Rheiner participated in the first meeting of the *Expressionistische Arbeitsgemeinschaft Dresden* in October 1917, one consequence of which was the foundation just two months later of the *Dresdner Verlag von 1917* under Schilling's directorship (ibid. 295). In the years that followed, the *Dresdner Verlag* would publish several collections of Rheiner's poetry and prose, as well *Kokain* and the lyric scene *Der inbrünstige Musikant* in separate editions (the latter originally published in Kiel by *Die schöne Rarität* in 1918, then again by the *Dresdner Verlag* a year later). When Rheiner moved to Dresden with his family in December 1918, it was the same publisher that offered him the editorship of *Menschen* (ibid. 300). Felixmüller's illustrations for *Kokain* and *Der inbrünstige Musikant*, reproduced in full in *KLPB*, amount to a little-known *tour de force* of late-Expressionist book-art, and one of the chief merits of Rietzschel's edition is precisely that it preserves the dynamic juxtaposition of Rheiner's text and Felixmüller's images.[66] Furthermore, Felixmüller certainly 'took notice' of Rheiner's death (cf. *KLPB* 285), which he commemorated with the portrait 'Der Tod des Dichters Walter Rheiner,' also reproduced in *KLPB* (2). In this painting Rheiner is depicted suspended in mid-air, floating out of an upper-storey window of a high-rise building against a backdrop of the bright yet eerie lights of night-time Berlin – a scene with possible allusions to both the Icarus episode in *Kokain* and the defenestration scene in 'Die Erniedrigung' (see 6.1 & 6.3). With one hand he is grasping at the net curtain above the window; with the other he is holding a hypodermic needle, symbol of the central role that drug abuse had played in both the life and death of the young poet. Through its stylization and sanitization of Rheiner's wretchedness, the portrait effectively consecrates the martyrdom of the *poeta dolorosus.*

As Rietzschel reports and St. Saveur confirms, the origins of Rheiner's drug addiction can be traced to his initial meeting with Becher in summer 1914 (Rietzschel 289, St. Saveur 133). Becher was one of a small group of pacifist artists who, against the current of popular sentiment, were firmly opposed to the 'great patriotic adventure' of the First World War even before it began (Haase 33). One of the strategies this group employed for avoiding conscription was to simulate infirmity through drug addiction. But the distinction between simulated and true addiction proved difficult to maintain, and as a consequence of this scheme several members of the group, including both Becher and Rheiner, developed very real addictions that led to very real infirmities. Of the two, Becher certainly came off less badly. Although he was forced on several occasions to undergo harrowing detoxification treatment, an experience he described in the poem 'Geheimrat B…' as a 'Kampf mit den grauseren Gespenstern-Schemen. / Tier-

66 All seven of Felixmüller's illustrations for *Kokain* are reproduced in *KNP*, but they are interspersed among the four stories included in that collection, while *K* includes just two of the seven.

Stimmen. Phantastischen Gesichten' (167), he eventually emerged from the episode with renewed physical vigour and reinforced conviction on questions of politics and social justice. Moreover, 'thanks' largely to his infirmity, he did in fact manage to avoid any sort of active involvement in the war. Rheiner, by contrast, was called up and sent to the Russian front in December 1914, where he found himself fighting '*Gen Brüder (Feinde nicht!)* die Gifte werfen' ('Der Morgen,' *KLPB* 84).

The cycle *Zwischen den Schlachten* documents the horror and trauma of Rheiner's experience on the front, his poeticization of this experience again being strongly suggestive of Heym's influence in both formal and thematic respects. 'Toten-Messe' is representative:

Nun liegen ihre Leiber halb verscharrt,
geborsten und verwittert tief im Sand.
Verworren züngelt Haar, hoch wächst die Hand,
greift in die Nacht, die auf den Zinnen harrt.

Verkohlte Städte schwelen lang vorbei,
und Brücken flattern schief und ausgezackt.
Die Sonne stürzt, schäumender Katarakt,
auf morsche Schädel, Augen fahl wie Blei.

Durch ihre Zähne pfeift ein süßer Wind,
der warm und rosig ist von frischem Blut.
(– In Abendröten weiden Lämmer gut. –)
Schon quellen sie verwesend aufwärts lind,

durchdringen, Freunde, sich mit ihrem Duft,
umarmen sich in lächelnder Spirale.
Die kühlen Sterne sind mit einem Male
ganz nah und kreisen singend durch die Luft.

Im Rauch verbrannter Zimmer nisten sie sich ein.
Sie fahren aufgelöst durch Ozeane.
Erkennen unten Schiffe, zitternd klein:
sie, des Planeten großgewölbte Fahne. (*KLPB* 86)

Here, the graphic depiction of decaying bodies that band together to form a community of the dead in a zombie-like afterlife, conveyed in elevated diction and with strict rhythmic regularity, are reminiscent of Heym's poems 'Die Heimat der Toten' and 'Die Morgue,' both included in *Mensch-*

heitsdämmerung (Pinthus 92–93, 97–99). In this and other poems of *Zwischen den Schlachten* Rheiner effectively takes up occupancy in what Rolleston describes as Heym's 'vast linguistic space for the dead, at once exalted and decomposing, biblical and clinical' (166). The second half of the poem offers a fresh response to the question Heym's corpses had posed in 'Die Morgue': 'In welche Dämmerung geht unser Flug?' (99). In the final stanza Rheiner deviates from his model, grafting an optimistic turn on to Heym's unmitigated horror. Whereas the dead in 'Toten-Messe' remain, in rarefied form ('aufgelöst'), in transcendent elevation, and become invested with symbolic significance for mankind as a whole ('des Planeten großgewölbte Fahne'), the flight of the dead in 'Die Morgue' is emptied of any redemptive function and ends with an anticlimactic 'return to the gutter' confirming the biological and social abjection of death:

> Im fernen Plan verlorner Himmelslande,
> Im Meere weit, wo fern die Woge flog,
> Wir flogen stolz in Abendrotes Brande
> Mit Segeln groß, die Sturm und Wetter bog.
>
> Was fanden wir im Glanz der Himmelsenden?
> Ein leeres Nichts. Nun schlappt uns das Gebein,
> Wie einen Pfennig in den leeren Händen
> Ein Bettler klappern läßt am Straßenrain. (ibid.)

Rheiner's exposure to the trauma of active military service was interrupted in 1916 for a period of detoxification treatment in Cologne, at the end of which he was sent – 'cured' – straight back to the front (Rietzschel 290). Then at the beginning of 1917 he was suddenly arrested and charged with 'dereliction of duty via self-inflicted incapacity for service.' His arrest had been occasioned, it seems, by the discovery of his name on the customer list of a Berlin drug dealer (ibid; see also St. Saveur 133–134). After a short spell in a military prison he was released and suspended from active service in early 1917. St. Saveur writes that he received a further call-up towards the end of the war, but he was declared unfit for service by a medical officer who, after perusing Rheiner's poetry, pronounced the judgement 'vollkommen irre' (138). Rheiner had survived the front, but the drug habit that he had cultivated in a failed attempt to avoid being sent there would overshadow the rest of his short life.

Whereas Trakl's appetite – or constitutional need – for transcendence through intoxication was such that he would try almost any drug available, and indeed went out of his way to gain access to a large number of different ones (see 7.1), Rheiner's addiction was 'limited' to two substances: cocaine and morphine. Indications of periodic alcohol abuse can also be identified, but nowhere is this given particular weight.[67] Accounts conflict regarding the history of his use of cocaine and morphine. Rietzschel documents that Rheiner's cocaine dependence began in 1914, and that he became addicted to morphine five years later (1–2). This chronology appears to be borne out, with the significant insertion of an extended period of abstinence between 1916 and 1919, in a statement to the Cologne court filed by Fo's lawyer W. Weinand in the divorce proceedings. This is dated 6 February 1925:

> Der Beklagte war bis zum Jahre 1916 Kokainist und ist 1916 vollständig geheilt entlassen worden. Die diesbezüglichen Akten liegen in der Krankenanstalt Lindenburg in Köln und können vom Gericht zugezogen werden, was hierdurch beantragt wird.
> Dass der Beklagte Kokainist gewesen war, hat sowohl der Beklagte als auch seine Mutter der Klägerin mitgeteilt. Vor 1919 ist der Beklagte jedoch niemals Morphinist gewesen. Dieses Laster hat er erst Mitte 1919 ausgeübt und gibt er selbst in seinem Schriftsatze vom 12. Januar 1925 zu, dass er seit mehreren Jahren Morphinist sei. Die Parteien haben im Jahre 1918 geheiratet, zur damaligen Zeit war der Beklagte, der wie schon ausgeführt ist, nur dem Kokainismus gefrönt hatte, schon seit 1916 vollkommen geheilt.
> Im Herbst 1919, nachdem die Parteien etwa 1½ Jahr lang verheiratet waren und er sich in der ersten Zeit gut geführt hatte, begann er Morphium zu spritzen und hat seit dieser Zeit nicht nur nicht für seine Frau und das Kind gesorgt, sondern auch eine ganze Reihe von betrügerischen Handlungen begangen, um Geld in die Finger zu bekommen, um so zu Morphium zu gelangen. (*K* 115)

---

67 Fo's divorce lawyer records, 'während seiner Morphiumentziehungen gab er [Rheiner] sich dauernd der sinnlosesten Trunkenheit hin und schlug in diesem Zustande auch die Klägerin häufig' (*K* 116). Despite this allegation of physical violence associated with Rheiner's alcohol abuse, the lawyer attributes only minor importance to this vice, which is especially striking by contrast with the detailed history of his cocaine and morphine use given in the same document. A further allusion to alcohol abuse can be found in Rheiner's final letter to his mother of 3 June 1925, in which he writes, 'ich bin gottseidank *nicht* rückfällig, weder in den alten Giften, noch etwa in Alkohol' (*KLPB* 281).

Naturally Fo's vested interest in demonstrating that Rheiner was 'clean' at the time of their marriage needs to be borne in mind here (had she knowingly married a junkie, she could have been held at least partially responsible for the failure of the marriage).[68] Notably, Weinand's case history was written explicitly in response to a contradictory version in Rheiner's own submission of 22 January 1925: 'Der Beklagte gibt an, [...] er sei bereits im Jahre 1916 Morphinist und Kokainist gewesen sei [sic]. Diese Tatsache habe sowohl er als auch seine Mutter seiner Ehefrau, der Klägerin mitgeteilt' (ibid.). It goes without saying that Rheiner himself, especially by 1925, was a highly unreliable witness. Yet further evidence can also be cited in support of his claim for earlier morphine use, and ironically enough, much of it is provided by his chief opponents in the debate: his estranged wife and mother-in-law. The latter's own testimony includes the statement, 'Ferner ist der Beklagte Morphinist [...]. Er muss dies schon als Junggeselle gewesen sein' (*K* 112–113), while in her 'Biographie', St. Saveur repeatedly refers to Rheiner's pre-1919 use of this drug:

> Rheiner kam ins Garnisonsgefängnis in Küstrin. Er erwartete das Schlimmste. Seine Mutter kam aus Köln, bewaffnet mit einem Attest von ihrem Hausarzt, der bestätigte, dass Rheiner schon lange an einem Leiden erkrankt war, welches dauernd *Morphium* zur Linderung seiner Schmerzen bedurfte. (134)

> Nach seinen Briefen zu urteilen, konnte ein moderner Mensch nur in Berlin seine Entwicklung fördern. Außerdem machte sich auch Rheiners Mutter, die wohl durch seine *Morphium*-Periode viel erlitten hatte, unangenehm bemerkbar. Auch um ihr zu entfliehen, ging er nach Berlin. (135)

> Da war der Musiker W.R. Heymann, [...] oder der vom Gift ausgemergelte Maler Höxter, und der andere Maler Ludwig Meidner, der den armen und vom *Morphium* verstörten und pfenniglosen Rheiner oft hatte in seinem Atelier schlafen lassen. (135–136) [NB: italics added in all three excerpts.]

To be sure, these references of both Olle and St. Saveur to *Morphium*, where for the sake of their own arguments they can only mean *Kokain*, may well

68 Although it contains certain elements that appear to contradict Weinand's version of events, St. Saveur's 'Biographie' underlines this point. Here, a paragraph describing Rheiner's near-miraculous 'cure' is immediately followed by an account of his first meeting with his future wife: 'Zu dieser Zeit lernte er im Hause seines Freundes, dem [sic] Musiker Jupp Hess, seine spätere Frau kennen, die am Kölner Musik-Konservatorium Gesang studierte' (134).

be simply the result of imprecision in expression and inadequate proofreading. In St. Saveur's biography, such a reading is more or less confirmed by her description of Rheiner's 1919 relapse: her statement 'diesmal war es Morphium' (140) only makes sense if it was a different drug on the previous occasion. Even so, a singular piece of circumstantial evidence strengthens the lingering doubt about the dating of Rheiner's morphine use. Not only St. Saveur but also Rietzschel, whose expression and proofreading are impeccable, specifically describe the Berlin dealer – identified by St. Saveur as Marga Gräber – on whose customer list Rheiner's name had been found in 1917, as a *morphine* dealer (St. Saveur 133, Rietzschel 290).

Thus, the possibility that at certain times Rheiner used cocaine and morphine concurrently following the relatively common pattern of stimulant–depressant alternation cannot be discounted. It should also be remembered that all the sources in Rheiner's case are concerned solely with documenting periods of abuse and addiction; no consideration is given to possible instances of limited recreational or experimental use such as that practised in the same years by Benn.[69] Although such questions must therefore remain open, one significant 'archipelago of certainty' (Morin) that emerges from this discussion is that Rheiner's most prolific literary activity coincided with the years immediately preceding, during and – if we accept Weinand's claim of a 'cure' in 1916 – following his cocaine addiction, whereas from 1920 onwards his output dried up almost entirely.[70] It would be misguided to infer a direct causal relationship between these circumstances. The literary inactivity of Rheiner's final years can only be explained by reference to a combination of factors, not least to the poet's increasingly dire financial and personal circumstances, and his apparent substitution of morphine for cocaine can hardly figure as especially prominent among them. Nonetheless, in line with Boon's characterization of cocaine (along with the other stimulants: caffeine and the amphetamines) as

69 For hints at possible cocaine use pre-dating 1914, see 'Der Tod des Schwärmers Gautier Fémin' (see 6.2). As far as morphine is concerned, Weinand qualifies Rheiner's claim that he had become addicted to this drug following 'experiments' with it by distinguishing between 'scientific' experiments and those undertaken in the pursuit of pleasurable effects. There was never anything scientific, he claims disdainfully, about Rheiner's so-called 'experiments' (*K* 114).

70 Although Rheiner's first publications came in 1915, one year after he became addicted to cocaine, the 1919 volume *Der bunte Tag* collects poems and short prose pieces from the period 1912–14, testifying to his creative output from these early years.

a 'technology of increased productivity' (171), it is conceivable that Rheiner's cocaine use contributed in some way to the creative energy of his most productive years, and that the historical correspondence between them is more than mere coincidence. Here, too, however, other factors were clearly no less important, and as with Benn (see 2.2), ultimately the link remains speculative. What is more apparent and propitious for this investigation is Rheiner's interest in 'writing on cocaine' in the other sense, that is, writing *about* it, rather than writing *under the influence of* it, and in this respect there is no question that this drug has unparalleled importance for his œuvre. However, to illuminate this aspect we must turn from his poetry to his works in a genre with which he identified less closely and in which, by his own account, he felt less secure of his own ability: narrative prose.

5.2 Literary Affinities and the Autobiographical Thread

At the beginning of the previous section, the question arose as to whether the privileging of Rheiner's prose, especially *Kokain*, over his poetry in editions published in recent decades can be seen as a reflection of the relative merits of his work in the respective genres, or whether other, external factors, notably the sensation-value of the drug theme, may have influenced this development. The subsequent discussion, by considering only the poetry in detail, has answered the question only partially. From this it has emerged that notwithstanding the lyricism of various lines and stanzas, and several poems that certainly deserve to be better known, whether because of their artistry or their value as documents of the Expressionist aesthetic ('Der Dichter in der Welt' and 'Expressionismus' being two obvious examples of the latter; see 1.2 & 5.1 respectively), ultimately we must extend Loerke's assessment of *Das tönende Herz* to Rheiner's poetry in general: it is stylistically inconsistent, overly derivative – on balance, *epigonenhaft* would not appear too harsh an epithet – and too often marred by the kind of rhetoric and high pathos that Sokel describes as recurrent shortcomings of 'naïve Expressionism' (*WiE* 18–19). How does the considerably smaller body of his prose works fare by comparison?[71]

One feature these have in common with the poetry is their thematic and stylistic similarity to the work of better known contemporaries. Several passages in *Kokain*, for example, echo Benn's *Rönne* stories, none more strongly than the series of southern associations the protagonist evokes while shooting up in a toilet cubicle of a Berlin railway station:

> Oben donnerte der Zug in die Halle (... sicherlich, dachte Tobias, Expreß zur Riviera, weiß schon: blaue Gestade, taubenumflattert, Pinien- und Orangenhain und der selige Berg: Santa Margherita...) und er nahm zwei neue Injektionen vor, in beide Oberschenkel je eine.
> Das erleichterte einen Augenblick: ... Riviera, dachte Tobias, Riviera, Santa Margherita... (*KLPB* 202)

Huder also notes parallels to Franz Kafka (83). The analogy he establishes between K. from Kafka's *Der Proceß* (written 1914–15, not published until 1925) and the title figure from Rheiner's 'Der Tod des Schwärmers Gautier Fémin' (written 1915, published 1918), however, is overstated. Huder's characterization of Fémin as 'wie K. von anonymen Gestalten gejagt, stets auf der Flucht und im technischen Gitter der Stadt vereinsamt' (83), sits uneasily with the text itself, in which he is described, at the height of his happiness, as 'grenzenlos ausgegossen in Nichtstun, Liebe, Spaziergänge, Musik, Cafés und Mond-Nächte' (*KLPB* 191), before descending rapidly into sullen resignation and apathy. Even more decisively for the overall effect of the story, the source of Fémin's troubles, unlike those of K., is spelled out without any ambiguity by the narrator (see 6.2), so that Fémin's predicament has none of the essential mystery of K.'s. Nonetheless, the broader parallel Huder draws attention to between Rheiner and Kafka has some pertinence. The fear of parental disapproval, such a central theme in the best known of Kafka's stories, 'Das Urteil' (1913) and 'Die Verwandlung' (1915), is also a key element in both *Kokain* and 'Die Erniedrigung' (see 6.3). A related but more specific parallel between this last story and the first chapter of *Der Proceß* is the motif of spying neighbours looking in through windows from across the street or courtyard, which in both texts

71 Considering Rietzschel's two volumes together, the number of pages occupied by the prose works (68, including Felixmüller's seven full-page illustrations of *Kokain*) is less than one third of that dedicated to the poetry (225).

appears symbolic of the protagonist's fear of disapproval by society at large (the same fear is also evident, although manifested differently, in *Kokain*). Whereas in *Der Proceß* the reader is left to infer that this motif reflects a tendency towards persecution mania on the part of the protagonist, in 'Die Erniedrigung' the same tendency is fully realised and gives rise to a startling hallucination:

> Er kam wieder dem Fenster nahe. Drunten staute sich die Menge, blickte aufmerksam herauf und befragte sich gegenseitig, murmelnd. Aber auch auf den Dächern der gegenüberliegenden Häuser, in allen Fenstern, auf allen Balkonen wimmelte es von Leuten, Männern und Frauen, zum Teil mit Fernrohren und Operngläsern, alle aber einzig seinethalben aufgestellt und ihm zuschauend. (*M* 105–106)

Although these similarities with Kafka's work are certainly striking, Rheiner's closest affinity as a prose writer, more clearly even than as a poet, is again with Georg Heym. The fact that this link has gone unremarked in previous scholarship is perhaps confirmation that Heym's prose works are not as well known as they should be, as his biographer Patrick Bridgwater has underlined (*PEB* 250). For present purposes, the most important reverberations with Heym's work – both his prose and his poetry – occur in 'Die Erniedrigung' and *Kokain*, and these will be accorded due consideration in the following chapter. To lay the groundwork for that analysis, some useful preliminary considerations can be made in relation to another of Rheiner's prose works, the early sketch 'Feuersbrunst' (*M* 91–94), the subject matter of which – the destruction of a house by fire – mirrors the final scene in one of Heym's most highly regarded stories, 'Der Dieb.' The question of Heym's possible influence on Rheiner, which appears undeniable in the later works (as in 'Toten-Messe'; see 5.1), becomes problematic in a comparative reading of these two texts. 'Der Dieb' was first published posthumously in a collection of Heym's stories of the same title in 1913, 'Feuersbrunst' not until six years later in *Der bunte Tag*, but the composition of both stories in fact dates to 1911 (making Rheiner just 16 or 17 upon composition of 'Feuersbrunst'), which would appear to exclude Heym's text as a possible source for Rheiner's. In this light, the Heym-like qualities of 'Feuersbrunst' are all the more remarkable, for the similarity in subject matter is merely the most obvious element they have in common. An assessment of the possible explanations for these parallels shall follow a more detailed comparison of the two texts.

'Feuersbrunst' is the account of an arsonist's attack on a 'large yellow villa' (*M* 91) surrounded by parkland on the outskirts of an unspecified town. It begins with the unnamed arsonist standing outside the villa's iron fence after he has left the building, continues with his satisfied recollection of the 'work' he has just completed in the house, leading into a metaphorically loaded description of the ecstasy that the growing flames had engendered in him ('Dann gingen hundert Sonnen auf und blendeten'; *M* 94), and ends by returning to the external perspective from which it had started for a more detached if no less stylized portrayal of the villa's final destruction: 'Das ganze Haus bäumte sich mit verzerrtem Antlitz und entsetzlicher Regsamkeit. Dann schlug es hintüber wie ein heimlich Erschlagener' (ibid.). The final scene of 'Der Dieb,' on the other hand, is set in a small house above Florence (2:91) rented by the unnamed thief of the *Mona Lisa* – the *Dieb* of the title, whose preparations for and execution of the theft of the famous painting occupy almost 20 of the story's 25 pages. Having just defaced the portrait in a frenzy of rage, gouging out the eyes and mouth with a kitchen knife in a mad attempt to free himself from the tyranny of its subject's smile, the thief collapses in exhaustion and despair (2:95). However, the torch with which he had initially singed the Mona Lisa's mouth (2:93) and then discarded starts a fire that eventually engulfs the whole house, along with the painting, the thief and several firemen who had entered the blaze to rescue him, only to become the victims of his final burst of destructive energy:

> Sie versuchten noch einmal, ihn herauszuziehen, aber der Alte ließ das Bild mit einer Hand los, riß eine glühende Sparre mit großen glühenden Nägeln über seinem Kopfe heraus und schlug sie dem einen Feuermann über das Gesicht, daß er zusammenbrach. (2:96–97)

Beyond the basic scenario of the house fire, the two stories have several content features in common: first and foremost the casting of an insane criminal as the protagonist, the chronicle of his crime as the basic organisational principle of the narrative, and at the end the depiction of his mad delight in the destruction he causes (Heym's firemen hear the thief's 'lautes Gelächter' as they desperately try to escape, 2:97). Within these equivalent frameworks, other similarities can be observed in detail, for example, the protagonists' fetishistic stroking, immediately prior to the fire, of the objects of their respective cathexes. In 'Der Dieb' this is – what else? – the

Mona Lisa's mouth: 'Er konnte es sich nicht versagen, ihn noch einmal zu streicheln, einmal noch leise mit dem Zeigefinger über diese Lippen zu fahren' (2:94). In 'Feuersbrunst' the object in question is the skin in which the arsonist carries his fuel:

> Und nun war es eine Wollust zu denken, daß man doch den Mut gehabt hatte und darin gewesen war im kostbaren Haus, in allen Stockwerken, von unten bis oben. Mitten in der Nacht, mit einem strotzenden großen Schlauch voll Petroleum. Er war weich und zärtlich anzufassen gewesen; das hatte man immer gemerkt, wenn man die Hände darüber gleiten ließ im Versteck und abwartete, daß das Herz langsamer schlüge. (*M* 91)

A further parallel is the appearance in both stories of a metaphorical dragon during the fire:

> 'Der Dieb': Nach einiger Zeit wieder sahen auf der Straße einige Betrunkene, die sich verirrt hatten, wie ein großer roter Feuerdrache oben auf dem Dache saß und mit seinen riesigen Flügeln auf den brennenden Sparren herumschlug. (2:95)

> 'Feuersbrunst': Die Fenster sprangen mit einem harten Ton ab, und hinter ihnen leckten riesige Zungen. – Der Drache war erwacht! Weit riß er die Augen auf in Todesnot und schrie stumm aus tobenden Schlünden und aufgerissenen Wunden. (*M* 94)

This common use of a given image points to broader stylistic parallels that are just as extensive as the similarities in content already described. Bridgwater emphasizes the prominence of visual imagery in Heym's prose (*PEB* 252); Sokel notes that it is 'teeming with metaphors' and especially similes, but that this is the narrator's only form of subjective participation in an otherwise depersonalized representation of things, thoughts and events: 'Heym never employs rhetorical commentary' (*PGE* 75). Rheiner adopts precisely the same kind of detached, metaphorical–descriptive narrative stance in 'Feuersbrunst'. The abundance of similes and other metaphors in the following description of the villa's parkland setting is illustrative, its overworked anthropomorphism symptomatic of the same stylistic tendency:

> Die Wege im Park blickten streng und einsam und fürchteten sich nicht; denn die Mauer stand ja vor ihnen wie eine erhobene Hand, – ein steinernes Verbot. Und der Mondschein, der über sie floß und sich mit der Grasfläche zu einem grünlich-weißen Teppich verwob, war wie ein heimtückischer Sumpf, in den man lautlos versinkt mit gekrallter Hand und zerrissenen Augen. Hinter der Mauer aber, in ihren tiefen

Schatten, standen ein paar schwarze schlanke Bäume wie geheime Wächter, die über einen herfallen, wenn man sich heranschleichen will. (*M* 91)

Last but not least, 'Der Dieb' and 'Feuersbrunst' are linked by their employment of what Sokel labels *figural perspective*, involving an apparent renunciation of narrative omniscience and conveying instead 'a distorted view of the world narrated from the very personal viewpoint of the main character' (*PGE* 82). In both stories this perspective is combined with heavy use of interior monologue, so that the character's thoughts are not distinguished from descriptions of external reality by quotation marks or other conventional means of signalling reported speech (ibid. 85). This technique results in a blurring of boundaries between interior and exterior, between subject and object, and so in the generation of ambiguity and uncertainty, most importantly – for these and other narratives by both Heym and Rheiner – regarding the distinction between normal perception and hallucination. Although in the years and decades that followed, interior monologue would become a distinguishing characteristic of Modernist narrative, in 1911 it was still highly innovative, and Heym, along with his contemporaries Kafka and Alfred Döblin, is considered one of its pioneers (ibid. 82). The opening lines of 'Feuersbrunst' are testament to Rheiner's command of this technique at a very young age:

Gewiß, es war eine Wonne, sich nun an die Eisenstäbe der Umzäunung zu schmiegen und den Kopf in die engen Zwischenräume zu pressen, soweit es ging. Wie ruhig das alles dalag! (*M* 91)

As a counterpoint to the numerous similarities listed here, it should be remembered that 'Feuersbrunst' is far more modest in both its scope and aims than 'Der Dieb', and whereas the latter is one of the masterpieces of Expressionist prose, the former, even within Rheiner's limited prose œuvre, remains a curio.[72] The relation between them might best be captured by the hypothetical contention that were its authorship unknown, 'Feuersbrunst' might easily be mistaken for a preparatory sketch for 'Der Dieb'. Although highlighting their difference in status, this observation also reinforces the perception of a fundamental connection between the two texts. Consid-

72 Rietzschel writes that *KLPB* contains 'die wesentlichen Prosatexte' (304), the exclusion of 'Feuersbrunst' indicating that for him it does not number among them. The exclusion of 'Die Erniedrigung' by the same criterion, however, is more questionable.

ering that they were apparently written in total isolation from one another, three possible explanations can be given for the similarities between them. The first is that this isolation may be only apparent and that the dating of 'Feuersbrunst' to 1911 may be inaccurate, so that Rheiner's text really does reflect its author's reading of Heym. Despite its neatness, this theory appears improbable given the lack of a compelling reason to think that it was dated inaccurately in the first place. A second possible explanation is a common source, but on reflection this also seems unsatisfactory, as even if a source could be determined for the shared content features (the house fire, the insane criminal etc), the formal parallels would likely remain unexplained. Thus, although the indebtedness of Heym's prose to the gothic horror of Edgar Allan Poe has been noted repeatedly (cf. Blunden 117, Bridgwater *PEB* 264), Heym's treatment of similar material differs fundamentally from his American model. Whereas 'Poe's narrative voice registers the shock and horror of a sensitive mind confronted by the ghastly,' the narrator in Heym's stories 'has deserted us, because Heym himself no longer believes in the civilization which the madman offends' (Blunden 117). In other words, Heym's adoption of figural perspective and interior monologue distinguishes him from Poe, but not, crucially, from Rheiner.

The third and perhaps most plausible explanation is that Rheiner's early experimentation with narrative prose led him to venture briefly, by comparison even tentatively, in a direction that, at the same time, Heym happened to be pursuing with great vigour and conviction. Telling in this respect is that among Rheiner's prose works, 'Feuersbrunst' is the only one whose concerns and approach conform with those of Heym's writing in this genre in such a wholesale manner. Indeed, after a further experiment with 20th-century gothic in 'Miramée' (*KNP* 70–74, *KLPB* 180–183), in which the first-person narrator discovers in the light of morning that his lover of the night just past is the victim of a ghastly wasting disease, in his next prose composition, the story 'Der Tod des Schwärmers Gautier Fémin' (*KNP* 60–68, *KLPB* 189–194), Rheiner would abandon Heym's metaphorical–descriptive method altogether, adopting instead a 'parabolic narrative' style, in which the narrator quite openly interjects opinions, reflections, conjecture and extra-narrative references into the story and is above all concerned with propagating a particular worldview, an approach associated with a quite distinct strand of Expressionism (especially the fictional and theoretical writings of Carl Einstein; see Sokel *PGE* 70–80). In his later works, notably 'Die Erniedrigung' and *Kokain*, Rheiner would return to Heym's themes and methods, but his deployment of them would be more selective and strategic (see 6.3). The Heym-like features in these texts are not for that reason any less important; on the contrary, the selective adaptation of predecessors' work for original purposes could well be read, as it can for both Heym and Trakl, as a sign of self-assurance in the creative writer.

The question of original purposes points to a key difference between Rheiner's prose and his poetry, in which, as suggested in our discussions of 'Expressionismus', 'Trauer', 'Näher, mein Bruder, zu dir!' and 'Toten-Messe' (see 5.1), such purposes become visible only sporadically. The presence of original elements in the prose, on the other hand, can be related to an autobiographical tendency that is evidently much stronger here than in the poetry. Nowhere is this impulse more visible than in the following passage from the novella *Kokain*, in which Rheiner stops just short of giving his protagonist's mother the name of his own, Ernestine Schnorrenberg: 'Und Sie, Frau Sch..., Eveline oder Ernestine mit dem schwer aussprechlichen Vatersnamen, Sie, teure Mutter, wie? ... mir schon wieder auf den Fersen?' (*KLPB* 204). The casting of suffering poets as the main characters in all his major works in this genre is certainly one of their most important autobiographical elements. In truth, the poet's suffering is a favourite theme in the poetry, as well – this congruity confirming that for Rheiner literary expression has a performative function, allowing him to re-enact the role as prophet and outcast he had cultivated for himself (see 5.1). In the prose, however, this role is filled out with mundane ('prosaic') details almost certainly based on the author's own experience, such as the humiliation to which he is subjected by unsympathetic editors: 'Das schlechte Gewissen, mit dem er um Geld bat im Café oder vor den Sesseln der Redakteure, die ihm erstaunt den Zigarrenrauch ins Gesicht bliesen und ihn verdrießlich abschüttelten' (*KLPB* 197).

Crucially, Rheiner's cocaine use is another main target of his autobiographical impulse, which appears to be implicitly confessional in nature (as opposed to De Quincey's, which is *explicitly* confessional) and is especially evident in all three of his largest complete works in prose: 'Der Tod des Schwärmers Gautier Fémin,' 'Die Erniedrigung' and *Kokain*. Weinand's chronology (see 5.1) would place the composition of the first of these, which Rietzschel dates to November 1915 (*KLPB* 189), squarely within the period of Rheiner's cocaine addiction, the second and third soon after his 1916 'cure' – 'Die Erniedrigung' was first published in *Die Aktion* in January 1918 (*M* 109–110); *Kokain* was written in summer of the same year (St. Saveur 137). All three of these works include direct references to the protagonist's cocaine use, and in the last two the physical, psychological and social degradation caused by cocaine addiction is the dominant theme. By contrast, not a single unambiguous reference to cocaine occurs in the poetry, the bulk of which was written over the same period. Occasional references to other psychoactive substances can be found: one memorable couplet from the 1917 cycle *Berlin*, referring perhaps to women forced into drug dealing and prostitution by wartime hardship, reads 'In den Alleen die Hunger-Frauen brennen; / Wein ist ihr Kuß, und Augen sind Haschisch' (*KLPB* 121), while 'Das zehnte Abendlied' from *Insel der Seligen*, written in spring 1918, contains the following stanza, which, like much of the cycle, again bespeaks Trakl's influence:

> Wir schlafen tief. Es nistet die Stirn im Stein
> des Hauses, das mit uns durch die Träume fährt,
> die uns der Sonne Wein noch schenkte,
> dunkel am Horizont: Mohnes Blüte! (*KLPB* 143)

This association brings to mind a broader parallel with Trakl, in whose verse very few of the very many intoxicants with which the poet was familiar find any mention, *Wein* and *Mohn* being the two exceptions (see 9.2). An important distinction, however, is that in Trakl's poetry states of intoxication are frequently invoked, whereas in this regard 'Das zehnte Abendlied' is unusual for Rheiner, who clearly did not consider drug use to be a particularly appropriate or fertile field for his poetic practice, either thematically or lexically. It is equally clear that he *did* consider it to be an appropriate and fertile field in both these respects for his prose.

The possibility that several poems treat the theme obliquely cannot be discounted, and the inclination to read certain poems in this way is strengthened by two factors. The first is their juxtaposition with both the prose texts and the 'biographical legend' that these serve to propagate and that, in Tomashevsky's words, 'the poet considers as a premise to his creations' (52; see 1.4). In other words, the prominence of a particular element in both the writer's biography and his works in one genre serve to make its absence in another conspicuous, giving rise to the suspicion that it is not really absent at all, only hidden in line with Jakobson's assertion that any literary work will 'include the situation [in which it was written] positively or negatively,' but 'is never indifferent to it' (320; see 1.4). The second factor that encourages the reading of Rheiner's poetry in relation to his drug habit is the recurrent use of the title *Kokain* by the editors of collections of his work (see 5.1). This is obviously not the result of any decision made by Rheiner himself – the only work to appear under that title during his lifetime was the novella – but it certainly can be considered a continuation of the 'biographical legend' initiated by the author himself, perpetuated posthumously in the first instance by Felixmüller and revived and extended in this way by his more recent editors. That marketing considerations have played a significant role here would appear beyond dispute, yet it is marketing designed to increase capital not merely within a commercial economy, but in the first instance within a literary-historical one, carving out a niche for Rheiner, the formerly 'forgotten Expressionist,' as the archetypal 'poet on cocaine,' whose works can be meaningfully collected under the name of that drug. The elevation of *Kokain* to a generic title unquestionably *does* affect the way in which the works included under it are read, acting in essence as a prism placed between the message and its addressee in the communicative pathway conceptualized by Jakobson (66; see 1.4).[73] There is a clear and inevitable implication that the drug named in the title of three of the four posthumous collections is somehow of central importance not only to Rheiner's life and his novella, but to his literary work as a whole (of which the novella is, in various respects, decidedly unrepresentative), suggesting a 'white thread' – as opposed to the red one of German phraseology – linking the diverse elements that make up his œuvre.

In view especially of the poetry's reticence about cocaine, it is apparent that this implication is, at least in part, misleading. Little is to be gained, for example, by contriving to read any of the four works discussed in detail in this chapter – 'Trauer', 'Näher, mein Bruder, zu dir!', 'Toten-Messe' or 'Feuersbrunst' – in direct relation to their author's drug habit. Yet a very obvious 'white thread' does indeed link the three major prose works, and it is surprising that this has not been remarked on in any previous study, especially considering the close correspondences between 'Die

73 Resch's assertion that 'Die Anrufung des Engels,' a poem that contains no readily recognizable references to psychoactive substances, is really concerned with the difficulty of articulating the complexity of drug experience, might be considered symptomatic of this effect (269; compare note 63).

Erniedrigung' and that 'Meilenstein der Drogenliteratur' (*K* 10) *Kokain*.[74] These three texts, then, will provide the 'archipelagos of certainty' (Morin, see 1.1) for the close readings of Rheiner's works featured in the following chapter. Our attempt to trace the extension of the 'white thread,' however, will be framed by two forays into the 'ocean of uncertainties' represented by the poetry. These are undertaken in the awareness that as far as the text–drug dynamic of Rheiner's œuvre is concerned, the works in question occupy a grey area, offering no more than intimations of a link to the drug theme that emerge via comparative readings with the key prose texts, but that their inclusion can provide a fuller picture of the relationship between Rheiner's writings and his drug habit than that which emerges from an exclusive focus on the prose. Furthermore, this extended selection of texts is intended to offer a perspective from which the development of the drug theme can be followed from earlier to later works. Just as Baudelaire's increasing scepticism about the efficacy of hashish as a creative tool can be traced from his earliest essay on the topic, 'Du Vin et du Hachish, comparés comme moyens de multiplication de l'individualité' (1851), through its various reworkings to the final version of *Les Paradis artificiels* (1860),[75] so too the texts by Rheiner chosen here can be read as chapters in a master narrative that follows the changing relationship between the poet's drug habit and his creative writing from its promising beginnings to its catastrophic conclusion. In this respect, the poems selected, although to an extent peripheral, would appear to confirm the tendency – and complete its trajectory – that already emerges from a comparative reading of the core stories. It must be underlined that our objective is not to reduce each text to a fragment of autobiography; the autobiographical master narrative emerges as an interpretative possibility only when the different works are seen in sequence and as elements of a textual cluster marking various stages in the development of Rheiner's œuvre.

---

74 A probable reason for this neglect is that 'Die Erniedrigung' is not included in *KLPB*, the major source for most scholars (compare note 72). This would also explain why this story is not mentioned in any of the surveys of drug literature, even those in which Rheiner features (see 1.3), despite its undeniable pertinence to those studies.

75 For a detailed discussion of Baudelaire's changing attitude to hashish, see Kupfer's *Göttliche Gifte*: 'Der [...] Vergleich der ersten und letzten Version seines Aufsatzes über das Haschisch zeigt deutlich die gedankliche Entwicklung Baudelaires, die, grob gesagt, aus einem hoffnungsvollen Drogenadepten einen entschiedenen Drogengegner werden ließ' (165).

6 Rheiner's Master Narrative of Addiction

6.1 Innocence and Experience

Rheiner's *Kokain* is divided into nine short chapters. The first of these narrates the evening-time struggle of the protagonist, Tobias, with his craving for the drug, a struggle that manifests itself in great agitation and restlessness: 'Er ging und ging, die Allee hinauf und hinab, fast schon zwei Stunden lang. / Die Normaluhr (ehernes Gespenst an der Straßenkreuzung) zeigte schon halb elf' (*KLPB* 195).[76] At a certain point he finds himself on the edge of a square: 'Geblendet stand er an der Schwelle des Platzes' (196). Here he stops to reflect on the degradation and humiliation of his life as an addict: his slovenly habits, his poverty and hunger, his paranoia and guilt, his resentment towards anyone and anything 'respectable' (196–197). Despite his acute consciousness of the state to which addiction has reduced him, the craving, now as ever, ultimately proves irresistible: 'Er hatte gekämpft, wie fast jeden Abend und war, wie immer, unterlegen' (198). He rings the night-bell at the chemist's, and despite the late hour and his lack of money, he is soon in possession of a 'small hexagonal bottle' containing 'the eternal poison' (ibid.). He goes into a café, perhaps the same one he had left earlier when the 'dämonische Unruhe' (197) of the early evening had become unbearable, and immediately goes to the bathroom where he gives himself three injections of the drug (198). The last paragraph of the chapter describes his re-entry into the café from the bathroom. With the cocaine in his bloodstream, his angst and agitation have been transformed into a euphoric self-confidence: 'Nun fühlte er sich frei und leicht, spielerisch, ein junger Gott!' (ibid.). The chapter ends as Tobias imagines himself soaring ecstatically into the night sky, the Icarus-simile foreshadowing his own protracted and deadly fall that forms the subject matter of the eight remaining chapters:

76 All citations from *Kokain* in this chapter refer to the version in *KLPB*.

> Ein Wink von ihm, und er würde, Ikarus, dem göttlichen Jüngling gleich, lächelnd an die Decke schweben, singend über den Baldachin des Vorgartens gleiten und auf zu den knisternden Sternen kreisen. (ibid.)

From the narratological point of view, perhaps the most remarkable feature of this chapter is the large amount of movement that occurs in such a limited textual space. The spatial progression that structures the narrative within the chapter (following Tobias's movements from one place to the next) can be represented graphically as follows:

[café][77] → street → square → chemist's → café (bathroom → main room) → sky

By comparison, the shorter narrative 'Die Erniedrigung' is divided into just three chapters, the first of which is further divided into two sections. The first of these, essentially an introduction to the story, consists of four paragraphs, the first containing the narrator's affirmation of the poet's status as plaything of divine and demonic forces (cited in 1.2), the second and third describing the nighttime homeward journey of the poet-protagonist, another Tobias, and the fourth his intravenous self-administration of cocaine in his bedroom immediately upon his arrival (100–101).[78] The pattern of restless movement ('unter seinem eiligen Schritt', 100) through an urban landscape (Tobias crosses a pontoon bridge before catching a tram) followed by multiple cocaine injections ('Kaum hatte er den Überrock abgeworfen, gab er sich zwei starke Spritzen,' 101) leading to an hallucinatory levitation ('Seine Füße hoben sich vom Boden, das Haar schäumte, er schwebte an der Zimmerdecke und trank den Glanz des Gaslichts,' ibid.) in the first section of the narrative is just one of numerous – previously unremarked – parallels linking this story with *Kokain*, the most obvious being the casting of a cocaine-addict called Tobias as the protagonist. It can be deduced from the markedly similar development of spatial progressions leading to the common goal of cocaine-induced relief and euphoria in the opening sections of the two narratives that Rheiner's textual enactment of

77 The square brackets indicate that this space is inserted into the progression retrospectively. The chapter opens with Tobias already walking up and down the street at half past ten at night, and only later in the chapter do we learn that he had spent the early evening at the café.

78 The typographical division of the first chapter (by extra line break) is shared by the versions printed in *KNP* and *K*, but not by that in *M*. Nonetheless, all citations from 'Die Erniedrigung' in this chapter refer to the version in *M*.

cocaine use tends to be driven by a strong spatial dynamic – in contrast, for example, to the predominantly cerebral dynamic of Benn's. This observation is borne out by the continuation of both stories, most obviously by the increasingly desperate roaming that fills *Kokain*, but more subtly also by the movement along a vertical axis, in the form of falling and climbing, that predominates in 'Die Erniedrigung,' informing the story from its title to the final collapse of the apartment building in which most of the action is set.

It is significant for this investigation, then, that a version of the spatial progression from *Kokain* outlined above, in its particulars more similar than that from 'Die Erniedrigung,' can be found in another of Rheiner's works, or rather two of his works that can be considered to form a pair: the early poems 'Die Straße' (*KLPB* 32) and 'Der Platz' (*KLPB* 33). These were originally published in 1915 (three years before both *Kokain* and 'Die Erniedrigung'), along with 'Miramée', in Franz Pfemfert's Expressionist journal *Die Aktion* (*KLPB* 238), and were later included in the collection *Das schmerzliche Meer* (Dresden, 1918). That they are to be read as a pair is suggested by two main factors: the apparent continuity of the lyric perspective from one poem to the next, and the almost exact repetition of the final clause of 'Die Straße' as the opening sentence of 'Der Platz.' Various other factors that reinforce this impression can be identified: the two poems' formal similarity (they are both sonnets in regular iambic pentameter), the semantic equivalence of their titles (they both denote an outdoor space defined by its social function), and more simply their placement in sequence by the poet in *Das schmerzliche Meer*.[79]

Die Straße

In meinem Hirn ist sie ein heller Pfad,
der unvermutet in die Wälder führt.
Oft bin ich stumm: ihr süßer Aufstieg rührt
mich fast zu Tränen, wenn in ihrem Bad

ich still verfließe. Wesen nahen sich,
die spülen leicht und einfach in mich ein.

79 Rietzschel has them in sequence and explains that 'die Gruppierung der ausgewählten Gedichte entspricht der Anordnung in den Erstausgaben' (304). Note that as these two poems are effectively treated here as a single work, for convenience the lines have been numbered as if dealing with a single poem.

Der Hunde, Pferde sanfter Widerschein
Verklärt mir Mensch und Ding, verklärt auch mich.

Die Häuser neigen sich, mein Ohr zu küssen,
und hoch wallt eine Frau durch mildes Feld;
ich werde ihr noch oft begegnen müssen.

Dann kommen Freunde sprudelnd mir entgegen
und gehn vorbei. Doch ich bin ganz erhellt
und groß und klar und wag nicht mich zu regen. (*KLPB* 32)

Der Platz

Ich wag mich nicht zu regen. Doch der Platz
dreht leise sich in meine weite Brust.
Im Innern blüht mir weiß und unbewußt
der hohen Bogenlampen langer Satz.

In ihrer Mitte schweb' ich lächelnd auf.
Aus meinen Händen fällt ein schmaler Regen
auf bunter Bahnen glückliches Bewegen,
und viele Menschen blicken still herauf.

Ich aber sauge aus beglänzten Läden,
aus Haus und Mensch, Getier und Untergrund,
der schwirrenden Gefühle Silberfäden.

Tief in sie eingehüllt, bin ich ganz bunt
und wunderbar erlöst und ohne Schäden
und kreise wie ein Mond am Himmelsrund. (*KLPB* 33)

'Die Straße' and 'Der Platz' can be numbered among the poems in which Rheiner's 'naturalistic-impressionistic' (*KLPB* 8) lyricism prevails over his acquired enthusiasm for 'Expressionist' contortions, and in line with the observation made in the previous chapter regarding his early poetry (see 5.1), many features of these poems are more reminiscent of Rilke than of any Expressionist model.[80] Thematically, the strongest affiliation is with the more subjective Rilke represented by *Das Stundenbuch* (1905), evident in the

80 The Rilkean features of 'Die Straße' and 'Der Platz' listed in this paragraph were first noted by Peter Russell.

lyric subject's sometimes precious self-consciousness and self-importance ('ich bin ganz erhellt / und groß und klar,' ll. 13–14), his intimate communion with external reality ('der Platz / dreht sich leise in meine weite Brust,' ll. 15–16), and his progression into a euphoric rapture with religious overtones ('wunderbar erlöst,' l. 27), as well as occasional bathos ('Die Häuser neigen sich, mein Ohr zu küssen,' l. 9). But these poems also integrate stylistic features characteristic of the more controlled and objective Rilke of *Neue Gedichte* (1907–08): the sonnet form; the deliberate, melodious assonance ('ihr süßer Aufstieg / rührt mich fast zu Tränen, wenn in ihrem Bad / ich still verfließe,' ll. 3–5); and the abundance of caesuras and enjambements (as in the last example).

The spatial progression contained in these two poems, when read together, can be summarized as follows:

street → square → sky

Clearly the larger setting of these two poems is quite different from that of either *Kokain* or 'Die Erniedrigung'. The first chapter of Rheiner's novella contains more or less direct references to various, easily recognizable Berlin landmarks (*die Kaiser-Wilhelm-Gedächtniskirche, das Café des Westens, Kantstraße*), while the opening paragraphs of the short story indicate, by more oblique means, a setting in another major city, Rheiner's native Cologne (especially in the colourful metaphor 'aufgeschreckter Riesen-Hase' used to describe the cathedral, 100).[81] The two poems, by contrast, evoke a provincial or even rural landscape, specifically a small town or village where the manifestations of human habitation (the street, the houses, the square, the shops) and the people themselves (the speaker, the woman, the friends, the people in the square) intermingle with the countryside and its animal life (the forests, the dogs and horses, the field, the 'creatures and subsoil'). The similarity between chapter 1 of the novella and the two poems lies in the individual spatial elements that make up these larger settings, and especially in the progression itself, that is, the movement of the speaker/protagonist from one space to the next. It is significant also that the titles of the two

81 The pontoon bridge that Tobias crosses can be seen as further evidence for a Cologne setting, as until 1915 such a bridge stood at the site of today's Deutzer Brücke. The visibility of the cathedral from the bridge is also consistent with Cologne's topography.

poems give particular prominence to these individual, more limited spaces over and above the broader geographical situation.

Notably, the two elements in the spatial progression from chapter 1 of *Kokain* that are absent from that of 'Die Straße'–'Der Platz,' the chemist's and the café, are the two that are most directly – *materially* – connected with cocaine. Tobias 'buys' the drug at the chemist's (on credit, but the promised payment will never be made), and then gives himself three injections of it in the bathroom of the café. In the other spaces he passes through in chapter 1, the narrative is chiefly concerned with the effects of the drug on his consciousness and lifestyle, rather than with its material presence in his possession or in his bloodstream. As Tobias paces the street in the vain attempt to give vent to the agitation brought on by his nightly craving and then stops in the square to reflect on the moral and social abasement to which his addiction has reduced him, he is in fact struggling to *avoid* the material presence of the drug, while on his imaginary flight into the Berlin sky that ends the chapter he manages to banish, if only momentarily, all thoughts of mere materiality from his consciousness. If we consider the two 'material' elements of the spatial progression as somehow distinct, a 'technical' addition made in order to introduce cocaine materially into the narrative, the remaining elements form a spatial continuum that is not only similar but identical to that of the two poems. The question that begs to be asked here, then, is whether the structural similarity between these texts points to a deeper thematic connection between them and specifically the possibility of aggregating 'Die Straße' and 'Der Platz' to the works informed, explicitly or implicitly, by their author's cocaine use. Further parallels between the texts can be identified to support such a view and to develop it further.

As already mentioned, the factor which more than any other unites the poems 'Die Straße' and 'Der Platz' is the continuity of the lyric perspective from one poem to the next. This continuity goes further than the mere repetition of first person pronouns. Rather, what is striking and particular about the lyric perspective is its dynamic relationship to its surroundings: the simple act of observation on the part of the speaker, as he walks along the street and stops in the square, becomes an increasingly intense physical, emotional and finally metaphysical interaction with the external environment. That the perspective is highly subjective is underlined at the very beginning of 'Die Straße': '*In meinem Hirn* ist sie ein heller Pfad' (l. 1, italics added). The images that follow show that this subjectivity is extraordinarily sensitive to external stimuli:

> [...] ihr süßer Aufstieg rührt
> mich fast zu Tränen [...] (ll. 3–4)
>
> Der Hunde, Pferde sanfter Widerschein
> Verklärt mir Mensch und Ding, verklärt auch mich. (ll. 7–8)

At certain points the relationship between mind and world appears to become entirely fluid: 'Wesen nahen sich, / die spülen leicht und einfach in mich ein' (ll. 5–6). As Tobias makes his way along the street at the beginning of *Kokain*, his perceptions of the scene around him display a similarly heightened receptivity and fluidity:

> Jetzt war die Nacht da. Flimmernd strahlte der Asphalt auf, wenn ein Automobil surrend an Tobias vorbeistob. Aus den Café-Vorgärten schwemmte eine süße Musik über ihn hin. Gesprächsfetzen wehten, ungehört von ihm, vorüber. Es war ein stetes Wandeln bunter, vornehmer Damen, diskreter Herren da, ein unaufhörlicher Verkehr lachender Equipagen und Autos: der melancholisch-heitere Abendgesang der großen düsteren Stadt, die auf ihre Art zu leben verstand. (196)

As in 'Die Straße,' in this passage from *Kokain* the environment is perceived as a flux ('ein stetes Wandeln [...] ein unaufhörlicher Verkehr') that surrounds and impresses itself on the consciousness of the observer in its never-ending movement ('an Tobias vorbei [...] über ihn hin').

At the same time, this passage highlights several significant differences between the poems and the novella, differences that indicate the specific ways in which chapter 1 of *Kokain* represents a variation on the scenes presented in 'Die Straße' and 'Der Platz.' Firstly, as far as the relationship between observer and environment is concerned, in 'Die Straße' the speaker's experience of his surroundings is evidently harmonious (consider especially Rheiner's use of such adjectives and adverbs as *hell*, *süß*, *still*, *leicht*, *einfach*, *mild*, *sprudelnd*) and intimate (the people he meets are 'friends'), and includes strong hints of erotic expectation and excitement (see especially lines 9–11). Tobias, by contrast, despite his physical centrality to the scene in which he finds himself, feels extraneous to it. The car 'flies past' him indifferently; the 'sweet' music emanating from the cafés clashes with his own distressed state of mind; he is excluded from the social interaction going on around him, and does not even register the 'scraps' of conversation that 'drift past'; the 'distinguished ladies' and 'discreet gentlemen' strolling by belong to a social stratum whose glitter and self-satisfied refinement are entirely foreign to the squalor and misery of his own existence. Although less developed in 'Die Erniedrigung,' a similar degree of alienation is expressed in the descriptions of the protagonist walking 'voll Grauen' (49) across the pontoon bridge and soon after sitting, 'verkrochen, in der Trambahn' (50). This contrast between harmonious integration and belonging on the one hand and alienation and discord on the other is reflected in subtle lexical differences between the texts. For example, whereas the street in 'Die Straße' is seen as a 'path', implying that it has a recognizable function (leading from one place to another, here from the village/town 'into the woods') within a greater social structure, in *Kokain* this functionality is no longer apparent – for Tobias the street is simply 'asphalt', cold and impersonal. The same contrast is also reflected in the difference in setting: the harmony and friendliness of the rural or provincial community are opposed to the anonymity and indifference of the metropolis.

These differences can be further elaborated in a comparison of the final stages of the spatial progression: in what we might call the ascension stage. As the speaker in 'Der Platz' 'floats smilingly upwards' (l. 19), his links to the community ('Haus und Mensch,' l. 24) and the natural environment ('Getier und Untergrund,' l. 24) are not severed but reinforced, as the physical bonds that previously determined his sense of belonging make way for metaphysical and emotional ones ('der schwirrenden Gefühle Silberfäden,' l. 25). Significantly, his transcendence is not an escape from but an apotheosis of the ties that define and limit his everyday life; in other words, a transcendental spiritual purpose is drawn from the speaker's integration in the community and environment. In this context his ascension takes on entirely positive religious-mystical overtones: the speaker is at once protected ('eingehüllt', l. 26) and redeemed ('wunderbar erlöst,' l. 27) by his emotional harmony with the external world. By contrast, Tobias in *Kokain* experiences his imaginary flight as a relief from the agitation brought on by his craving for cocaine and as an escape ('Nun fühlte er sich *frei*,' 198, italics added) from the 'spaces' that this agitation causes him to 'hate': 'Und doch siegte immer diese Unruhe, die, wenn sie kam, ihm alle Räume verhaßt machte – sein chambre garnie so gut wie das Café oder den großen Raum der Straßen und Plätze' (196). In an interesting variation on this theme, in

'Die Erniedrigung' cocaine provides the protagonist with an escape from an acute sense of claustrophobia, that is, a suffocating lack of space:

> Noch war er nicht zu Bett, so fühlte er schon das dunkle Tuch von oben auf sich herniederschweben, das ihn fest einwickelte, Mund, Nase, Ohr und Lunge dick verhüllend und ihn in eine Ecke drückte. Dort schrumpfte er ganz klein zusammen. Die Augen rissen sich auf; die Pupillen weiteten sich zu zwei unabsehbaren schwarzen Schächten… Ah! Den Druck vom Körper fort! – Hastig nahm er zwei weitere Spritzen. – (101)

As for the speaker in 'Der Platz,' for Tobias in *Kokain* the ascension stage is imbued with definite religious overtones. He feels like 'a young god' (198), and compares himself to Icarus, 'the divine youth' (ibid.), whose fateful flight from the labyrinth of Crete with his father Daedalus was also, it should be noted, an escape.[82] However, the religious element introduced at the end of chapter 1 of the novella is not, as in the earlier poem, characterized by cosmic harmony and miraculous redemption, but by hubris and impending disaster, and indeed Tobias's intoxicated euphoria turns out to be painfully short-lived. Just a few lines later, at the beginning of chapter 2, his good humour evaporates in the face of the threat represented by '*jene Nacht, seine Nacht, die mit schwarzem Faustschlag diese kurzen Minuten des heiteren Rausches zertrümmerte*' (ibid.).

This combination of similarities in general structure and differences in specific detail between the two poems on the one hand and the two prose works, especially *Kokain*, on the other certainly supports a view of the first chapter of the novella as a reworking of the street→square→sky progression first employed in the poems. Evidence for a potential role for cocaine in 'Die Straße' and 'Der Platz,' however, remains elusive. Indeed, a first impression may suggest that one of the most significant aspects of Rheiner's reworking is precisely the introduction of the drug into the text of the novella, which brings with it the introduction of the chemist's and less directly of the café into the basic progression. From this it might in turn be deduced that the prose text is, quite simply and as its title would indicate, 'about' cocaine, whereas the poems are not. Closer consideration, however, brings this view into question. For although cocaine is indeed materially present in chapter 1 of the novella, within that chapter it is not once named directly. This is remarkable considering that, in one way or

82 For the story of Icarus, see Ovid, *Metamorphoses* VIII, ll. 183–235.

another, it is central to each of the various stages in the development of the chapter: Tobias's craving for cocaine gives rise to his agitation on the street; his addiction to cocaine has brought about the degradation of his day-to-day life that he reflects on in the square; he 'buys' cocaine at the chemist's and administers it to himself intravenously in the café bathroom; and at the end of the chapter cocaine intoxication causes the exultation of his imaginary flight to the stars. Yet none of this is stated directly. Rather, the reader infers the centrality of cocaine in each stage from the title of the novella, an inference that is confirmed retrospectively by the events narrated in the following chapters. The word *Kokain* itself becomes a nucleus around which the text revolves without coming into direct contact. The closest that chapter 1 comes to naming the drug, while Tobias is clasping the newly acquired bottle in his hands, is the circumlocution 'das ewige Gift' (198). The first mention of cocaine, in chapter 2, gives some clue as to the reasons for this reticence. At this point Tobias is seated in the café, and his euphoria has given way to the paranoia that he is the object of the other customers' derision:

> Angestrengt horchte er hin … und da, war es nicht da? Hatte er nicht eben deutlich das Wort vernommen, das fatale Wort, das riesenhaft über die Firmamente dieser seiner Nächte gespannt war und (im Klang schon erbarmungslose Maschine) ihn langsam zerhackte: - *Kokain! … Ko-ka-in!*
> Stück für Stück hackte es ab von ihm, bis er dereinst bald ganz zermalmt sein wird. (200)

For Tobias the very word *Kokain* has become taboo, a 'fatal word' that has come to represent the destructive power, mechanical in its relentlessness, that the substance it denotes wields over his body and mind. Evidently the narrative, which slips, Heym-like, between metaphorically loaded description and interior monologue, shares in his reluctance to enunciate this 'fatal word.'[83]

Although there is no reason to attribute the same lexical taboo to the speaker in 'Die Straße' and 'Der Platz,' it is now evident that the absence of the word *Kokain* from the text is in fact a further point of similarity rather

83 'Die Erniedrigung,' in which the drug is named only twice, shares the novella's reticence in this respect, even without drawing specific attention to it. More frequent is the metonymic *Spritze*, which on its first occurrence is expanded parenthetically by a pharmacological designation, the formality of which can be seen as a further distancing strategy: 'zwei starke Spritzen (Sol. hydro. Cocaine 0,06)' (101).

than a point of difference between the two poems and chapter 1 of Rheiner's novella, and that this absence by no means precludes a role for the drug in the text. Might, therefore, the centrality of cocaine *despite its own absence* be another, more subtle parallel between the two poems of 1915 and the first chapter of the novella written three years later? That 'Die Straße' and 'Der Platz' depict an experience of intoxication of some kind is indisputable. The dynamic fluidity of the lyric perspective already discussed is clearly symptomatic of an abnormal state of consciousness, as is the apparent seamlessness of the transitions between visual, emotional, physical and metaphysical levels of experience. Furthermore, the lyric subject's description of himself in the final lines of 'Die Straße' as 'ganz erhellt / und groß und klar' (ll. 13–14), and more generally his euphoria and self-importance, in particular his feeling of almost divine singularity, can all be considered consistent with the effects of cocaine intoxication. All the evidence, then, both textual and intertextual, would seem to point in the direction of cocaine intoxication as the pharmacological agent for the speaker's peculiar state of mind. Nonetheless, the evidence remains circumstantial, and it must be remembered that the text is concerned with the state of mind itself, rather than its pharmacological agent. In this respect, 'Die Straße' and 'Der Platz' are comparable to Benn's cocaine poems (see 3.1–3.4), only without the wish to challenge the sober bourgeois creed that is implicit in Benn's 'shameless' confession of having taken cocaine. On the contrary, they propose an idyllic (if intoxicated) view of social harmony. In such a context it is perhaps unsurprising that the drug should remain unnamed.

Further, it can be argued that Rheiner's depiction of intoxication detached from its agent is consistent with the Romantic tradition, discussed in 1.2, according to which intrigue in the text–drug relationship is generated by means of an information *lack*. Indeed, the 'cocaine link' between these two poems and the first chapter of Rheiner's novella is comparable to the 'hashish link' Boon identifies between two well-known works by Baudelaire, likewise one in poetry and the other in prose: 'Correspondances' and *Les Paradis artificiels*. Boon writes that

> when we read the beautiful poem 'Corréspondences' [sic!], a cornerstone of Symbolist aesthetics, we find no mention of hashish in the poem. But when we read the hashish chapter of *Les paradis artificiels*, we find passages identical in imagery and meaning to parts of this poem that are presented explicitly as being the products of hashish intoxication

> […] Anyone having read both texts would connect them immediately, but they are separated by a divide, which can only be bridged mythically, in secret. (45)

Boon argues that Baudelaire's reticence about intoxicants in his poetry – which applied not only to hashish but to opium as well – 'contributes to a certain literary myth' about drugs, surrounding them with an aura of mystery and secrecy and giving them an almost godly or diabolical unspeakability (ibid.).[84] We might add that such reticence also 'contributes to a certain literary myth' regarding poetry itself, namely that it has the capacity to articulate relationships, or 'correspondences', that are less tangible yet more profound than the merely prosaic cause-and-effect that, for example, links intoxicants with intoxication. Baudelaire is universally recognized as one of the most important forerunners of literary Modernism, as well as a major influence on the poets of Expressionism,[85] and his drug-related reticence was evidently one aspect of his art that his Expressionist heirs, even Benn in a roundabout way, considered worthy of emulation. Trakl's poetry provides perhaps the most complete realization of this tendency; his 'intoxicated' language suggests, in the subtlest ways, correspondences with the experience of psychoactive drugs without ever reducing this relationship to one of cause and effect (see 9.1–9.2). Benn, on the other hand, iconoclastically turns Baudelaire's practice on its head: his poetic prose of the Expressionist period is drug-reticent in the extreme (consider especially the *Rönne* stories; see 4.1), whereas one of the most startling features of his poetry is that it states the drug connection most prosaically: 'O Nacht! Ich nahm schon Kokain' (*GW* 1:53; see 3.1–3.3). In view of the numerous and far-reaching parallels between Rheiner's poems 'Die Straße' and 'Der Platz' and the first chapter of *Kokain*, it can be argued that they manifest the same kind of 'secret' connection to cocaine that Baudelaire's 'Correspondances' does to hashish. It is a relationship that remains – mystically – unspoken, 'ungenannt […] und nicht zu nennen,'

84 Boon, whose primary concern is to distinguish the literary projects associated with individual drugs and to play down the common features that unite them under the rubric 'drugs in literature,' initially writes that this 'myth' concerns narcotics in particular, but then perhaps unwittingly illustrates its wider applicability by giving the example cited here of a 'secret' relationship between Baudelaire's poem and hashish, a drug he deals with separately and to which he ascribes a different literary project.

85 Rheiner was no exception in this regard. He uses Baudelaire's sonnet 'La Mort des pauvres' as an epigraph to *Kokain*, and Rietzschel provides an incomplete poetic translation of the same poem found among Rheiner's unpublished works (195).

like the angel in 'Die Anrufung des Engels' (*KLPB* 79). For Rheiner the act of naming, as this poem makes clear, inevitably involves profanity: '*Kein Donner trübt / solche Sprache, die der Mund nicht kennet, / der nur lügen kann und ewig lügt*' (ibid.; italics in the original).

In view of this admittedly hidden link between these two poems and the drug to which their author was addicted, they can be considered, with the qualifications already stipulated, the first element in the master narrative tracing the changing relationship between the poet's drug habit and his creative writing. Read as such, they suggest that at its outset, despite the turmoil in other areas of Rheiner's life deriving from his involvement in the First World War, this relationship was for the most part a felicitous one. The depiction of transcendence through intoxication that these two poems offer gives no inkling of the suffering, or Icarus-like fall, that would follow, and the fact that the source of the speaker's euphoria remains undisclosed suggests that he is himself oblivious to the prospect of disastrous consequences. This prospect is painfully evident, by contrast, in Tobias's formulation 'das ewige Gift' (198).

6.2 The Decadent Drug

Of the six prose pieces that Rietzschel includes in *KLPB*, the two longest, the novella *Kokain* and the short story 'Der Tod des Schwärmers Gautier Fémin' (neither of which is particularly long by other standards), are both tales of cocaine users who end up shooting themselves. But the similarity between the two works ends there. *Kokain* is an unrelentingly grim account of an addict's suffering and despair with a plot that is strictly linear: Tobias's distress becomes increasingly intense until finally he kills himself. The style is modelled on that with which Rheiner had experimented as a teenager in 'Feuersbrunst' and is most recognizably associated with Heym, who at the same time was using it to perfection in his own short prose (see 5.2): paratactic and teeming with metaphors that inject a degree of subjectivity into a description-oriented narrative (cf. Sokel *PGE* 75–76). Its artistry, especially by the standards of Rheiner's self-proclaimed 'language-revolutionary radicalism' (*KLPB* 8), remains understated throughout, and the impression the novella creates is less that of an inspired creative act or literary performance than of an anguished attempt to expel the story from its narrator's consciousness.

By contrast, the narrative of 'Der Tod des Schwärmers Gautier Fémin,' written in November 1915 while Rheiner was on active military duty, is very much a self-consciously literary performance. Indeed, *style* is of central thematic concern to the whole story, which, although disguised as an elegy on the premature death of a friend, in effect amounts to a celebration of the aesthetic shift from one artistic movement to another, and on a broader scale of the cultural shift from one historical epoch to another: from the art-for-art's-sake doctrine of *fin-de-siècle* Decadence, depicted as enervated and sterile, to the revolutionary and messianic fervour of Expressionism (specifically 'light Expressionism'; see 5.1). This ulterior significance is hinted at in the story's subtitle, 'Ein Abschied und eine Begrüßung' (*KLPB* 189),[86] and links it to poems such as 'Expressionismus' and 'Der Dichter in der Welt' as first and foremost an articulation of Rheiner's literary credo and poetic self-image.

The first two of the story's three chapters are set in Paris on the eve of the First World War, and recount the failed love affair between Fémin and the exotic and sensual salon-socialite Erid, a Norwegian singer and music student. The protagonist Fémin embodies the decadent cult of beauty, and his very name implies 'effeminate aesthete' (by combining the name of the originator of 'l'art pour l'art,' Théophile Gautier, with the first two syllables of the French *féminine*). His first mistake, as the narrator tells us in the opening paragraph, is

> daß er zu leicht und ausschließlich an 'das Schöne' glaubte: ein Begriff, oder (wie er mich stets verbesserte) ein Erlebnis, mit dem er keineswegs irgendwelche ethischen oder auch nur praktischen Ziele verband. Ästhet also, betonte er des öfteren, daß das Schöne einzig um seiner selbst willen dasei, fremd jeder Tendenz, abgekehrt von allem realen Betrieb, wenngleich mitten in ihm (einem aus Schutt und Schmutz ausgegrabenen Torso gleich) vollendet, manifestiert. (189)

Fémin's blind faith in the pure existence of 'the beautiful' in an ugly world is described as his second mistake and, by his own admission, as if in recognition of his status of living anachronism, 'die innere Ursache seines notwendigen Todes' (ibid.). The immediate, 'external' cause of his suicide is his

86 All further citations from 'Der Tod des Schwärmers Gautier Fémin' in this chapter refer to the version in *KLPB*.

repudiation by Erid, who proves to be entirely unsuited to the role of objective correlative for his belief in the mystical power of beauty, a belief that she seems to share only for the short period of their initial infatuation. Flattered by the attention but indifferent to the theoretical ideal that motivates it, she soon tires of Fémin's adoration and returns to drinking tea with her husband, as well as becoming involved in a number of new erotic intrigues with Fémin's own friends. Fémin himself is devastated but steadfast in his convictions: 'Er gab die Person auf, glaubte aber noch an die Sache' (192). His dream of achieving 'most magnificent soul-fusion' (191) with Erid has failed, he claims in full seriousness, because of her 'Seelenklappenfehler' (192).

By contrast with the prose works in which Rheiner applies Heym's narrative method – such as 'Feuersbrunst', 'Die Erniedrigung' and *Kokain* – 'Der Tod des Schwärmers Gautier Fémin' is narrated in the first person, and the narrator plays a minor role in the action rather than standing entirely outside it. The narrator is a friend of Fémin, part of a circle that in addition to these two includes the 'decadent painter' Coret and the student Lebref. Throughout the first two chapters his tone is light and ironic, alternating swiftly and elegantly between matter-of-fact description, lyrical playfulness and mild mockery of his friend's grandiloquence. The final sentence of chapter 1 is illustrative:

> Nach wiederholten Fällen schlechtentschuldigten Fernbleibens von seiner Arbeit, nach erster mystischer Fahrt im Bette der Geliebten (… Weltenfahrzeug im unendlichen gesichteerfüllten Raum! …) verschlafen und verklärt am Pult hockend, fand er sich am Abend singenden Mai-Endes, leise erschrocken, doch rasch besänftigt, an den Häusern der Rue de la Banque zu den großen Boulevards hintreibend: entlassen, letztes Gehalt in der Tasche. (190–191)

The construction of the narrative displays a similar degree of easy sophistication, combining – into a seamless chronological account – the narrator's own suppositions ('Es ist möglich,' 190) and observations ('Nicht lange darauf sah man,' ibid.) with knowledge that he comes by only later ('Später erfuhr ich von ihm,' ibid.). The narrator subtly draws attention to his own role as a performer at the very beginning of the story by issuing a kind of disclaimer, a statement not of what the story is about, but of what it is *not* about: 'Ich will nicht behaupten, daß mein Freund Gautier Fémin, Bureaubeamter im Hause Dreyfus & Cie. in Paris, von jeher romantischer Schwärmer gewesen sei' (189). The effect is in fact the opposite of that stated: the reader is asked to reflect on whether Fémin may have always been a 'romantic sentimentalist,' an idea that would never have occurred without the narrator's suggestion. Such narrative mischievousness, however, proves to be merely a foreshadowing of what is to come, for in chapter 3 the narrator's performance hijacks the story entirely, dramatically relegating Fémin's romantic longing, and with it the whole over-refined chic of Parisian salon society, to the annals of cultural history:

> Seine willentlich exponierte Silhouette, aufgereckt einen Augenblick, zerbrach im Getöse und Gebrüll, – herausgeschleudert aus dem europäischen Feld. Gautier Fémin ist tot! (193)

In place of Fémin's defunct aestheticism, the narrator heralds the arrival of a new, irresistibly dynamic, violently self-confident and politically radical (if ideologically indefinite) movement that will emerge from the ruins of the old system and of which, considering his use of the first person plural, he evidently considers himself the flag-bearer:

> Wir aber schreiten aus! En avant! En avant! Wir umkreisen die fünfzehn Fronten der europäischen Völker: Aviatiker, kristalline Scheinwerfer, Säulen dröhnend im Sonnen-Aufgang! Zerrissenste irdischste Dionyse, sammeln wir uns an den enormen Städte-Pfeilern rasender Gewölbe Europas – […] Schon in den Metropolen baun sich neue Barrikaden (… und wieder: die Untergrundbahnen brechen herauf und sprühen empor! ein Bahnhof schwebt in der Luft! …), überwallt von dem zehnfarbenen, firmamenthaften Banner unendlich gewollter, *gewollter* Zukunft! (193–194)

The transformation in the cultural environment is reflected in microcosm in the transformation of the two main characters. In the course of the story Fémin turns from a dreamy idealist into a corpse, a disillusioned victim of 'necessary' suicide. His last words are recorded as 'Ich bin nichts für diese Erde! – Notwendig mein Tod! – Machen wir Schluß!' (193). The narrator, on the other hand, appears in the first two chapters as an ironic yet affectionate commentator of his friend's misadventures, as well as a pragmatic and informed *engagé*: 'Nicht interessierten ihn [Fémin] unsere, seiner Freunde, allerirdischste real-soziale und politische Erörterungen der Kunst' (191). By the end of the story he has changed into an Expressionist zealot proclaiming the dawn of a fabulous new era. This last transformation, the unmasking of the narrator in his sudden abandonment of all modesty, subtlety and restraint, is the more unsettling. Recovering from the shock effect, the reader may in fact regret the passing of the stylish prose of chapters 1 and 2, and it is doubtful whether the 'radikal expressionistische Symphonie' (8) that replaces it can generate the same level of sympathy. In this respect the narrator's Expressionist 'Begrüßung' (189) is in fact undone by his own uncontrolled exuberance.

Historically, the connection established in 'Der Tod des Schwärmers Gautier Fémin' between drug use and French *fin-de-siècle* Decadence is well-founded. In the last two decades of the 19th century the recreational use of morphine, hashish, opium and to a lesser extent cocaine increased significantly throughout Europe and North America, but nowhere more so than in France, where it extended from bohemian and artistic circles to a wide section of the population and became, for the first time, both a fashionable status symbol and a serious social problem (Kupfer *GG* 180–183). In his 1926 characterisation of *fin de siècle* Paris, Oscar Schmitz not only makes the same connection between the literary scene and drug use, but describes a decadent type to which Rheiner's Fémin conforms exactly:

> Man war dekadent und wollte es sein. Man sagte von der Literatur: Tout est dit, il n'y a plus rien à dire. So flüchteten sie sich in Mystik und Magie, und nicht selten wurde zu gefährlichen Berauschungsmitteln gegriffen wie Opium und Haschisch. (cited in Springer *N* 30)

Here Schmitz does not mention cocaine by name, but significantly Maier places Paris at the head of a list of European cities where cocaine use was common in artistic circles during the first decade of the 20th century: 'Es ist allgemein bekannt, daß damals schon in gewissen Orten, besonders in dekadenten Künstlerzirkeln, z.B. Paris, London, München und Berlin, häufiger Kokain geschnupft wurde' (62). What is surprising about 'Der Tod des Schwärmers Gautier Fémin,' therefore, is not so much the link made between cocaine use and the obsolete movement of Decadence, but its apparent exclusion from the fresh and vibrant one of Expressionism (which, as Springer notes, in many respects 'continued the tradition of this epoch'; *NBDE* 30). While the narrator and his friends discuss, passionately but soberly, the practical importance of art and are swept along in the current of large-scale social and political upheavals, Gautier Fémin closes himself off in his own fantasy world, and when this collapses he descends into a narcosis-like stupor that insulates him from the increasing turmoil around him. At both stages of this process he uses cocaine to help shut out the external world:

> 1. In Haschisch- und Kokain-Räuschen (die ihm Kellner auf Montmartre gegen gutes Trinkgeld verschafften) träumte er bald fabelhafteste Seelen-Fusion mit ihr [seiner Geliebten], ekstatisch verflochtene Zukunft, aufgerichtete Säule, eiffelturmgleich, vollendeter Einheit, Schönheit zweier Wesen. (191)
>
> 2. Dann wieder dumpf, kokaingesättigt, versunken, unberührt von anderem:– selbst von plötzlich nahenden Wirbeln politischer Komplikationen, die uns andere hinrissen in erfüllte Abende, treibende Menschenflüsse auf den Boulevards Montmartre und Poissonnière, illuminierte Telegramme, Abfahrt der Ausländer am Ost- und Nordbahnhof, plötzlich auf die Straßenzüge niederstürmende Trikoloren, nächtliche Fackel-Demonstrationen im Blitz des Eiffelturms, Massenreden und -gesang in den rotbestrahlten Himmel. (192)

In the narrator's view, the new generation of Expressionist militants represented by the *wir* of the final chapter is presumably high enough on its own adrenalin not to need any further, 'artificial' stimulation.

Unusually, then, in this story drug use in general and cocaine use in particular are characterized not as dangerous but simply as *passé*, symptomatic of an outmoded attitude to art and life. We may note that this is opposed to Benn's presentation of the drug, in his poems and plays of the two years subsequent to Rheiner's composition of 'Der Tod des Schwärmers Gautier Fémin,' as a key to a radically new aesthetic perspective and a means of liberating the artist from the oppressive norms of rational thought and social convention, in other words of accessing an 'Expressionist' as opposed to a 'Decadent' mindset (see 3.1–4.3). Despite this basic inversion, one significant point of similarity can be observed between Rheiner's story and Benn's works: intoxication causes the cocaine user to retreat into his own private world of thoughts, or rather to become so preoccupied with the ideas streaming through his head and with his own sense of self-importance that he becomes indifferent to all other considerations. 'Cocaine-sated' torpidity similar to that of Gautier Fémin can be seen in other fictional users as well, for example the protagonist of Pitigrilli's 1921 novel *Cocaina*, who feels, when intoxicated, that he would gladly 'let everything collapse, and not lift a finger' (74).[87] The essential dissimilarity in the aesthetic function of cocaine between Benn's works and Rheiner's story is not,

---

87 'Lasciare che tutto crolli, e non sollevare un dito.'

therefore, a result of the drug's different effects on different users in different settings (as a drug–set–setting analysis might suggest; see 1.3), but arises rather from differing conceptions of the Expressionist aesthetic. For Benn, the desired perspective emerges when the *individual*, in particular the poet or artist, is able to break out of the straitjacket of conventional, 'logical' psychology through 'Ich-Zerfall', the violent disruption of his own selfhood, and cocaine is portrayed as a tool that can aid in this process. The wider social and political ramifications are given little weight. In 'Der Tod des Schwärmers Gautier Fémin,' the narrator's vision of the Expressionist revolution is intrinsically *social*. The narrator himself, an *ich* for the first three-quarters of the story, is ultimately absorbed into the *wir* of the new movement. From his point of view, the use of a 'self-centred' drug like cocaine is inevitably seen as characteristic of the decadence of the old social structure now in its death-throes.

As far as its author's history of drug use is concerned, the setting of the story in pre-War Paris raises an interesting question. In 1912 Rheiner, aged just 17, had spent several months in the city as an employee of the grain wholesaler Dreyfus & Cie, the same company specified as Fémin's employer in the opening sentence of the story (189). This autobiographical reference suggests that other aspects of the work may also be drawn from Rheiner's own experience of the French capital. Whether this experience included exposure to Fémin's drugs cocaine and hashish is impossible to determine conclusively, but seems likely given the writer's evident familiarity with the method and ease of procuring such substances in that city: 'In Haschisch- und Kokain-Räuschen (die ihm Kellner auf Montmartre gegen gutes Trinkgeld verschafften) träumte er bald fabelhafteste Seelen-Fusion mit ihr' (191). Historical studies confirm that Montmartre was indeed the centre of the illicit drug trade in Paris at that time (e.g. Boon 63; Castoldi 157).[88] The inference is that Rheiner's acquaintance with cocaine may well predate, by at least two years, his first trip to Berlin and his fateful meeting with Becher and the other Expressionists. What is more certain is that by the time he came to write the story in November 1915, Rheiner had become a regular user, and from this perspective, 'Der Tod des Schwärmers Gautier Fémin' invites interpretation as a form of distance-taking, an im-

88 This trade was illicit not because the sale of cocaine was illegal (it would become so only a few years later), but because by law the drug could be obtained only from chemists.

plicit attempt to relegate drug use to the past along with an artistic ideal, and indeed a whole system of thought and way of life, that had been overtaken by more progressive cultural-historical currents. Here cocaine use is portrayed as just one, almost incidental trapping in the lifestyle of the 'romantischer Schwärmer' (189), and the implication is that it could be expected to disappear along with the social conditions that allow such a lifestyle to exist. However, the problem would prove to be much more deeply rooted, and the next chapter in the master narrative of Rheiner's addiction would represent a more urgent attempt to free himself from the drug's hold.

6.3 Two Portraits of the Addict as a Madman

We have already mentioned the 'close correspondences' between Rheiner's story 'Die Erniedrigung' and his novella *Kokain*, first published within months of one another in 1918 (see 5.2), and several of these correspondences have already emerged more or less incidentally at various points in this discussion. These can be summarised as follows: that the protagonist is a cocaine addict called Tobias (see 6.2)[89]; that the physical, psychological and social degradation brought about by cocaine addiction is the main theme (see 5.2); that the textual enactment of cocaine use is driven by a strong spatial dynamic that operates first along a horizontal and then along a vertical axis (see 6.2); that both works appear to embody an autobiographical impulse (5.2); that their most obvious autobiographical features include the protagonist's feelings of guilt and shame towards mother and sister-figures (see 5.1); and that as far as their place in Rheiner's literary development is concerned, they reflect a selective and strategic re-deployment – following the break evident in 'Der Tod des Schwärmers Gautier

89 The Biblical story in which Tobias exorcises a murderous demon possessing his wife Sarah and then cures his devout father's blindness, from the apocryphal Book of Tobit, promotes ideals of benevolence and prayer with assurances that God is merciful to the long-suffering and righteous. Therefore, Rheiner's choice of name seems ironic.

Fémin' – of a narrative model the author had experimented with several years previously, notably in the sketch 'Feuersbrunst', and that can be associated with the prose works of Georg Heym (see 5.2). In the discussion that follows, the relationship between these two works, the manner and extent of their borrowings from Heym, and their place in Rheiner's œuvre will be investigated in more depth.

This list of parallels between 'Die Erniedrigung' and *Kokain* made above is by no means exhaustive, and several other correspondences warrant attention. For example, the two narratives have a very similar temporal structure, both tracing their protagonists' tormented final hours over the course of one night, ending early the next morning with their respective deaths (in truth, the protagonist of 'Die Erniedrigung' shows signs of life in the work's final lines, despite having fallen several storeys onto asphalt; nonetheless, the story carries the parenthetical subtitle *Ein Totentanz* and the final chapter is entitled, also parenthetically, 'Requiem'). Similarities in detail can also be noted within this overall framework, such as that dawn in both works is experienced as malevolent: in 'Die Erniedrigung' the rays of the new day's sunlight are likened to 'millions of needles' (*M* 105), while in *Kokain* the day's hostility is directed at Tobias personally: 'Der Tag quoll mächtig empor und grollte ihm dumpf' (*KLPB* 218). A further parallel can be observed at the beginning of the temporal progression, with both narratives drawing attention to the time of day: Tobias's nighttime trek is introduced in 'Die Erniedrigung' by the exclamation 'Ein Uhr durch!'(*M* 100), and in *Kokain* by the spectral image of a public clock: 'Die Normaluhr (ehernes Gespenst an der Straßenkreuzung) zeigte schon halb elf' (*KLPB* 195), with further references interspersed through the novella charting the increasing lateness of the hour: first midnight (*KLPB* 203), later half past 12 (*KLPB* 206), then half past two (*KLPB* 212). In both narratives, this lateness can perhaps be read as a first signal of the protagonist's alienation from the bourgeoisie, whose work ethic would normally impose more conservative bedtimes. The first chapter of *Kokain* relates a reflection by the protagonist containing a further reference to clock time that supports this interpretation: 'Was war dies: das Aufstehen morgens um zehn oder elf Uhr, manchmal auch mittags; dies Aufstehen mit dem tiefen Ekel vor seinem Zimmer, vor seinen Büchern, seinen Kleidern, seiner eigenen Person?' (*KLPB* 196–197). The autobiographical basis of these works is underlined when this passage is read against Fo's letter of October 1920 cited above (see 5.1), in which the poet is criticised for staying in bed until 11 o'clock, when in his wife's view he should have been out looking for gainful employment (*KLPB* 262).

In addition to the initial time reference just described, we have already identified a common basic structure in the walking scenes with which the two narratives open: restless movement through an urban landscape followed by multiple cocaine injections leading to an hallucinatory levitation (see 6.1). The shift evident here in Tobias's mood from agitation to euphoria can be linked to a larger pattern informing both narratives, which repeatedly record fluctuations in the protagonist's state of mind. The general tendency is towards increasing agitation or derangement, from which cocaine injections provide all too temporary relief while perpetuating the addiction that has given rise to his psychological lability in the first place. This vicious circularity is alluded to at the beginning of *Kokain*, where Tobias is described as 'ergriffen von jener düsteren Unruhe, die immer wiederkam und ihn desto mehr quälte, je mehr er ihr zu entfliehen oder sie zu betäuben suchte' (*KLPB* 196). The brevity of the relief cocaine provides on two specific occasions is underlined rhetorically in 'Die Erniedrigung' by use of the conjunctional adverb *doch*:

1. Hastig nahm er zwei weitere Spritzen. –
   Sofort ward ihm wohler und unendlich ruhig. Die Augen schlossen sich. *Doch* dann gingen sie wieder wie zwei dunkle Monde auf: weit! weit! (*M* 101; italics added)

2. Schnell nahm er eine Spritze.
   Nun schwieg es ein wenig. *Doch* plötzlich klingelte es (mitten in der Nacht!), die Tür ging, jemand trat nebenan ins Zimmer. (*M* 102; italics added)

The same rhetorical gesture is used in *Kokain* in a description of the generic pattern:

> Wie oft, war er auch diesmal dort [ins Café] hingeflohen vor dem Zergehen der sommerlichen Sonne, das weich über den nahen Himmel rann und seine Unruhe zum Irrsinn zu steigern drohte.
> Und *doch* siegte immer diese Unruhe, die, wenn sie kam, ihm alle Räume verhaßt machte. (*KLPB* 196; italics added)

The reference to the threat of insanity (*Irrsinn*) in this last passage signals that the protagonists' alternating states of agitation and calm can be linked to the other symptoms of substance-induced psychosis they display in the course of their respective stories. Two such symptoms are especially salient:

paranoid delusions and misperceptions, whether as illusions (misperception of external stimuli) or hallucinations (perception in the absence of external stimuli). As far as paranoid delusions are concerned, three related manifestations can be identified, all of which occur in both texts, albeit with variations in form and emphasis: first, the protagonist's perception of his cocaine addiction as an object of moral condemnation (by both his family and society in general); second, his perception of his cocaine addiction as an object of surveillance; and third, in a grotesque extension of this, his perception of his cocaine addiction as a public spectacle. In 'Die Erniedrigung,' which is set mainly in the Cologne flat that Tobias shares with his mother and sister, the protagonist sees his two immediate family members as the primary sources of disapprobation and is haunted by visions of their reproaches, as in this example involving his sister: 'Die Schwester, Ly, hatte sich hinter den Kleidern am Garderobenständer verborgen und schnalzte mißbilligend mit der Zunge' (*M* 104). Later in the story, when Tobias is standing at his bedroom window confronting the crowd that has gathered to watch him, a similarly moralizing (if more openly aggressive) attitude is attributed to a leading representative of a public institution:

> Jetzt wandten sich plötzlich alle Polizisten um und schauten scharf nach Tobias; einer trat vor (die Menschenmenge rauschte, ein Meer) und (es war der Polizeihauptmann in glitzernder Uniform) schrie herüber: 'He! Sie! Sie da! Zum Donnerwetter! Lassen Sie das jetzt sein! Schämen Sie sich nicht!? … Sie Tier!!' (*M* 106)

In *Kokain*, which is set mainly on the streets of Berlin, this development is inverted, with expressions of reprobation from strangers preceding and outnumbering those from family members, as in the sequence of auditory hallucinations Tobias is subject to after climbing the staircase to the landing outside the apartment of his friend Marion:

> *'Das muß endlich aufhören … Es ist ein Skandal … Das Schwein ruiniert sich und seine Angehörigen … Ins Irrenhaus mit dem Subjekt! … Wir werden ihn ins Automobil schaffen … Packen Sie ihn nur gleich! … Und daß er nicht die Flasche austrinkt, das bringt der Kerl fertig …'*
> Tobias zitterte. Schweiß rann ihm (… oder war es Blut?). Er hörte die Stimme seiner Mutter, während das Licht wieder erlosch:
> *'Tobias, mein Sohn! Tobias, ich flehe dich an! … Tobias, Tobias! …… Tobias ……!'* (*KLPB* 210; italics in the original)

In his paranoia, Tobias perceives members of the public he encounters by chance while roaming about the city not only as judges and vilifiers, but also as spies, undercover policemen or informants for his mother. When in chapter 4 he enters a public toilet at an intersection of the Kurfürstendamm, for example, he convinces himself that an elderly gentleman just preparing to leave the rotunda is somehow involved in a coordinated operation aimed at his capture and committal to a psychiatric institution:

> Tobias fühlte sich beobachtet. [...] Um Gottes Willen! Das war ein Detektiv, ein Sanitätsbeamter, ein Abgesandter der Mutter, der er vorhin begegnet war und die sich vor ihm verbarg! [...] Gewißlich standen sie jetzt draußen im Kreis um die Rotunde, ein schweigender Kordon. Handschellen klirrten, Zwangsjacke war zum Überwerfen bereit. [...] In letzter Wirrnis zu allem entschlossen, verließ er schließlich die Bude und wankte ins Freie hinaus.
> Er war sehr erstaunt, niemand vorzufinden, der auf ihn lauerte. (*KLPB* 205–206)

In 'Die Erniedrigung,' Tobias continues to feel watched within his own bedroom, even with the curtains drawn and the door closed:

> Halt! man könnte ihn beobachten! ... Er verhüllte sorgfältig die Fenster, schloß die Zimmertür ab und hing seinen Hut an die Klinke. – Doch die Photographien auf der Kommode konnten den geheimen Beobachtern vielleicht als Spiegel dienen! (*M* 102)

With the photographs laid flat so they can no longer function as mirrors for external observers, Tobias begins to suspect that his room has been infiltrated, specifically that his sister is spying on him from under the sofa:

> Er schreckte auf und sah sich um. Doch sofort warf er den Körper wieder zurück, denn unter dem Sofa bewegte sich etwas ... Sollte es seine Schwester sein, die der schlafenden Mutter Lichtsignale gab über seinen Zustand und die Anzahl der Spritzen? ... Er sprang auf, suchte unter dem Sofa, nahm eine neue Spritze, lachte (es war die Katze), löschte das Gaslicht und legte sich von neuem zu Bett. (ibid.)

Even the realization that the only other living creature in his room is the cat, however, is insufficient to free Tobias from the *idée fixe* that he is being spied on. His paranoia is so acute that it is easier for him to believe that the cat herself is party to the elaborate surveillance operation than to accept that no such operation exists. When he gets up again after a sleepless night we are told that he trips over the cat, 'die aufrecht saß, in beiden Vorderpfoten kleine Spiegel hielt und Lichtsignale gab' (*M* 103)! Later on we learn that the cat, 'walking sardonically' and 'with ironic paws' over the 'thousand heads' in the crowd beneath Tobias's window, has a name singularly well suited to her role as a spy: Iris (*M* 106).

The shift in the protagonists' perceptions of their cocaine addictions from objects of condemnation and surveillance to sources of entertainment – with a distinctly voyeuristic slant – for the general public is one of degree rather than of kind, and as such can be interpreted as a further sign of the acuteness of their respective paranoias. Both Tobiases experience the physical and psychological degradation brought about by their addictive illnesses as a very public loss of face, a loss they equate with farcical theatrical productions in which they unwittingly play the starring roles. In *Kokain* the theatrical metaphor is explicit and extended:

> Das war seine Mutter und seine Schwester. Aber waren die nicht in Köln?
> Gewiß, die mußten eigentlich in Köln sein! Aber wer weiß? Vielleicht hatte sie der Herr Bahnhofsvorsteher telegraphisch nach Berlin gerufen, damit die Mutter ihren Sohn, die Schwester ihren Bruder sehen könne, teilnehmen könne an dem unterhaltenden Schauspiel, das das Publikum von Berlin W allabendlich genoß, interessanter und billiger als im Palast-Theater oder in Nelsons Künstlerspielen, an der amüsanten Tragikomödie: *'Der Kloakenprinz' oder: 'Mein Gott, mein Gott, warum hast du mich verlassen.'* (*KLPB* 203–204)

Whereas here the theatricality remains metaphorical, in 'Die Erniedrigung' it is enacted diegetically in the accumulation of spectators, some even equipped with appropriate optical aids, in front of Tobias's window, as described in the passage already cited above as representative of Rheiner's affinities with Kafka (see 5.2).

In addition to the violent mood swings and paranoid delusions already described, visual and auditory illusions and hallucinations can be identified as the third important symptom of mental imbalance linking the two protagonists. Several examples of such illusions and hallucinations are evident in the excerpts cited above to illustrate the various manifestations of their paranoia: in *Kokain*, the condemnatory voices Tobias hears emanating from the bottom of the stairwell while cowering on Marion's landing, or the vision of his mother and sister on a Berlin street when he knows they must really be in Cologne; in 'Die Erniedrigung,' the policeman's public remonstrance, or the appearance of the cat using small mirrors to communicate with an unseen observer. An especially striking parallel between the two works is that they both contain passages in which the protagonist manifests doubts about the reliability of his own sensory perception, in effect an acknowledgment of his own susceptibility to illusions and hallucinations. In both these passages, he crawls around on the floor in search of something, stopping to examine every object he encounters to make sure that it is not the one in question. In 'Die Erniedrigung,' the primary object of his search appears to be his sister, even though Tobias has just seen her body lying smashed on the street below after she had jumped – for no apparent reason – through his bedroom window:

> Tobias suchte krampfhaft auf dem Fußboden herum. Was suchte er doch? … Nadeln, die Schwester, oder einen Teil des anmutigen, zerschmetterten Körperchens? Seine Hände und Knie waren voll Schmutz, denn die müde Mutter reinigte längst nicht mehr Tobias' Zimmer. Unzählige Streichhölzer, Watte, Kerzen- und Blutstropfen lagen herum. Tobias nahm alles in die Finger, nestelte daran und betrachtete es genauest. Er hatte Angst, alle diese Gegenstände könnten die Schwester sein, und er sähe nur so falsch … (*M* 105)

In *Kokain*, Tobias gets up from the bed Marion has prepared for him to look for another bottle of cocaine solution he already knows is not there, 'aber sein Wunsch siegte sinnlos über die Logik' (*KLPB* 218):

> Er stieg vom Bett und suchte, auf den Knieen rutschend, sich mit einem Blut, das in dicken Tropfen auf dem Fußboden vor dem Bette lag, besudelnd, das Zimmer ab. Er traute nicht der Kraft seiner Augen. Er betastete jeden Gegenstand, nahm ihn in die Hand und hielt ihn dicht vor die Augen. Konnte das nicht eine Kokainflasche sein, oder jenes, oder dies? Wer sagte ihm, daß ihn seine Augen nicht trogen! *War das, was wie ein Pantoffel aussah, wirklich ein Pantoffel, nichts anderes? Wer konnte es wissen?* (ibid.; italics in the original)

If, as these passages demonstrate, the protagonists share an awareness of the malfunction of their own cognitive apparatus, they also share an intense fear of insanity and its consequences, in particular institutionalization. In 'Die Erniedrigung' this fear is evident in Tobias's response – 'O Gott! Der Arzt!' (*M* 103) – to the (probably hallucinatory) conversation he overhears between his mother, sister and the chemist Herr Pagenstecher:

> Die Mutter weinte. Jetzt hörte Tobias ganz deutlich die Schwester sprechen: 'Ist das nicht fürchterlich mit Tobias? … Wie er die Augen aufreißt! Man sollte einen Arzt holen! Er wird wahnsinnig!' Der Apotheker nickte traurig. Die Mutter schluchzte: 'Ja, Herr Pagenstecher, holen Sie den Arzt!' Der Apotheker wandte sich und ging. (ibid.)

The lie he tells his mother shortly afterwards – 'Ich habe nur eine einzige Spritze genommen!' (*M* 104) – is to all appearances a feeble attempt to dissuade her from pursuing medical intervention. In the more extended narrative *Kokain*, fear of madness becomes a recurrent motif and effectively frames Tobias's story, with the initial threat of an intensification of his 'Unruhe zum Irrsinn' (*KLPB* 196) mirrored in the final chapter, immediately before his suicide, by the realization that his psychological decline is now unstoppable: 'Ausgefetzt würde er hinstehlen sein Leben lang, vom Morgen bis zum Abend, der ihm einst den Wahnsinn bringen würde' (*KLPB* 224). The intervening narrative contains several more expressions of this fear. First, Tobias's misadventure in the public toilet leads him to implore the elderly gentleman he mistakenly believes is spying on him not to call the enforcers he is sure are lurking with a straightjacket ready to bundle him off: 'Ich versichere Ihnen, wirklich, glauben Sie mir: *ich bin nicht wahnsinnig! Noch nicht!* Auch nicht betrunken oder vergiftet! Glauben Sie mir! Pfeifen Sie nicht Ihren Leuten! Lassen Sie mich gehen!' (*KLPB* 206; italics in the original). Second, the discussion Tobias hallucinates on the landing outside Marion's apartment is similarly concerned with his capture and transport to an asylum (*KLPB* 210). Third, lying in bed in Marion's apartment, he convinces himself that the shadows he can see moving on the ceiling are being cast either by thieves attempting to break in or by policemen coming to arrest him. Here the most pressing reason for the addict's fear of committal is revealed: 'Waren es Detektive, so würden sie beide in Schutzhaft genommen werden, und gegen ihn, Tobias, würde man Anklage erheben. Er würde in eine Anstalt kommen, jahrelang, und kein Kokain mehr erhalten' (*KLPB* 215). Marion's reaction to these ravings echoes the family's worried conversation with the chemist from 'Die Erniedrigung': 'Marion begann an seinem Verstand zu zweifeln. – *Ist's schon so weit mit ihm?* dachte sie' (*KLPB* 216; italics in the original). A fourth and final reference to Tobias's 'Angst vor dem Irrenhaus' (*KLPB* 217) occurs shortly afterwards when he has drained the final drops of cocaine solution from his bottle, only here this fear evaporates in the face of an even more urgent problem:

> Vergessen die Furcht vor den Einbrechern oder Detektiven, erloschen die Angst vor dem Irrenhaus! Nur eines erfüllte ihn, nur eines brannte sein Inneres aus:– der unbeugsame, unerbittliche, unwiderstehliche, dieser metaphysisch-unergründliche Trieb, der Wunsch nach dem Gift, das ihm Atem und Leben, Luft und Trank, Sein und Zeit bedeutete! (ibid.)

At this point Tobias becomes walking testimony to the annihilation of the personality as a consequence of addictive illness, to *Ich-Zerfall* gone horribly wrong. His fear of madness may have been suspended, but this suspension is itself symptomatic of his lack of control over his own cognitive processes, and so an ironic confirmation of his mental illness. Despite his desperate assertion, '*ich bin nicht wahnsinnig! Noch nicht!*' (*KLPB* 206), the weight of textual evidence makes it clear that both he and his namesake in the short story have already reached an advanced stage of substance-induced psychosis. Indeed, we are now in a position to recognise the most fundamental similarity between these two works as their portrayal of the cocaine addict as a madman. Considering this observation alongside the affinity already established between Rheiner's short prose and Heym's (see 5.2), it will come as no surprise that Heym's own portrait of a madman, the tale 'Der Irre' (first published posthumously alongside 'Der Dieb' in 1913), presents itself as a likely model for Rheiner's narratives.

To begin with, we might note the various basic structural features linking 'Der Irre' with 'Die Erniedrigung' and *Kokain*. As far as its temporal structure is concerned, Heym's plot, like Rheiner's, traces the protagonist's final hours in a linear progression that ends with his violent death, and like *Kokain*, 'Der Irre' has an episodic plot structure reminiscent of the *Stationendrama*-form popular among Expressionist playwrights. Following its protagonist's movement through the urban landscape – 'Er kam durch ein paar volle Straßen, über einen Platz, wieder durch Straßen' (2:31) – 'Der Irre,' like Rheiner's stories, emphasises his psychological detachment from it, as well as the unease it generates in him: 'Da waren ziemlich viele Menschen, die an ihm vorübergingen, ohne auf ihn zu achten. Eine elektrische Bahn fuhr vorbei. / Ihn überkam das Gefühl einer grenzenlosen Verlassenheit, das Heimweh packte ihn mit aller Gewalt' (2:28). This homesickness is replicated in both 'Die Erniedrigung' and *Kokain*:

> 'Die Erniedrigung': Nicht konnte er es erwarten, nach Hause zu kommen. (*M* 101)
>
> *Kokain*: Oh, nun wünschte er zu Hause zu sein. (*KLPB* 208)

The prowling of Heym's mad protagonist, which begins with his release from an asylum on the periphery of an unspecified town, from there taking him ever closer to its centre, operates spatially along both horizontal and vertical axes, culminating, as in 'Die Erniedrigung,' in a final fall witnessed by a crowd that has gathered for the show. Significant correspondences can be noted not only in the basic patterns of movement themselves, but also in their representation; for example, the madman's final elevation is depicted metaphorically as suspension above a luminous ocean similar to that into which Tobias falls towards the end of Rheiner's short story:

> 'Der Irre': Unter ihm in dem Ozean war ein riesiges Licht. Er mußte jetzt herabtauchen, jetzt war es Zeit, auf das Meer zu sinken. (2:33)

> 'Die Erniedrigung': Im Stürzen sah er noch, wie drüben alle Balkone abbröckelten und mit den Zuschauern pfeifend in die Tiefe fuhren. … Im Ozean von Getöse und Licht versank alles … (*M* 107)

Several of the qualities we have identified as common to the two Tobiases can also be seen in Heym's unnamed protagonist. Like theirs, his mood is highly unstable and characterised by sudden and mostly unprovoked shifts ('mit einem Mal schlug seine Stimmung um', 2:23) between states of agitation – in his case manifested as murderous aggression – and calm. A striking lexical correspondence is evident in the evocations of the latter state in the three texts.

> 'Der Irre': Ein unendlicher Friede, eine ewige Ruhe zitterte unter diesem ewigen Himmel. (2:33)

> 'Die Erniedrigung': Sofort ward ihm wohler und unendlich ruhig. (*M* 101)

> *Kokain*: Er war ganz ruhig geworden und unendlich müde. (*KLPB* 220)

In all three cases the infinity-topos is heavily infused with irony; despite its perception as 'unendlich', this calm will last only until the next mood swing and will in fact prove to be of all too limited duration. Further correspondences can be observed between Rheiner's and Heym's depictions of their respective protagonist's moments of euphoria, as well as their fits of rage. Following Tobias's first three injections in *Kokain*, we are told: 'Nun fühlte er sich frei und leicht, spielerisch, ein junger Gott!' (*KLPB* 198); Heym's madman, upon the sight of his first victim's blood, experiences an equivalent apotheosis: 'Das berauschte ihn, machte ihn zu einem Gott' (2:23). On the other hand, Tobias flies off the handle when Marion, confronted with her friend's physical degradation as he undresses before going to bed, is overcome by nausea: 'Tobias, ratlos und verzweifelt, begann laut zu brüllen' (*KLPB* 213); the anger of Heym's protagonist towards his wife, whom he blames for his committal to the asylum from which he has just been released, is expressed in the same way: 'Er fing an zu schreien. Er brüllte wie besessen' (2:30).

A related feature linking the three characters is their attribution of their own psychological instability to an external agency; in other words, all three see themselves as possessed. In *Kokain* Tobias's victimhood, his reduction to an object of possession, is attendant upon the use of the statal passive in the description of him as 'ergriffen von jener düsteren Unruhe, die immer wiederkam und ihn desto mehr quälte, je mehr er ihr zu entfliehen oder sie zu betäuben suchte' (*KLPB* 196). In this way, Tobias ('er') is rhetorically constructed as distinct from his own agitation ('sie'), by which he is 'ergriffen'. In 'Die Erniedrigung,' the state of possession is presented as physiological internalization, with a 'macabre' craving for cocaine having taken up residence in the protagonist's spinal column: 'ein makabrer Drang, ein unergründliches, unbegreifliches, unwiderstehliches Sehnen nach dem Gift im Rückgrat' (*M* 101). In 'Der Irre,' the possessing agency is apprehended metaphorically as a wild animal; as in 'Die Erniedrigung,' it is viscerally located, and as in 'Kokain', the protagonist's resistance to its malign power proves futile:

> Er fühlte, daß in ihm wieder die Wut aufkommen wollte. Er fürchtete sich vor dieser dunklen Tollheit. Pfui, jetzt wird sie mich gleich wieder haben, dachte er. Ihn schwindelte, er hielt sich an einem Baum und schloß die Augen.
> Plötzlich sah er das Tier wieder, das in ihm saß. Unten zwischen dem Magen, wie eine große Hyäne. Hatte die einen Rachen. Und das Aas wollte raus. Ja, ja, du mußt raus. Jetzt war er selber das Tier, und auf allen vieren kroch er die Straße entlang. (2:25)

Heym's protagonist takes on animal form on several further occasions, appearing variously as a jackal, a fish, an orang-utan, and in his final and most extended metaphorical incarnation, as 'a great white bird' ('Teufel, was war es doch schön, ein Vogel zu sein. Warum war er nicht schon lange ein Vogel geworden?'; 2:33). Although less pronounced, tendencies towards the animalization of the protagonist (a motif famously taken to its extreme in Kafka's 'Die Verwandlung,' first published in 1915) can be observed in both of Rheiner's narratives, as well. In 'Kokain', Tobias characterizes himself as '*die stinkende Kellerassel, das Klärichtvieh*' (*KLPB* 202; italics in the original), while a more generic animal epithet is applied to him in the reproof he ascribes to one of the customers at the café: 'Diese Bestie pumpt sich jeden Abend mit Kokain voll!' (*KLPB* 200). This echoes the final insult aimed at his namesake by the policeman in 'Die Erniedrigung': 'Sie Tier!!' (*M* 106). An even more striking parallel between 'Die Erniedrigung' and 'Der Irre' is the casting of anthropomorphized animals as secondary characters. In this respect, the cat's mirror-signalling cameo in the former is analogous to the protagonist's belief in the latter that a rat he finds scurrying through his abandoned apartment is really his wife, with whom he is determined to get even ('er hatte ja mit seiner Frau abzurechnen'; 2:24):

> Aber da war sie ja, da lief sie ja herum. Sie sah aus wie eine große graue Ratte. So also sah sie aus. Sie lief immer an der Küchenwand entlang, und er riß eine eiserne Platte von dem Ofen und warf sie nach der Ratte. (2:30)

This scene highlights a further feature the three narratives have in common: the protagonist's search for a particular woman character is an important plot element in each. In 'Der Irre' the woman in question is his wife, in 'Die Erniedrigung' his sister ('alle diese Gegenstände könnten die Schwester sein, und er sähe nur so falsch'; *M* 105), and in *Kokain* his friend Marion, 'dies milde Geschöpf, das einzige, das ihn nicht verstieß, ihn, den Paria ohne Freunde, den jedes Haus ausspie wie einen eklen Auswurf' (*KLPB* 222). A certain qualification is necessary here in so far as the hostility of Heym's protagonist towards the object of his search contrasts sharply with the good will of Rheiner's towards theirs; moreover, each of their searches has a quite different motivation. Whereas the visit made by Heym's protagonist to his former place of residence is driven by a thirst for violent revenge, Tobias's scrabbling about on the floor in 'Die Erniedrigung' appears to be prompted by concern for his sister's welfare, while in *Kokain* it is the addict's need for refuge, solace and not least a reprieve from his sense of – characteristically Expressionist – existential isolation ('Wohin, wohin, mein Gott, in seiner Not! Barhäuptig stand er unter den Sternen'; *KLPB* 208) that leads him to seek out his 'goldene Freundin aus dem Café' (*KLPB* 209).[90] Nonetheless, despite these substantial differences in motivation, equally substantial similarities are evident in the modes in which these searches are enacted as narrative, especially between 'Der Irre' and *Kokain*. In both these works, the protagonist is shown walking across town

90 For Marion's role as a Maria-figure and mother substitute, see Atai 61–62.

to the apartment building where the relevant female character lives (*Kokain*) or is presumed to be living ('Der Irre'), but in order to reach this destination has to overcome his own tendency to distraction that threatens to throw him off course:

> 'Der Irre': Ja, wo nun hin? / Da fiel ihm seine Aufgabe wieder ein. Er hatte ja mit seiner Frau abzurechnen. (2:24)

> *Kokain*: Fast hatte er schon vergessen, was er hier wollte, als sich Schritte dem Hause näherten. (*KLPB* 209)

Once at the building, both have to climb stairs to get to the female character's apartment, and during this ascent, fear of discovery by other residents of the building prompts both to proceed with exaggerated caution:

> 'Der Irre': Er ging die Stiege hinauf. Überall roch es nach Essen. Er schlich auf den Zehenspitzen weiter. Als er unter sich eine Tür aufgehen hörte, zog er auch noch die Schuhe aus. (2:28–29)

> *Kokain*: Tobias schlich zagend zum vierten Stock empor, mit tödlicher Angst vor jedem Treppenabsatz, der ihn an einer Wohnung vorbeiführte. (*KLPB* 210)

When repeated knocking on the apartment door (*Kokain*) or ringing the bell ('Der Irre') brings no response, both bend down to the keyhole:

> 'Der Irre': Er bückte sich, um durch das Schlüsselloch zu sehen, da war aber alles schwarz. (2:29)

> *Kokain*: Er beugte sich zum Schlüsselloch nieder und rief 'Marion! Marion!' mit unterdrückter Stimme hinein. (*KLPB* 212)

Inside the apartment, both become enraged and vent their anger by yelling, as already described. Finally, within the apartment building the protagonist either becomes ('Der Irre') or sees himself as (*Kokain*) an object of public persecution. In this respect, Tobias's hallucination of the conversation between his putative pursuers (cited above) corresponds to the formation in 'Der Irre' of a crowd intent upon putting an end to the madman's rampage. In the depiction of this pursuit the two narratives converge lexically once again:

'Der Irre': Überall klapperten die Türen, überall entstand Lärm. Jetzt kam es schon die Treppe herauf. (2:30)

Kokain: Tapp, tapp, tapp! Man stieg die Treppen herauf, regelmäßig, immer näher. (*KLPB* 210)

The portrayal of the protagonist within an apartment building as an object of physical assault by members of the public (as opposed to the imaginary assault in *Kokain*) links 'Der Irre' with 'Die Erniedrigung.' In the latter, the assault comes about as the spectators gathered on the street and on nearby balconies become increasingly aggressive towards Tobias, who is standing at his window: 'Einige sprangen von den Balkonen herunter und kletterten eilig an der Fassade des Hauses empor, auf Tobias' Zimmerfenster zu' (*M* 106). This sudden display of prodigious, almost superhuman athleticism can be identified as a further element of congruence with 'Der Irre,' only here it is displayed by the protagonist himself, rather than his assailants, and provides his means of escape from their assault:

Mit ein paar großen Sätzen sprang der Irrsinnige wie ein riesiger Orang-Utan mitten über das Volk hinweg. Er raste die Treppen hinauf, kam an die Bodenleiter, schwang sich auf das Dach, kroch über ein paar Mauern, um Schornsteine, verschwand in einer Luke, stürzte eine Treppe hinunter und befand sich plötzlich auf einem grünen Platz. (2:30)

The parallels between the three protagonists – which already cover their patterns of movement and thought, as well as their relationships to other characters and to their physical and social environment – can be extended to include their physical appearance, as well. The first observation to be made here is that the three works display, in effect, a negative equivalence, in that none dwells at length on the protagonist's physical features as objects worthy in themselves of particular narrative attention, a lack consistent at a general level with the essentializing tendency of Expressionism, as apparent in its representation of human subjects as in any other respect,[91] and in particular with the demands of the figural perspective employed. Nonetheless, in so far as a character's physical appearance can be assessed in the reactions it elicits from other characters, Rheiner's characterization once again follows Heym's closely, with both 'Der Irre' and *Kokain* describ-

91 As early as 1913 Kurt Hiller identified the defining characteristic of Expressionism as 'die konzentrierte Hervortreibung des voluntarisch Wesentlichen' (cited in Best 4).

ing panicked acts of flight (and screaming) provoked by the mere sight of the protagonist:

> 'Der Irre': Die Frau sah sich um. Als sie da einen Mann auf Händen und Füßen hinter sich herlaufen sah, das wirre Haar in dem dicken Gesicht, weiß von Staub, da ließ sie ihren Wagen stehen und laut schreiend rannte sie die Straße hinunter. (2:25)

> *Kokain*: Dabei verzerrte sich sein Gesicht, und die Schläfen spielten wie Wellen. War nicht neulich, auf dem Alexanderplatz, eine alte hinkende Frau schreiend vor ihm geflüchtet, als sie dieses fratzenschneidende Gesicht sah? (*KLPB* 214)

Consistent with such responses, one quality all three narratives underline is the protagonist's state of dirtiness and dishevelment, which can be considered a further symptom of his failure to conform with society's behavioural norms:

> 'Der Irre': Er trat aus den Halmen heraus, allenthalben klebte Stroh an seinem Anzug und an seinem Haar. [...] Und die Kletten, die an seiner Hose saßen, flogen in weiten Bögen ab. (2:22)

> 'Die Erniedrigung': Seine Hände und Knie waren voll Schmutz, denn die müde Mutter reinigte längst nicht mehr Tobias' Zimmer. (*M* 105)

> *Kokain*: Dann betrachtete er seinen schmierigen Anzug, die schadhaften Stiefel. Durch die Ärmel des hellen Jacketts drangen Blutflecke; auch die Hose zeigte Spuren. (*KLPB* 223)

The more specific image of bloodstained clothing evident in the last of these passages is a motif that *Kokain* shares with 'Der Irre.' Moreover, in both narratives the protagonist is shown trying either to remove (*Kokain*) or to hide ('Der Irre') such stains to make himself presentable, signalling an at least passing recognition of the need to bring himself into line with normative behaviour for the purpose of successful social functioning.

> 'Der Irre': Er ging also auf den Schutzmann los. Plötzlich merkte er, daß auf seiner Weste noch ein großer Blutfleck war. Na, den durfte der Schutzmann aber nicht zu sehen kriegen. Und er knöpfte seinen Rock zu. (2:28)

> *Kokain*: Hatten diese Menschen, dieses Gebräu aus Hohn und Schadenfreude, nichts anderes zu tun, als ihm aufzulauern, sich am Bahnhof aufzustellen um Mitternacht, um dies Schauspiel zu genießen:– wie er, der Kokainist, aus seiner Kloake gekrochen

kam, mit blutenden Armen und Beinen, an die sich das Hemd festklebte? Fluch über sie! Fluch über seinen hellen Anzug ... Da: waren das nicht schon Blutflecke?
Er feuchtete die Fingerspitzen an und wollte so die Flecken fortreiben. (*KLPB* 203)

A distinction not apparent from the comparison of these two passages is that whereas Tobias's clothes are stained by his own blood, those of Heym's madman are stained by the blood of his victims, even if he does not recognise it as such: ' "Aber pfui, bin ich schmutzig." Er besah sich. "Wo kommt denn das viele Blut her?" ' (2:27). Thus, if the bloodstains in 'Der Irre' continue to bear witness to the madman's acts of violence upon others even after these appear to have been dismissed from his consciousness, recurrent references to the protagonist's bleeding in *Kokain* serve as visible reminders of the violence the addict insistently inflicts upon himself, as well as of the imminent threat of his own physical disintegration. In 'Die Erniedrigung' this same threat is realized in a hallucination of massive and uncontrollable bleeding prompted by an accident with a syringe:

Er setzte sich aufs Bett und gab sich zwei Injektionen hintereinander. Bei der zweiten hatte er die Nadel zu tief eingestochen; flink quoll ein dünnes, hellrotes Rinnsal, kroch vom Oberarm bis zum Handgelenk, tropfte auf den Schenkel und lief das Bein entlang bis zur Fußsohle. Es sah aus wie Eisenbahnlinien auf einer Landkarte. Die Watte tränkte sich rot, so oft Tobias das Blut zu stillen versuchte. Höhnisches Gerinn! Schließlich schien ihm, als ob er aus tausend Stichen und allen Körperöffnungen blute. Todesangst packte ihn. Er ließ den Strömen ihren Lauf.– (*M* 104–105)

In their totality, these correspondences make compelling evidence for considering 'Der Irre,' the story of a madman whose insanity is never explained, as a major source for 'Die Erniedrigung' and *Kokain*, two stories of madmen whose insanity is caused by drug abuse. To paraphrase Pinthus, 'hier wird kräftig geheymt' (see 5.1). Yet perhaps the most recognisable Heym-like feature in Rheiner's narratives is derived not from 'Der Irre,' but from the monumental visions of the modern city as a playground for divine and demonic forces associated in particular with three of Heym's most famous poems, 'Der Gott der Stadt,' 'Die Dämonen der Städte' and 'Der Krieg' (Pinthus 42–43, 51–52, 79–80). Among Heym's prose works, the fullest articulation of such a vision can be found in 'Der Dieb,' whose links to one of Rheiner's early prose sketches have already been discussed (see 5.2). This tale's many Biblical references, products of the protagonist's delusional conviction that he has been chosen to fight God's final, apocalyptic battle against the forces of evil, suggest it as another probable source for 'Die Erniedrigung' and *Kokain*. In particular, the first paragraph, in which the titular thief proclaims his self-appointment in prayer ('ich bin Dein Werkzeug für und für, von nun an bis in Ewigkeit'; 2:72), mirrors the narrator's exposition of the poet's divine calling at the beginning of 'Die Erniedrigung' (see 1.2), while the thief's later belief that he has been abandoned by God is shared by Tobias in *Kokain*, a link underlined by the citation in both works of Mark 15,34: 'Mein Gott, mein Gott, warum hast du mich verlassen?' (Heym 2:75; *KLPB* 204, N.B. Rheiner's citation is italicized).[92]

In truth, the main action of 'Die Erniedrigung' takes a metaphysical turn only in the last of the story's three chapters. Much shorter than the previous two, this takes up from the collapse of Tobias's apartment block and the surrounding buildings at the end of chapter 2: 'Der Apotheker (…seht's ihr denn nicht? …) ist CHRISTUS JESUS, der über den zerfallenen Häusern und über den verfallenen Menschen sitzet und mitleidig den Kopf schüttelt' (ibid.). An analogous image of a deity atop the ruins of a fallen city occurs near the end of 'Der Krieg':

> Eine große Stadt versank im gelben Rauch,
> Warf sich lautlos in des Abgrunds Bauch.
> Aber riesig über glühenden Trümmern steht
> Der in wilde Himmel dreimal seine Fackel dreht. (Pinthus 79)

Although the sympathy of Rheiner's chemist-cum-Christ contrasts with the destructive fury of Heym's god of war (certainly closer to the Old Testament God), the link between them is reinforced by their appropriation of the moon as an aid to self-expression:

92 Another noteworthy link between *Kokain* and 'Der Dieb' is the spinning-top simile used to describe the protagonist's state of confusion and agitation:

> 'Der Dieb': Sein Gehirn drehte sich wie ein Kreisel in der Enge seines Schädels herum. (2:83)

> *Kokain*: Dann kam der große Fluch, der Abend, der ihn einspann und die dämonische Unruhe brachte, die ihn wie einen Kreisel sich um sich selbst drehen ließ. (*KLPB* 197)

'Der Krieg': In der Dämmrung steht er, groß und unbekannt,
Und den Mond zerdrückt er in der schwarzen Hand. (ibid.)

'Die Erniedrigung': Aus seiner Ulstertasche zieht er eine große Mond-Harfe. Er weint, und wie die Tränen auf die Saiten fallen, erklingt es leise:

> Du Menschensohn! Nicht spendet der Himmel Blick
> und gutes Wort zu tödlichem Jammertanz.
>> Ein Marter-Regen, dumpfe Tränen,
>> kränzen (o Bitternis!) eure Häupter! (*M* 107)

Kokain can be considered even closer to Heym's eschatological visions in that the diety presiding over the city is distinctly malevolent, a 'demon' apprehended by Tobias as a brutal parody of the Biblical God:

> Ja, siehe, da standen die bebenden Sterne wieder still, einen Augenblick lang. – Heiliges Gift! Heiliges Gift! – Das fühlte Tobias und sah den Dämon, der ihm ebenso vertraut wie schrecklich war, weit über dem nächtigen Himmel stehen. Er wußte und flüsterte es ins Firmament hinauf:
> *'Du bist der Tod, die Gnade und das Leben. Du hast keinen Gott neben dir!'* (*KLPB* 205; italics in the original)

Heym's thief experiences something very similar: 'Er sah herauf, und da sah er den ganzen Himmel mit Dämonen erfüllt' (2:83). In Rheiner's novella, the supernaturally charged atmosphere (and with it the protagonist's self-image as a victim of divine persecution) becomes apparent at a relatively early stage, when the buoyancy of Tobias's cocaine-fuelled trip in the café is abruptly deflated by his realization that 'the night' is lurking literally just beyond the smoke from his own cigarette:

> Doch da er aufschaute, *sah er die Nacht drohen* hinter dem aromatischen Qualm, den sein Mund ausstieß, – *jene Nacht, seine Nacht, die mit schwarzem Faustschlag diese kurzen Minuten des heiteren Rausches zertrümmerte* und sich selbst unerbittlich heranschob mit jenem *neuen düsteren Qual-Rausch, dessen rhapsodischen Gesang, endlos gedehnt, sie ihm von jetzt an in die Ohren gellte.* (*KLPB* 199–200; italics in the original)

The image of the 'Faustschlag' itself echoes the final stanza of Heym's 'Der Gott der Stadt':

> Er streckt ins Dunkel seine Fleischerfaust.
> Er schüttelt sie. Ein Meer von Feuer jagt

Durch eine Straße. Und der Glutqualm braust
Und frißt sie auf, bis spät der Morgen tagt. (Pinthus 43)

This particular association is strengthened by the reappearance of the fist image in a description of dawn in the city later in the story:

Sollte er wiederum, wie öfter schon, die ganze Nacht herumirren, um schließlich den grauen Morgen am Spreekanal zu finden oder an der Gasanstalt, die dann wie eine Faust aus den Nebeln stiege? (*KLPB* 208)

Through the novella the ominous supernatural presence impinges repeatedly on the protagonist's consciousness, and despite the variety of forms it assumes – it appears not only as a demon and the night, but also as a father-figure and a giant animal – links to Heym's urban demonography are consistently evident. Note, for example, the 'black brow' of the impassive father-figure filling Marion's windows, seemingly a direct allusion to the opening couplet of 'Der Gott der Stadt':

'Der Gott der Stadt': Auf einem Häuserblocke sitzt er breit.
Die Winde lagern schwarz um seine Stirn. (Pinthus 42)

Kokain: Nein! Niemand hörte diesen verzweifelten Menschen, *am wenigsten jener gütige Vater, dessen unerbittliche schwarze Stirn vor den großen Atelierfenstern stand, starr, unberührt, unbeweglich!* (*KLPB* 213; italics in the original)

Further, Heym's choice of the verb *lagern* in the same couplet is replicated in Rheiner's final incarnation of this force as a giant animal looming above the city, in the same posture adopted by the supernatural beings in all three of Heym's poems:

Das Gift nur, das sein Schicksal war, lagerte wie ein riesiges Tier über der ganzen Stadt, über den Horizonten und über seinem Dasein: – unentrinnbar, *Charybdis, die ihn schlürfte.* (*KLPB* 224; italics in the original)

If Rheiner's depiction of the *beseelte Stadt* in his two 1918 narratives is modelled closely on Heym's poetry of 1910–11, this last passage highlights the one key ingredient that Rheiner has added to Heym's recipe: 'das Gift.' Bridgwater's analysis of Heym's technique provides a useful basis for understanding the mechanics of this addition:

> It is ironical that as man is increasingly depersonalized by the hostility of his environment, the abstractions of which this hostility consists are themselves personified. As a result, man's fears become more real than anything else about him; he is overshadowed by the megalopolis in which he lives, this being personified in a succession of monstrous 'deities'. (*PEB* 221)

In contrast to Heym's, what Rheiner's deities personify is more than simply an abstract fear generated by the disorientation and spiritual impoverishment associated with the rapid urban growth of the late 19th and early 20th centuries; to be precise, Rheiner's personifications incorporate this fear – which is why Heym's poems lend themselves so well as templates for them – but subsume it to a more specific malaise: cocaine addiction. This effect is achieved in *Kokain* by the representation of the 'poison' itself as a giant demon whose identity is in turn blurred with both night in the city and an amorphous father-figure of unmistakably Christian heritage. In 'Die Erniedrigung' it is brought about more succinctly via the identification of the chemist, the dispenser of poisons ('der Apotheker, von dem er das Cocain bezog'; *M* 103), with Christ, whose second coming follows the city's apocalyptic collapse. This thematic integration of cocaine addiction into what by 1918 could be considered orthodox Expressionist portrayals of the *cité maudite* (Huder notes the similarity of Rheiner's depiction of Berlin in *Kokain* to the graphic representations of the city by Georg Grosz and Frans Masereel, but not to the literary ones by Heym; 84) is what makes these two narratives extraordinary within the canons of both drug literature and Expressionism. The principle Rheiner applies here is equivalent to the one we have already observed in his depictions of the main characters in these stories: just as he seems to use Heym's madman as a prototype for his protagonists, filling the gap represented by the unspecified cause of his madness with cocaine abuse, so too he seems to take Heym's visions of the demon-infested metropolis as the basis for his settings, only adding cocaine addiction to the abstract fears that Heym's demons already personify.

These two elements, the first concerning the protagonist, the second the setting, constitute, in Kantian terminology, the basis of the single 'aesthetic idea,' of which 'Die Erniedrigung' and *Kokain* can be said to represent different elaborations. If this identity of aesthetic idea underlies the numerous and far-reaching similarities between the works as described here, it remains to be seen, first, how the two elaborations differ, and second, what these differences reveal about the role these texts play in the master narrative of Rheiner's addiction. As it happens, the most obvious differences between the two narratives, most of which have already been touched on in passing – one is set in Cologne, the other in Berlin, one mainly in an apartment, the other mainly on the street; one is substantially longer than the other, etc. – are largely superficial and not especially revealing. Indeed, these create the impression that 'Die Erniedrigung' stands as a mere preparatory sketch or trial-run for the fuller, definitive treatment of the same material in *Kokain*.

A more complex dimension to the relationship between the two works emerges, however, when a subtle difference in their narrative strategies is considered. In both, the basic model is the figural perspective employed by Heym in both 'Der Irre' and 'Der Dieb,' generating 'a distorted view of the world narrated from the very personal viewpoint of the main character' (Sokel *PGE* 82; see 5.2). The distortions of this view are particularly marked in Rheiner's narratives, in the same way as they are in Heym's, due to the insanity of the character in question. In 'Die Erniedrigung' this technique is applied consistently from the second paragraph onwards, with a conspicuous and disconcerting lack of narrative commentary to explain, by reference to a reality external to the protagonist's mind, such bizarre and paradoxical occurrences as the X-ray vision into the next room afforded by his hand mirror (*M* 102–103), his cat's role as a spy (*M* 103), the random suicide (*M* 104) and equally random resurrection (*M* 106) of his sister, the revelation of the chemist as Jesus Christ (*M* 107), etc. The first of these is even tagged with the parenthetical remark that Tobias gave the matter no more thought ('über die er nicht weiter nachdachte'; *M* 103), evidently signalling that it therefore merits no more thought – or explanation – from the narrator either. By refusing to offer the reader the reassurance of sane points of reference to oppose to the protagonist's madness, the narrator, here as in Heym's stories, configures his narrative as an implicit challenge to normative, bourgeois rationalism (evincing moreover a clear parallel to Benn's more overt sympathy for 'disreputable' psychological states such as 'Nervenschwäche, Ermüdbarkeit, Psychasthenie'; *GW* 8:1875, see 3.1).

In *Kokain*, a technically slight yet thematically significant adjustment to this stance can be noted, in so far as at several key moments the protagonist's view is qualified, corrected or explained. In his use of such terms as 'Halluzinationen' (*KLPB* 210) and 'Spuk' (*KLPB* 212) to describe Tobias's perceptions, the narrator occasionally steps back, effectively taking a diagnostic distance from his protagonist and contributing to a reduction in the dominance of the latter's perspective. The story is crafted in such a way, however, that these corrections and explanations occur mostly on the diegetic level; integrated into the plot, they consist either in Tobias's recognition of his own misperception or in a rational rebuttal by another character of his misinterpretation of particular events. The most important instance of self-correction is Tobias's belated realization that the figures standing on the street corner opposite the railway station, whom he had taken to be his mother and sister, are really just billboards:

> Schnell atmend entwand er sich dieser neuen Gefahr und schoß auf die Straßenecke zu, wo die beiden Damen standen.
> Standen? Standen?
> Er sah nur zwei Reklameschilder, in Schwarz und Gold, die ihm unverschämt entgegenleuchteten. Keine Frauen da, kein Mensch! (*KLPB* 204)

The first occurrence of an explanation by another character is the response given by the elderly gentleman from the public toilet to Tobias's appeal not to whistle to the would-be captors he is convinced are waiting to ambush him:

> Verwundert maß ihn der Herr vom Kopf bis zu den Füßen. Er trat einen Schritt zurück und sagte:
> 'Wie meinen Sie? Ich verstehe Sie nicht. Was gehen Sie mich denn an? Ich pfeife meinem Hunde.' (*KLPB* 206)

The same dynamic can be observed in the methodical explanation Marion offers, in the hope of calming Tobias's nerves, of the shadows on her ceiling he attributes to either robbers or detectives:

> 'Natürlich doch, das sind die Schatten der Bäume unten und der Schornsteine und Windfänge auf dem Dach. Die Bogenlampe schwingt unten im Wind, und das bewegt die Schatten. Geh schlafen, leg dich nieder!' (*KLPB* 216)

The insertion into the narrative of these voices of sanity that compete with the protagonist's perspective, exposing its distortions and calling his hallucinations by name, amounts to a substantial deviation from the technique employed in 'Die Erniedrigung'; the surreal elements in the short story remain surreal, in the novella they are largely defused by rational explanations. For this reason, notwithstanding all the similarities between them, the two texts generate quite different overall effects. Far from rearticulating the challenge the short story issues to normative, bourgeois rationalism, the disruption of figural perspective in the novella functions as an attempt to reassert the authority of reason in the face of the addict's accelerating derangement. In this respect, the short story can be said to conform much more closely to the experimental trend that gave Expressionism its revolutionary dynamism and its place at the forefront of European avant-garde movements of the early 20th century (in several respects 'Die Erniedrigung' anticipates Luis Buñuel's classic Surrealist film *Un chien andalou* of 1929), whereas the novella emerges from the comparison as an essentially conservative text that draws heavily on Expressionist themes and techniques yet to a significant extent deactivates their radical implications. A parallel can be drawn to the trend we have observed in Benn scholarship towards taming the idiosyncrasies of the works under discussion by reconciling them to the familiar conditions of empirical reality (see 2.1), only here the conciliatory trend is built into the work itself. From this viewpoint, *Kokain* sits ambivalently between its own Expressionist and anti-Expressionist tendencies.

When we broaden the terms of comparison chronologically to include not only the novella's direct antecedent 'Die Erniedrigung,' but also the revolutionary fervour that had exploded in the last chapter of 'Der Tod des Schwärmers Gautier Fémin,' written three years earlier in 1915, as well as the avowal of radicalism Rheiner would issue in his preface to *Der bunte Tag* a year later in 1919 (*KLPB* 8), this conservative turn in *Kokain* becomes all the more surprising. If 'Der Tod des Schwärmers Gautier Fémin' styles itself as a call to the barricades ('Schon in den Metropolen baun sich neue Barrikaden'; *KLPB* 194), then for the sake of the comparison we could extend this metaphor to say that *Kokain* dismantles its own barricades as they are being erected. Indeed, of all the works examined in this study, it is clearly the one that is most willing to compromise with the sober, respectable bourgeois ethos that it nominally installs as the addict-poet's natural enemy ('dieses Gebräu aus Hohn und Schadenfreude'; *KLPB* 203), much more so even than Benn's 'Die Eroberung' with its plea, 'Nehmt mich auf in die Gemeinschaft!' (*GW* 5:1193), which is delivered in an altogether more prickly narrative package. The novella's ambivalence is perhaps most visible in Tobias's wistful contemplation of the suburban housing development he observes from Marion's window in the peace of morning. If only briefly, the text hints here at the prospect of domestic bliss as an alternative to the poet's 'Aasleben' (*KLPB* 202), if only he could get the demonic monkey off his back:

> Hier wurde noch gebaut. Grundstücke, mit Drahtgittern umhegt und mit schmutzigem Gras bewachsen, lagen da. Asphaltierte Straßen, in denen noch keine Häuser standen, kreuzten sich und liefen geruhsam im Glanz der Morgensonne hin. *Vögel sangen mild.* Ein tiefes Blau stand am Himmel und sandte linden Hauch. Schäfchenwolken wanderten langsam im Azur.
> Marion brachte die Suppe, die dick und nahrhaft war und ihm wohl mundete. (*KLPB* 220–222; italics in the original)

The singing of birds, usually prettified in the diminutive 'Vöglein', is a recurrent motif that functions as a reminder, even at the worst moments in Tobias's story (including, ironically, immediately after the announcement that his brain has been splattered against the walls and staircase of the entrance-way that represents the terminus of his painful journey; *KLPB* 224) of the petit-bourgeois idyll as an alternative and more desirable mode of being in the world.

This major thematic reconfiguration, amounting indeed to a thematic anomaly in Rheiner's literary development, throws doubt on the view of *Kokain* as simply a full and final treatment of the material tested in 'Die Erniedrigung.' If *Kokain* not only elaborates, but also – in an almost reactionary narrative gesture in the Expressionist context – de-radicalizes the aesthetic idea developed in 'Die Erniedrigung,' it follows that in all probability this re-elaboration was targeted primarily not at aesthetic refinement, but at the more successful fulfilment of another function. The particular combination of textual and the extra-textual circumstances (to which the texts themselves, by means of their autobiographical orientation, repeatedly refer) indicate that this function is most likely a therapeutic, purgative one.[93] A view of 'Die Erniedrigung' and *Kokain* as two attempts at self-therapy aimed at Rheiner's writing-out of his own cocaine addiction would certainly account for the apparent anomalies we have identified in the development from one work to the next: in the first, the author treats the material in a

93 The therapeutic intention of Rheiner's composition of *Kokain* is confirmed by St. Saveur: 'Während des Sommers [1918] schrieb Rheiner die Novelle *Kokain*, womit er sich von diesem Erlebnis befreien wollte. Fo las sie, hielt aber vieles für dichterische Phantasie, so wenig wusste sie von diesen Dingen' (137). This would necessarily imply that Weinand's claim of a 'complete cure' in 1916, made in 1925 on Fo's behalf, was exaggerated (*K* 115, see 5.1).

manner consistent with the Expressionist methods already assimilated and practised in previous works, but when this does not produce a satisfactory cure, he tries again, only this time adjusting his methods – even if this means compromising their aesthetic rationale – to increase his chances of success. In particular, a therapeutic reading would explain the shift from a pure to an impure figural perspective that we have identified as the most fundamental difference between the two works, in so far as this suggests an attempt by the author to rein in the psychologically volatile elements in his own narrative. Whereas the depersonalized narrative of 'Die Erniedrigung,' with its deference to Tobias's perspective and its willingness to leave ambiguities and paradoxes unresolved, bespeaks the narrator's own – and by proxy, the author's – self-assurance, the insistence in *Kokain* on correcting the addict's misapprehensions by reference to authoritative voices of reason suggests a wish to establish a critical distance from the protagonist's diseased mind.

A purgative function of literary expression is one of the possibilities allowed for by the notion of 'the multiform interpenetration of the word and the situation,' highlighting in particular the potential for 'mutual influence' of an author's life and work (Jakobson 320, see 1.4). According to this view, a literary work can do more than passively reflect the writer's situation; it can play an active part in shaping it. In the German literary tradition, perhaps the most renowned manifestation of the purgative function is Goethe's writing-out of the emotional turbulence of his youth in the novel *Die Leiden des jungen Werthers*. This interpretation was put forward by the author himself in *Dichtung und Wahrheit*, in which he reflects on the effect that the composition of *Werther* had had on his perturbed state of mind:

> Ich hatte mich durch diese Komposition, mehr als durch jede andere, aus einem stürmischen Elemente gerettet [...] Ich fühlte mich, wie nach einer Generalbeichte, wieder froh und frei, und zu einem neuen Leben berechtigt. Das alte Hausmittel war mir diesmal vortrefflich zustatten gekommen. (9:588)

Rheiner's novella gives us good reason to suspect that the author was consciously seeking to imitate Goethe's cathartic precedent, for Tobias's suicide closely resembles Werther's: Goethe's protagonist, just like Rheiner's, ends up literally blowing his own brains out, an act that stands as a symbolic purging of the character – and more importantly of his 'sufferings' – by the author. Significantly, David Ebin recognizes this kind of confessional, writing-as-therapy approach and its potential failings as characteristic of a certain direction of drug-related literature:

> It may be that words reflect the effort of the writer to be rid of the drug-experience, to put himself outside of it. It may be that this effort is only partially successful and that this explains why in some writings the sound of two voices is heard simultaneously; that of the observer and that of the experiencer. (143)

In its pitting of substance-induced psychosis against sober reason, *Kokain*'s heteroglossia clearly conforms to Ebin's model.

The extent to which the author sincerely hopes to effect a cure for his ills by writing about them is open to question, and it cannot be discounted that in any given case the *purgative function* may operate first and foremost as a *purgative conceit*, a performative strategy for the author's shaping of his own 'biographical legend' (Tomashevsky 52). Even without considering the implications of a view of the text as authorial performance, the situation is already complicated by the possibility suggested by Derrida that the elaboration of drug experience in writing may function not only therapeutically, but concurrently as a surrogate for that experience – the latter function counteracting the former (*RD* 25). Whatever its degree of sincerity or contamination, with hindsight it goes without saying that Rheiner's creative therapy was far less successful than Goethe's. Whether he gained some short-term respite from his affliction by 'putting himself outside of it' is uncertain. It is certain, however, that in the long term *Kokain* proved less therapeutic than prophetic. Rheiner's circumstances immediately preceding his death just seven years after the publication of his novella bear an uncanny resemblance to those of Tobias as he portrayed them in *Kokain*, as can be gathered from his final letter, written in June 1925 just nine days before his fatal morphine overdose (*KLPB* 278–282). Homeless, jobless and with few prospects of improving his situation, by the time he wrote this letter Rheiner had already turned his thoughts to suicide: 'Ich bin auch fest entschlossen, mir lieber dieses elende Jammerleben voll Schmerz und Kummer vom Halse zu schaffen, als *so* zu leben!' (*KLPB* 281). Whatever value can be attached to his claim that after a prolonged spell of institutionalized detoxification he was 'gottseidank nicht rückfällig, weder in den alten Giften, noch etwa in Alkohol' (ibid.), sure enough he would soon turn to the 'old poisons' once again to end it all. In a logical extension of Tomashevsky's theory (51), the manner of Rheiner's death, as much as the phenomena of his life, testify to the penetration of his own 'literary clichés' into his biography.

6.4 Rheiner's Final Chapter

The Rönne-like Mediterranean reverie Tobias experiences in the toilet of a Berlin railway station momentarily distracts him from his sufferings, but the addict's thoughts return abruptly to the hopelessness of his immediate situation in the form of a death-wish, as if in recognition of the impossibility of ever realizing his dream of the Riviera:

> Das erleichterte einen Augenblick: … Riviera, dachte Tobias, Riviera, Santa Margherita…
> Dann betete er, murmelnd: *Gib, lieber Herr von Gott, du selige Excellenz, gib, daß ich bei der nächsten Injektion lautlos verrecke!* (*KLPB* 202)

In March 1925 Rheiner formulated a death wish of his own, a short poem of just eight lines that represents the brief final chapter in the master narrative of his drug use:

> Komm, holder Schnee! Verschütte dies schwere Herz!
> Mit deiner Gnade zaubre die Träne starr,
> so aus der ewigen Quelle rinnet,
> täglich geboren, geliebt noch immer.
>
> O gib, daß mir aus dieser verlorenen Qual,
> der bittern, werde das große, das ernste Grab,
> darin ich mich zur Ruhe finde:
> weinende, liebend erlöste Seele. (172)

In both these texts the speaker portrays death as the only escape from his suffering and openly wishes for a swift demise. Yet the contrast in tone between them could not be more pronounced. Tobias's appeal is tinged with a wry, world-weary humour, most evident in the ironically aristocratic address 'Herr von Gott' and the sudden shift in register from the apparent solemnity of his prayer to the crudely colloquial 'verrecken'. By contrast, the poem 'Komm, holder Schnee!' exhibits a lyricism reminiscent of

Rheiner's earliest poetry, while in its form and diction it draws heavily on Romantic models, in which yearning for the grave is a stock motif. It displays especially close affinities to the first Harper's Song from Goethe's *Wilhelm Meisters Lehrjahre* (1795), 'Wer sich der Einsamkeit ergibt,' in which the pathos attendant upon the figure of the grave as a refuge from anguish is similarly augmented by an association with love. The second of this poem's two stanzas reads:

Es schleicht ein Liebender lauschend sacht,
Ob seine Freundin allein?
So überschleicht bei Tag und Nacht
Mich einsamen die Pein,
Mich einsamen die Qual.
Ach, werd ich erst einmal
Einsam in Grabe sein,
Da läßt sie mich allein!

The strong Goethean influence on 'Komm, holder Schnee!' (which indirectly adds weight to the hypothesis of an attempt to emulate Goethe's cure-by-writing in *Kokain*) would appear startlingly atavistic if we were to take Rheiner's claim for 'language revolutionary' status at face value (*KLPB* 8). His abandonment here of all revolutionary pretensions is further evidence, rather, for our view of the poet's ostensible commitment to Expressionism as essentially self-effacing (see 5.1). In truth, his adoption of a neo-Romantic posture in this poem is no less so; this merely attests further to the stifling of his own voice under the weight of existing poetic models. Nonetheless, a case can be made for considering Rheiner's use of literary precedents here as equivalent to that we have observed in his prose works 'Die Erniedrigung' and *Kokain*, that is, as involving the addition of cocaine as a key autobiographical element (see 6.3). As this element remains unstated, the case is admittedly less clear-cut, yet as in our comparison of the two early poems 'Die Straße' and 'Der Platz' with the first chapter of *Kokain* (see 6.1), the thematic correlation between 'Komm, holder Schnee!' and the station scene from the novella invites reflection on whether the central role of Tobias's cocaine problem in the latter can be taken to suggest a hidden role for the drug in the former.[94]

94 Note also that Grimm includes this poem (*K* 145) as the last among only five interspersed through his edition, which deliberately foregrounds the role of drugs in Rheiner's biography and work (see 5.1). This placement accentuates any 'cocaine link'

To explore this question in more depth, two different approaches may be adopted. The first involves reading the poem as confessional and thus assuming a straightforward identity of poet and speaker. Although such an assumption can only be made with the utmost caution, and indeed the identity of poet and speaker can never be more than a plausible hypothesis, the text itself offers no evident basis for any interpretation other than an autobiographical one. On the contrary, its lyricism, like that which Tomashevsky observes in Pushkin's poems, depends on the reader's assumption that he is reading 'not the words of an abstract author, but those of a living person' (50). Once the poem is placed in the context of Rheiner's biography, the thematic centrality of drug addiction becomes more or less self-evident. After all, his addiction was the most important single factor behind the 'forlorn anguish' referred to at the beginning of the second stanza, and is particularly relevant here because at the time of writing this poem Rheiner was nearing the end of a six-month period of detoxification treatment at a nursing home in Bonn.

Second, although there is no unequivocal reference to the drug within the poem, a case can be made of considering cocaine as a thematic element of 'Komm, holder Schnee!' even independently of the extratextual evidence. In such a reading the drug theme relates not to the cause of the speaker's 'anguish', but to the agency of the escape-through-death he longs for. In the passage from *Kokain*, Tobias prays that his end will be brought about by his next injection of cocaine. In 'Komm, holder Schnee!' the agent of death is the snow that features as the addressee. All the reader learns about this snow, however, is that the speaker considers it *hold* ('fair' or 'sweet'), endowed with apparently divine grace ('Mit deiner Gnade,' l. 2) and magical powers ('zaubre die Träne starr,' l. 2), and most importantly that by causing death it can put an end to his suffering. In contrast to Trakl's 'Delirium' and 'Winternacht' (see 10.1–10.2), and to Rheiner's own Traklesque poem 'Schnee' of 1917 (*KLPB* 36), in this poem there is no evocation of a scene in which the snow can logically be assimilated as part of the landscape. Naturally, the reader is free to imagine such a scene in any case; perhaps the speaker is standing at a window watching the snow fall, perhaps outside walking through the snow, or considering his state of mind, perhaps even lying in it. But there is nothing in the poem to exclude

that might be attributed to it on the basis of Rheiner's work alone – a further instance of editorial influence on the interpretation of possible drug motifs (see 1.4 and 5.2).

the possibility that the word *Schnee* is being used here in a figurative sense, that is, to denote cocaine; moreover, as the etymological dictionaries confirm, this meaning was already well established by the time this poem was written in 1925 (see 1.1). In the absence of further contextual factors that might give a clue as to the more precise nature of the snow being addressed, neither of its possible meanings is activated at the expense of the other, and so both can be considered latent.

With this inherent ambiguity in the text–drug relationship, this flickering of meaning that is neither entirely present nor entirely absent, 'Komm, holder Schnee!' represents a return from the concrete and often painfully direct, *prosaic* descriptiveness of *Kokain* to the mythical and *poetic* unspeakability of drug experience associated with 'Die Straße' and 'Der Platz.' The obvious and crucial difference is that the optimism and vitality of the earlier poems has given way, in 'Komm, holder Schnee!', to a profound pessimism. Both 'Der Platz' and 'Komm, holder Schnee!' speak of redemption, but whereas in the former this redemption comes about through ecstatic cosmic communion, in the latter the most that the speaker can hope for is redemption through annihilation.

The resigned melancholy dominant in this poem – Rheiner's last and one of only a handful written in the last five years of his life – also permeates his letters of this period. By the time he wrote 'Komm, holder Schnee,' his personal and literary aspirations already lay in ruins. Whether this should be seen as a consequence or a cause of his inability to control his long-standing drug habit is impossible to determine; vicious circularity is again the most probable scenario. Even if, as his last letter indicates (see 6.3), the detoxification treatment of late 1924 and early 1925 was successful in weaning him from his physical dependence on 'the old poisons' (*KLPB* 281), in the end it did nothing more than delay the inevitable. After his release Rheiner clearly lacked the strength and resolve to start a new, sober life, and was also terrified by the prospect of slipping back into his old one: 'Ich *mag* das alte Leben, wenn auch gottseidank, gottseidank *ohne* Morph. oder Kokain *nicht* weiterführen' (ibid.). Just three months after the composition of his poetic death wish Rheiner would commit suicide by overdose, an event commemorated in his friend Felixmüller's painting 'Der Tod des Dichters Walter Rheiner' (see 5.1). With its overt drug symbolism this work would enshrine its subject as the quintessentially intoxicated Expressionist poet and ensure that his biographical legend would become – in Tomashevsky's words (54) – 'an inescapable concomitant to his poetry.'

Part Three: Georg Trakl

One must always be intoxicated. That's the main thing: it's the only issue. In order not to feel the horrible burden of Time which breaks your shoulders and bows you to the earth, you must become intoxicated without respite.
– Baudelaire, 'Enivrez-vous' [95]

95 'Il faut être toujours ivre. Tout est là: c'est l'unique question. Pour ne pas sentir l'horrible fardeau du Temps qui brise vos épaules et vous penche vers la terre, il faut vous enivrer sans trêve' (*Oc* 286). Tr. Peschel, 'Foreword' to *Intoxication and Literature* (5).

7 The Life and Death of an Austrian Drug-Eater

7.1 'Lost between Melancholy and Drunkenness'

Mention of Georg Trakl's (1887–1914) death by cocaine overdose is almost *de rigeur* in biographical summaries, yet as a key element of his 'literary' biography (see 1.4) this overdose stands in splendid isolation: even in specialist Trakl scholarship, cocaine is usually mentioned only in connection with his death. This occurred in the evening of 3 November 1914, and is described in his medical file (*HkA* 2:728–730), complete with exclamation mark, as 'Suicid durch Cocainintoxication!'[96] At the time Trakl, just 27 years old and deeply traumatized by his brief but intense experience of the carnage of the First World War, was under observation in a military hospital in Kraków due to his unstable psychological condition. Whether his death truly was suicide or rather an accidental overdose is just one of the many points of contention that surround the life and work of this poet whose relatively small body of austere yet deeply resonant verse continues, almost a century later, to exert its unique fascination on readers and to provoke astonishingly diverse responses from critics. One thing we can say with certainty about the overdose that killed him is that it was the culminating act in an unrelenting process of drug and alcohol-based self-destruction that had a major influence over the course of the poet's brief adult life. 'Ein starker Trinker und Drogenesser' is the characterization offered by Trakl's close friend, mentor and publisher Ludwig von Ficker, a man by no means given to cheap sensationalizing, least of all in matters concerning his brilliant protégé (*DD* 31; cited in Weichselbaum 45).[97] Trakl, it would seem, belonged to that 'certain number of beings of most acute sensibility,' for whom, as the Surrealist poet Roger Gilbert-Lecomte put it

96 The same document, *Vormerkblatt mit der Krankengeschichte* of the *K. und k. Reservespital Nr. 1 Jaroslau*, dated 4 November 1914, gives '*intoxicatio cocainum*' as Trakl's 'morbidity schema diagnosis.'

97 The account of Trakl's drug use given in the following pages draws substantially on the documentary evidence reproduced in Weichselbaum's biography.

in 1930, '*drugs are an inescapable necessity*,' and who 'cannot survive except by destroying themselves' (cited in Castoldi 143–144). When these circumstances are considered, the question of intention in Trakl's fatal cocaine overdose becomes almost incidental, for it seems doubtful that his unrelenting self-poisoning could have ended any other way.

A crucial point that emerges immediately, then, is the extensive and multifarious nature of Trakl's drug experience. Commentators have traditionally described him as a 'drug addict' without considering it necessary to specify which drug or drugs he was addicted to. Even Heselhaus, one of the few who see a direct link between Trakl's drug use and his poetic activity (see 1.3 and 8.1), never moves beyond the blanket term *Drogen* (228–257). A similar tendency to vagueness is typical of direct testimonies to Trakl's drug use, many of which refer generically to *Drogen*, *Gifte*, or *Trunkenheit* (literally 'drunkenness', but this meaning can extend to 'intoxication' more generally; see 9.2). By way of illustration we might mention, in addition to Ficker's characterization given above, that Ficker's wife is said to have complained about Trakl's 'vieles Giftnehmen' (Szklenar 233). Also, Trakl's friend Karl Röck noted that Trakl was 'schwer vergiftet' on his return from Berlin in April 1914 (Szklenar 232). Trakl himself, in a letter to Karl Borromaeus Heinrich of January 1914, describes himself as lost 'zwischen Trübsinn und Trunkenheit' (*HkA* 1:532). References to a range of specific psychoactive substances have also been documented, but apart from wine, no individual substance is mentioned with particular frequency. There are indications that Trakl's two drugs of preference were alcohol and Veronal, the first barbiturate to be marketed for medicinal purposes (Weichselbaum 48), but he is known to have taken chloroform, ether, morphine, opium and cocaine as well, and it has been suggested that he was perhaps also familiar with curare and even mescaline (for curare see Orendi-Hinze 382; for mescaline see Kupfer *GG* 228–231). Clearly, for Trakl the imperative to achieve intoxication in any form – to go 'anywhere out of the world,' as Baudelaire puts it in his prose poem of that name – was more important than such considerations as the particular effects and relative merits of individual drugs. Moreover, when we consider how many different substances he is known to have used, it seems probable that variety and curiosity were significant factors influencing his choice of intoxicants.

In the histories of the drug–literature association that have been published in recent years (see 1.3), there has been a tendency to categorize writers and 'creative projects' according to their association with a single drug or class of drug (narcotics, stimulants, hallucinogens, etc.), and in two separate studies Trakl has been made to fit into this scheme as a 'writer on cocaine' (Boon 185; Castoldi 159–160). Given that in truth only limited specific evidence exists for his use of this drug, this categorization is evidently the result of editorial convenience rather than historical accuracy. Indeed, the essential and irreducible diversity of Trakl's drug use highlights the over-simplification inherent in the approach underlying such studies. It is true that different drugs have often radically different effects, but their fundamental similarity is that they all lift the user out of his 'normal' state of consciousness, and all the evidence suggests that for Trakl this was the most important consideration. For him drugs represented, as Klaus Stark puts it in his medical analysis, 'Vehikel zur Flucht aus einer aktuell unerträglichen Lebenswirklichkeit' (Stark 101; cited in Weichselbaum 48). The premise of the present study, then, is that it is necessary to see Trakl's cocaine use in this context: as just one element in a wide-ranging and above all relentless quest for intoxication that began while he was still a teenager and that ended with his 'Suicid durch Cocainintoxication' in November 1914.

Among writers of the modern period with such a broad experience of psychoactive substances, Trakl is unusual in that he never treated the drug question systematically or in detail, whether in fictional or essay form. This is hardly surprising, as outside his poetry he never in fact treated any question systematically or in detail, and left nothing in the way of autobiographical reflection apart from what can be gathered from his letters, which are invariably brief rather than newsy or discursive. As a result, although it is well established that he had a prodigious appetite for intoxicants of all descriptions, the specific evidence of his drug consumption is patchy and much of it, as the examples already cited illustrate, is second-hand. Trakl's first reference to his own drug use is contained in his earliest surviving letter, written between the end of August and the middle of September 1905 to his friend Karl von Kalmár (*HkA* 1:469). Even then drug taking was evidently not a new experience for him, for Trakl writes of having 'once again taken refuge in chloroform.' Trakl's younger brother Fritz would later confirm that Georg had started using drugs at a 'very early' stage: 'Ich erinnere mich, daß er als Junge seine Zigaretten mit Opiumlösung bestrich' (Bondy 9; cited in Weichselbaum 45). Trakl himself would claim, while hospitalized in Kraków in 1914, that his mother was also an 'Opiumesserin' (*HkA* 2:729), and so it is conceivable that his first exposure to this drug occurred while observing her in his childhood. It has also been mooted that one of Trakl's classmates, the son of a chemist, introduced him to drug taking and became his regular supplier during his school days (Basil 49).[98] In any case, the letter to Kalmár demonstrates that by the age of 18 Trakl both had direct experience of the suffering caused by drug abuse and was aware of its very real dangers. With hindsight the presentiment of catastrophe he expresses here appears uncanny in its accuracy:

> Um über die nachträgliche Abspannung der Nerven hinwegzukommen habe ich leider wieder zum Chloroform meine Zuflucht genommen. Die Wirkung war furchtbar. Seit acht Tagen leide ich daran – meine Nerven sind zum Zerreißen. Aber ich wiederstehe [sic] der Versuchung, mich durch solche Mittel wieder zu beruhigen, denn ich sehe die Katastrophe zu nahe. (*HkA* 1:469)

Another significant feature of this letter is that it clearly spells out the negative motivation for Trakl's drug taking: he presents chloroform not as a key to 'artificial paradises,' but more prosaically as a means of coping with nervous exhaustion. It is almost certain, however, that the young poet's predilection for this kind of medicine was determined in large part by his wish to cultivate a transgressive, bohemian image, and further reinforced by his desire to imitate literary role models. Chief among these was Baudelaire, who exerted an especially strong influence on Trakl at this time, as is evident in the parallels between Trakl's 1905 poem 'Der Heilige' (1:254) and the French poet's 'La Prière d'un païen' (Weichselbaum 47).

With regard to Trakl's motivation for taking drugs, his biographer Hans Weichselbaum remarks:

> Ihr Konsum schafft für kurze Zeit eine Erleichterung, nach deren Ende die seelischen Spannungen umso deutlicher zutage treten. Diese Funktion eines Fluchthelfers aus schmerzhaften inneren Zuständen haben die Drogen für Trakl beibehalten. Es ging ihm nicht um innere Erlebnisse, um Bewußtseinserweiterung oder um Rauscherleben in der Gruppe. Er hat Drogen, ausgenommen am Anfang, immer allein genommen. Sein Ziel war, das Bewußtsein zu dämpfen. (48)

---

98 Weichselbaum names Gustav Müller, Trakl's classmate until 1904, as the most likely candidate for the young Trakl's supplier. Müller's father was a chemist in Oberndorf near Salzburg (47).

Weichselbaum is right to emphasize that for Trakl intoxication was – and remained – primarily a means of escape from 'the bitterness of the world,' to borrow a phrase from an aphorism the poet penned in August 1914 (*SW* 4ii:323). This emphasis is important because it further distinguishes Trakl from the majority of drug-taking writers, for whom the appeal of intoxicants arises chiefly from intellectual curiosity, the quest for enlightenment or a radically new perspective on the world, or simply the pursuit of pleasure. Naturally, all such positive motivations presuppose that 'normal', sober consciousness is somehow deficient, or at least that our experience or knowledge of the world can be enriched through the exploration of alternative states, but only very few writers have found normality so intolerably painful – and escape through drugs therefore such an 'inescapable necessity' (Gilbert-Lecomte) – as did Trakl. That said, Weichselbaum's assertion that Trakl was not concerned with 'inner experiences' is simplistic and requires some qualification. It is clear that Trakl's intention was neither a meticulous investigation of drug-induced visions in the manner, say, of De Quincey, nor a systematic appraisal of intoxicants as aids to artistic creativity as undertaken by Baudelaire. But it seems equally clear that if for Trakl intoxication represented a painless alternative to sobriety, it also represented something more than that. If we accept that his sole objective was to 'subdue consciousness,' as Weichselbaum concludes, then it becomes difficult to account for his evident curiosity in experimenting with ever-new psychoactive substances, and practically impossible to account for his use of a stimulant such as cocaine, which he is known to have taken in large quantities towards the end of his life (*HkA* 2:730).

The first part of the aphorism cited above offers a more complete picture of the value Trakl saw in alternative states of consciousness: 'Gefühl in den Augenblicken totenähnlichen Seins: Alle Menschen sind der Liebe wert: Erwachend fühlst du die Bitternis der Welt' (*SW* 4ii:323). Waking consciousness is the consciousness of bitterness. Alternative states represent the suppression of this consciousness and for this reason are described as 'death-like', but crucially they involve more than just suppression: they also contain an intuitive awareness ('Gefühl') of something indisputably life-affirming ('Alle Menschen sind der Liebe wert'). A similarly positive emotional value is attributed to states of intoxication in certain of Trakl's poems. 'Herrlich: betrunken zu taumeln in dämmernden Wald,' for example, is a line that appears in the poem 'Zu Abend mein Herz' (*SW* 2:124–128). Significantly, the positive value of intoxication in Trakl's poetry is not only emotional. The poem 'Amen' (*SW* 2:421–422) hints, by means of the collocation of 'angel' and 'poppy', at a metaphysical significance for opium intoxication: 'In der Stille / Tun sich eines Engels blaue Mohnaugen auf'; while the phrase 'Flöten weich und trunken' from the poem 'Verwandlung' (*SW* 2:29–42) suggests a link between intoxication and musicality. A fuller discussion of the role of intoxication in Trakl's poetry follows in chapter 9. At this point suffice it to say that there was evidently more to Trakl's attraction to drugs than the subduing of consciousness.

A decisive moment in the development of Trakl's drug habit came with his decision to embark on a career in pharmacy, beginning in autumn 1905 with a three-year apprenticeship at a local chemist's. A number of reasons can be given for his career choice (Weichselbaum 51). For one thing, pharmacy was a 'respectable' occupation – and one which would therefore satisfy the expectations of his family – for which it was not necessary to have completed the final, eighth class of secondary school. Trakl had left the *Salzburger k.k. Staatsgymnasium* at the end of the academic year 1904–05, rather than repeat the seventh class after failing Latin, Greek and mathematics. Another factor was the reduction in the required duration of military service for training pharmacists from three years to one. Ease of access to the full range of available pharmaceuticals was no doubt another advantage that Trakl saw in this decision. Despite the premonition of 'catastrophe' he had formulated in the letter to Kalmár just a few weeks earlier, from this point on the 'temptation' to soothe his nerves by means of drugs in moments of distress had effectively become impossible to resist. In the years that followed, such moments of distress became increasingly frequent and acute, in particular once he moved from the familiar environment of his native Salzburg to the imperial capital Vienna in September 1908, where he completed two years of pharmacy studies at university followed by one year of military service. He vividly evokes one such 'nightmarish' anxiety attack in a letter to his elder sister Hermine written shortly after his arrival in Vienna:

> Ich glaube, es müßte furchtbar sein, immer so zu leben, im Vollgefühl all der animalischen Triebe, die das Leben durch die Zeiten wälzen. Ich habe die fürchterlichsten Möglichkeiten in mir gefühlt, gerochen, getastet und im Blute die Dämonen heulen hören, die tausend Teufel mit ihren Stacheln, die das Fleisch wahnsinnig machen. Welch entsetzlicher Alp! (*HkA* 1:472)

Trakl's younger sister Margarethe Jeanne, known as Grete or Gretl, was also a student in Vienna during Trakl's university years. A talented pianist, she was enrolled at the *k.k. Akademie für Musik und darstellende Kunst.* Trakl's relationship with Grete was especially close and had been ever since their childhood. Whether this relationship ever became incestuous is a question that has caused much debate in Trakl scholarship – especially in view of the prominent sister figure in Trakl's poetry – but seems improbable in the light of the comments on the matter made by Erhard Buschbeck, who was a close and long-standing friend of both Georg and Grete. The following passage appears in a letter from Buschbeck to Röck of August 1938. Note also the curious detail regarding his friend's tendency to confession while under the influence of alcohol, apparently confirming for Trakl the validity of Cicero's famous adage 'in vino veritas':

> Zwischen Trakl und seiner Schwester Grete hat es niemals so etwas wie eine Blutschuld gegeben, was diesbezüglich in Gedichten steht, ist lediglich ein Aufrücken von Gedankensünde, die niemals in die Realität herübergegriffen hat. Es war bei ihm wie bei ihr eine geistige Leidenschaft zur Schuld, nie eine andere. Trakl war in jenen Jahren, um die es sich handelt, durchaus zu Confessionen geneigt und hat sie oft, namentlich in trunkenem Zustand, abgelegt. Aber selbst wenn er diesbezüglich geschwiegen hätte, seine Schwester Grete, mit der wir wirklich befreundet waren, war in erotischen Dingen von solcher Offenheit, daß sie eine solche Sache keineswegs verschwiegen hätte. […] Nochmals: ich habe dabei nicht die furchtbare Schädigung, die das äußere Ansehen Trakls erleiden würde, im Auge, sondern einzig und allein die Wahrheit, die wir kennen. (Röck 7:10; cited in Weichselbaum 58)

It is certain, however, that Trakl introduced his younger sister to drug taking, and it seems most likely that this occurred while they were both studying in Vienna (Weichselbaum 82). Grete soon became an addict and remained one, despite two spells of detoxification treatment, until her suicide in 1917. Grete's drug habit, which had a devastating effect on all aspects of her life, is often named as one concrete source of the deep and unremitting sense of guilt that plagued Trakl throughout his life (e.g. Basil 78; Kupfer *GG* 229; Weichselbaum 59).

The three years that followed Trakl's completion of military service in September 1911 and preceded his enlistment in August 1914 were characterized on the one hand by the maturation of his literary talent and the production of a body of poetry of astonishing originality, and on the other hand by instability, angst and increasing financial difficulty as he moved restlessly between Salzburg, Vienna and Innsbruck in search of regular employment. His various attempts at establishing himself in paid work all ended – with remarkable suddenness – in total failure. In these circumstances his emotional and psychological equilibrium was more delicate than ever, and consequently his drug use became even greater, which in turn can only have exacerbated his anxiety and his inability to cope with everyday life. A letter to Ficker of November 1913 encapsulates Trakl's state of mind in his moments of dejection, and also underlines the role intoxication continued to play for him as a refuge from distress:

> Ich bin seit einer Woche in Wien. Meine Angelegenheiten sind ganz ungeklärt. Ich habe jetzt 2 Tage und 2 Nächte geschlafen und habe heute noch eine recht arge Veronalvergiftung. In meiner Wirrnis und all' der Verzweiflung der letzten Zeit weiß ich nun gar nicht mehr, wie ich noch leben soll. Ich habe hier wohl hilfsbereite Menschen getroffen; aber mir will es erscheinen, jene können mir nicht helfen und es wird alles im Dunklen enden. (*HkA* 1:526)

In parallel with his manifold drug use, Trakl's consumption of alcohol is also known to have reached alarming proportions in this period. 'Ich habe in der letzten Zeit ein Meer von Wein verschlungen, Schnaps und Bier,' he wrote to Ficker just the day after describing his 'Veronal poisoning' (*HkA* 1:527). Röck recorded in a diary entry of October 1913 that Trakl spent 200 crowns per month on drugs and alcohol, two crowns per day just for 'Weintrinken und Rauchen' (2:32). 'Wie viele Leute leben mit diesem Geld ganz,' commented Röck, who nonetheless continued to lend Trakl money. However, neither Trakl's drug and alcohol abuse nor his chronic pessimism seems to have impeded his literary activity in any way. Indeed, it is clear from his biography that his drug habit, his tendency to melancholy and despair, and the refinement of his poetic technique all developed in parallel over the course of his short life, with all three showing a marked intensification over the final years. A letter to Karl Kraus of December 1913 testifies to Trakl's ability to write beautiful poetry in such seemingly unfavourable conditions:

> In diesen Tagen rasender Betrunkenheit und verbrecherischer Melancholie sind einige Verse entstanden, die ich Sie bitte, entgegenzunehmen, als Ausdruck der Verehrung für einen Mann, der, wie keiner der Welt ein Beispiel gibt. (*HkA* 1:530)

In the letter this introduction is followed by the first version of the poem 'Ein Winterabend' (*SW* 3:404–414; see 9.2).

The documentary evidence of Trakl's cocaine use is restricted to the months of his active military service in Galicia and his hospitalization in Kraków, that is, the period from the end of August to the beginning of November 1914. It is probable that he had begun taking – or had at least tried – cocaine before then, as this was a readily available pharmaceutical in the years before the First World War (see 1.2), without however leaving any written record of this experience. It should be added that he did not personally leave any written record of his cocaine experience in Galicia either. Rather, this is documented only in his medical file (*HkA* 2:728–730), without which there would be no conclusive evidence whatsoever of Trakl's cocaine use at any point in his life. In this document cocaine intoxication is listed twice as the cause of Trakl's death, and in the description of his movements and behaviour prior to his admission to hospital we find the following remark: 'Ob er sich auffällig benommen hätte, weiß er nicht, getrunken hat er nicht aber sehr viel Cocain zu sich genommen' (*HkA* 2:730). We can presume that the second part of this sentence, like the first, is based on Trakl's own declarations (there is no other obvious source), and hence that the shift from the subjunctive mood to the indicative is merely the result of grammatical imprecision. In any case, although previous studies have given no particular weight to this statement, it has significant implications for the evaluation of Trakl's famously maladjusted mental condition. Even if such a posthumous evaluation seems a near-futile task, and one of questionable value for achieving a better understanding of Trakl's poetry (see 9.1), for better or worse it has become one of the highest priorities of Trakl research over the last few decades (see 1.3). The hypothesis that the poet was schizophrenic, a problematic theory that has nonetheless become so ingrained in Trakl scholarship as to be mistaken in more recent scholarship for historical fact,[99] is based to a great extent on

99 Williams writes, 'shortly before he died at age twenty-seven of a self-administered overdose of cocaine [...] Trakl was clinically diagnosed as suffering from dementia praecox, schizophrenia in today's psychiatric terms' (135). This claim is undocumented, and its only possible source seems to be a letter of 15 November 1914, that is, in fact 12 days *after* Trakl's death, sent by the authorities of the Kraków hospital to the poet's brother Wilhelm in response to his enquiries (*HkA* 2:736). No evidence of such a diagnosis, however, can be found in Trakl's medical file, in any other of the documents collected in the *Historisch-kritische Ausgabe* of his works, or those referred to in Weichselbaum's extremely thorough biography. By contrast, Ficker's account of his visit to Kraków suggests that Trakl's doctor had arrived at a much less 'clinical' diagnosis of the case: 'aus der Unterredung mit dem Arzt, dem bei der Briefzensur

records of his eccentric and seemingly delusional behaviour during the final months of his life. In response to this conviction, then, and with reference to the statement cited above of Trakl's heavy cocaine use (abuse is perhaps a better word, not least in view of the outcome) in this final period, it seems pertinent to note that the superficial symptoms of acute cocaine intoxication bear a strong resemblance to those of paranoid schizophrenia, and that misdiagnoses of cocaine addicts as schizophrenics – even in living patients – are not uncommon, as medical studies show:

> Psychiatric complications commonly reported in association with cocaine use include anxiety, depression, paranoia, delirium, psychosis, and suicide. A toxic psychosis may be misdiagnosed as paranoid schizophrenia. (Burnett and Adler)

Maier, writing in 1926, documents instances of such misdiagnoses that predate even Trakl's fatal overdose (63–64).

These considerations should not be taken as an attempt to arrive at a fresh diagnosis of Trakl's condition. Rather, the point is that whatever the root cause or causes of the breakdown that led to his hospitalization (the immediate cause was the trauma resulting from active duty on the frontline; see 8.2), his emotional and psychological instability must have been severely exacerbated by the cocaine abuse documented in his medical report. By the same token, factors from earlier periods of his life that are often listed as early signs of his hypothetical decline into schizophrenia – insomnia, hallucinations, paranoid delusions, his sharp swings in mood and sudden shifts between sociability and withdrawal – might also be seen in large part as results of his increasingly intense drug abuse. In other words, the drug addiction that is often mentioned as a *symptom* of Trakl's psychological imbalance (e.g. Spoerri 93f.; Kleefeld 39–48) was almost certainly also one of its major *causes*.

---

auch einige Gedichte Trakls zu Gesicht gekommen waren, war mir haften geblieben, daß er diesen Fall zum Kapitel "Genie und Wahnsinn" rechne, womit er anzudeuten schien, daß weiter Vorsicht und Beobachtung geboten sei' (*A* 200).

7.2 Poetry, Biography, Reality

In short, Trakl lived what Seymour-Smith describes as 'an almost completely deranged life' (579), and it is clear that drug taking was one of the major contributors to its derangement. But what of his poetry? How, if at all, can Trakl's habitual intoxication and its effects on the various aspects of his life be related to his poetic production? This question points to a broader one that for many years has been one of the main sources of disagreement among Trakl critics: the link between Trakl's life and his works, and therefore the validity of a critical approach to his poetry that foregrounds elements of the poet's biography. At one end of the spectrum are those who claim that the full significance of Trakl's poetry cannot be grasped without reference to biographical factors. Williams, for example, writes:

> It is – especially in Trakl's case – a naïve and limiting mistake, I believe, to valorize the aesthetic autonomy of this seemingly self-contained verse by interpreting it in total (New-Critical, formalist [see 1.4]) isolation of the poet's trauma-filled existence of clinically diagnosed schizophrenia [see 7.1], drug addiction, alcoholism, and, ultimately, suicide. (122)

On the other hand, others maintain that biographically oriented interpretations themselves tend to be 'naïve and limiting.' Maria Carolina Foi argues that 'precisely because [Trakl's] existence was so brief and tormented, it is easy to run the risk of interpreting his life and his work reductively, according to a relationship of cause and effect' (ix).[100]

This controversy is entwined with another issue that has caused divergence of opinion in critical circles, namely the relationship between the world as depicted in Trakl's poetry and the world as humans, in particular Trakl's readers, normally perceive it. Curiously, it is the critics who adopt a biographical approach to the poetry who generally claim that it has only a very tenuous relationship, or no relationship whatsoever, to 'reality', by which they mean the world outside this poetry (the term is confusing, as it implies that Trakl's poetry is somehow less real than other things). In the passage cited above, for example, Williams talks of the 'aesthetic autonomy'

100 'Proprio perchè la sua esistenza è stata così breve e tormentata, è facile correre il rischio di interpretare riduttivamente, secondo un rapporto di causa ed effetto, la sua vita e la sua opera.'

of Trakl's 'seemingly self-contained verse,' and later in the same work he states that Trakl's 'signs do not point to the elements of nature' (275). We find the same idea expressed in earlier studies as well: 'Trakls Sprache und Dichtung [...] erfaßt nie außersprachliche Wirklichkeit, sondern ihre Wirklichkeit liegt in ihr selbst' (Kaufmann 67). Esselborn and Kurrik both characterize the development of Trakl's poetry from his earlier to his later work as a drifting away from external reference. Esselborn writes that in Trakl's later poems the reader is confronted with the 'Welt einer fast hermetischen Lyrik [...], die um unbewußte Erfahrung kreist' (222). Philipp takes an even more extreme view, suggesting that Trakl's poetry achieves 'Entleerung der Wortinhalte' (137), effectively rendering words meaningless. In the majority of such studies, the negation of a referential function for Trakl's poetry, or the limitation of this function to a purely psychic or linguistic level of experience, is interpreted as symptomatic of the poet's own increasingly tenuous 'grip on reality,' whether this tenuousness is then attributed to schizophrenia (as, for example, by Kurrik), 'metanoia' (Sharp), an Oedipal imbalance (Kleefeld), or a combination of debilitating factors (Williams).

On the other hand, those critics who attach only peripheral importance to biographical factors have been more inclined to see Trakl's poetry as grounded in the world as it is experienced not only by the writer but by the reader as well. Steinkamp, for example, shows how Trakl uses landscape images to create coherent spatial and temporal structures based on position and movement in a recognizable environment and the linear succession of stages in the day and year (for other studies that affirm or assume a referential function for Trakl's poetry, see 1.3). According to this view, the poetry's psychic, metaphysical and cultural implications represent a secondary level of meaning grafted onto Trakl's depictions of scenes that at the most basic level fall within the conventional parameters of human experience:

> Wir meinen [...], daß es Trakl bei der Verwendung von landschaftlichen Bildern stets um beides geht: elementar um die Gestaltung von Naturräumen und den in ihnen ablaufenden Prozessen und, umfassender, um die Verwendung von Landschaftsbildern und Landschaftsräumen als Sinnbilder für Verlust, Entfremdung und Verfall. (Steinkamp 22)

The first of these interpretive positions is certainly the more problematic. The idea that Trakl's 'signs do not point to the elements of nature' (Williams 275) appears untenable when considered alongside the poetry itself, as the majority of Trakl's poems consist predominantly of signs that most emphatically *do* point to elements of nature. Consider, to cite just one representative example, the opening lines of the poem 'Die Sonne' (SW 3:385–393), written in December 1913:

> Täglich kommt die gelbe Sonne über den Hügel.
> Schön ist der Wald, das dunkle Tier,
> Der Mensch; Jäger oder Hirt.

The error underlying the view that such passages depict an exclusively psychic level of experience might be explained with reference to Jakobson's remark, already cited in 1.4, that in poetry 'the supremacy of the poetic function over the referential function does not obliterate the reference but makes it ambiguous' (85). It is perhaps the notorious idiosyncrasy of Trakl's poetic language and the assumption that this idiosyncrasy is equivalent to hermetic 'self-containment' that has led such a large number of critics to mistake the ambiguity of its external reference for the obliteration thereof.

The present study, then, aligns itself with the second of the two critical approaches outlined above, which affirms the poetry's referential function while recognizing that the features most characteristic of Trakl's distinctive style serve precisely to enhance the poetic ambiguity of this function. We also note that in this sense Trakl must be considered a supremely Modernist poet, in that one distinguishing trait of the Modernist aesthetic is precisely the elevation of referential ambiguity from a 'corollary feature' of poetic expression (Jakobson 85) to one of its principal ends. As already indicated, adherents of the second approach have traditionally played down the importance of biographical factors, regarding them distrustfully, as Foi does in her cautionary statement (ix), as stepping stones to reductive interpretation. However, this distrust must in turn be considered an exaggerated if understandable reaction to the interpretive contortions of Trakl's would-be psychiatrists, and a more balanced perspective is called for, one that, in line with the general methodological considerations made in 1.4, succumbs neither to 'vulgar *biographism*' nor to 'vulgar *antibiographism*' (Jakobson 320). In the course of those same considerations, we have observed that the subjective nature of Trakl's style means that his poetry 'plays on the potential [non-textual] reality' of its own references (Tomashevsky 55), and the fact that its subjectivity is manifested in an unusual and detached way (with which we shall concern ourselves in detail in 9.1) serves if anything to strengthen the impulse it sends its readers to look 'beyond the work to its creator' (ibid. 48). This 'structural role' (ibid. 50) that the tension between biography and work plays within the poetry itself would seem to be the most compelling reason for recognizing biographical data as a legitimate point of reference in its interpretation. That such reasoning does not figure more prominently in the scholarship might be linked to the tendency among Trakl's biographically oriented critics to downplay the poetry's referentiality. Not only are possible references to the 'the elements of nature' (Williams 275) overlooked, but possible references to elements of the poet's biography are, too.

One critic who seems almost disappointed that the biographical references in Trakl's poetry are not more direct or more visible is Boon. Although his discussion of Trakl extends to only a few lines within his wide-reaching 'History of Writers on Drugs,' his position warrants attention here both because of his interest in authorial drug use and because of the particular difficulty he encounters in bringing this interest to bear on Trakl's poetry. This difficulty arises, he states, because 'it is hard to draw solid conclusions' concerning the 'influence' of Trakl's drug use on his poetry (185). Boon evidently sees this situation as an impasse, and having noted that 'Trakl's fascination with the French Symbolists could in itself have resulted in many of the drug-like effects found in his writing' (ibid.) – as if these two factors were mutually exclusive! – he concludes his analysis before it has even begun. In the light of the present discussion, it is clear that this impasse results from the analytical approach adopted, one that sees its objective as revealing and classifying biographical causes for literary effects, or inferring 'an unknown situation from a work,' as Jakobson puts it (320). Nowhere, it would seem, are the shortcomings of the 'vulgar biographical' approach exposed more starkly than in confrontation with Trakl's poetry.

In our own reading of this poetry, then, it will be important to bear in mind Peter von Matt's warning: 'Die Biographie bietet reichlich Entsprechungen, Analogien, Parallelen zum Werk, nicht aber den gesuchten Schlüssel' (67). Two elements of this statement are worth elaborating because they indicate paths leading beyond the interpretive dead end in which Boon finds himself. First, the biographical *Schlüsselsuche* that von Matt recognizes as futile should itself be viewed not as a whim of those scholars who choose to pursue it (Brik might describe them as 'maniacs'; see 1.3), but rather, in accordance with Tomashevsky's analysis (see 1.4), as a response conditioned both by literary conventions as they have developed since the 18th century and more particularly by the configuration of textual subjectivity within the poetry itself. Thus, although the 'key' itself may not exist, important features of the poetry might be illuminated by accounting for the textual conditions that prompt or encourage the search for it. Second, as long as we steer clear of the assumption that the relationship between biographical drug experience and literary work is one of simple cause and effect, then we may take the fact that a given work was produced by a writer who had a particular relationship to such-and-such a drug as the point of departure for a potentially fruitful investigation of it. 'Correspondences, analogies, or parallels' may emerge that enrich our appreciation of the work, and when they do not, their very absence may be significant. From this perspective, the question is not primarily one of possible *influence*, but one of possible *congruence*.

Although Heselhaus does not explicitly formulate this influence–congruence distinction, an intuition of it seems to underlie the hesitancy in his remark concerning the decisive developments in Trakl's poetic style that became evident in late 1912 and early 1913: 'wenn es nicht mißverständlich wäre, würde ich von Drogentraum-Gedichten sprechen' (240). Heselhaus goes on to elaborate this qualification in his discussion of the poem 'Abendlied' (*SW* 2:335–341): Trakl's 'Verfahren läßt sich ziemlich sicher aus Drogenträumen erklären; womit aber nicht gesagt sein soll, daß es sich bei solchen Gedichten um Aufzeichnungen derartiger Träume handelt' (241). In other words, a degree of congruence between drug experience and poetry does not necessarily indicate the direct derivation of the latter from the former. Rather, there is something about Trakl's 'procedure' ('Verfahren') that is reminiscent of – congruent with – the experience of drug-induced intoxication. The risk of poetological reduction attendant upon this observaton can be avoided if by 'procedure' we understand the procedure of the text, meaning the way its elements combine and interact, rather than – like Heselhaus – the procedure of the writer during composition. In what aspects of Trakl's textual procedure does this congruence lie? In chapter 9 we shall attempt to answer this question by investigating the underlying correspondences between the stylistic idiosyncrasies of Trakl's poetry and the characteristics of intoxicated consciousness. This broadening of our perspective to consider the role of other intoxicants and intoxication as a generic state in Trakl's poetry is also a necessary consequence of the view of his cocaine use described in 7.1 as just one element in his wide-ranging and compulsive quest for intoxication. Moreover, it gives us scope to consider the reasons for the poetry's reticence concerning a large number of the psychoactive substances with which, in his day-to-day existence, the poet himself was intimately familiar.

This more general discussion of the role of drugs and intoxication in Trakl's poetry is framed by two other chapters concerned with possible relationships between his literary work and cocaine in particular. With regard to this drug, we are immediately confronted with the question of absence alluded to above. For of the three writers whose works are considered in this study, Trakl stands out as the only one never to have used the word *Kokain* in his writings. His poetry can be situated, therefore – alongside Stevenson's 'great nineteenth-century cocaine book' (Boon 181–182; see 1.2) – at the outer limit of the body of texts that could be labelled the canon of cocaine literature, and one aim of the following discussion is to explore, in relation to Trakl's works, the subtextual dynamics of inclusion and exclusion that make a grey area of that limit. How, then, is one to go about analyzing the role of a drug in an œuvre in which it does not appear? Previous studies have adopted two different approaches, each with its own merits and limitations, both of which will be applied and appraised in our own analysis. Following Heselhaus (229) and Castoldi (160) we might, for example, investigate the hypothesis that the poetry contains symbolic, enciphered references to the drug rather than direct ones, or we might, like Kupfer (*GG* 228–231), look for correspondences to the cognitive and perceptual characteristics associated with particular drugs in the way Trakl's speaker views both the world and himself. A further possibility is suggested by another of the salient points to have emerged from the biographical account of Trakl's drug habit in 7.1. As we have seen, the evidence of Trakl's cocaine use is restricted to one relatively brief period, that is, the last few months of his life, and this circumstance may be taken as an invitation to approach the two poems dated to this period with this fact in mind. As the contemporaneity of the writing of these poems and Trakl's documented cocaine use is the most solid and irrefutable link between his poetry and this drug, this is also the most appropriate point at which to begin. By confronting us with manifestations of Trakl's themes and techniques in individual poems, these readings have the additional purpose of providing a basis – and a ready source of examples – for the more general remarks that follow in chapter 9.

8 The Poems of Trakl's 'Cocaine Period'

8.1 A Delirious Seascape

Ficker records that it was on the second afternoon of his visit to the Kraków military hospital of late October 1914 that Trakl introduced him to his latest – and as it turned out, last – poems:

> 'Wollen Sie hören, was ich im Feld geschrieben habe?,' fragte er nach einer Weile. 'Es ist blutwenig,' setzte er hinzu […]. Und nun las mir Trakl leise, mit der schlicht hinsagenden Stimme, die ihm eigen war, zwei Gedichte vor: 'Klage' und 'Grodek' – dieses, das sein letztes bleiben sollte, noch in einer Fassung, darin der Schluß, der Ausblick auf das Schicksal der ungeborenen Enkel, etwas breiter angelegt war und noch nicht jene jähe perspektivische Verkürzung aufwies, in die hinein dann Trakls Blick förmlich gebrochen und aus der Welt gehoben schien. Ich war erschüttert. (*A* 204–205)

Here, then, are two poems that we can collocate in the period in which Trakl is known to have taken 'sehr viel Cocain zu sich' (*HkA* 2:730). Moreover, Ficker's record of an earlier, longer version of 'Grodek', no longer extant, demonstrates that although Trakl composed these poems 'in the field,' he continued to revise and rework them during his time in hospital following Ficker's visit, a period in which his access to (and abuse of) cocaine is confirmed by the circumstances of his death, which occurred only a few days later. The first of these poems reads as follows:

Klage

Schlaf und Tod, die düstern Adler
Umrauschen nachtlang dieses Haupt:
Des Menschen goldnes Bildnis
Verschlänge die eisige Woge
Der Ewigkeit. An schaurigen Riffen
Zerschellt der purpurne Leib
Und es klagt die dunkle Stimme
Über dem Meer.

Schwester stürmischer Schwermut
Sieh ein ängstlicher Kahn versinkt
Unter Sternen,
Dem schweigenden Antlitz der Nacht. (*SW* 4:327–332)

Even a cursory reading of 'Klage' will suffice to understand why Boon should think that 'it is hard to draw solid conclusions' concerning the 'influence' of Trakl's drug use on his poetry (185). Despite the historical link between this poem and Trakl's cocaine abuse, to suggest that 'Klage' is 'about' cocaine in any conventional sense would be a hopelessly arbitrary and ultimately unhelpful position. One detail in this poem that might be seen as an oblique reference to intoxication, although not necessarily to cocaine intoxication, is the image of the 'anxious boat' in line 10, for Heselhaus writes that *Kahnsymbolik* is one of the means by which this state is represented in Trakl's poetry (229). Although he does not elaborate as to why boat imagery should be read in this way, the most obvious explanation is an intertextual one: Trakl's *Kahn* is a descendant of Rimbaud's *bateau ivre*. Such a derivation is supported by Rimbaud's status as not only one of Trakl's major influences, but also one of his main sources of poetic 'raw material' (e.g. Böschenstein 9–27; Grimm 271–313). The poem 'Le bateau ivre' (1871) is one of Rimbaud's most celebrated works, and the boat that features in this poem stands as a relatively transparent metaphor for intoxicated consciousness (Peschel *AR* 65–80; Kupfer *GG* 179–180). By extension, the different kinds and colours of water that it passes over have been seen as metaphorical representations of different intoxicants: wine, absinthe and hashish (ibid.). The resonance of Rimbaud's metaphor in Trakl's poetry is particularly strong in the poems 'Siebengesang des Todes' (*SW* 4i:137–145) and 'Frühling der Seele' (*SW* 3:374–384), in which the *Kahn* image is explicitly linked to the opium symbol 'poppy' and 'drunkenness' respectively:

Auf schwärzlichem Kahn fuhr jener schimmernde Ströme hinab,
Purpurner Sterne voll, und es sank
Friedlich das ergrünte Gezweig auf ihn,
Mohn aus silberner Wolke. ('Siebengesang des Todes')

O sanfte Trunkenheit
Im gleitenden Kahn. ('Frühling der Seele')

In 'Klage', however, we find no such obvious lexical complement that would activate an equivalent metaphorical meaning in this poem. Less obvious ones will be identified in the course of our reading, but these emerge only from more detailed analysis.

Moreover, such an interpretation of the *Kahn* image in 'Klage' would have to be weighed against its significantly stronger intertextual reverberation with the 'Schleier der Maja' passage from Arthur Schopenhauer's *Die Welt als Wille und Vorstellung*, quoted in the opening chapter of another of Trakl's favourite books, Nietzsche's *Die Geburt der Tragödie*:[101]

> Wie auf dem tobenden Meere, das, nach allen Seiten unbegrenzt, heulend Wellenberge erhebt und senkt, auf einem Kahn ein Schiffer sitzt, dem schwachen Fahrzeug vertrauend; so sitzt, mitten in einer Welt von Qualen, ruhig der einzelne Mensch, gestützt und vertrauend auf das principium individuationis. (Nietzsche 3:23)

Indeed, the same cursory reading of 'Klage' that suffices to understand Boon's difficulty also suffices to recognize the poem as a direct response to Schopenhauer's nautical simile. The basic scenario of a man in a small boat on a stormy sea is the same, only the calm of Schopenhauer's mariner and his trust in his craft have been replaced by fear (l. 10), the realization that the boat is sinking (ibid.) and the prospect of being smashed against reefs (ll. 5–6). Trakl's poem would thus seem to depict what happens when the illusion or *Schleier* of psychic safety offered by Schopenhauer's *principium individuationis* collapses. Certainly, these two intertextual echoings and their attendant symbolic connotations are by no means mutually exclusive; there is no reason why Trakl's *Kahn* should not be read in relation both to Rimbaud's and to Schopenhauer's precedents. Even so, the very symbolic openness of this image is itself illustrative of the difficulty interpreters face in pinning down Trakl's drug references, and once again the need to proceed systematically from areas of greater to lesser certainty is underlined in order to avoid wild or reductive interpretations. Let us therefore take a step back and approach the question of the poem's possible relationship to its author's cocaine abuse via an analysis of its thematic and stylistic elements.

---

101 Trakl's most recent editors Eberhard Sauermann and Hermann Zwerschina single out *Die Geburt der Tragödie* as one of the poet's main sources in their 'Editorischer Bericht' and trace its influence through his writings (*SW* 1:17–18). The Schopenhauer quote is among the passages they mention, but strangely not in relation to 'Klage'.

As the reader may deduce from the title, the dominant theme of 'Klage' is death, and the poem itself is an elegiac expression of sorrow in the face of death. The death theme is introduced directly in the opening words 'Schlaf und Tod' (l. 1). Ingo Leiß and Hermann Stadler note that Trakl's combination of sleep and death may be read as a mythological reference: in Greek myth the twin brothers Hypnos and Thanatos, the gods of sleep and death respectively, accompany the dead to the underworld, and in the fine arts they are usually portrayed as winged youths (398). In 'Klage' these two states are equated with 'gloomy eagles' circling the speaker's head. This type of opening, featuring birds that seem to be visible or audible to the lyric subject, as well as symbolic of his psychological condition, is not new for Trakl. The first image of the poem 'Anif' (*SW* 3:326–332), although without the menace of 'Klage', is similar: 'Erinnerung: Möven, gleitend über den dunklen Himmel / Männlicher Schwermut.' However, in contrast with the melancholy but deliberate remembrance symbolized by the 'gliding' seagulls in 'Anif', the 'swishing' of the eagles around the speaker's head in 'Klage' implies a delirium-like, highly unstable state of mind, in which consciousness itself – here represented metonymically by its seat, the head – is precarious, threatened with extinction through 'sleep and death.'

In this context, the root *-rausch-* of the verb 'umrauschen' (l. 2), the primary function of which is to convey the sound and movement of the 'gloomy eagles,' acquires added significance, hinting at a link between intoxication – *Rausch* – and the lyric subject's mental state. Thus, while the primary meaning of line 2 might be rendered by the translation 'swish all night around this head,' on a secondary level another meaning suggests itself: 'surround this head all night with intoxication.' Such a self-contained doubling of the predicate would mirror the explicit doubling of the subject, with the primary meaning of line 2 more closely aligned with the 'gloomy eagles' and the secondary one with 'sleep and death.' However, this secondary meaning is no more than an embedded suggestion, a connotation rather than a denotation, and as such it is uncertain whether the link between the speaker's state of mind and intoxication is one of equivalence (he *is* intoxicated) or metaphorical association (he *is as if* intoxicated). On the other hand, the word 'umrauschen' and its potential semantic permutations are highlighted by this word's formal importance to the text: it determines the phonetic pattern of the whole poem, which is dominated by sibilants, in particular the hushing *-sch-* sound both denoted by and contained in the onomatopoeic 'umrau*sch*en':

> ***Sch***laf und Tod, die dü***s***tern Adler
> Umrau***sch***en nachtlang die***s***e***s*** Haupt:
> Des Men***sch***en goldne***s*** Bildni***s***
> Ver***sch***länge die ei***s***ige Woge
> Der Ewigkeit. An ***sch***aurigen Riffen
> Zer***sch***ellt der purpurne Leib
> Und e***s*** klagt die dunkle ***S***timme
> Über dem Meer.
> ***Sch***wester ***s***türmischer ***Sch***wermut
> ***S***ieh ein äng***s***tlicher Kahn ver***s***inkt
> Unter ***S***ternen,
> Dem ***sch***weigenden Antlit***z*** der Nacht.

The colon ending line 2 indicates that the following ten lines embody or enact this *Umrauschen der Adler* textually, as the sound pattern confirms. In addition to the recurrence of 'swishing' sibilants illustrated above, we should also note the prominence of dental–liquid consonant pairings that echo the *-dl-* combination of 'A*dl*er': 'nach*tl*ang' (l. 2), 'go*ld*nes' (l. 3), 'Bi*ld*nis' (l. 3), 'zersche*llt*' (l. 6), 'k*l*ag*t*' (l. 7), '*d*unk*l*e' (l. 7), 'ängs*tl*icher' (l. 10), and 'An*tl*itz' (l. 12).

From the thematic point of view, the images that follow the introductory couplet develop different aspects of the death theme introduced in the opening line. The 'icy wave of eternity' that would engulf 'man's golden portrait' implies the futility of human achievement, in particular the helplessness of the intellect and its attributes – ambition, optimism, religious faith and philosophical ideal, any or all of which may be read into 'Des Menschen goldnes Bildnis' (l. 3) – when confronted with the endlessness of time. The enigmatically subjunctive mood of the verb 'verschlänge' (l. 4) strengthens the impression that this image encapsulates the mind contemplating its own demise. By contrast, the more concrete indicative mood of the verb 'zerschellt' (l. 6) in the following image underlines the stark physicality of the destruction of the body as it is dashed against 'gruesome reefs.' The body's 'purple' colour suggests its bloody and battered condition and underlines how far removed it is from the 'golden' ideal of the portrait in line 3. It would appear that the only function of the lyric subject's 'smashed' body still under his control is his 'voice', while all that remains of his 'engulfed' intellect is the capacity to 'lament', and so in lines 7 and 8 we find a lament within a lament, the echoing of the title underlining that these lines contain the crucial, self-defining moment of the poem – the final act of self-assertion on the speaker's part before his annihilation: 'Und es klagt die dunkle Stimme / Über dem Meer' (ll. 7–8). Notably, the second of these lines is the only one in the body of the poem –in this sense there is a further link to the title – that does not make phonetic reference to the dominant sound patterns established in the opening lines. This phonetic peculiarity highlights the thematic importance of this image, for line 8 represents a break in the swishing of the eagles and hence a momentary reassertion of the speaker's control over his own state of mind. The oppressive swishing, however, asserts itself with renewed vigour in line 9 and is maintained throughout the last sentence, which articulates the final destruction of both mind and body in the image of the sinking boat, an event that the speaker calls upon a sister-figure to witness. This invocation is particularly meaningful in view of the indifference of the natural and divine spheres to the fate of the individual, manifested in the last line in the 'silent face of night.' A comparison between the sister's and the night's reactions to the sinking of the boat is encouraged by an exchange of attributes: the meteorological term 'stormy' is used to describe the sister's melancholy, whereas the night acquires a 'mute face.' The contrast between the night's silent indifference and the sister's 'stormy melancholy' suggests that human solidarity and compassion, rather than religious faith or cosmic harmony, are the only genuine sources of solace in the face of death.

The images that make up this poem are connected not only by common sound pattern or their contribution to the development of the death theme; rather, the most fundamental link between them is that they cohere to create a scene with a recognizable setting in time and place. The temporal setting is night, to which explicit references occur at both the beginning and end of the poem: 'nachtlang' (l. 2) and 'Nacht' (l. 12). Further, oblique references to night can be seen in the words 'Schlaf' (l. 1), 'düstern' (l. 1), 'dunkle' (l. 7) and 'Sternen' (l. 11). The spatial setting is at sea, which is named directly in line 8 and to which implicit references are contained in the words 'Woge' (l. 4), 'Riffen' (l. 5), and 'Kahn' (l. 10). Other words in the poem that are consistent with and help to fill out the depiction of the seascape include 'Adler' (l. 1), 'Verschlänge' (l. 4), 'eisige' (l. 4), 'Zerschellt' (l. 6), 'stürmischer' (l. 9), 'versinkt' (l. 10), and 'Sternen' (l. 11). Leiß and Stadler remark: 'Ungewöhnlich ist, daß Trakl eine einheitliche Bildwelt – die des "Meeres" – verwendet, in die selbst die Adler sich einordnen lassen' (399). However, the assertion that Trakl's employment of a unified sphere of imagery in 'Klage' is unusual must be considered inaccurate, for as Steinkamp demonstrates in her analysis of Trakl's 'landscape code' (46ff.), one of the characteristic features of what is regarded as his mature verse is precisely that the images contained in these poems represent contiguous elements of a given setting as they are perceived from a certain – whether static or mobile – standpoint within that setting.

No definite setting is evident in the majority of poems from Trakl's first phase, that is, those collected in the *Sammlung 1909* (*HkA* 1:213–256).[102] But in a small number of these poems – 'Herbst' (*SW* 1:224–228) is one example – and in the majority of poems from the second phase, those written between 1910 and early 1912 and included in the collection *Gedichte* of 1913 (*HkA* 1:9–73), the lyric voice seems to emanate from a perspective based in or around a garden; thus, Steinkamp characterizes the garden as the dominant landscape of Trakl's second phase (70–75). In certain poems from the second and most of those from the third phase, spanning from late 1912 to the first two months of 1914 and represented by the posthumous collection *Sebastian im Traum* of 1915 (*HkA* 1:75–150), the perspective becomes mobile as the speaker typically sets off on foot through the countryside, an environment that Steinkamp labels 'Hügel und Ebene' (92–100). In the fourth and final phase, corresponding to the poems written between March and October 1914 and published in Ficker's journal *Der Brenner* in 1914–15 (*HkA* 1:143–168), the speaker takes refuge in the mountains, from where he can observe both his immediate alpine surroundings and the scenes of war and destruction in the *Hügel-und-Ebene* environment of the previous phase now visible in the valley below. Steinkamp designates this characteristic spatial structure of the fourth phase 'Gebirge und Tal' (111–117). What is unusual about 'Klage', therefore, is not that Trakl employs a unified sphere of imagery, as Leiß and Stadler claim, but his choice of setting, the sea, which is untypical not only of the fourth phase, to which this poem belongs, but of Trakl's poetry as a whole. We should also note that even in Trakl's other poems featuring boat imagery, such as the two cited above, 'Siebengesang des Todes' and 'Früh-

102 The generally accepted division of Trakl's work into four phases was first proposed by Esselborn (39–40). This division reflects the arrangement of the poems in the *Historisch-kritische Ausgabe*, which is referenced here for this reason; bibliographical references for individual poems, on the other hand, refer to the more recent *Sämtliche Werke*.

ling der Seele,' the boat is not at sea, but on a river that traverses the more familiar landscape of *Hügel und Ebene.*

This unusual choice of setting has important thematic implications. In Trakl's earlier poems the sum of natural features and processes evident in the rural landscape represents a model of meaningful and harmonious existence, and the human figures populating them are either integrated in the landscape (characteristically as farmers, shepherds, hunters, etc.) or alienated from it (and may be variously designated as sick, mad, blind, leprous, homeless, beggars, travellers, etc.; Steinkamp 228–232). In poems depicting alienated human figures, the natural environment continues to function as an ideal of cosmic harmony, and alienation from this harmony, reflected in images of decay and decline in the natural world, causes them great suffering, so that such figures typically aspire to return to an original state of naïve integration. Kaspar Hauser in the poem 'Kaspar Hauser Lied' (*SW* 3:312–325) and *der Abgeschiedene* in the poem 'Gesang des Abgeschiedenen' (*SW* 4i:152–162) are two representatives of this type. Even in the war poems of Trakl's fourth phase, the absolute disharmony of war is resolved as the bodies and spirits of the dead soldiers are mythically reintegrated into the landscape, as the following lines from the poem 'Im Osten' (*SW* 4:319–322) illustrate:

> Mit zerbrochenen Brauen, silbernen Armen
> Winkt sterbenden Soldaten die Nacht.
> Im Schatten der herbstlichen Esche
> Seufzen die Geister der Erschlagenen.

The hostile sea-setting of 'Klage' represents a significant deviation from Trakl's familiar view of the relationship between man and nature. Far from evoking an original harmony between the two, this poem emphasizes human fragility confronted with the overwhelming power of cosmic forces, which are entirely indifferent to the fate of the individual. Pertinent here is the contrast between the 'waving' night of the poem 'Im Osten' and the 'silent face' of night in 'Klage'. In the latter poem death is brought about not by conflict between men, as in the other poems of Trakl's fourth phase, but by the forces of nature themselves. The effect is a much more pessimistic, existentialist vision of the human condition; the implication is that the life of the individual acquires meaning not from its integration into a higher cosmic or metaphysical order – the speaker's faith in which would seem to have evaporated – but must generate its own, either through compassion and solidarity, represented here by the appeal to the sister, or through self-expression, in this case a 'dark voice' that projects its song of sorrow 'over the sea.'

We are now in a position to assess possible relationships between 'Klage' and its author's cocaine abuse of the period during which it was composed. For the sake of balance this assessment can usefully be integrated into one of the poem's biographical referentiality more generally. Indeed, it might seem paradoxical to suggest that a poem with a maritime setting can be considered to refer to the situation of its author writing in landlocked Galicia, but this would be a hasty judgement. We have already noted that this setting, and more importantly the particular use that Trakl makes of it, point not to the author's boating experience but to his reading of Nietzsche (and perhaps Rimbaud); the poem's intertextual resonance itself can thus be identified as a first element implying an image of its author that corresponds with our knowledge of his biography – not as a sailor (which we know he was not), but as a reader of Nietzsche and Rimbaud (which we know he was). Three further elements can be identified in the text that contribute both to the biographical correspondence of the poem's authorial image and to its idiosyncratic mechanism for the projection of this. The most obvious is the sister figure of line 9. Although the thematic function of this figure can be considered independently of its biographical valence, as it has been in our own analysis above, it is notable that the same function could hypothetically be fulfilled equally well by a different figure: a mother, brother, friend, etc. For this reason, the suspicion is likely to occur even to readers unfamiliar with Trakl's biography that the selection of *Schwester* for this role over other possible candidates is, at least in part, biographically determined (in part it is also phonetically determined), and consultation of any biographical summary (e.g. 7.1) can only strengthen this impression.

The last two biographically relevant elements in 'Klage' relate to the unusual way in which textual subjectivity is manifested in Trakl's poetry in general, one of our main concerns in the next chapter (see 9.1), so brief consideration will suffice here. The first is the phrase 'dieses Haupt' in line 2; in the absence of the pronoun *ich* this stands, lexically speaking, as the most direct self-reference in the poem, especially considering that no points of reference are offered for an interpretation of the demonstrative adjective 'dieses' alternative to 'belonging to the speaker.' The second is the coherence of the lyric perspective generated by what Leiß and Stadler call the poem's 'einheitliche Bildwelt' (399). The combined effect of these two elements is to indicate that the agitated state of mind evoked in the poem, combining delirium with acute existential angst, can be attributed to its speaker. The potential biographical significance of these elements – the potential, that is, for postulating a degree of identity between speaker and author – can be seen, following Tomashevsky's argument (see 1.4), as implicit in their very subjectiveness, and this potential is reinforced, which is not to say definitively activated, by their combination with the other biographical elements already discussed.

At this point, finally, the poem's composition during the period of its author's cocaine abuse assumes pertinence to our interpretation. If the poem itself hints, in the ways we have described, at a degree of identity between its speaker's and its author's states of mind, then the biographical circumstances associated with the author's psychological lability become integral factors contributing to the 'mutual tension' between 'word and situation' (Jakobson 320; see 1.4). The poem does not refer to these circumstances directly, but by oblique means it draws attention to their role in the poet's biography. Within this constellation, the poem's title also assumes potential biographical significance, suggesting that the text it names represents an attempt by the writer to sublimate his suffering through poetic self-expression, just as the speaker does in the lines we have identified as the poem's thematic core. For the poem itself the circumstances behind its author's suffering – the trauma of his frontline experience (see 8.2), but also his heavy cocaine use that came about in response to it (see 7.1) – thus become 'significant absences.' It is prudent here to reaffirm the point, made at the outset of this analysis, that this poem is no more 'about' its author's cocaine abuse than it is 'about' cocaine in any other sense. Nonetheless, with reference to Jakobson's theoretical remarks on the relationship between literary works and the situations in which they are produced, we can conclude that even if 'Klage' contains Trakl's cocaine abuse only 'negatively', the nature and extent of the poem's biographical investment indicate that the poem is far from 'indifferent to it' (320; see 1.4).

Let us now turn to the second poem Trakl recited to Ficker from his hospital bed in Kraków in late October 1914.

8.2 On the Road to Black Decay

The second of the two poems Trakl composed 'in the field' in the autumn of 1914 and revised in hospital in Kraków is the much-anthologized 'Grodek'. The title of this poem refers to the Battle of Gródek-Rawa Ruska of 6–11 September 1914, one of the first major battles on the Eastern Front in the First World War. During Ficker's stay in Kraków, Trakl recounted that for two days during this battle he had been left in sole care of a group of 90 wounded and dying soldiers, a task for which he lacked the necessary equipment, training and fortitude (Ficker *A* 200–201). The trauma associated with these days, during which he witnessed a mass hanging and one of the wounded soldiers shooting himself in the head, triggered the breakdown that led to his hospitalization. This choice of title, by implying that the poem can be read as a response to the author's actual experience at the place after which it is named, constitutes a more direct biographical reference than any of those we have identified in 'Klage'. The revised version of 'Grodek' that Trakl posted to Ficker shortly before his fatal overdose is the only one to have survived:

Grodek
2. Fassung

Am Abend tönen die herbstlichen Wälder
Von tödlichen Waffen, die goldnen Ebenen
Und blauen Seen, darüber die Sonne
Düstrer hinrollt; umfängt die Nacht
Sterbende Krieger, die wilde Klage
Ihrer zerbrochenen Münder.
Doch stille sammelt im Weidengrund
Rotes Gewölk, darin ein zürnender Gott wohnt
Das vergoßne Blut sich, mondne Kühle;
Alle Straßen münden in schwarze Verwesung.
Unter goldnem Gezweig der Nacht und Sternen
Es schwankt der Schwester Schatten durch den schweigenden Hain,
Zu grüßen die Geister der Helden, die blutenden Häupter;
Und leise tönen im Rohr die dunkeln Flöten des Herbstes.
O stolzere Trauer! ihr ehernen Altäre
Die heiße Flamme des Geistes nährt heute ein gewaltiger Schmerz,
Die ungebornen Enkel. (1:167)

The influence of Trakl's cocaine abuse on the poetic activity of his final months is certainly no more obvious in 'Grodek' than in 'Klage'. If anything it is less so, for 'Grodek' does not display the same direct and ongoing concern with the state of mind of its speaker as 'Klage', in which this state can be described as delirious and perhaps intoxicated. Despite the unambiguous biographical reference in its title and its evocation of the wartime violence and bloodshed that prompted its author's breakdown, this poem is in fact less subjectively oriented than its immediate predecessor. We might summarize this difference by saying that if 'Klage' has a centripetal dynamic that tends towards the sublimation of its author's suffering, then 'Grodek' has a centrifugal one that tends towards its mythologization.

As far as its possible relationship to the poet's cocaine consumption is concerned, we might also note that in 'Grodek' there is no image with such well-established drug associations as the 'anxious boat' that is used as a metaphor for the speaker's condition in the text discussed in 8.1. This particular image would appear out of place in 'Grodek', as in this poem Trakl returns to the *Hügel-und-Ebene* environment familiar from the poems of his third phase. The breadth of the perspective, which takes in a plurality of 'forests', 'plains' and 'lakes' (ll. 1–3), suggests that the speaker may be observing the battle scene from a topographically elevated position similar to the mountain refuges evoked in several earlier poems of the fourth phase (compare 'Das Gewitter,' *SW* 4ii:132–149; 'Die Schwermut,' *SW* 4ii:215–232; and 'Die Nacht,' *SW* 4ii:249–260). In this respect, 'Grodek' can be considered more consistent with – and the final embodiment of – the general patterns governing the development of the lyric perspective in Trakl's poetry from the second phase onwards.

One important similarity between 'Grodek' and 'Klage' is the theme of annihilation, here stated most succinctly in line 10: 'Alle Straßen münden in schwarze Verwesung.' In 'Grodek', however, the manifestation of this theme is transferred from the personal to the social and cultural domain. Thus, whereas in 'Klage' the poem's final image conveys the destruction of the individual, the final image of 'Grodek' evokes the genocidal extinction of future generations ('Die ungebornen Enkel,' l. 17). In this way the carnage of one particular battle depicted in the first half of the poem becomes a symbolic cause of seemingly apocalyptic destruction. This shift from the specific and historical to the universal and mythical occurs gradually over the course of the poem, in which the progression of cultural-historical events on the battlefield is superimposed on a natural temporal progression from early evening (at the beginning of the poem the sun is still in the sky, although 'rolling more gloomily'; l. 3) via the 'red cloud' (l. 8) of sunset, to night (named directly in lines 4 and 11). Steinkamp identifies the stages in the cultural sequence of 'Grodek' as battle (ll. 1–6), death (ll. 7–10), honouring the dead (ll. 11–14) and the destruction of future generations (ll. 15–17), with the transition from one stage to the next indicated syntactically by a new sentence (189–191).

The opening lines of the poem are marked by a striking disparity between the visual and auditory perceptions of the speaker: the idyllic evening landscape of 'autumnal forests,' 'golden plains' and 'blue lakes' is offset by the violent sounds of battle emanating from it ('tönen die herbstlichen Wälder / Von tödlichen Waffen,' ll. 1–2). This incongruity of sight and sound underlines the alienation of man, here perceived aurally, from the cosmic harmony embodied in the natural environment, perceived visually. In this poem, as in the other war poems of Trakl's fourth phase, this alienation extends to the whole of human civilization, manifesting itself in the self-destructive conflict of battle. Once again (compare the lines from 'Im Osten' cited in 8.1), in 'Grodek' dying brings reintegration into the natural order, and at this point perceptual congruity is also reestablished – the speaker can both see and hear the 'dying warriors': 'umfängt die Nacht / Sterbende Krieger, die wilde Klage / Ihrer zerbrochenen Münder' (ll. 4–6). In terms of theme as well as setting, then, 'Grodek' represents a return to the more familiar standpoint of Trakl's earlier work. In the remaining lines of this poem, however, Trakl develops and radicalizes the consequences of this thematic position as never before.

The poem's second sentence, spanning lines 7 to 10, is remarkable for its distorted syntax, which highlights the transition initiated here from the depiction of a particular historical event, the Battle of Gródek-Rawa Ruska, conveyed in more neutrally descriptive language, to a mythopoeic elaboration of its universal significance. In particular, the main verb 'sammelt' (l. 7) appears to have a triple subject – 'Rotes Gewölk' (l. 8), 'Das vergoßne Blut' (l. 9), and 'mondne Kühle' (l. 9) – although the syntactic equivalence of these three noun phrases is brought into question by their relative disjointedness. Further, their status as subjects is made ambiguous by their distance from the main verb, especially 'Das vergoßne Blut' and 'mondne Kühle,' and in the case of 'Rotes Gewölk' and 'mondne Kühle' by their separation from the reflexive pronoun 'sich' (l. 9), which is itself positioned at a most unnatural two-line distance from the verb it reflects. The Latinate complexity of this construction, resonant of the epics and sagas of past epochs, itself contributes to the poem's extension into a mythical and transhistorical dimension. It is significant also that what most disturbs the syntactic flow of this sentence is a 'raging god' who 'lives' in 'red cloud' (l. 8). The appearance of this god provides a fresh perspective on the battle scene described in the opening: it is no longer simply a manifestation of human folly, but becomes part of a larger metaphysical scheme, in which both men and gods (note the indefinite article in 'ein zürnender Gott,' indicating that this god is one of several) have parts to play. In this context the 'spilt blood' of the dead soldiers may be understood as a sacrificial offering to appease the wrath of the 'raging god.' At this point in the poem the process of reintegration of the dead soldiers into the natural environment seems to be complete. As their 'spilt blood' collects in the 'pasture land' (l. 7), commingling – grammatically at least – with the 'red cloud' and 'lunar coolness,' the 'wild lament' (l. 5) of the dying is stilled ('Doch stille,' l. 7). The second main clause in this sentence summarizes and explicates the universal law that the bloodshed at Grodek has come to epitomize: 'Alle Straßen münden in schwarze Verwesung' (l. 10). The rhetorical power of this formulation is enhanced by its syntactic simplicity, which stands out after the convolution of the preceding lines, and its semantic clarity is also – by the standards of Trakl's poetry – extraordinary. It substantiates what is merely suggested in earlier poems, namely that for Trakl, the flux of the world is a manifestation of the terminal process that governs all forms of life, whether human, animal, or vegetable, individual or social, all of which are condemned to decay and death. The reassimilation of the dead into nature as depicted in lines 7 to 9, therefore, does not bring redemption and does not reverse or arrest but simply confirms the inevitability of decline.

The third sentence introduces a new human element in the form of the 'sister's shade' (l. 12), which 'sways through the silent grove' (l. 12) to 'greet the ghosts of heroes' (l. 13). The transformation of the dead soldiers into 'the ghosts of heroes,' in combination with the supernatural meeting between a 'shade' and 'ghosts', reinforces the mythical dimension of the scene developed in the previous sentence. The sister's appearance itself might be read as a mythical allusion, as Martin Swales notes (192): in Norse myth the Valkyries would ride over battlefields to claim the spirits of dead heroes and escort them to Valhalla. That her meeting with the dead soldiers takes place in a grove, a characteristic site of pagan worship, adds to the mythical import of this image, as does the adjective 'schweigend' (l. 12) used to describe it, as this implicitly attributes the power of speech to a group of trees and so intensifies the atmosphere of *beseelte Natur* already established in the night's embrace of dying soldiers. The figure of the sister has a similar function to that she assumes in 'Klage' (see 8.1), suggesting a reassertion of intimacy and solidarity in human relations; in 'Grodek' this contrasts with the conflict that has dominated to this point and resulted in so much suffering ('die wilde Klage / Ihrer zerbrochenen Münder,' ll. 5–6) and death ('Sterbende Krieger,' l. 5). In this context, the sibilant alliteration associated with her arrival takes on a soothing quality, the opposite of its threatening character in 'Klage': 'Es *sch*wankt der *Sch*wester *Sch*atten durch den *sch*weigenden Hain' (l. 12). The idea that her homage to the dead amounts to a pantheistic ritual deriving from an original concord between humanity and the natural world is inherent in line 13, in which the sounds of nature provide a musical accompaniment to her movement: 'Und leise tönen im Rohr die dunkeln Flöten des Herbstes.' The repetition of the verb 'tönen', previously used in line 1, underlines the contrast between the two sources of sound associated with it: on one hand the 'deadly weapons' (l. 2) symptomatic of the degenerate state of civilization, and on the other the 'dark flutes of autumn' (l. 13) that symbolize the essential and mysterious powers of nature, the 'quiet' (l. 13) autumnal decline of which towards winter at once mirrors and offsets the self-destructive collapse of human society.

Although the deaths of the individual soldiers result in the reintegration of their corpses into a greater cosmic order – the order of 'schwarze Verwesung' (l. 10) – this brings no consolation for the human species as a whole, which faces a bleak fate: the annihilation of future generations ('Die ungebornen Enkel,' l. 17). The comparative degree of the adjective in the formulation 'prouder grief' (l. 15) at the beginning of the poem's final sentence can perhaps be related to this distinction between individual and collective destinies. Whereas the sister can take pride in the heroism of the soldiers' deaths, thus ennobling her grief, the speaker's grief for the downfall of humankind is unrelieved by any such notions of honour, purpose or deliverance, so that all he is left with is a 'violent pain' (l. 16). This pain is described as 'nourishing the hot flame of the spirit' (l. 16), a formulation with ambivalent implications. The collocation of 'flame' and 'violent pain' suggests destruction by fire, but at the same time this is described as a source of spiritual 'nourishment', and so might be interpreted as the force underlying the articulation of the 'violent pain' in the poem

'Grodek' itself. The speaker's grief, like the sister's, is ritualized in the invocation of 'brazen altars' (l. 15), and this, in connection with the phrase 'hot flame,' also suggesting a religious rite, links his historically specific ('heute', l. 16) grief and the elegy that it has inspired – that is, this poem – to the same greater mythical and metaphysical system in which the events depicted earlier in the poem have already been placed.

Significantly, this occurs without any further development of the battlefield setting, and Steinkamp argues that the absence of landscape words in the final three lines of this, Trakl's last poem, points to the ultimate failure of the landscape code that had dominated his poetry since the second phase, in particular to its inadequacy for articulating the decline of human civilization in the universal and ahistorical terms of natural and organic processes (272). This conclusion is questionable, however, for the lines in question cannot be considered in isolation from the rest of the poem, and the absence of landscape words in the final sentence is meaningful precisely because of its contrast to the preceding images in which landscape words are predominant. In this regard, the use of an adjective with a metallic referent such as 'ehern' (l. 15) can be likened to the use of other words with the semantic feature 'metal' in earlier poems, where this indicates human alienation from the order intrinsic in the natural world. Representative examples include 'Auf meine Stirne tritt kaltes *Metall*' from 'De Profundis' (*SW* 2:111–123), 'O des Menschen verweste Gestalt: gefügt aus kalten *Metallen*' from 'Siebengesang des Todes' (*SW* 4i:137–145), and 'Über stürzenden Städten / Von *Stahl*' from 'Der Schlaf' (*SW* 4i:13–24). The point is that the negation of landscape is a variation allowed for by Trakl's landscape code, and as the final lines of 'Grodek' illustrate, the thematic weight of this negation depends on its affirmation in other parts of the poem. It is not, therefore, a failure of Trakl's code, but a variant application of it, an opposition not *to* the code but *of* the code.

With respect to the thematic peculiarity of 'Grodek' in relation to Trakl's earlier poems, Steinkamp's observations are more convincing:

> Sah er [der Traklsche Sprecher] in den landschaftlichen Abläufen des Tages in 'Nacht' und 'Kühle' und jenen des Jahres in 'Herbst' und 'Verwesung' bislang – in den Landschaftsgedichten ab der ersten Entwicklungsphase – eine Vorbedeutung seines eigenen Endes und allgemein einer kulturellen Endzeit, so wird nun, im unmittelbar erlebten Mord der Völker auf dem Schlachtfeld von 'Grodek', diese Ahnung zur erschütternden Gewißheit. (191)

We should add that the same thematic radicalization – the climactic realization of what had previously been mere intimations of destruction – can be seen in 'Klage' too, so that this can be identified as the factor that links and distinguishes the two poems Trakl composed in the final weeks of his life. In both, the processes of decline and disintegration manifested in his earlier poems are amplified into acts of slaughter and extermination.

At this point we cannot but note a biographical parallel of direct relevance to this investigation, namely a concomitant tendency to radicalization in important aspects of the poet's life. Just as the collapse that followed Trakl's involvement in the Battle of Gródek-Rawa Ruska represented a radicalization of the psychological instability that had always accompanied his extraordinarily acute sensibility, so too his intense cocaine use of the same period amounted to a radicalization of the self-destructive pattern that was always inherent in his drug habit. Although any attempt to place these biographical and poetic developments in a relationship of straightforward cause and effect would misrepresent their complex and reciprocal actions and reactions, to deny any link between them would imply a willful misreading of the biographical referentiality that, as we have seen, is inscribed into the texts themselves. A meaningful way forward, therefore, is to enhance and refine our appreciation of the connections themselves, in particular of the extent to which Trakl's conception of the poetic intersected with his experience of intoxication, and for this task a considered account of his stylistic idiosyncrasies is now indispensable.

9 Trakl's Poetics of Intoxication

9.1 Aspects of an Intoxicated Style

In order to identify and analyze the characteristic aspects of Trakl's poetic style, we might start by considering their overall effect. Pertinent in this respect is the remark of Leiß and Stadler discussed in 8.1 that 'Klage' is atypical because its images belong to a uniform 'Bildwelt' (399). From this we can infer that in their view Trakl's poetry normally consists of disparate images arranged arbitrarily, and this inference is confirmed by their description of the elements of earlier poems as 'exchangeable': 'kein einziges Glied wäre – wie in früheren Gedichten – austauschbar' (398). This notion is problematic not least because it subverts the very integrity of the text – suggesting, it might be argued, a failure to apprehend its integrity – yet it is by no means uncommon among Trakl critics. In his discussion of the poem 'Gesang einer gefangenen Amsel' (*SW* 4i:290–300), Williams formulates a similar idea:

> This constellation of loosely connected images seems to be somewhat randomly arranged. It appears that one could almost rearrange the order of various lines without appreciably altering the import of the poem. [...] Each image or trope appears to stand relatively independently of the surrounding tropes and images. The contextual background in and against which images and phrases ordinarily take on significance provides no immediately apparent clues as to how things fit together. (24–25)

Arguing along similar lines, Philipp writes of the 'Auflösung von Kontiguitätsverhältnissen in der Dichtung Trakls' (137). Even if we consider such responses erroneous, their recurrence testifies to the often disconcerting peculiarity of Trakl's poetic language.

In response to claims for the interchangeability of Trakl's images, their 'relative independence' of one another, and the 'dissolution of contiguity relationships' in his poetry, a small number of scholars have adopted the opposite view, asserting the intrinsic coherence of Trakl's poems, even if for some the apprehension of this coherence remains a matter of intuition:

'it seems to be demonstrable that [Trakl's poetry] succeeds in achieving (at its best) a full coherence. But such demonstrations cannot be made in familiar critical terms' (Seymour-Smith 661). Steinkamp's text-semantic approach (32–34), based on the structuralist theories of Algirdas Julius Greimas and Werner Kallmeyer, has provided perhaps the most comprehensive demonstration of the coherence of Trakl's poetry. Following this method, Steinkamp identifies key lexemes in Trakl's poems that contribute to the depiction and development of the temporal and spatial characteristics of a particular scene and by extension to the thematic structure of the poem in question. In this way she arrives at, among other things, the results outlined in 8.1 concerning the typical settings of Trakl's poems in each of his four phases. She also succeeds in showing that Trakl's images are neither independent, exchangeable, nor arranged arbitrarily, but put together rather in accordance with a definite structural principle. Steinkamp's analysis, published in 1988, represents at once a revival of an older direction of critical thought, represented for example by Klaus Simon's 1955 *Traum und Orpheus*, and a major step forward for Trakl scholarship, which in the 1970s and for much of the 1980s had become bogged down with convictions of the poetry's incomprehensibility, non-referentiality and randomness cultivated in parallel with speculation about the writer's mental health. Indeed, the persisting strength of these convictions is such that Steinkamp's work has yet to receive due recognition, as can be seen from the claims for the exchangeability and arbitrary arrangement of Trakl's images made in more recent studies such as those by Williams (1993) and Leiß and Stadler (1997).

One reservation that Steinkamp's study might provoke is this: her understandable determination to demonstrate the coherence of Trakl's poetry is such that she tends to minimize the importance of the factors that have caused so many critics to be convinced of its incoherence. In other words, apart from noting the poetry's 'enciphered' appearance (52), she does not give particular weight to the effects generated by the *elusiveness* of its coherence, although these effects certainly contribute substantially to the peculiar fascination of Trakl's poems. In regard to the much-discussed question of subjectivity in Trakl's poetry, for example, Steinkamp counters the commonly held view that the almost complete disappearance of the pronoun *ich* from the later poems amounts to a dissolution of subjectivity – Esselborn's 'Entsubjektivierung' (194) – or even a schizophrenic collapse, by showing how Trakl gradually replaces the explicit first person pronouns of his early works with a 'homogenous direction of perception and movement' (121) in the later ones, while maintaining a distinct 'perspective of human experience' (37) inherent in the point of view of the lyric subject in each poem:

> Diese Perspektivierung im Raum durch eine kohärente Beobachtungs- und Bewegungsrichtung kann als für Trakl typische Gestaltung der lyrischen Erlebnisdimension angesehen werden. Sie löst für seine Dichtung (besonders ab der zweiten Entwicklungsphase) das traditionelle Konzept des personal auftretenden lyrischen Ich ab. (121)

To illuminate Trakl's procedure further, a useful analogy can be made with Jakobson's vivid characterization of subjectivity in the works of Pasternak:

> The first person is thrust into the background. But it is only an apparent relegation – here too the eternal [first person] hero of the lyric is present. It is merely a case of his being metonymically presented; in the same way, no railway train can be seen in Chaplin's *A Woman of Paris*, but we are aware of its arrival from the reactions of the people in front of the cameras – as if the invisible, transparent train were making its way between the screen and the audience. Similarly, in Pasternak's poetry, images of the surrounding world function as contiguous reflections, or metonymical expressions, of the poet's self. (307)

Although only rarely represented by a pronoun, the role of the speaker as lyric subject in Trakl's poetry is not only apparent in the spatial and temporal continuity of the perspective, but is often manifest in references to bodily parts or functions, physical position or movement, and mental activity. All of these are present in 'Klage': body parts in the phrases 'dieses Haupt' (l. 2) and 'der purpurne Leib' (l. 6); the linguistic faculty in 'die dunkle Stimme' (l. 7); physical position in 'über dem Meer' (l. 8) and 'unter Sternen' (l. 11); and mental activity in the opening couplet with its final colon (ll. 1–2). In 'Grodek', with its emphasis on the social and universal over the individual, the only part of the speaker to appear directly is his 'Geist' (l. 16), although as this is preceded by the impersonal determinate article 'des' rather than a possessive adjective, even this is not unambiguously his own. What this poem illustrates, however, is that the other human figures who appear in Trakl's poetry are portrayed in the same, curiously disjointed way. Thus, the wounded soldiers are represented metonymically by 'die wilde Klage / Ihrer zerbrochenen Münder' (ll. 5–6), and later as ghosts by 'die blutenden Häupter' (l. 13), while the sister who pays homage to them is merely a 'Schatten' (l. 12). Furthermore, in numerous poems the subject is designated nominally if not pronominally, for example as a 'Wanderer' in several poems of the third, *Hügel-und-Ebene* phase. In 'Klage' the 'ängstlicher Kahn' of line 11 might be read as a metaphorical designation of the lyric subject, a kind of 'Wanderer' at sea, and the anthropomorphic quality of this image is reinforced by the emotive adjective 'ängstlicher' that qualifies the normally inanimate 'Kahn'.

Steinkamp's observations on the nature of subjectivity in Trakl's poetry are valuable, therefore, not least as a foil to the many commentators who would interpret the poems as symptoms of their author's psychic disintegration. However, once it has been established that Trakl's poetic dissent from the convention of expressing subjectivity by means of personal pronouns is the result of stylistic choice rather than a symptom of pathology (and we should also note that his letters exhibit none of the schizophrenic symptoms that have been detected in his poetry, as Kleefeld has the good sense to point out), the question remains as to the reasons for and effects of such a radical shift. Steinkamp mentions Trakl's quest for a 'universal form' that will 'say and mean more' (expressions taken from his letter to Buschbeck of late autumn 1911, 1:485–486), his desire to create a perspective with which the reader can identify, as one motivation for this stylistic feature (37, 96). But this is only a partial explanation. After all, to generate a 'coherent direction of observation and movement' by means of which the reader can participate vicariously in the lyric perspective, it is not strictly necessary to do away with the lyric *ich*. Indeed, the simplest – and certainly the most conventional – way to generate such a perspective would be through the repeated use of a personal pronoun, whether *ich* or a less egocentric alternative, such as *du*. One unusual feature of the prose poem 'Winternacht' (*SW* 3:352–368; see 10.2) is Trakl's quite uncharacteristic use of the pronoun *du* for precisely this purpose. His avoidance of this technique in the vast majority of his poems must point to a deeper significance for his relinquishment of pronoun-based subjectivity.

Although it is exaggerated, then, to claim that Trakl's poetry manifests a complete dissolution of subjectivity, and fallacious to draw from this that the poet himself must have been schizophrenic, it must be acknowledged that the development of Trakl's poetic language from his earlier to his later works displays a significant qualitative shift in subjectivity. Clearly, the subjectivity of a mature Trakl poem is less self-assured, less self-evident, more aware its own precariousness, and more prone to fragmentation than that expressed by the *ich* of his more 'conventional' early poems. In the poems of the third and fourth phases especially, this subjectivity often appears threatened with collapse, without however reaching the state of total dissolution indicated by Esselborn's 'Entsubjektivierung'. Even when the pronoun *ich* occurs, such as in the late prose poem 'Offenbarung und Untergang' (*SW* 4ii:49–71), this stands in ironic contrast with the speaker's perception of his own tendency to psychic disintegration: 'und da ich mit silbernen Fingern mich über die schweigenden Wasser bog, sah ich daß mich mein Antlitz verlassen.' Only rarely in Trakl's poetry does the instability of subjectivity achieve such drastic and direct expression as in this rewriting of the Narcissus myth; usually its expression is more subtle, as in 'Klage' and 'Grodek', being implicit in the absence of a unifying pronoun and its replacement by what appear to be fragments of subjectivity: typically body parts or functions and mental processes that take on an uncommonly detached and autonomous quality. This instability must be considered one of the chief characteristics of the poetic state of mind manifested in Trakl's poems from the second phase onwards, a state typically associated also with a melancholy mood of reflection on the processes of decay and decline in the natural world, and by extension on the loss of cultural ties and metaphysical meaning in the human sphere. Indeed, the speaker's apprehension of instability in his own selfhood is consistent with his sensitivity to loss and decay in his natural environment and in human society – it is the same sensitivity applied to his own person.

In the context of this discussion, we should underline that the instability of textual subjectivity as outlined here represents one of the most significant correspondences between Trakl's poetry and the cognitive effects of psychoactive drugs. Distortion of subjectivity is among the most frequently recurring motifs in the canon of drug literature, and although its forms are as many and varied as the works of which that canon consists, it represents a thread that links literary texts produced in entirely diverse historical and cultural environments, from the multitude of 'alien natures' that, haunting De Quincey's opiate dreams, appear within 'what he once thought the inviolable sanctuary of himself' (*EM*), to the divided hero of Philip K. Dick's *A Scanner Darkly*, an undercover narcotics agent who, placing himself under surveillance, becomes both the subject and object of his investigation. One of this theme's most succinct formulations can be found in the essay 'A Fundamental Experiment' by French poet-turned-mystic-philosopher René Daumal. As a consequence of his own experiences with various psychoactive substances, Daumal warns emphatically that 'It's I, I who am at stake' (cited in Plant 159). For Nietzsche, on the other hand, the suspension of subjectivity resulting from a neurochemical surge, whether this is prompted by the administration of drugs or occurs spontaneously in response to seasonal change, is the key quality of 'Dionysian' intoxication: 'Entweder durch den Einfluß des narkotischen Getränkes [...] oder bei dem gewaltigen, die ganze Natur lustvoll durchdringenden Nahen des Frühlings, erwachen jene dionysischen Regungen, in deren Steigerung das Subjektive zu völliger Selbstvergessenheit hinschwindet' (3:24). In 'Kokain' (see 3.3–3.4), Benn responds enthusiastically to the same phenomenon, hailing the drug-induced collapse of the ego as a welcome escape from the pointlessness and hypocrisy of day-to-day existence: 'Den Ich-Zerfall, den süßen, tiefersehnten, / den gibst du mir.' Although not explicitly 'given' by cocaine or any other drug, Trakl's virtual abandonment of the pronoun *ich* from his second phase onwards, in conjunction with the various other techniques described here that serve to destabilize, obscure, fragment, or simply de-familiarize the subjectivity in his poems, is certainly analogous in its *effect* to the transformations of subjectivity in these other, openly drug-informed texts. In particular, Trakl's distinctive tendency to limit his depiction of human figures to body parts or functions, where the reader would normally expect 'whole' individuals, can be considered consonant with an intoxicated perspective. The sensation that individual body parts have become disconnected and autonomous is one of the characteristic effects that many psychoactive drugs, including cocaine when taken in prolonged and excessive doses, exercise on the consciousness of the user. In *Masse und Macht* (1960), Elias Canetti writes:

> *Dissoziative* Körpergefühle sind von anderen Krankheiten her bekannt. Die beharrliche Tendenz des Delirs auf das Konkrete und Kleine hin, die sich im Kokain-Delir zum 'mikroskopisch' Kleinen steigern kann, hat etwas von einer Dissoziation des Körpers in seine Zellen. (416)

Benn describes a similar drug-induced perceptual shift in 'Provoziertes Leben':

> Das Komplexe wird brüchig, man sieht durch die Risse: 'Ich hatte ein ganz eigenartiges Muskelgefühl. *Ich hätte jeden einzelnen Muskel getrennt aus dem Körper herausnehmen können.*' (3:897–898)

Another distinctive stylistic feature of Trakl's language that contributes significantly to the masking of his poetry's underlying coherence, and thus to the impression of its 'randomness', is his tendency to formulate seemingly enigmatic word combinations. Whereas the range of his poetic vocabulary is famously limited, and with few exceptions the lexical items that make up his vocabulary belong to the language of everyday speech, his word combinations tend to be innovative, semantically unconventional, and may often appear cryptic or even paradoxical (Wellmann 315–345). Syntactically speaking, many of Trakl's surprising word combinations consist in collocations of attributive adjective and noun, and of particular interest in this connection is his use of adjectives that denote qualities of colour or light, one of the most striking and discussed aspects of his style. As Seymour-Smith observes, Trakl 'used colour more than any poet before or since' (577). Phrases such as 'ein blaues Wild' ('Elis', *SW* 2:443–455), 'das rote Gold' ('Nachts', *SW* 2:434–436), 'der schwarze Schnee' ('Delirium', *SW* 2:321–324), 'der weißen Enkel' ('Der Abend,' *SW* 4ii:247–248), 'die dunkeln Flöten' ('Grodek') and 'mit silbernen Fingern' ('Offenbarung und Untergang') appear esoteric, while even less disconcerting formulations such as 'goldnes Bildnis' and 'der purpurne Leib' (both from 'Klage') have marked but not entirely clear symbolic overtones. Another recurrent and related syntactic form involves a nominalized adjective such as 'ein reines Blau' ('Der Herbst des Einsamen,' *SW* 3:21–25), 'ein Goldnes' ('Passion', *SW* 4i:107–124), or 'ein Dunkles' ('Siebengesang des Todes,' *SW* 4i:137–145).

Predictably, Trakl's colours have provoked a wide variety of critical responses. These can be divided into three broad categories. First, certain commentators have attempted to overcome the semantic difficulty associated with Trakl's colour adjectives by arguing that their function is not primarily – or not at all – descriptive. For instance, Philipp ascribes a metalinguistic significance to Trakl's use of colour: the word is revealed in its function as 'Bezeichnung einer Farbe' (123). Iris Denneler adopts a biographical–poetological viewpoint, astonishing both in its originality and its improbability, characterizing colour as a psychological stimulus to poetic composition: 'Hineinschreiben und meditatives Sich-Versetzen in bestimmte Farbbereiche dienen zur Schaffung eines Farbklimas und zur Steigerung der Leistungsfähigkeit während der Gedichtproduktion' (90). In another, no less problematic biographical interpretation, Esselborn sees a mysterious psychological connection between the abundance of colour in Trakl's poetry and the guilt that the poet felt as a consequence of his hypothetically incestuous relationship with his sister Grete (248; see 7.1). Second, a more common approach, and one which has the merit of being based primarily on a response to the text rather than to the biography of its author, has been to emphasize the symbolic implications of Trakl's colours, the aim being to provide a determinate figurative reference to compensate for the apparent lack of a determinate literal one.[103] Hermann von Coelln, for example, reads Trakl's images as purely symbolic and claims that 'die Bilder, sofern sie eine vordergründige, gegenständliche Wirklichkeit bezeichnen, von sich aus keine Aussagekraft besitzen' (184). The adjective *blau* and its potential associations have been the object of particular scrutiny in this regard (e.g. Becht 108–131), although what exactly this colour symbolizes has proved difficult to pin down. No single meaning has been determined, whether religious, philosophical, emotional, or from any other field, that fits with all the different uses Trakl makes of this word, as certain adherents of this approach have come to admit: 'Je nach dem Kontext, in dem die Farbe steht, kann "blau" Unschuld, Reinheit, Ursprung, Helligkeit bedeuten oder auch einen anderen Sinn erlangen' (Gorgé 43; cited in Steinkamp 293). Even in a given context, claims such as 'in this poem blue means innocent' or 'here blue symbolizes purity' would be arbitrarily and unacceptably limiting, and would ultimately reveal nothing about the peculiarity of Trakl's technique. Significantly, then, this second approach leads not to a determinate symbolic meaning, as was the original intention, but to a form of semantic anarchy – the conclusion that a word like *blau* can mean just about anything at all.

More substantial and convincing results have been achieved by the few scholars who first grapple with the difficulties posed by the literal meaning of Trakl's puzzling lexical formulations, and then use this as a basis to explore their possible symbolic associations. Pioneering work of this type was undertaken by Schneider in his 1954 study *Der bildhafte Ausdruck*. His commentary on the line 'Wandert ein Dunkles in Abend und Untergang' from the poem 'Siebengesang des Todes' is illustrative. According to Schneider, the enigmatic gender-neutral 'ein Dunkles'

103 This approach has been adopted, for example, by Becht, Blass, Bolli, von Coelln and Goldmann.

> gibt […] etwas Objektives wieder, wie etwa die Blässe des 'bleichen Menschen' oder die Verschwommenheit des in der Dämmerung wandelnden Spaziergängers. […] Andererseits enthält sie aber auch mehr als einen objektiven Befund, als die bloße Charakteristik der Sache. […] Tatsächlich hebt der Dichter durch seine Metapher gleichsam die Körpergrenze des Menschen auf, so daß sie zu merkwürdig gewichtlosen und verschwommenen Schemen werden. (95–97)

From these observations Schneider astutely draws the conclusion that 'die Verschwommenheit des nächtlichen Spaziergängers' can, for Trakl, be identified as a 'feststehendes Merkmal des Menschlichen' (97). Schneider's method of progressing from literal to symbolic levels of meaning serves as one model for Steinkamp's more recent examination of Trakl's colour adjectives, with respect to which her text-semantic approach has once again provided arguably the most thorough and systematic elucidation of the poet's idiosyncrasies. Steinkamp argues that in Trakl's landscape code, colours usually function on a primary level as 'implicit' or 'idiolectical' time indicators; they give the reader information about the time of day or year in the scene depicted in a poem, and in this sense they complement his more conventional time indicators, prevalent among which are *Abend*, *Nacht*, *Herbst* and *Winter* (146–147). Brighter colours normally suggest daylight – otherwise these colours would not be visible (consider the 'golden plains' and 'blue lakes' at the beginning of 'Grodek', seen as the sun rolls 'more gloomily' across the sky). Green is generally associated with spring or summer; red, brown and gold with autumn (again note the prominence of gold in 'Grodek'). Black and white are winter colours but also the colours of the night; things often appear white, silver or crystalline in the moonlight (for example, in the lines from 'Im Osten' cited in 8.1: 'mit zerbrochenen Brauen, silbernen Armen / Winkt sterbenden Soldaten die Nacht'). The colour blue has special status. In the phrase 'ein blaues Wild' ('Elis'), the description of the 'deer' as 'blue', certainly an unusual colour for a deer, tells the reader that the quality of light in the scene depicted is such that even this normally brown animal seems to take on a bluish hue. The time of day associated with such light is evening (a similar effect may also occur on a clear night), and in the poem in question the adverbial phrase 'am Abend' appears just two lines previous to 'ein blaues Wild.' Steinkamp extends her investigation of this colour to the entire body of Trakl's poetry, systematically assessing the position of the word *blau* in the temporal progression of individual poems, and in this way is able to confirm a consistent connection between blue and evening:

> In der Mehrzahl der Gedichte, in denen Trakl sein idiolektales Zeitwort 'blau' einsetzt, stellt sich die Zeiterfahrung des Sprechers etwa so dar: Auf der Schwelle zwischen Tag und Nacht, in den frühen Abendstunden (meist eines Herbsttages) mit ihren Resten an Tageslicht, [...] antizipiert der Traklsche Sprecher einen jahreszeitlichen Übergang, in der Regel vom Herbst mit seinen letzten Anzeichen landschaftlichen Lebens zum Winter und seinen ersten Vorboten von landschaftlicher Öde und Todesstarre. Soviel läßt sich zur elementaren Bedeutung der Farbe Blau bei Trakl sagen. (169)

Steinkamp derives the secondary, symbolic meaning of the word *blau* directly from this primary, literal meaning:

> Innerhalb der umfassenderen Zeitschichten in Trakls Gedichten, nämlich auf der Ebene von Lebensgeschichte und Kulturgeschichte [...], nimmt die 'blaue Stunde' noch eine spezifische Traklsche Bedeutung an. Sie läßt sich dann verstehen als eine (an bestimmte tages- und jahreszeitliche Verhältnisse gebundene) Zeit der Besinnung, in der der Sprecher nachdenkt über Veränderung und Verlust innerhalb seiner eigenen Lebensgeschichte oder – umfassender noch – über Wandel und Kontinuitätsbruch innerhalb der Geschichte seines (abendländischen) Kulturkreises. (ibid.)

In other words, the colour blue is associated with the poetic apprehension of a process of dissolution that is tangible and organic on the one hand and broadly existential, social and cosmic on the other.

This is a further aspect of Trakl's style, then, with respect to which Steinkamp succeeds in demonstrating the poetry's underlying coherence. As with the question of textual subjectivity discussed above, the only significant objection that can be raised against her analysis of Trakl's colours is that it does not adequately account for the evident difficulty of grasping this coherence, or to put it differently, for the conspicuous dissimilarity between the coherence of Trakl's style and the type of coherence that the reader would habitually expect. The 'procedure', to use Heselhaus's term (241), is clear, but the question as to what effects are achieved by this procedure remains open. It is important, then, that in regard also to Trakl's use of colour, a striking parallel can be noted between these effects and the effects of psychoactive drugs. This parallel has tempted Kupfer into conjecture about the nature of the poet's own drug use:

> Die Betonung farblicher Reize ist ein hervorstechendes Merkmal der reifen Lyrik Georg Trakls [...]. Wenn die These zutreffen sollte, daß er auch mit dem Meskalin vertraut war, so kann diese Tatsache kaum überraschen, da diese Droge für ihre un-

> gewöhnlich intensiven Farbvisionen bekannt ist und, wie Huxley versichert, eine über den Rausch hinaus anhaltende Veränderung der Wahrnehmung bewirkt. (*GG* 230)

Two points are to be noted here. First, although it is true that among psychoactive drugs the hallucinogens in general and mescaline in particular bring about a particularly intense sensitivity to colour, a change in colour receptivity, and consequently an increased colour awareness, is in fact characteristic of intoxicated perception generally, as Kupfer himself has emphasized: 'Da Farben einen der stärksten visuellen Reize bewirken, erfährt auch ihre Wahrnehmung im Rausch eine besondere Akzentuierung' (*kP* 247). Indeed, a 'particular accentuation' on colour was evident in drug-associated literary texts – in Rimbaud's 'Le Bateau ivre' of 1871, to name just one example – long before the mescaline alkaloid was first isolated in 1894. In connection to coca in particular, we might note physicist Paolo Mantegazza's observations, dating from 1859, on the perceptual alteration induced by a large dose of the drug: 'I was at that time fully aware of myself, but I felt isolated from the external world and saw images that were more bizarre and splendid, in terms of colour, than could ever be imagined' (41). Trakl's use of colour, therefore, can be considered a significant correspondence between his poetry and the experience of intoxication regardless of the validity of Kupfer's mescaline hypothesis. Second, in the passage cited above Kupfer falls into the now all-too familiar trap of attempting to explain away the peculiarities of the text by positing an unmediated causal relationship between biography and work. In this sense the mescaline hypothesis is analogous to – and shares the shortcomings of – the schizophrenia theories that in recent decades have threatened to overrun the field of Trakl scholarship. Fortunately, Kupfer's reflection on Trakl's colourful style leads him to a more substantial insight that implicitly casts doubt on his own biographical speculation:

> Die auffällige Bedeutung von Farben, die sich in der Lyrik Trakls bis zuletzt erhalten hat, ist ein gutes Beispiel, an dem sich zeigen läßt, wie die Wahrnehmung des Drogenrausches und die Bestrebungen der expressionistischen Weltdeutung sich zuweilen auf einer gemeinsamen Linie treffen können: Die Befreiung von den einengenden Formen und Begriffen, durch die das rohe Ensemble der von uns wahrgenommen Welt in ein rationales Koordinatensystem einzementiert wurde, ist dem drogenberauschten Visionär ein ebensolches Anliegen wie dem expressionistischen Künstler. Die Farbe ist ein solcher von aller Gegenständlichkeit befreiter Stoff, der die hinter den Dingen liegende Welt gewissermaßen 'pur' erleben läßt. (*GG* 230–231)

In view of Kupfer's use of such formulations as 'Befreiung von den eineng-enden Formen und Begriffen' and 'in ein rationales Koordinatensystem einzementiert,' his description of the common ground between Expressionism and intoxication appears closer to Benn's poetics than to Trakl's (the idea of perceptual 'purity', on the other hand, is a phenomenologically dubious reworking of William Blake's 'cleansing of the doors of perception' as described in 'The Marriage of Heaven and Hell'). In contrast to Benn, with Trakl the emphasis is less on 'liberation' than on disintegration and decline. In any case, the gist of Kupfer's argument is sound, and his point concerning the 'liberation of colour' as a point of intersection between intoxicated perception and the Expressionist aesthetic is a useful extension of the affinity between them already noted by Springer (*N* 28–29 & *KMR* 43; see 1.2). To be sure, Trakl's poetry is just one of the numerous manifestations of 'intoxicated' colouring in Expressionist art: Benn also proclaimed 'eine Befreundung für Blau, welch Glück, welch reines Erlebnis!' (GW 8:1879; see 3.1); while the disruption of 'sober' colour perception was one of the guiding principles of Expressionist painting, a tenet implicit in the very name of the Munich-based school *Der blaue Reiter*. In Trakl's poetry the dominance of colour and light – in 'Klage' we find 'düstern', 'goldnes', 'purpurne', 'dunkle'; in 'Grodek' 'goldnen', 'blauen', 'düstrer', 'rotes', 'schwarze', 'goldnem' and 'dunkeln' – is a further manifestation of the abnormal cognition underlying the speaker's perspective, in which the conventional parameters for the classification and elaboration of sensory material have been shifted, as in the experience of intoxication, so that the articulation of this perspective paints an defamiliarized and often disconcerting picture of the world. It remains, nonetheless, a picture of the world, as opposed to a 'random' montage of symbols detached from their original referents, and it displays a deep-rooted if unusual coherence in its relation to the world.

The final aspect of Trakl's poetic style of particular interest here is closely related to those already discussed: ambiguity. This is in effect a more generic characteristic of his verse, one to which the other features described here – the subversion of textual subjectivity, the enigmatic lexical collocations, the prevalence of colour and light – all contribute. Once again, Steinkamp's findings provide a useful foundation for our own investigation of this aspect. As with her work on colour, she bases her analysis of the ambiguity in Trakl's style on the identification and distinction of different levels of meaning or 'isotopes' within individual texts. She cites Kallmeyer's definition of this term, derived in turn from Greimas:

> Der Begriff der Isotopie beschreibt die 'semantische Tektonik von Texten [...]. Die jeweils über ein dominantes und damit rekurrentes [semantisches] Merkmal verbundenen Lexeme eines Textes' konstituieren dessen Isotopieebenen: 'Ein Text läßt sich semantisch als ein Gefüge von 1 bis n Isotopieebenen definieren.' (225; cf. Kallmeyer 147)

As Steinkamp demonstrates, landscape is the dominant isotope in the majority of Trakl's poems from the second phase onwards – hence her coinage 'landscape code' to describe his poetic idiolect – while secondary isotopes characteristically include human presence, culture-civilization, and religion. In order to generate meaning on one of these secondary levels, Trakl typically and increasingly chooses lexemes that have a semantic link to the dominant landscape isotope as well as the relevant secondary isotope. For example, words that straddle the isotopes 'landscape' and 'human presence' include *Landmann*, *Hirte*, and *Magd*; for 'culture-civilization' we find *Hof*, *Zaun*, and *Sensen*; for 'religion' *Kreuz*, *Hain*, and *Brot und Wein* (Steinkamp 225–226). We might expand on Steinkamp's observations by noting that a particular lexeme's relevance to a secondary isotope is not always evident when it is considered in isolation from its context in the poem. To employ Ferdinand de Saussure's terminology, often this relevance is apparent in the *parole*, the use of a word in a specific context, but not in the *langue*, its predetermined meaning in the linguistic code. Thus, the word *Adler* contains no implicit reference to the isotope 'state of mind,' but as we have seen, in the poem 'Klage' it assumes – in particular by means of its syntactic correlation with the word *Haupt* – a metaphorical function in this isotope that complements its primary role, derived from its literal meaning, in the isotope 'seascape'. By exploiting and augmenting the polysemantic quality of words in this way, Trakl is able to achieve the extreme lexical economy and powerful semantic suggestiveness for which his poetry is renowned.

As far as the stylistic peculiarity of Trakl's ambiguity is concerned, however, Steinkamp's observations tell only half the story. For the coexistence and interplay of different levels of meaning in a literary text is not in itself anything remarkable, especially not in poetry, where it may, as Jakobson shows, be considered standard. Yet clearly there *is* something remarkable about the ambiguity we find in Trakl's poetry, as Martin Heidegger notes in his 1953 Trakl essay: 'Die Sprache des Gedichtes ist wesenhaft mehrdeutig und dies auf ihre eigene Weise' (70). We may postulate that what is truly distinctive about Trakl's style is that his poems combine a multi-layered 'isotopic' structure, as described by Steinkamp, with a high degree of semantic openness both on and between each of the levels of meaning in the text. In linguistic terms, we can say that Trakl's language is characterized by a radical semantic underdetermination, where the term semantic underdetermination refers to the difference between what is said and what is implicated in a given utterance, a gap that the addressee, whether the reader or listener, is required to bridge. Semantic underdetermination is widespread in all forms of language use,[104] but Trakl consistently amplifies it to produce ambiguity.

To illustrate this point, let us reconsider two of Trakl's 'difficult' formulations already mentioned in connection with his use of colour and light. We have seen that it is legitimate, in accordance with both the rules of Trakl's landscape code and the overall temporal structure of the texts in question, to interpret the phrase 'ein blaues Wild' as 'a deer seen in the bluish light of evening' (Steinkamp) and the phrase 'ein Dunkles' as 'an indistinct human figure in the darkness' (Schneider). Yet there remains in each case a considerable and indisputable gap between what is said and what – according to these readings – is meant. In most imaginable contexts outside Trakl's poetry this gap would be unacceptably large, in so far as it cannot be bridged by the conventional procedures of propositional development, but only by the idiolectical procedures of the poetry itself, and the result would be incomprehensibility. Indeed, even within Trakl's poetry, as we have already seen, numerous critics have concluded that such formulations are essentially meaningless or have an exclusively figurative significance. Certainly the gap is large enough to require that any determinate reading or prose paraphrase, even plausible and well-founded ones such as Steinkamp's and Schneider's, be bracketed and question-marked. Crucially, the meaning these critics extrapolate is latent rather than explicit and does not exclude the possibility of alternative, complementary, or even contradictory interpretations; on the contrary, the semantic openness of such formulations acts as a stimulus for the reader to explore this very possibility.

104 For a linguistic analysis of this phenomenon, see Mendoza Ibáñez.

A similar effect to that achieved by unusual lexical or morphological formulations, as in these two noun phrases, may be achieved by other means as well, such as by a surprising – semantically underdetermined – choice of grammatical category. Examples we have already seen include the subjunctive mood of the verb 'verschlänge' (l. 4) in 'Klage' and the comparative degree of the adjective 'stolzere' (l. 15) in 'Grodek', where the indicative mood and the positive degree respectively would make the meaning less opaque. In both poems the reasons for the choice of grammatical category are not immediately obvious, thus inviting the reader to reflect on various interpretive possibilities. Swales limits his commentary on the phrase 'O stolzere Trauer' to making this invitation explicit: 'what is the force of the comparative in 'O stolzere Trauer'? What kind of greater pride is this? We are left with uncertainty' (192). Similar questions might be asked about the subjunctive mood of 'verschlänge' in 'Klage'. Answers can be given, such as those put forward in the discussions of 'Klage' and 'Grodek' in 8.1 and 8.2, but even when these cohere with the general themes and structure of the poem, they do not reconcile Trakl's grammatical eccentricities to linguistic normality, and so formulations such as 'verschlänge' and 'stolzere' retain a residual strangeness. Recognizing the semantic openness characteristic of Trakl's style, Bridgwater writes that 'any poem by Trakl is the sum total of its probable interpretations' (*GT* 108). But as these examples show, Trakl's stylistic idiosyncrasies serve to anticipate and subvert even the most plausible interpretations. In other words, Trakl's semantic underdetermination has important implications not just for the quantity but above all for the quality of meaning in his poetry.

The mechanics of Trakl's stylistic ambiguity are made even more complex by the extension of this radical semantic underdetermination to the relationship between various levels of meaning in a given text. To illustrate this feature, let us consider once again the opening couplet of 'Klage': 'Schlaf und Tod, die düstern Adler / Umrauschen nachtlang dieses Haupt.' The first line establishes a metaphorical equivalence between the two noun phrases in apposition that form the subject of the clause: 'sleep and death' on the one hand and 'the gloomy eagles' on the other. But in contrast to most metaphorical relationships, it is not immediately apparent which of the two elements constitutes the source domain and which the target domain, or where the boundary is to be drawn between diegetic and non-diegetic levels within the text – in other words, which element the reader is meant to understand as really present in the 'scene' of the poem and which is meant to provide a merely metaphorical frame of reference. In theory this ambiguity could be resolved or diminished by a slight rearrangement of the words, for example, by the insertion of a preposition such as *wie* (to create a simile) or statal verb such as *sind.* The reader might also expect it to be clarified in the subsequent development of the poem, by the explication of one of these levels of meaning as merely metaphorical or non-diegetic at a later point in the text. But as we have seen in 8.1, in fact they are both developed – so that we can classify 'sleep and death' as belonging to a larger 'state of mind' isotope and 'the gloomy eagles' as part of a 'seascape' isotope – and become increasingly entwined without any resolution to the semantic problem posed in the opening line. The non-resolution of this ambiguity, therefore, becomes an integral quality of the poem, and because of it each level of meaning effectively acquires *both* a literal function and a metaphorical one.

The overall effect of this isotopic blurring might be described as 'conceptual synaesthesia,' in that each isotope is apprehended, paradoxically and irreducibly, in terms of the other. A similar phenomenon, characterized by the same conceptual synaesthesia, by apparent 'errors and transpositions of ideas,' is described by Baudelaire in *Les Paradis artificiels* as the dominant feature of one state of hashish intoxication (*Pa* 47). This correspondence is significant because it illustrates that Trakl's distinctive technique for generating ambiguity, perhaps the most intriguing and potentially perplexing aspect of his style, gives rise to a *textual* effect analogous to a *cognitive* one experienced during drug-induced intoxication. To suggest that the 'transpositions of ideas' in Trakl's poetry are the result of a fortuitous arrangement of unrelated images is to misapprehend the essence of his verbal craftsmanship and the intoxicated aesthetic it serves.

Considered in their totality, Trakl's poetic strategies for generating ambiguity amount to a decisive deviation from the conventional parameters of language use. More important, this linguistic, specifically semantic idiosyncrasy stems from and embodies a more fundamental perceptual and cognitive deviance in the consciousness of the lyric subject. In particular, 'Klage' portrays not so much an external scene with metaphorical correspondences to the speaker's state of mind, which would be true if it were simply a question of the co-existence of various levels of meaning, as a continuum of physical and psychic experience. In this sense also 'Klage' is representative of Trakl's mature work, which, as Sharp puts it, typically presents a 'fusion of landscape and mind-scape' (*PM* 196). Describing the same effect, Seymour-Smith claims that Trakl's poetry 'successfully turns the mind inside out' (661). Here we can observe a further significant correspondence with the perceptual and ontological conditions of intoxicated consciousness, colourfully described by Octavio Paz in *Corriente Alterna* (1967):

> Drugs provoke the vision of the universal correspondence of all things, arouse the powers of analogy, set objects in motion, make the world a vast poem shaped by rhymes and rhythms. Drugs snatch us out of everyday reality, blur our perception, alter our sensations, and, in a word, put the entire universe in a state of suspension. (76)

A comparable effect is created by and in Trakl's poetic language. It, too, seems to 'put the entire universe in a state of suspension,' to 'set objects in motion,' and it does so by setting meaning in motion, accentuating its inherently elusive qualities, exploiting its latencies and ambiguities, and transgressing semantic norms, in short, by weaving a web of sound and sense, signifiers and signifieds, whose elements intertwine in complex and incantatory patterns.

These reflections confirm that the parallels between Trakl's poetry and the state of intoxication relate to several of the most essential and idiosyncratic aspects of his style, so much so that we might reasonably speak, with reference to this style, of a 'poetics of intoxication.' This notion lends more weight and clarity to the proposition made in 7.1 that there must have been more to Trakl's interest in states of intoxication than the simple matter of subduing consciousness, that for him there was in fact a positive – we might now call it 'poetic' – value in such states. As far as his poetry itself is concerned, the stylistic features of Trakl's language discussed here combine to produce a semantic undercurrent of intoxication that runs through his poems. As in Kallmeyer's definition of textual isotopes referred to above, according to which lexemes with a common semantic feature combine to create a distinct level of meaning in a given text, so too the stylistic aspects of a Trakl poem that share a correspondence to the experience of intoxication, considered together in a reading of the full text, generate a semantic level of their own. Certainly, an isotope generated stylistically is less tangible and less precise than one generated lexically, so that we might more appropriately describe it as subtextual than textual, but it is no less important to the larger semantic structure of the poem and hence to the overall reading effect. For the same reason, it is a level of meaning that inevitably disappears from any paraphrase of Trakl's poetry into more familiar prosaic language, in so far that the primary purpose of any such paraphrase is to nullify the strangeness of his style. Although stylistic in nature, Trakl's undercurrent of intoxication has effects that may become apparent on the lexical level: it may serve to activate or semi-activate the semantic feature 'intoxication' in certain lexical items in which this feature is not immediately apparent. The verb 'umrauschen' (l. 3) and the noun phrase 'ängstlicher Kahn' (l. 11) from the poem 'Klage' are examples of such items. This last point will be of central importance to the investigation of a possible textual role for cocaine in Trakl's poetry that follows in 10.1 and 10.2.

Taking the non-occurrence of cocaine in the poems of Trakl's 'cocaine period' as our point of departure (see 8.1 and 8.2), so far we have seen how his 'poetics of intoxication' operates independently – and despite the absence of – explicit references to states of intoxication or intoxicants themselves. However, Trakl's poetry is by no means devoid of such references, and in this respect Boon's observation that 'there are few direct mentions of substances in the poems' is potentially misleading (185). In fact references – admittedly, not always direct – to psychoactive substances and their effects occur with greater frequency in Trakl's poetry than, for example, in Benn's, even if there is nothing of the confessional *ich-nahm-schon-Kokain* variety that might be taken as an easy point of reference for the critic intent upon demonstrating a causal relationship between biography and work. In order to broaden and fill out our picture of the correspondences between text and drug, let us now consider the psychoactive substances that – in contrast to cocaine – have a tangible presence on the surface level of Trakl's verse.

9.2 Wine, Poppy, Dark Poisons: Trakl's Poetic Intoxicants

Trakl's pre-eminent poetic intoxicant – the only one his poetry names directly – is wine, and *Wein* is among the most frequently recurring words in his pared-down poetic lexicon, especially in the poems of the second and third phases, collected in *Gedichte* and *Sebastian im Traum* (see 8.1). The reason for its privileged status in relation to other intoxicants is easily grasped when we consider that, from the semantic point of view, *Wein* represents a nodal point for several of Trakl's dominant themes, linking the predominantly subtextual intoxication isotope (see 9.1) with landscape, seasonal progression, and horticultural activity on the one hand, and with religion and myth on the other. In a number of poems *Wein* is used on a primary level to describe features of the landscape, that is, it functions as a metonym for 'grapes', 'grapevine', or 'vineyard'. The poem 'Verfall' (*SW* 1:224–228) provides one example: 'Es schwankt der rote Wein an rostigen Gittern.' Here, the redness of the 'wine', that is, the grapevine, suggests the onset of autumnal decay that characteristically mirrors the cultural decay manifest in the 'rostigen Gittern.' Other poems in which *Wein* is used in the portrayal of landscape include 'Frauensegen' (*SW* 1:433–436), 'Verklärter Herbst' (*SW* 2:47–50), and the long poem 'Helian' (*SW* 2:230–263). In these poems, the use of *Wein* in place of *Weintrauben*, *Weinrebe*, or *Weingarten* emphasizes the natural and irreducible connection between the plant and the intoxicating beverage produced from its fruit. In other poems the activity associated with wine production is invoked, and this activity invariably represents the highpoint – the autumnal fruition – of rural life in naïve but meaningful synchrony with the rhythms of seasonal change. References to activities such as the harvesting and pressing of grapes typically occur in contexts that suggest peacefulness, fulfilment, and a mystical, unconscious symbiosis between man and nature. In the poem 'Im Herbst' (*SW* 1:385–389) from *Gedichte*, for example, we find: 'Da zeigt der Mensch sich froh und lind. / Heut keltern sie den braunen Wein.' The later poem 'Der Herbst des Einsamen' from *Sebastian im Traum* offers a more direct and complex articulation of the metaphysical fulfilment represented by the process of wine production: 'Gekeltert ist der Wein, die milde Stille / Erfüllt von leiser Antwort dunkler Fragen.' In 'Helian' the same metaphysical significance is implicit in the collocation 'Brot und Wein,' an unmistakable reference to the Christian sacrament of the Eucharist:

> In kahlen Gezweigen feiert der Himmel.
> In reinen Händen trägt der Landmann Brot und Wein
> Und friedlich reifen die Früchte in sonniger Kammer.

The poem 'Der Spaziergang' (*SW* 1:524–531) contains a similar image: 'Und Brot und Wein sind süß von harten Mühn.' In these poems, the integration of Christian imagery into a pantheistic vision of rural life confirms Seymour-Smith's impression that Trakl's 'use of Christian material seems [...] a pagan use' (582).

In other poems, the same *Brot-und-Wein* formulation occurs in connection with images of pain, alienation, and destruction. In such contexts, the mystical harmony implicit in the collocation of the two Eucharistic elements represents a source of consolation in existential hardship. In 'Menschheit' (*SW* 2:106–110), a series of images suggesting warfare and bloodshed ('Ein Trommelwirbel, dunkler Krieger Stirnen, / Schritte durch Blutnebel; schwarzes Eisen schellt') is followed by Trakl's most direct invocation of the Christian significance of bread and wine deriving from the Last Supper: 'Es wohnt in Brot und Wein ein sanftes Schweigen / Und jene sind versammelt zwölf an Zahl.' A more oblique reference to the metaphysical power of the Eucharist can be found in 'Ein Winterabend,' in the final stanza of which a luminous vision of bread and wine is contrasted with the wandering and pain that immediately precede it:

> Wanderer tritt still herein;
> Schmerz versteinerte die Schwelle.
> Da erglänzt in reiner Helle
> Auf dem Tische Brot und Wein. (*SW* 3:404–414)

The same contrast occurs – featuring a more explicit allusion to divine grace – in 'Gesang des Abgeschiedenen':

> [...] denn geheiligt ist Brot und Wein
> Von Gottes Händen, und es schaut aus nächtigen Augen
> Stille dich der Bruder an, daß er ruhe von dorniger Wanderschaft. (*SW* 4i:152–162)

Even when unaccompanied by bread, so that its religious overtones are less pronounced, wine offers consolation and even joy, albeit tinged with melancholy, to the speaker and other figures in Trakl's poems, in particular as the focal point of companionship and festivity. Illustrative examples of social drinking can be found in 'Abend in Lans' (*SW* 3:201–208) and 'Helian':

> [...] Unter getünchten Bogen,
> Wo die Schwalbe aus und ein flog, tranken wir feurigen Wein.
> Schön: o Schwermut und pupurnes Lachen. ('Abend in Lans')

> Abends auf der Terasse betranken wir uns mit braunem Wein.
> Rötlich glüht der Pfirsich im Laub;
> Sanfte Sonate, frohes Lachen. ('Helian')

In the final line of 'Unterwegs' (*SW* 2:471–482), even the unseemly act of collapsing drunk in the gutter acquires a peculiar metaphysical dignity, as it is portrayed as the moment in which poetic consciousness, or the 'frightened soul's lonely string playing,' resigns itself to its own extinction: 'Erstirbt der bangen Seele einsames Saitenspiel. / Laß, wenn trunken von Wein das Haupt in die Gosse sinkt.' It is significant that Trakl goes to the trouble of specifying the source of the speaker's intoxication, for if he were interested simply in conveying the squalor of passing out drunk, this would be unnecessary. The implication is that intoxication produced by wine represents an enduring connection to the idyllic rural life of the *Landmänner* who in other poems are shown producing the beverage, and the act of drinking wine is an expression of nostalgia for that life and the unconscious harmony with nature it represents. This notion is conveyed more directly in 'Dämmerung' (*SW* 2:54–57), in which 'sick' people glide through an autumnal landscape recalling a 'golden' past, and wine features prominently in their recollection:

> Durch Herbstgebräuntes weiche Kranke gleiten.
> Ihr wächsern-runder Blick sinnt goldner Zeiten,
> Erfüllt von Träumerei und Ruh und Wein.

Although Trakl never states the matter so plainly, the role that wine plays for his alienated human figures might usefully be compared with that it plays for Harry Haller, the protagonist of Hesse's *Steppenwolf*:

> Ich liebe am meisten ganz reine, leichte, bescheidene Landweine ohne besonderen Namen, man kann viel davon vertragen, und sie schmecken so gut und freundlich nach Land und Erde und Himmel und Gehölz [...] Auch das war wunderlich, daß da irgendwo in grünen Tälern von gesunden braven Menschen Reben gebaut wurden und Wein gekeltert wurde, damit hier und dort in der Welt, weit von ihnen entfernt, einige enttäuschte, still schöppelnde Bürger und ratlose Steppenwölfe sich ein wenig Mut und Laune aus ihren Bechern saugen konnten. (45–46)

In Trakl's poetic lexicon, just as wine is favoured over other intoxicants, so too the state of intoxication is more often than not equated with drunkenness, which is manifested in a range of syntactical variants. As well as the noun *Trunkenheit*, the reader encounters the participles *betrunken* and *trunken* used both adjectivally and adverbially, the verb *betrinken* in various forms, and the animate participial nouns *der Betrunkene* and *der Trunkene*. Thematically, in certain poems drunkenness is equated with oblivion as relief from existential torment, but as we have just seen in the final line of 'Unterwegs', it is oblivion as more than just negation; rather it may acquire, depending on the context, a positive moral, social, aesthetic, or even metaphysical significance. In most poems featuring drunkenness it is in fact this positive value that is emphasized. The following short poem from *Gedichte* is representative:

> Zu Abend mein Herz
>
> Am Abend hört man den Schrei der Fledermäuse.
> Zwei Rappen springen auf der Wiese.
> Der rote Ahorn rauscht.
> Dem Wanderer erscheint die kleine Schenke am Weg.
> Herrlich schmecken junger Wein und Nüsse.
> Herrlich: betrunken zu taumeln in dämmernden Wald.
> Durch schwarzes Geäst tönen schmerzliche Glocken.
> Auf das Gesicht tropft Tau. (*SW* 2:124–128)

Here the speaker's 'marvellous' drunkenness contrasts with his 'painful' observations of autumnal and evening decline that fill the rest of the poem. All the images are conditioned by the opening 'Am Abend,' which defines the beauty of the scene as evanescent. Even images like that of the cavorting horses in line 2 or the red maple in line 3, considered in the evening and autumnal context of the poem, are tinged with the awareness of their imminent loss, so that only superficially are they less ominous than the 'scream of bats' (l. 1) and the 'painful' chiming of bells (l. 7). It is notable in this context that what is 'marvellous' about the speaker's intoxication is not just the anaesthetic effect of drunkenness, but 'staggering drunk *into the darkening forest*' (note the accusative of direction) – that is, confronting the dark reality of decline in an intoxicated state of mind. It is marvellous because it transforms this confrontation into an aesthetic experience of decline, just as the poem itself represents an aesthetic experience of decline. The positive value of drunkenness is not that it changes or erases the content of the speaker's consciousness, which remains painful, but that it gives his consciousness an intoxicated-aesthetic form. It does not so much relieve his pain as contribute to the same kind of sublimation of it that we have already observed in 'Klage' (see 8.1). It is sublimation in the Nietzschean sense: for Trakl, the acceptance and artistic elaboration of painful reality becomes, metaphysically, the only meaningful response to the inevitability of decay. On a thematic level, then, this poem reinforces the fundamental link between intoxicated and poetic consciousness that is manifested stylistically in so many aspects of Trakl's poetic language (see 9.1).

In 'Zu Abend mein Herz,' as in various other poems including 'Helian' and 'Unterwegs', drunkenness is attributed explicitly to the consumption of wine. In others there are factors in addition to or other than wine that produce drunkenness, and yet others in which its causes are unspecified. In such texts drunkenness, that is, alcohol intoxication, assumes a broader semantic function as a metonym for intoxication as a generic state. In other words, although wine is Trakl's preferred poetic intoxicant, it is just one of numerous substances or other stimuli that are linked by their capacity to bring about the altered and privileged state of consciousness he refers to as *Trunkenheit*. 'Stunde des Grams' (*SW* 3:369–373) offers one example of wine working in conjunction with another agent to produce drunkenness: here, 'the stony head' of the 'lonely one' is described as 'trunken von Wein und nächtigem Wohllaut.' The idea that sound – and by inference the sonic art of poetry – can give rise to or itself *be* a form of drunkenness is conveyed in other poems as well. One version of 'An Novalis' (*SW* 3:304–311) talks of 'das trunkene Saitenspiel' of Trakl's illustrious predecessor. In 'Verwandlung' we find 'Flöten weich und trunken,' which in a previous version of the same poem appear as 'Klänge, weich und trunken.' Such formulations support the notion that Trakl attributes not only a poetic value to intoxication, but also an intoxicating value to poetry.

Another repeatedly invoked source of drunkenness is *Mohn* or *Mohnsaft*, an indirect but undisguised reference to the poppy-derivative opium. With its allusions to opiate drugs, Trakl's *Mohn* imagery taps into a literary heritage that in the German Romantic tradition alone stretches from Novalis's 'Hymnen an die Nacht' (1799–1800) to Benn's *Rönne* stories (1915–16; see 3.1, 4.1), and whose broader cultural and religious roots have been traced as far back as antiquity (Kupfer *kP* 14–16). The poems 'Sebastian im Traum' (*SW* 3:229–234), 'Geistliche Dämmerung' (*SW* 3:68–76), 'Verklärung' (*SW* 3:333–344), and the last version of 'An Angela' (*SW* 1:543–557) all provide examples of poppy-induced drunkenness. Whereas in poems such as 'Verfall' Trakl uses the intoxicant *Wein* to stand for the plant it derives from, in his *Mohn-Trunkenheit* collocations this metonymy is reversed, so that it is the plant that stands for the intoxicant produced from it. Despite the reversal, the effects of these two circumlocutions are essentially the same: both underline the organic link between plant and intoxicant, between the natural world and human consciousness, and so contribute to Trakl's 'fusion of landscape and mind-scape' (Sharp *PM* 196). It is not surprising, then, to find that Trakl's poetic poppy-intoxication shares several of the positive values attributed to his wine-induced drunkenness. A single image from the opening section of 'Sebastian im Traum,' with its apposition of poppy juice and birdsong, embodies the threefold consonance of opium intoxication, elegiac lyricism, and nature: 'Trunken vom Safte des Mohns, der Klage der Drossel.' A similar link is made in another poem, 'Verklärung':

> Stille wohnt
> An deinem Mund der herbstliche Mond,
> Trunken von Mohnsaft dunkler Gesang.

The intertwining sound patterns of these three lines (note especially the recurrence of nasal and dental consonants in combination with dark vowels: *wohnt*, *Mund*, *Mond*, *trunken*, *Mohn*, *dunkler*) point to the thematic intermingling of the various elements denoted, an effect strengthened by the unusual – and ambiguity-generating – arrangement of the clause's syntactical components. As there is no comma separating them, the adjectival phrase 'Trunken von Mohnsaft' seems to modify the noun phrase 'dunkler Gesang' that follows, yet the uninflected ending of the adjective 'trunken' (contrast 'dunkler') indicates that it may be postpositive. Its referent, therefore, could also be 'der herbstliche Mond' or even 'deinem Mund' from the preceding line. On the other hand, it might be read as an adverbial phrase, in which case its referent is the verb 'wohnt' of two lines earlier.

The thematic overlap between *Wein* and *Mohn* also extends to the sphere of religious significance, although when *Mohn* is used in place of *Wein* in combination with Christian imagery, this significance may acquire a sacrilegious nuance, suggesting a critique of the dogmatism of institutionalized religion. Thus, in the poem 'Träumerei am Abend' (*SW* 1:558–562) opium intoxication stimulates a religious insight that in ecclesiastical doctrine would normally be associated with the taking of bread and wine during Communion: 'Dem einsam Sinnenden löst weißer Mohn die Glieder, / Daß er Gerechtes schaut und Gottes tiefe Freude.' The same connection between opium-affected vision and religious experience, manifested in an allusion to the rosary and the presence of an angel, finds even more potent expression in 'Amen' (*SW* 2:421–422):

> Braune Perlen rinnen durch die erstorbenen Finger.
> In der Stille
> Tun sich eines Engels blaue Mohnaugen auf.

One distinction between *Wein* and *Mohn* – a distinction of emphasis rather than of kind, for we are still dealing with aspects of the privileged state of 'drunkenness' – concerns the poppy's narcotic and especially oneiric properties. Trakl makes most evident use of these in 'Unterwegs': 'Deine Lider sind schwer von Mohn und träumen leise auf meiner Stirne.' The association between opium and dreaming is also exploited in the final line of 'Im Spital' (*SW* 1:454–468): 'Im Garten flattert traumhaft weißer Mohn.' In this line, in contrast to the poems in which the poppy or its juice are specified as the cause of drunkenness, the flower's association with the opiate drugs remains implicit as a subtextual influence that adds to the dreamlike effect of the whole. Here the poppy reference is integrated into the depiction of landscape, with the emphasis on the flower's decorative characteristics, specifically its colour. Another poem with an equivalent poppy image is 'Frauensegen': 'Weiß verblüht der Mohn am Zaun.' In 'Sommer' (*SW* 3:261–264) the final line of the first stanza reads, quite simply, 'der rote Mohn.'

A further cause of Trakl's poetic drunkenness that merits close consideration is that which occurs in the second and third of the three published versions of 'Nachtseele' (*SW* 2:77–92), in which the moon is described as 'trunken von dunklen Giften.' Significantly, in the transition from Trakl's third to his fourth phase, these same 'dark poisons' supplant wine and poppy juice as his dominant poetic intoxicants, a development that coincides with the tendencies to radicalization in both his poetry and biography identified in the previous chapter (see 8.2). They first appear in a manuscript version of the prose poem 'Winternacht' (see 10.2) dating from December 1913, only to be replaced by 'purple wine' in the definitive version included in *Sebastian im Traum.* They then resurface in another prose poem of the same collection, 'Traum und Umnachtung' (*SW* 4i:25–76), in conjunction with a dreamy cosmic-maternal vision of contrasting whiteness: 'Tief ist der Schlummer in dunklen Giften, erfüllt von Sternen und dem weißen Antlitz der Mutter, dem steinernen.' Composed in January 1914, 'Traum und Umnachtung' is the final text of *Sebastian im Traum*, and the appearance of 'dark poisons' in this work foreshadows their prominence in two poems of Trakl's following and final period, a period in which the role of *Wein* and *Mohn* is reduced to a peripheral one – each is mentioned only once in the prose poem 'Offenbarung und Untergang.' In addition to the use of the phrase *dunkle Gifte* in 'Nachtseele', written in the late spring of 1914, it also appears in the opening lines of 'Der Schlaf,' which dates from June of the same year. In this poem the same 'dark poisons' are elevated to the role of lyric addressee, and Trakl highlights the thematic import of this image by means of a dark–white contrast even starker than that used in 'Traum und Umnachtung':

Der Schlaf

Verflucht ihr dunklen Gifte,
Weißer Schlaf!
Dieser höchst seltsame Garten
Dämmernder Bäume
Erfüllt von Schlangen, Nachtfaltern,
Spinnen, Fledermäusen.
Fremdling! Dein verlorner Schatten
Im Abendrot.
Ein finsterer Korsar
Im salzigen Meer der Trübsal.
Aufflattern weiße Vögel am Nachtsaum
Über stürzenden Städten
Von Stahl.

The crucial difference between *Wein* and *Mohn* on the one hand and *dunkle Gifte* on the other lies firstly in the latter's dissociation of intoxication from the natural world. As with Trakl's metal imagery discussed in relation to the final lines of 'Grodek' (see 8.2), the negation – or non-affirmation – of his familiar landscape code in the formulation 'dark poisons' suggests alienation from the cosmic harmony this code embodies. In 'Der Schlaf' the 'dark poisons' of the first line seem to offer access to a form of phantasmagoric *Ersatznatur*, one in which the equilibrium of Trakl's earlier pastoral landscapes has been disrupted by an unnatural, almost nightmarish proliferation of animal life (ll. 5–6). The speaker's alienation ('Fremdling!', l. 7) is merely confirmed, and the poem concludes with an image of nature distancing itself from the collapse of civilization (ll. 11–13). The drastic and wholly uncharacteristic shifts in setting (*Garten* → *Meer* → *Städte*) further underline the unnatural and disruptive influence of the 'dark poisons.' The second important factor that distinguishes Trakl's *dunkle Gifte* from the intoxicants that dominate his earlier poems is their harmful, even diabolic quality. In 'Der Schlaf' this is emphasized by the epithet 'verflucht' (l. 1), which suggests the malevolent influence of supernatural powers. Even without this imprecation, the phrase *dunkle Gifte*, more than either *Wein* or *Mohn*, draws attention to the seed of destruction that – both morphologically and physiologically – in*toxic*ation carries within itself. Thus it may be seen as Trakl's most succinct poetic response to the problem that Michael Cooke formulates with reference to the opium use of Coleridge and De Quincey: 'the rhetoric of intoxication must cope with the paradox that self-transcendence and self-abasement lie embedded in each other' (27–28).

The expression *dunkle Gifte* can be further distinguished from *Wein* and *Mohn* for the plurality and non-specificity of its referent. The 'dark poisons' it refers to generically could well include wine and opium, but equally any number of other substances that this phrase qualifies rather than names. It is curious, then, that 'Der Schlaf' is one of the two poems that Castoldi cites in support of his perhaps surprising claim that the influence of Trakl's cocaine use in particular is manifested 'explicitly' in his verse (160; Castoldi's claim might be considered an extension of the position taken by Springer, who had already included 'Der Schlaf' in the Expressionist section of his anthology of cocaine literature, 46; see 1.3). It might reasonably be objected that such a reading arbitrarily reduces the essential semantic openness of Trakl's formulation, rendering determinate a phrase that draws its poetic suggestiveness from its very indeterminacy. However, if we accept the premise that the meaning Castoldi sees in 'Der Schlaf' is neither exclusive nor definitive but latent, an evaluation of the factors that speak for and against this interpretation may open up new directions of enquiry into the relationship between drug and text.

Most important among the factors that support Castoldi's reading is the colour and light imagery associated with Trakl's 'poisons'. It has already been established (see 9.1) that an unusual emphasis on the perception of colour is both symptomatic of intoxicated consciousness and a recurrent motif of drug-related literature. Furthermore, various texts – including, most pertinently, certain poems of Trakl's foremost poetic role model Rimbaud (see 8.1, 9.1) – exhibit a tendency to associate individual colours and shades with particular psychoactive substances. With cocaine this association is particularly strong due to the distinctive whiteness of its crystals. 'It was very white and twinkled like crystal, resembling naphthalene,' records Vadim Maslennikov, the protagonist of Ageev's *Roman s kokainom*, recalling his first sight of the drug (128).[105] 'Exquisite, white poison,' is one characterization offered in Pitigrilli's *Cocaina* (241).[106] The combination of black with white in the colour-coding of cocaine, highlighted for example in the title of Antonin's essay 'Blanche et noire,' is the result of an association by opposition that seems particularly apposite in view of the 'black' perils the drug embodies. It is the same association that Castoldi has in mind in his cocaine-oriented reading of the Trakl poems he discusses: 'the ambiguous aspect of the drug, seductive and terrible at the same time, is frequently translated into the opposition of white and black' (160).[107] Returning to 'Der Schlaf,' then, the drug most likely to be brought to mind by the striking *dunkel-weiß* contrast Trakl employs in the opening lines of this poem is, as Castoldi suggests, cocaine. Notably, similar shade contrasts can also be found in Trakl's other poems featuring *dunkle Gifte*: in 'Traum und Umnachtung,' as already mentioned, there is the image of the 'mother's white face,' and in 'Nachtseele' the same phrase is immediately followed by a metaphorical description of the moon as a 'silver mask.' We should also add that reading the white and silver imagery in these poems in contradistinction to the 'darkness' of Trakl's 'poisons' can be considered complementary with the meaning such images acquire in the poet's landscape code as time indicators for winter and night (see 9.1). Just as *Wein* and *Mohn* are linked, whether directly or by nostalgia, to autumn and summer respectively (grapes are harvested and pressed in autumn, while poppies flower in summer, as in the poem 'Sommer'), in Trakl's fourth phase *dunkle Gifte* become the representative intoxicants of the wintry desolation he typically draws in black and white.

---

105 ‹Он был очень бел и сверкал кристаллически, напоминая нафталин.›

106 'Bianco, squisito veleno.'

107 'L'aspetto ambiguo della droga, seduttivo e terribile al tempo stesso, si traduce frequentemente nell'opposizione di bianco e nero.'

The main factor that may appear to contradict Castoldi's notion that 'Der Schlaf' contains an allusion to a powerful stimulant like cocaine is the association of *dunkle Gifte* with sleep, an association made not only in this poem, but also in the other two in which this phrase occurs. When we consider, however, that cocaine is at best only one of the several 'poisons' this phrase encompasses, this apparent contradiction becomes less significant, for the soporific effects may be attributed to other substances involved. We might also question the meaning of the formulation 'weißer Schlaf' (l. 2), yet another of Trakl's enigmatically coloured noun phrases. 'White sleep' can hardly denote sleep in any normal sense, and indeed the poem as a whole suggests that the state depicted is a form of delirium, such as that which might be produced by a cocktail of different drugs or 'dark poisons.' A state of delirious half-sleep is in fact characteristic of multiple addictions in which the user takes depressants or narcotics to counteract the side-effects of stimulants, or vice-versa, in the process reinforcing the intoxicating – and toxic – effect of the drugs already taken. The combination of caffeine and alcohol is a widespread, socially and legally sanctioned example of the same practice. An instance of such drug abuse involving cocaine in combination with a sedative can be found in Pitigrilli's *Cocaina*:

> Tito's nights were restless: in the evening he took strong doses of chloral to control the insomnia produced by the drug [cocaine] from which he did not know how to detach himself. But his indomitable insomnia and the useless narcosis engendered a hallucinatory exaltation: he spent long hours in a state of wakefulness in which he felt he was dreaming, and in a state of sleep that gave him the sensation of being awake.[108] (188)

Considering the strange and rapidly shifting imagery of 'Der Schlaf,' the reader has good reason to think that Trakl's 'white sleep' denotes a state of 'hallucinatory exaltation' similar to that depicted in this passage. The crucial distinction is that whereas the voice describing Tito's delirium belongs to a detached and dispassionate narrator who systematically distinguishes causes and effects, calls things by the names that his sober consciousness assigns them, and does not participate in the hallucinations he refers to, the voice

108 'Le notti di Tito furono agitate: la sera prendeva forti dosi di cloralio per dominare l'insonnia prodotta dalla droga da cui non sapeva staccarsi. Ma dall'indomabile insonnia e dall'inutile narcosi nasceva una esaltazione allucinatoria: passava lunghe ore in una veglia in cui gli pareva di sognare, e in uno stato di sonno che gli dava la sensazione d'essere desto.'

in Trakl's poem appears to emanate from the delirium itself, so that the speaker's 'hallucinatory exaltation' is enacted in the same language in which it is presented. In this state of mind causal relationships lose their primacy, and this is reflected in the wording of the poem: the prominence of precisely such a relationship was reduced with Trakl's correction of the second line, 'weißer Schlaf,' which in the original draft version reads 'erzeugend weißen Schlaf.' By the same token, whereas in Pitigrilli's text the narrator clearly states which substances have given rise to Tito's delirium, leaving the reader in no doubt that the protagonist has taken cocaine and chloral, in 'Der Schlaf' the agents of intoxication are stylized so as to conform with the obscure and sinister – that is, 'dark' and 'poisonous' – significance they acquire in the speaker's delirious-cum-mystical perspective. Thus, although the justification for Castoldi's theory that these lines contain an allusion to cocaine is – considering the extreme lexical concentration of the context – relatively substantial, it must be underlined that Trakl's lyric subject has no interest in naming this drug, or in making his allusion to it unambiguous.

These observations on Trakl's poetic intoxicants demonstrate the important thematic role of intoxication in his poetry, which coincides with and amplifies its dominant stylistic one. They also confirm that the intoxicants named in his poetry are chosen in accordance with the same criteria which govern his lexical selection generally. In other words, this choice is determined by how well these intoxicants conform with and extend the mythopoeic parameters of his landscape code, more than by any confessional imperative to document – or even to *seem* to document – his own drug usage. Wine is supremely suitable to Trakl's poetic ends because of its pastoral and religious associations; the poppy is both a colourful flower and a long-established symbol of opiate dreams; the phrase 'dark poisons' carries overtones of mystery and impending doom. A word like cocaine simply does not have the same resonance or heritage; nor, for that matter, do words like alcohol, beer, schnaps, chloroform, barbiturate, Veronal, morphine, even opium, all of which denote psychoactive substances the poet himself is known to have consumed in considerable quantities (see 7.1). However, we have also established that several distinctive features of Trakl's poetry point beyond the intoxicants it names directly to the broader significance of intoxication as a privileged existential condition, as well as to the numerous means that can be employed to attain it. In addition to the stylistic traits discussed in 9.1, these features include the apparent interchangeability of religious and mystical associations between *Wein* and *Mohn*, the diversity of Trakl's agents of drunkenness, the use of the word *Trunkenheit* as a metonym for intoxication, and the plurality and non-specificity of the phrase *dunkle Gifte*. We have also touched on the possibility of reading enciphered allusions to drugs – and specifically to cocaine – in other image patterns, such as patterns of colour and light, where the plausibility of such readings depends to a great extent on their contextual vicinity to the other features listed here. Chapter 10 will develop this last approach, examining another of Trakl's dominant image patterns that might be read as incorporating an allusion to cocaine.

10 Black Snow: the Shadow of a White Drug

10.1 Performing Derangement

Castoldi's assertion that Trakl's contrasting black and white imagery 'translates' the 'ambiguous aspect' of cocaine, discussed in relation to the poem 'Der Schlaf' in 9.2, points to another potential sphere of reference to the same drug in Trakl's poetry, one that is distinct from the patterns of intoxication imagery outlined in the previous section, but related to the phrase *dunkle Gifte* by its colour associations: Trakl's most 'felicitous' expression of this same black and white opposition, Castoldi writes, is 'the image of black snow' (160).[109] For an explicit if rather grandiloquent elaboration of this analogy, we may refer to Antonin's comparison of cocaine to a snow drift that masks the crevasses endangering those who cross it:

> As for cocaine, it is white and black. Made up of little white crystals, it resembles snow, but despite its appearance, it's snow that you are more likely to sink into than slide over. Like a fine field of powder snow, cocaine invites you to ski or snowboard across it. But this snow hides crevasses, and the abysses are all black.[110] (225)

Castoldi cites the first quatrain of the poem 'Delirium', written in January 1913, to illustrate the validity of a similar metaphorical interpretation of Trakl's black-snow image. Here the text of the poem is given in full:

Delirium

Der schwarze Schnee, der von den Dächern rinnt;
Ein roter Finger taucht in deine Stirne
Ins kahle Zimmer sinken blaue Firne,

109 'L'immagine di una neve nera.'

110 'La cocaïne, elle, est blanche et noire. Constituée de fins cristaux blancs, la cocaïne rappelle la neige, mais c'est une neige, malgré les apparences, dans laquelle on s'enfonce plus qu'on ne glisse. La cocaïne, comme un beau champ de poudreuse, invite à la godille et au surf. Mais la neige masque les crevasses et tous les abysses sont noirs.' Tr. Jeremy Macey.

Die Liebender erstorbene Spiegel sind.
In schwere Stücke bricht das Haupt und sinnt
Den Schatten nach im Spiegel blauer Firne,
Dem kalten Lächeln einer toten Dirne.
In Nelkendüften weint der Abendwind.

A curious piece of documentary evidence, unremarked by Castoldi, tantalizingly hints at a concrete connection between this poem and the poet's drug habits. 'Delirium' and another poem, 'Am Rand eines alten Brunnens' (*SW* 3:26–27), the definitive version of which dates from July 1913, together represent the finished products of what Trakl scholars have labelled the <Delirien> mini-cycle, a name given in view of Trakl's use of elements from 'Delirien' (*SW* 2:315–320), the 'mother' poem of the cycle, in the composition of these other two poems.[111] The first manuscript version of 'Delirien', a sketch consisting of just three lines of verse, was pencilled on the reverse side of a letter to Trakl from Buschbeck, dated 17 January 1913. These lines appear on the right-hand side of the bottom half of the page, written lengthways with the first line against the right edge of the paper. On the left-hand side of the same piece of paper, also written lengthways with the first line against the left edge – thus on the page reading bottom-to-top rather than, like the poem, top-to-bottom – and similarly pencilled in Trakl's hand, there appears the following list of various medicinal and psychoactive agents and related paraphernalia: 'Aspirin / Morph. (Pulver) / Sublimat. (Glas) / Doverische Pulver / Xeroform / Kal. Chloric. / Codeinpulver / Formanwatte / Veronal.' We can do no more than speculate about the purpose of this list and its relationship to the poetic idea that germinated alongside it. Is the spatial proximity of these two texts merely coincidental, or might it be indicative of some deeper connection between them? One thing is certain: a mixture of the 'dark poisons' named in Trakl's list would be potent enough to bring about the 'deliria' referred to in the title of his poem. Furthermore, although the incidental writings that appear on the same piece of paper as the original sketch for a poem can have little if any bearing on our interpretation of the final text, Castoldi's suggestion that 'Delirium' manifests the 'significant part of [Trakl's] inspiration' (160) that the poet drew from his cocaine use is

111 For a graphic representation of the development of the <Delirien> mini-cycle, see *HkA* 2:395. The description of the manuscript given here is based on that in *HkA* 2:394; the equivalent description in *SW* does not mention the list discussed here.

not helped by the absence of cocaine from this list. Once again, the biographical question of drug influence proves impossibly slippery.

The draft versions of the text itself may further modify our perspective on a potential relationship between this poem and cocaine. In the first of the two versions of this poem, as well as in the second version of 'Delirien', the third stanza of which forms the basis for the first quatrain of 'Delirium', what 'runs from the roofs' (l. 1) is not 'der schwarze Schnee' (l. 1), but 'der schwarze Kot,' a phrase which can hardly be taken as an allusion to cocaine, or to any other drug for that matter. It is likely that 'der schwarze Kot' is a reworking of the following line from Rimbaud's 'Mauvais sang' (1873): 'Dans les villes la boue m'apparaissait soudainement rouge et noire.' In the German translation by Klammer Trakl is known to have possessed, this is rendered as: 'In den Städten schien mir der Kot plötzlich rot und schwarz' (*LD* 187; cited in *SW* 2:316). Whatever the derivation, even if we accept that the black–white contrast of the first image in this poem contains an enciphered allusion to cocaine, the fact that this contrast was introduced only in the final revision of the text would suggest that 'Delirium' was not originally conceived as a poem about cocaine intoxication, thus casting further doubt on Castoldi's cocaine-inspiration theory.

On the other hand, it can be argued that the generation of such an allusion represents one enrichment of the text resulting from Trakl's eventual substitution of 'Schnee' for 'Kot.' This substitution brings other enrichments, too, that are no less significant to the poem's thematic configuration. Apart from the purely rhetorical force of the oxymoronic 'black snow,' we must also consider that this same oxymoron makes the first line of the poem ambiguous. Whereas 'black filth' makes no particular demands on the reader, black being one of the colours most easily associated with filth, 'black snow' is enigmatic and therefore loaded with symbolic suggestiveness. No less important is the consideration that the word 'snow' reinforces the poem's seasonal setting, so that 'Delirium' becomes – from the outset – a winter poem. By extension, whereas 'black filth falling from the roofs' embodies only the corruption of civilization, 'black snow falling from the roofs' underlines the parallel corruption of the natural and human domains, both of which must ultimately succumb to the same fate of 'schwarze Verwesung,' as Trakl would proclaim in 'Grodek' (see 8.2).

It is evident, then, that Trakl's black-snow motif is neither primarily nor unambiguously a reference to cocaine. In addition to the text-historical factors already mentioned, the fact that the snow of 'Delirium' is described as 'running from the roofs' is the most obvious sign that its referent is closer to snow in the original, meteorological sense of the word than snow as a moniker for cocaine. This observation, however, does not invalidate Castoldi's reading of 'black snow' as a poetic 'translation' of the 'seductive and terrible aspect' of this drug; it merely qualifies it with the condition that at best this translation occurs on a secondary and figurative level of meaning. The elusiveness of an assumed reference to cocaine in 'Delirium' can perhaps be better appreciated by comparison to the snow imagery used in other texts discussed in this study. In Benn's *Pameelen* plays (see 4.1–4.3), which similarly feature patterns of imagery based on the words *Firn* and *Schnee*, the impression that beyond their literal significance, on a secondary level these patterns can also be read as allusions to cocaine is supported by more explicit references to the drug in each of these two texts, references that words such as *Firn* and *Schnee* echo and reinforce. By contrast, in Walter Rheiner's poem 'Komm, holder Schnee!' (see 6.4), as in 'Delirium', there is no explicit reference to the drug. But at the same time there is nothing that would appear to complicate a reading that posits a straightforward snow–cocaine equivalence, such as the relative clause 'der von den Dächern rinnt' that qualifies the black snow of 'Delirium'. The speaker in Rheiner's poem seeks spiritual absolution through death, and the only characteristic attributed to the snow that is presented as the lyric addressee and provider of this absolution is the adjective *hold*, which in itself does not give the reader any clue about the material qualities of the snow in question. As a result, Rheiner's snow seems to remain caught in the balance – at a primary level – between its meteorological and psychoactive referents, either of which could, in its own way, be used to satisfy his death wish.

In 'Delirium' the situation is more complex, as the contextual factors acting on the phrase 'Der schwarze Schnee' are both numerous and heterogeneous. To assess the validity of reading this image as an allusion to cocaine, and thus to characterize more precisely the relationship between Trakl's poetry and this drug, we shall now undertake a semantic analysis of these contextual influences. This analysis also has wider relevance as a case study of how Trakl's extreme lexical economy produces the extraordinary semantic resonance for which his poetry is known, as a similar analytical model could conceivably be applied to any of his 'difficult' images. The following diagram summarizes the complex set of contextual influences on the image of black snow in 'Delirium':

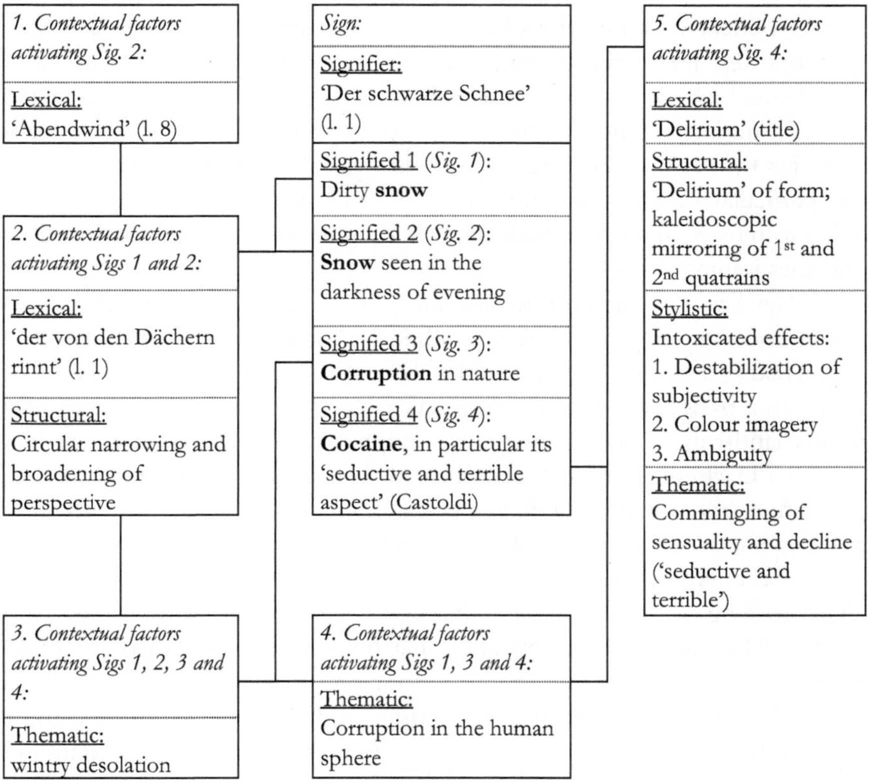

The central cell in the diagram represents the linguistic sign under discussion, that is, the phrase 'der schwarze Schnee.' Its representation is based on Saussure's well-known division of the sign into two constituent parts: the signifier and the signified. However, as it is not immediately apparent what is signified by the paradoxical collocation 'black snow,' the reader is obliged to look for clues in the surrounding text. Clues are indeed available, but these do not point to a single determinate meaning, rather to at least four possible meanings involving various degrees of figurativeness. These have been listed, starting from the most literal, under the line separating signifier from signifieds. As in Lacan's revision of Saussure's original sign diagram, the solidity of this line conveys the fundamental and irremediable break between these two elements, a break that is nowhere more evident than in Trakl's 'essentially ambiguous' poetry (Heidegger 70; see 9.1). The dotted lines between individual signifieds, by contrast, indicate that the meanings listed not only coexist but also interrelate and overlap, the correspondences and tensions between them contributing to the distinctive semantic texture of the poem. The cells surrounding the sign and numbered anticlockwise 1 to 5 represent the textual clues that may influence the reader's understanding of the phrase 'black snow.' Each of these cells contains the set of contextual factors that serve to activate or semi-activate the particular signified or combination of signifieds indicated in italics. The relationships between signifieds and these contextual sets are illustrated by the lines joining the cells.

The first two of the four meanings listed (signifieds 1 and 2) posit a literal understanding of the word 'Schnee', in contradiction with the view that Trakl's 'signs do not point to the elements of nature' (Williams 275; see 7.2). On a basic level, the poem depicts a scene in which snow is part of a wintry landscape. This interpretation is supported by the relative clause 'der von den Dächern rinnt' (cell 2), which further defines the setting as one of habitation (roofs imply buildings), perhaps a town or village. Crucially, the sight of snow 'running from the roofs' coincides with the range of perceptions that might be made in such a setting. Further contextual support for a literal reading of 'Schnee' is provided by the circular structure of the poem (cell 2). The point of view appears to narrow from an outdoor perspective, taking in 'roofs' and 'snow', to an indoor one focusing on elements of a domestic environment, such as the 'room' and 'mirrors', before widening again in the final line with its reference to the sound of the wind: 'weint der Abendwind.' It is probable that this same structural principle was the reason for Trakl's inversion of the last two lines in the first draft of the poem, when he reformulated 'Mit Nelken Düften füllt den Abendwind / Das fremde Lächeln einer toten Dirne,' replacing it with a version much closer to the definitive one by moving 'Abendwind' from line seven to line eight: 'Dem fremden Lächeln einer kalten Dirne. / In Nelkendüften weint der Abendwind.' Further, a literal reading of 'Schnee' coheres with the theme of wintry desolation that runs right through the poem (cell 3). This theme is manifested in the dominance of lexemes with the semantic features 'decline', 'death', and 'cold': 'schwarz' (l. 1), 'Schnee' (l. 1), 'taucht' (l. 2), 'kahl' (l. 3), 'sinken' (l. 3), 'blau' (ll. 3 and 6), 'Firne' (ll. 3 and 6), 'erstorben' (l. 4), 'bricht' (l. 5), 'kalt' (l. 7), 'tot' (l. 7), 'weint' (l. 8), 'Abend' (l. 8).

The major difficulty with an interpretation of this kind emerges when the reader comes to account for the adjective 'schwarz'. The text itself offers only vague hints as to why the snow should appear – literally – black. First, it may be dirty, perhaps with soot, an idea that gains some credibility from the winter setting among roofs, and probably therefore among chimneys. Another factor that supports, albeit indirectly, a black–dirty equivalence is the theme of corruption in civilization (cell 4), which links such images as the bare room (l. 3), the dead mirrors (l. 4), the breaking head (l. 5), the shadowy presences (l. 6), and the dead prostitute (l. 7). A level of pollution that causes the snow to appear dirty would be compatible with the state of social degeneration implied by these images. On the other hand, following Steinkamp's evaluation of Trakl's colour adjectives as idiolectical time markers (see 9.1), 'black snow' might be interpreted as an indicator of the time of day as well as the season, in so far that blackness implies the absence of daylight. Line 8 of the poem explicitly names 'evening' as the time at which the poem is set (cell 1), so that a possible retrospective interpretation of the 'black snow' of line one might be 'snow seen in the darkness of evening.' Both these readings draw a certain plausibility from the textual evidence supporting them, but in neither case is this evidence strong enough for the meaning in question to be considered determinate, for dirty snow or snow seen in the darkness may appear off-white, but hardly black. The persisting deficiency of these signifieds (*dirty* or *evening* snow) in relation to the signifier (*black* snow) represents a semantic gap that the reader can only fill by attributing additional, more figurative meaning to the phrase 'der schwarze Schnee.'

The meaning listed as 'signified 3' is essentially an amalgamation and abstraction of the previous two. Here we are following the method advocated by Schneider and Steinkamp of progressing from a literal dimension of meaning to a related symbolic one (see 9.1). Regardless of its relation to the scene being depicted, that is, its function at the level Saussure labels *parole*, in general usage – at the level he calls *langue* – the word snow is inseparably associated with whiteness, as this is both the natural condition and most conspicuous characteristic of its referent. Compare, for example, the cliché 'as white as snow,' which has Biblical pedigree,[112] or the use of the adjective snowy as a synonym for white. Therefore, Trakl's use of the adjective black to describe the snow in 'Delirium' suggests that its natural condition has been corrupted. Indeed, con-

112 It occurs in Numbers 12:10; 2 Kings 5:27; Psalms 68:14; Isaiah 1:18; Daniel 7:9; Matthew 28:3; Mark 9:3; and Revelation 1:14.

sidering the Biblical link between snow and whiteness, it may even be taken as a sign that the environment in which it occurs is literally God-forsaken. Pertinent here is also the common metaphorical association of whiteness with purity – employed, for example, in Psalms 51:7: 'wash me, and I shall be whiter than snow' – and, by contrast, blackness with impurity. In the specific context of the poem, a reading of the black-snow image as symbolic of corruption in nature accords with the two dominant thematic patterns already identified: wintry desolation and corruption in society (cells 3 and 4). In so far as they develop and expand the same theme, these contextual correspondences confirm that the corruption evoked in this image is not limited specifically to the snow itself, but is symptomatic of an advanced state of decay in the natural environment, indeed in the cosmos as a whole.

The symbolic potential of this image, however, has not yet been exhausted, for there is another set of contextual factors (cell 5) that, seen in relation to the black-snow image, opens a further semantic domain within the poem, namely Castoldi's interpretation of black snow as an allusion to cocaine, in particular to this drug's 'seductive and terrible aspect' (signified 4). Most conspicuous among the textual clues in this set is the title of the poem itself, 'Delirium', a naming of the state of mind that we have seen manifested in the linguistic structures of other poems, such as 'Klage' and 'Der Schlaf' (see 8.1 and 9.2 respectively). Within Trakl's poetic idiolect, *Delirium* can be related to *Trunkenheit* as an altered form of consciousness involving an aesthetic or poetic apprehension of the world – note that in 'Delirium' the form in which the speaker's state of mind manifests itself is an entirely regular and archetypally poetic iambic pentameter. What distinguishes *Delirium* from *Trunkenheit*, however, is that whereas the latter is normally linked to such positive factors as pastoral equanimity, festive drinking, song, opiate dreaminess, or stoical resignation to decline (see 9.2), the former is invariably associated with angst and alienation. In this respect, the relationship of *Delirium* to *Trunkenheit* is comparable to that of *dunkle Gifte* to *Wein* and *Mohn*, outlined in 9.2; whereas with *Trunkenheit* the emphasis is on intoxication as transcendence, with *Delirium* it is on intoxication as poisoning. With delirium as with drunkenness, there are numerous possible agents or catalysts that may be involved in bringing this state about, and these are sometimes specified – such as the 'dark poisons' in the poem 'Der Schlaf' – sometimes not. The poem under discussion belongs to the latter category, so that the juxtaposition of the word *Delirium* in the title with the image of black snow in the first line can be read as a hint as to what this agent – or one of these agents – might be.

As in 'Klage' and 'Der Schlaf,' in 'Delirium' the phonetic and syntactical structures of the poem embody the delirious consciousness of the speaker, thus reinforcing the contextual predisposition for reading the phrase 'der schwarze Schnee' as a drug-related symbol. In this poem the structural manifestation of the delirium theme is aided by one of Trakl's favourite devices for displacing and distorting subjectivity: the mirror. The word *Spiegel* occurs twice in the poem, once in line four in the plural, and then again in line six, this time in the singular. On both occasions the mirrors are equated with the 'blue snows' that in line 3 are described as sinking into the 'bare room.' As if this equation in itself were not delirious enough, in line 4 the mirrors are described as 'dead', while the mirror in line 6 reflects the images not of objects or people themselves, but of their shadows: 'und sinnt / den Schatten nach im Spiegel blauer Firne.' The distorting mirror is more than just a prominent thematic motif in 'Delirium'; it is also the poem's primary structural principle, as words and images from the first quatrain reappear, half-reflected and half-transfigured, in the second. This mirror structure is also the basis for the poem's rhyme scheme – *abbaabba* – in which two of the mirrored pairs, the endings of lines 4 and 5 (*sind–sinnt*) and lines 3 and 6 (*Firne–Firne*), are phonetically identical. The kaleidoscopic effect of the whole is evocative of a delirious state of mind similar to the cocaine-induced 'hallucinatory exaltation' discussed in relation to 'Der Schlaf' (Pitigrilli 188; see 3.2).

Other contextual factors that similarly contribute to expanding the semantic potential of the black-snow image of line 1 to comprehend an allusion to cocaine include the stylistic features examined in 9.1 and designated generically as constituting Trakl's poetics of intoxication. These can be divided into three main types, corresponding to points 1–3 in the diagram and below: destabilization of subjectivity, colour imagery, and ambiguity. The poem 'Delirium' exemplifies how these features combine to generate a semantic undercurrent of intoxication that runs through the poem.

1. As far as textual subjectivity is concerned, we might first observe the complete absence of personal pronouns from the text. The only gesture towards pronominal subjectivity is the possessive adjective in the phrase '*deine* Stirne' of line 2, but even this assumes a strangely

detached quality in its isolation from any pronominal referent. At the same time, there are two nominal references to human subjects, 'Liebender' (l. 4) and the 'tote Dirne' (l. 7), as well as numerous metonymical references in the form of body parts and mental functions: 'Finger' (l. 2), 'Stirne' (l. 2), 'Haupt' (l. 5), 'sinnt' (l. 5), 'Schatten' (l. 6), and 'Lächeln' (l. 7). The description of the head in line 5 as 'breaking into heavy pieces' is an especially direct reference to the fragmentation of subjectivity; drawing out Castoldi's interpretation, this might be read as the moment in which the drug symbolized by the 'black snow' of line 1 achieves its maximum neurochemical impact. Further, it is possible that the speaker and the prostitute of line 7 together can be identified with the lovers who, in the inverted genitive construction of line 4, are associated with the 'dead mirrors,' especially as the link between these two images is underlined by the repetition of the death motif: '*erstorbene* Spiegel'–'*tote* Dirne.' So much remains unsaid about these figures and the link between them, however, that this identification must remain tentative, and the uncertainty associated with it is itself a major contributor to the destabilization of subjectivity in the poem.

2. In addition to the cocaine symbolism Castoldi sees in the black–white contrast of the snow image itself, we should also note the dominance of colour imagery throughout the poem. This dominance is consistent with the perceptual peculiarities of an intoxicated perspective: 'der *schwarze* Schnee' (l. 1), 'ein *roter* Finger' (l. 2), '*blaue* Firne' (ll. 3 and 6).
3. With regard to ambiguity, 'Delirium' features Trakl's characteristic combination of a multi-layered semantic structure with radical semantic underdetermination on and between individual layers of meaning. As this analysis shows in relation to a single image from the poem, different levels of meaning involving various degrees of figurativeness coexist and interact, partly reinforcing and partly contradicting one another, without offering the 'prosaic' comfort of determinate meaning. Other lexical formulations in the text that are both semantically opaque and symbolically suggestive include 'ein roter Finger,' 'blaue Firne,' and 'erstorbene Spiegel.' Noteworthy in the poem as a whole is the accentuated blurring of the distinction between the categories 'exterior' and 'interior'. This observation applies both on the environmental level to the distinction between outdoors and indoors – in line 3 the granular snow of the 'blaue Firne' sinks into the

'bare room' – and on the human level to the distinction between mind and body, most obviously in line 2 in the 'dipping' of a 'red finger' into 'your forehead.' The overall effect is a 'blurring of the perceptions' and a 'setting in motion of objects' equivalent to that which Paz attributes to drugged consciousness (76; see 9.1).

Castoldi's claim that the colour contrast in Trakl's black-snow image 'translates' in particular the 'seductive and terrible aspect' of cocaine finds a contextual correspondence in the theme of the commingling of sensuality and decline, or in Freudian terminology, the pleasure principle and the death drive. Explicit references to eroticism and death are juxtaposed in line 4 ('Liebender erstorbene Spiegel') and line 7 ('Dem kalten Lächeln einer toten Dirne'), while line 8 suggests that the morbid yet erotically charged mood governing the human presence in the poem extends to nature as well, as the wind 'cries' in 'carnation fragrances.' We should also note a further correspondence between Castoldi's interpretation of 'der schwarze Schnee' as a symbol for cocaine and the theme of corruption in the human sphere (cell 4), and by extension the theme of wintry decline (cell 3): *Delirium*-inducing drug abuse, like the assumption of 'dark poisons' (see 9.2), may be considered a symptom of decay on a broader social or anthropological scale, which is in turn subsidiary to the universal drift towards 'schwarze Verwesung' (see 8.2).

In summary, two salient points need to be underlined in the light of this discussion of 'Delirium', the first concerning the weakness of Castoldi's reading, and the second its strength. The tenuous and ultimately unfruitful claim that Trakl 'derived a significant part of his inspiration' from his experience of cocaine appears, in the absence of any sort of documentary evidence to support it, contrived to make this poet fit neatly into Castoldi's outline of the historical development of cocaine-inspired literature. Furthermore, the related, biographically reductive claim that this influence is 'explicit', for example, in the image of black snow in 'Delirium' misrepresents the most distinctive stylistic features of the poetry itself, features that privilege and enhance the latent and elusive – as opposed to 'explicit' – qualities of meaning. Second, however, once these distinctive features and their effects have been grasped, the affirmation of a referential relationship between the black-snow image of 'Delirium' and cocaine points to a level of latent meaning that displays a complex set of connections with other aspects of the text, enriches the semantic configuration of the whole, and owing to its very elusiveness, reinforces the poem's symbolic resonance. In 'Delirium', therefore, cocaine intoxication might best be characterized as a shadowy subtext, another significant absence, a meaning that – in much the same way as the speaker himself (see 9.1) – is never really there, but presented metaphorically as black snow and metonymically in a series of contextual correspondences and effects. Only in this way, by becoming intangible, mysterious, and sinister, does cocaine obtain the mythopoeic force of Trakl's other poetic intoxicants.

10.2 Listening in the Snow

'Delirium' is by no means the only Trakl poem featuring prominent snow imagery. *Schnee* can in fact be counted among Trakl's most frequently recurring landscape words, especially in the poems of the third and fourth phases, at which point his treatment of wintry desolation as the final stage in the seasonal–existential progression characteristic of his poetry acquires both greater urgency and more refined articulation. The question arises, then, as to what extent the considerations made in 10.1 with regard to the relationship between cocaine and the black-snow image of 'Delirium' are relevant to Trakl's snow imagery in general. Naturally, the contextual factors influencing the activation of the semantic possibilities of the word *Schnee* vary, sometimes considerably, from one poem to the next. Thus, although Trakl's snow is usually integrated into a larger depiction of a wintry landscape, as in 'Delirium', significant variables include the degree of difficulty associated with a purely literal understanding of the word and consequently the degree of its symbolic suggestiveness. Whereas in the line 'Sah, daß Schnee fiel in kahles Gezweig' from 'Kaspar Hauser Lied' (*SW* 3:312–325), a literal reading presents no apparent difficulty, the same cannot be said for the snow image that occurs in the poem 'Im Dorf' (*SW* 2:403–413), owing to the snow's 'Delirium'-like blackness and its mysterious fluttering 'through the arms' of the 'Bäurin': 'Durch ihre Arme rieselt schwarzer Schnee.' The snow that appears in the following couplet from 'Helian' – placed in an indoor setting, collocated with leprosy, and enigmatically sinking from Helian's forehead – takes this difficulty to an even higher level: 'Da Helians Seele sich im rosigen Spiegel beschaut / Und Schnee und Aussatz von seiner Stirne sinken.'

Despite such variations, several contextual factors can be identified that recur frequently in connection with Trakl's snow imagery and that, as established in 10.1, might be linked with a latent drug or in particular cocaine symbolism. Notable among these are the stylistic features characteristic of Trakl's poetics of intoxication (see 9.1). Points 1–3 below correspond to the same tabulation of these features employed in the discussion of 'Delirium' in 10.1:

1. In regard to the destabilization of textual subjectivity, we find that Trakl's snow imagery very often involves contact between or commingling of snow and body parts, or bodily disintegration, effects consistent with the 'dissociative bodily sensations' (Canetti 416) of cocaine delirium. Illustrative examples can be found in the lines cited above from 'Im Dorf' and 'Helian', featuring the *Bäurin*'s arms and Helian's forehead respectively. Poems with similar image combinations include 'Sonja' (*SW* 3:39–42), 'Dezember' (*SW* 3:77–93), 'So leise läuten' (*SW* 4i:265–269), and 'Vorhölle' (*SW* 4ii:11–30):

   Schnee, der ihre *Wangen* feuchtet. ('Sonja')

   Spinnen fielen aus ihren *Augen* / Und roter Schnee. ('Dezember')

   Es weht von Gestirnen / Ein scheeiger Wind durch *dein Haar*. ('So leise läuten')

   Ein *Herz* / Erstarrt in schneeiger Stille. ('Vorhölle')

   The last of these might be read with hindsight as a chilling premonition of the poet's own fate. 'Vorhölle' was composed in April 1914, little over six months before Trakl suffered cardiac paralysis as the result of a cocaine overdose.[113]
2. Oxymoronic blackness or darkness is another recurrent motif. In addition to the examples already cited from 'Delirium' and 'Im Dorf,' others can be found in the poems 'Im Frühling' (*SW* 3:253–260),

113 On Trakl's death certificate the cause of his death was transformed from the '*intoxicatio cocainum*' of his medical file into the euphemistic 'Herzlähmung' (see 2:732–33).

'Geburt' (*SW* 3:415–417), and 'O die entlaubten Buchen' (*SW* 3:265–269):

> Leise sank von *dunklen* Schritten der Schnee. ('Im Frühling')
>
> Gebirge: *Schwärze*, Schweigen und Schnee. ('Geburt')
>
> O die entlaubten Buchen und der *schwärzliche* Schnee. ('O die entlaubten Buchen')

Other colours, especially red and its compounds, are often linked with Trakl's snow as well. Note, for example, the 'red snow' in the line from 'Dezember' cited in point 1 above. Other poems featuring similar colour patterns include, once again, 'Geburt' and 'O die entlaubten Buchen':

> Schnee, der leise aus *purpurner* Wolke sinkt. ('Geburt')
>
> Und das Wohnen in *rosigem* Schnee. ('O die entlaubten Buchen')

3. Trakl's characteristic amplification of poetic ambiguity in the relationship between signifiers and signifieds can often be observed in connection with his snow imagery. Relevant here is the difficulty mentioned above in assimilating certain of his snow images to a literal reading of the word *Schnee*, whether because of the snow's unusual, seemingly unnatural relation to body parts or colours, which can be seen in several images already cited, or for any other reason. The snow image from 'Helian', involving the association of snow and leprosy, is surely among the most disconcerting of all, and an analysis of it reveals one of Trakl's most ingenious ambiguity-generating mechanisms. The combination of *Schnee* and *Aussatz* is derived from the Bible, in several verses of which snow is used in similes describing the flaky white skin symptomatic of leprosy (Exodus 4:6; Numbers 12:10; 2 Kings 5:27; cf. *SW* 2:201). In adapting this collocation, Trakl eliminates the comparison underlying its Biblical use. In this way he replaces the original, readily comprehensible association through similarity between the two terms (snow-*like* leprosy) with a highly enigmatic association through contiguity (snow *and* leprosy), so that not only the target domain (leprosy) but also the source domain (snow) of

the Biblical simile become, seemingly, present in the scene of the poem, 'sinking' together from Helian's 'forehead'.[114] This outright substitution of metonymic for metaphoric association can be seen as a radical extension of one of poetry's inherent and most distinctive qualities. As Jakobson explains, 'in poetry, where similarity is superinduced upon contiguity, any metonymy is slightly metaphoric, and any metaphor has a metonymic tint' (85).

The poem in which these and other contextual factors combine to produce perhaps the strongest allusion to cocaine intoxication in all of Trakl's œuvre is 'Rosiger Spiegel: ein häßliches Bild':

Rosiger Spiegel: ein häßliches Bild,
Das im schwarzen Rücken erscheint,
Blut aus brochenen Augen weint
Lästernd mit toten Schlangen spielt.

Schnee rinnt durch das starrende Hemd
Purpurn über das schwarze Gesicht,
Das in schwere Stücken[115] zerbricht
Von Planeten, verstorben und fremd.

Spinne im schwarzen Rücken erscheint
Wollust, dein Antlitz verstorben und fremd.
Blut rinnt durch das starrende Hemd
Schnee aus brochenen Augen weint.

---

114 A similar mechanism underlies Georg Samsa's metamorphosis in Kafka's story 'Die Verwandlung,' first published two years after 'Helian' in 1915, in which Samsa, an insect-like individual with no 'backbone' (Seymour-Smith 610), finds himself transformed into an insect. As in Trakl's poem, the metaphorical intrudes upon the literal.

115 The phrase 'in schwere Stücken' is ungrammatical. The accusative adjective *schwere* does not agree in case with its noun referent *Stücken*, which is dative. We can exclude the possibility that this is a deliberate ambiguity. Syntactical ambiguities typically arise in Trakl's poetry when several words or phrases may fulfil the same function; in line 9 of this poem, for example, the verb *erscheint* has three possible subjects: *Spinne*, *Wollust*, and *dein Antlitz*. With the phrase 'in schwere Stücken,' by contrast, it is not a choice between various, grammatical readings, as here no grammatical reading is possible. It seems more likely, therefore, that the final *-n* in *Stücken* was simply a slip of the pen that was overlooked in revisions of the poem. In line 5 of 'Delirium' the same phrase is unambiguously accusative: 'In schwere Stücke.'

This poem, one of Trakl's most gruesome, dates from the winter of 1912–13, the same period as 'Helian', with which it shares the 'rosy mirror' of its first line. The poems that make up the <Delirien> mini-cycle were written in this period as well. Indeed, 'Rosiger Spiegel' has various key features in common with 'Delirium', including several that may contribute to the contextual activation of a cocaine reference in the poem's snow imagery. First and most generally, 'Rosiger Spiegel' may be added to the list of Trakl poems embodying a state of delirium, fraught with an acute existential menace, that is crafted into the poem's language and so attributable to the consciousness of an implicit speaker. This list already includes the poem 'Der Schlaf' (see 9.2), with which 'Rosiger Spiegel' shares the – perhaps hallucinated, certainly menacing – appearance of snakes and spiders. As in 'Delirium', the production of the delirious effect is based in large part on the thematic and structural elaboration of the distorting-mirror motif. In 'Rosiger Spiegel' the functioning of the mirror is deformed just as radically as in 'Delirium': the 'ugly image' of line 1 and the 'spider' of line 9 appear not in the glass, but in the 'black back.' Once again, the mirror is not only a prominent image in the poem, but also its dominant structural principle, as meanings, sounds, words, and even entire phrases are recycled and recombined in what becomes a kaleidoscopic succession of reverberating images and rhymes. The colour black appears in every stanza, as does a word meaning dead (*tot* in the first stanza, *verstorben* in the second and third). The third stanza consists mostly of rearranged material from the first two, and the last two lines are simply an inversion of lines 3 and 5, only that *Blut* and *Schnee* have exchanged predicates. The *abba* rhyme scheme of each quatrain gives sonic expression to the same mirror motif. The echo effect of this scheme intensifies in the final stanza, which reproduces the *b*-rhyme of the first stanza as its *a*-rhyme and the *a*-rhyme of the second as its *b*-rhyme.

Moreover, 'Rosiger Spiegel' conforms fully to the stylistic principles of Trakl's poetics of intoxication (see 9.1). As in 'Delirium', a single possessive adjective – '*dein* Antlitz' (l. 10) – is the only manifestation of the conventional, pronominal variety of textual subjectivity (the familiarity it suggests is immediately undermined by the repetition of the adjective 'fremd' to describe the same face). For the most part subjectivity is expressed by means of fragmentary, metonymical references to human presence: 'Blut' (ll. 3 and 11), 'Augen' (ll. 3 and 12), 'weint' (ll. 3 and 12), 'spielt' (l. 4), 'Hemd' (ll. 5 and 11), 'Gesicht' (l. 6), 'Wollust' (l. 10), and 'Antlitz' (l. 10). The psychological precariousness of the lyric subject conveyed in this manner is accompanied and reinforced by images evoking physical disintegration and death: the repeated references to blood, the shattering face of the second stanza, the dead countenance of the third. The broken eyes of the first and third stanzas, by playing on the idiom 'seine Augen brechen' (see 1.1), combine both these motifs in a single image. Further, colour imagery is as prominent in 'Rosiger Spiegel' as elsewhere in Trakl's poetry. The implicit whiteness of the snow is once again offset, albeit less directly than in 'Delirium', by recurrent references to black and shades of red (*rosig*, *purpurn*, *Blut*). Finally, 'Rosiger Spiegel' has a characteristically intricate semantic structure that generates ambiguity through both the multiplication and destabilization of meaning. The first of this poem's numerous semantically underdetermined features is the rosiness of the mirror in line 1. This might be read – tentatively – as a sign that the images which usually appear in it are excessively optimistic (the German *rosig* is used figuratively in the same way as the English *rosy*), perhaps comparable to the image of illusory wholeness and integrity, the identification with which represents the defining characteristic of the early phase of psychic development Lacan calls the Mirror Stage. It follows that the 'ugly image' of disintegration and angst that appears in the black back of Trakl's rosy mirror may be closer to the true condition of the human subject, reflecting a deeper, ordinarily unconscious reality that belies the rosy appearance of normality. On the other hand, the word *rosig* might be read – no less tentatively – in relation to the symbolic value of the rose as a metaphor for erotic love, and thus in relation to the poem's thematic linking of sensuality and death (expressed most directly in line 10 in the juxtaposition of 'voluptuousness' and a 'dead face'), which constitutes yet another parallel between 'Rosiger Spiegel' and 'Delirium'.

The snow images of lines 5 and 12 themselves represent another of this poem's problematic semantic features. Significantly, 'Rosiger Spiegel' is one of the few poems in which Trakl does not integrate the word *Schnee* into a larger depiction of landscape. Indeed, unusually for his mature poetry and in contrast to 'Delirium', in 'Rosiger Spiegel' there is no landscape other than these two references to snow, and very little in the way of setting – of indications of place and time – beyond the rosy mirror and its black back. Thus, although the two levels of physical and psychic experience flow, as ever, seamlessly together, what the poem presents is less Trakl's characteristic 'fusion of landscape and mind-scape' (Sharp *PM* 196) than a fusion of *body*-scape and mind-scape, creating a surreal effect of spatial and temporal suspension combined with a painfully extreme physicality. In this context, the link between the signifier *Schnee* and its primary, landscape-related signified is made even less secure than in the opening line of 'Delirium', and the word's semantic potential is opened up. Further, the last two lines of the third stanza, in their rearrangement of lines 3 and 5, establish a definite if enigmatic equivalence between snow and blood, both of which are described, alternately, as 'crying from broken eyes' and 'running through the stiffening shirt.' Although the precise nature and extent of this equivalence remains uncertain, the reader may use it to account, at least partially, for yet another difficulty, namely the colour attributed to the snow in line 6, in which it runs 'purple over the black face.' The same snow–blood equivalence also underlines the thematic connection between snow and bodily disintegration, one of the main contextual factors contributing to the generation of a latent cocaine symbolism in Trakl's snow imagery, a connection that is also inherent in the poem's final image: 'Schnee aus brochenen Augen weint' (l. 12). To sum up, even if there can clearly be no straightforward identification between cocaine and the snow imagery of 'Rosiger Spiegel,' which remains indeterminate and elusive, the convergence of contextual factors described here is sufficient to suggest and sustain a veiled reference to cocaine intoxication in this same image pattern, and not least among these factors are the very indeterminacy and elusiveness that make a straightforward identification impossible.

If the absence of landscape in 'Rosiger Spiegel' is decisive in extending the semantic scope of its snow imagery to encompass an allusion to the snow-like drug cocaine, it is appropriate that we balance our perspective by considering the relevance of the same symbolic possibilities to a poem in which snow imagery is unequivocally incorporated into the development of setting. Perhaps the most suitable text for this purpose, the one in which snow imagery is most dominant, is the prose poem 'Winternacht':

> Winternacht
>
> Es ist Schnee gefallen. Nach Mitternacht verläßt du betrunken von purpurnem Wein den dunklen Bezirk der Menschen, die rote Flamme ihres Herdes. O die Finsternis!
> Schwarzer Frost. Die Erde ist hart, nach Bitterem schmeckt die Luft. Deine Sterne schließen sich zu bösen Zeichen.
> Mit versteinerten Schritten stampfst du am Bahndamm hin, mit runden Augen, wie ein Soldat, der eine schwarze Schanze stürmt. Avanti!
> Bitterer Schnee und Mond!

Ein roter Wolf, den ein Engel würgt. Deine Beine klirren schreitend wie blaues Eis und ein Lächeln voll Trauer und Hochmut hat dein Antlitz versteinert und die Stirne erbleicht vor der Wollust des Frostes;

oder sie neigt sich schweigend über den Schlaf eines Wächters, der in seiner hölzernen Hütte hinsank.

Frost und Rauch. Ein weißes Sternenhemd verbrennt die tragenden Schultern und Gottes Geier zerfleischen dein metallenes Herz.

O der steinerne Hügel. Stille schmilzt und vergessen der kühle Leib im silbernen Schnee hin.

Schwarz ist der Schlaf. Das Ohr folgt lange den Pfaden der Sterne im Eis.

Beim Erwachen klangen die Glocken im Dorf. Aus dem östlichen Tor trat silbern der rosige Tag.

'Winternacht' is one of just a handful of prose poems of Trakl's authorship. It was written in December 1913, and the narrative idea it develops possibly has an autobiographical basis in an episode of that same month. According to Erwin Mahrholdt, one night the poet had set off on foot along the railway line from Hall in Tirol, only to fall asleep in the snow before reaching Ficker's home at Mühlau bei Innsbruck, where he was staying at the time (33). Doubt has been cast on the factuality of Mahrholdt's account by the editors of *Sämtliche Werke*: 'Die von Erwin Mahrholdt in "Erinnerung an Georg Trakl" (S. 33) referierte Anekdote, das im Gedicht "Winternacht" Geschilderte habe Trakl persönlich erlebt, läßt sich nicht verifizieren' (*SW* 3:352). A letter Trakl had written to Ficker a year earlier suggests a possible error in Mahrholdt's dating, or alternatively that the incident he records was not an isolated one. With reference to a previous stay in Innsbruck, Trakl wrote that 'der Weg nach Mühlau ist weit und voll Gefahren für den Trunkenen. Auch kann er sich leicht verirren und hat am Ende nicht, wo er das Haupt zum Schlaf hinlegt' (*HkA* 1:498).

Trakl's atypical formal preference for prose over verse in 'Winternacht' is perhaps indicative of the text's dominant narrative impulse. The opening and closing paragraphs provide this work with a rudimentary narrative trajectory. The scene opens some time 'after midnight' as the lyric persona leaves 'the dark precinct of men,' and finishes at daybreak as the village bells signal re-entry into the social sphere abandoned at the beginning. The Homerically 'rosy' dawn of the last paragraph recalls the 'red flame' that the subject had left in the first to set off alone into the darkness. The experience contained within these two limits is essentially solitary, the only human presence encountered that of the sleeping watchman. Even this encounter, as the subject's forehead 'bows silently' over the sleeping figure, is more mystical than social, and the watchman, asleep and 'sunk down in his hut,' might in fact be considered a fellow solitary traveller who has similarly detached himself from the 'dark precinct of men.' Two other peculiarities of 'Winternacht' can be related to the dominance of the text's narrative function. First, the temporal progression the prose poem follows is not terminal, but ends with awakening and the dawn of a new day: 'Beim Erwachen klangen die Glocken im Dorf. Aus dem östlichen Tor trat silbern der rosige Tag.' Such a *dénouement* is necessary to convey the notion of an entire night spent in the open air, and in particular, in the snow. Notably, however, the new dawn of the final lines is dissociated from the rest of the text – so that it functions almost as a postscript – by a shift from the present tense, which lends immediacy to the scenes described, to the past tense, which creates distance and confirms that the perspective in these last two sentences is that of a detached, *post-factum* narrator. Second, the repeated use of the personal pronoun *du* and its related possessive adjectives ('*deine* Sterne,' '*deine* Beine,' '*dein* Antlitz') offers Trakl's reader the rare comfort of unambiguous textual subjectivity. Even here, however, this comfort is relative, for in the second half of 'Winternacht' the *du*-subject disappears, and the possessive adjectives of the first half are for the most part replaced by impersonal definite articles ('*die* Stirne,' '*die* tragenden Schultern,' '*der* kühle Leib,' '*der* Schlaf,' '*Das* Ohr'; '*dein* metallenes Herz' is the sole exception). The reader is left with a more familiar but less tangible coherence of 'observation and movement' (Steinkamp 121; see 9.1), supported by references to body parts or functions ('Das Ohr *folgt*'), and mental activity ('der *Schlaf*,' 'Beim *Erwachen*').

This substitution of metonymical for pronominal subjectivity is illustrative of a more general tendency to poetic stylization in the language of 'Winternacht'. While its use of prose accords with the dominance of the text's narrative function, its prosaic impulse is tempered by a contradictory one, namely the impulse to assimilate the episode narrated to the mythical-aesthetic outlook that characterizes Trakl's poetry. This second impulse finds expression not only in the – unusually subtle – defamiliarization of subjectivity already described, but also in this prose poem's conformity with the other stylistic criteria attributable to Trakl's poetics of intoxication (see 9.1). Thus, colour and light imagery is prominent throughout, and broadly follows the black–white–red pattern associated with Trakl's snow poetry and already observed in 'Delirium' and 'Rosiger Spiegel': 'von *purpurnem* Wein'; 'den *dunklen* Bezirk'; 'die *rote* Flamme'; 'die *Finsternis*'; '*Schwarzer*

Frost'; '*schwarze* Schanze'; 'Ein *roter* Wolf'; '*blaues* Eis'; 'die Stirne *erbleicht*'; 'Ein *weißes* Sternenhemd'; 'im *silbernen* Schnee'; '*Schwarz* ist der Schlaf'; 'trat *silbern* der *rosige* Tag.' Further, although 'Winternacht' contains a lower concentration of puzzling, semantically underdetermined lexical combinations than most Trakl poems, phrases such as 'Ein roter Wolf' and 'dein metallenes Herz,' which resist purely literal interpretation, open a figurative dimension of meaning in the prose poem and suggest that its other, ostensibly more straightforward images may hide deeper, symbolic significance. Similarly, as in so much of Trakl's work, in 'Winternacht' there are no discernible dividing lines between observation, hallucination and imagination, or as they are manifested in this work, between physical and metaphysical levels of experience. The lyric persona's night-time trek through the winter landscape of this prose poem is punctuated by a series of mystical-religious visions: the ominous 'evil signs' formed by the stars; a 'red wolf' being strangled by an angel; and 'God's vultures' that tear at the persona's 'metal heart.' But these hallucinatory visions are not presented as such; rather, they are indivisibly incorporated into the perceptual continuum of the whole, and in the text their ontological status is no different from that of the embankment, the watchman and his wooden hut, the stony hill, or the snow itself. As well as affording these visions a strangely real aspect, this fusion of physical and metaphysical, observation and hallucination, creates ontological uncertainty about the seemingly concrete environmental and human features named in the text, and gives an aura of mystical significance to these, too. Thus, 'der steinerne Hügel,' where the persona's journey reaches its premature end, might be read symbolically as an allusion to Golgotha, and 'die tragenden Schultern' of the previous paragraph as an allusion to Christ's bearing the cross.

On a primary level, the snow imagery of 'Winternacht' contributes to the portrayal of landscape, and the opening sentence, 'Es ist Schnee gefallen,' sets the wintry scene for the episode that follows. In particular, snow imagery combines with references to frost and ice to emphasize the coldness of the setting, a coldness that impinges variously on all the senses, from the hardness of the earth – subsequently echoed in images of stone and metal – and the bitter taste of the air, to the ice-like rattle of the persona's stride, and the silence that 'melts' as the stony hill comes into view. However, in view of the intoxicated effects embedded in the language of this prose poem, and more specifically of the ambiguity that, as described above, informs its semantic texture, here too the reader may be tempted to see a shadowy reference to cocaine intoxication in its recurrent snow imagery. That intoxication of some sort plays a role in 'Winternacht' is stated directly: the *Du* is introduced in the second sentence as 'betrunken von purpurnem Wein.' The manuscript version shows that Trakl originally conceived this phrase as 'trunken von dunklen Giften,' which, in its plurality and indefiniteness (see 9.2), would have made a symbolic reading of this prose poem's snow imagery of the sort under consideration here that much more plausible. (We may speculate, on the basis of the observations made in 9.2 regarding Trakl's poetic intoxicants, that his substitution of 'purple wine' for 'dark poisons' in 'Winternacht' was motivated by this phrase's textual proximity to the 'dark precinct of men,' as throughout Trakl's poetry wine is by far the most social of his intoxicants.) Even the reader of the final version has good reason to think that the wine referred to in the opening paragraph is not the sole agent of the persona's intoxication. Whereas the narrative point of view, projected in 'Winternacht' onto the second person subject, is distinguished by acuity of perception and heightened sensitivity to touch ('Die Erde ist hart') and taste ('nach Bitterem schmeckt die Luft'), as well as colour, the consumption of alcohol tends to dull the senses rather than sharpen them, just as it would usually blunt the imagination rather than inspire the kind of vivid and powerful visions of divine wrath described here. Even the sleep that seems to overtake the lyric persona towards the end of 'Winternacht' can hardly be equated with the insensibility that normally results from alcohol abuse. Despite apparent physical exhaustion, the persona's sensory and imaginative faculties continue to function apace: 'Das Ohr folgt lange den Pfaden der Sterne im Eis.' All these elements are in fact more consistent with the effects of stimulant drugs than alcohol, and so add to the validity of a reading that posits a subtextual reference to cocaine intoxication in the snow imagery of this prose poem. The question arises, also, as to whether the repeated references to bitterness, and in particular the exclamation 'Bitterer Schnee und Mond!,' can be understood in relation not only to the harshness of the cold, but also to the characteristically bitter taste of cocaine. Even if the cocaine symbolism is more heavily disguised in 'Winternacht' than in a poem like 'Rosiger Spiegel,' it corresponds with and so reinforces the mystical, almost eschatological significance that this text attributes to a winter night spent in the snow.

The reflections contained in this chapter may provoke the objection that they attempt to ascribe symbolic meaning to an image pattern occurring in texts that not only never make this symbolic value explicit, but whose author may never have intended to generate such meaning. Indeed, the possibility that Trakl never consciously formulated the metaphorical link between snow and cocaine, long since popularized in the ever-fertile jargon of drug use, is a real one, especially when we consider that our knowledge concerning his exposure to and use of cocaine is so limited, and that the word *Schnee* is already loaded with associations relevant to his dominant poetic themes – nature, landscape, winter, desolation, whiteness, coldness, purity, pestilence (via its Biblical connection with leprosy) – which could themselves explain the appeal this word held for him. However, even if we set aside the interpretive perils of attempting to reconstruct authorial intention, an approach that usually has the unspoken goal of containing and classifying a text's semantic possibilities, we might respond that such an objection itself implies a misreading of Trakl's poetics, and specifically a failure to grasp the semantic openness and elusiveness cultivated in his poetic language, features which anticipate and frustrate precisely such attempts at prosaic containment. To say that Trakl's language – and his snow imagery in particular – is 'semantically open' is not to say that it could mean anything, and could therefore also symbolize cocaine. Rather, in a given poem, as we have seen with 'Delirium', 'Rosiger Spiegel' and 'Winternacht', contextual features can be identified that variously support or subvert different but not unlimited readings, both literal and figurative, of a particular word, phrase, or image pattern, resulting in a complex, dynamic, and in this sense 'open' relationship between text and meaning. In this poetic system, the contextual features that support an implicit cocaine symbolism in Trakl's snow imagery are subtle but significant, and such a symbolism can in turn be considered coherent, not least in its subtlety, with his poetry's dominant thematic concerns. Only in the poet's biography does the drug materialize, become self-evident, real and deadly, as well as prosaic, even banal.

Summary of Findings

Benn, Rheiner and Trakl can be linked not only by their more or less deliberate affinities with Expressionism and their use of cocaine during the First World War, but also by their innovative handling of themes and motifs that, as we have seen in the introductory chapter, by the beginning of the 20th century were already well established in the literary representation of drugs and intoxication. Their status as heirs to the drug-literature tradition that had asserted itself most vigorously in the previous century can be derived from their integration of more or less explicit drug imagery into the elaboration of themes such as escape from suffering or the 'dull routine of existence' (Doyle 90), rebellion against social and cognitive norms, and the pursuit of alternative, poetically fertile forms of consciousness, themes that for the most part they inform with a Modernist emphasis on the instability of subjectivity, perception and meaning. Moreover, we have observed that all three develop or play off the poetic tradition of drug-related reticence, a 'poetic' device that may also be used in prose, privileging allusion, evasion and ambiguity as *semantic* instruments of *ontological* elevation.

Despite these important similarities, we have also seen that each poet treats the drug theme distinctively in accordance with his individual thematic and stylistic concerns, and the differences between them are readily apparent in their representations – whether direct or indirect – of cocaine, the one drug they are all known to have taken. In particular, it is apparent that the affinity Springer identifies between the Expressionist aesthetic and the cognitive and emotive characteristics of cocaine intoxication (*N* 28–29 & *KMR* 43) is exploited to a significant degree, among the works examined, only in the poems and plays associated with Benn's 1916 'episode with cocaine.' Rheiner's 'Der Tod des Schwärmers Gautier Fémin,' on the other hand, implicitly distances Expressionism from cocaine by instead associating the drug with the newly obsolete Decadent movement, while in his two narratives 'Die Erniedrigung' and *Kokain* the thematic emphasis lies less on the feelings of euphoria or vitality occasioned by individual hits than on the physical and psychological degradation of cocaine addiction. In Rheiner's poetry, as in Trakl's, cocaine is never even mentioned. Clearly, Springer's postulate of a generic relationship between

Expressionism and cocaine intoxication is not in itself sufficient – and could even be misleading – for understanding the relationships between specific authors or works associated with Expressionism and the same drug. A nuanced appreciation of them can only be achieved, rather, via a detailed consideration of individual writers and texts that displays sensitivity to biographical, textual and contextual particularities, as well as to the often complex but hidden interplay of these elements. The analyses contained in the three parts of the present study are intended to contribute to such an appreciation. Its main findings are summarized below.

In part 1 we have considered the difficulty of determining not only the scope of Benn's drug use, but also his estimation of drug use as an aid to artistic creativity. This difficulty arises from the inconsistencies and self-contradictions in both the relevant autobiographical material and Benn's substantial essayistic reflections on the drug question. We have argued that his evasiveness in this regard is itself an important element of his literary enterprise, in which the impossibility of adequately explaining the creative process in rational terms, and indeed the more general inadequacy of reason as a means of apprehending the complexity and flux of experience, is juxtaposed with his 'prelogical' concept of 'mystical participation,' a more primitive, intuitive, ecstatic, fertile consciousness, of which art – and poetry in particular – is the most significant manifestation in the modern era. In view of Benn's biographical 'entanglements', we have proposed a reading of his literary works that feature cocaine and correspond historically with their author's alleged 'brief episode' with the same drug, as constituting an autonomous textual 'episode'. This consists of the two poems 'O Nacht' and 'Kokain' and the two plays *Der Vermessungsdirigent* and *Karandasch*, all products of Benn's 'Brussels spring.' In our analyses of these texts, we have observed how Benn's representation of cocaine and cocaine use is conditioned by other interests, and the different ways in which the drug is assimilated into his elaboration of these. Of greatest importance in this regard is his key theme of transcendence via regression, as well as his associated notion of the transcendental-regressive power of poetic language. The portrayal of cocaine in each text offers, in effect, a variation on a common theme. 'O Nacht,' 'Kokain' and *Karandasch* all depict and enact the psycholinguistic effects of increasingly intense cocaine intoxication, and their common ground extends to direct structural and lexical correspondences. In *Der Vermessungsdirigent* the character Picasso claims to have taken cocaine in large quantities for reasons analogous with the intentions expressed by the cocaine users in the other three works – to achieve a radically new (for Benn radically *old*), mystical-artistic perspective.

In part 2 we have characterized Rheiner's drug addiction as one of several debilitating influences that eventually put paid not only to his literary ambition, but to all other aspects of his life. More specifically, we have emphasized the role that cocaine use played in his self-stylization as an Expressionist *poeta dolorosus*, a status that provided the thematic substance for much of his work in both poetry and prose, yet that ultimately and ironically proved detrimental to both the scope and originality of his literary achievement. Rheiner's devotion to Expressionism is evident not least in the extent to which his own poetic expression came to be modelled on that of the movement's more established representatives; that his imitations are usually convincing (to greater or lesser degrees) is testament to his underlying but underdeveloped lyric talent. The most important among his numerous Expressionist sources is Heym, an importance that is underlined when the relatively small body of Rheiner's narrative prose is added to the equation. The Heym connection becomes especially pertinent in relation to 'Die Erniedrigung' and *Kokain*, the two works in which Rheiner paints his most detailed portraits of the poet as a cocaine addict. The correspondences these display with Heym's work encompass such a range of features that their basic compositional principle could be expressed, with only slight exaggeration, in the formula 'Heym plus cocaine.' At the same time, the very deliberate autobiographical elements in their depictions of the addict's suffering suggest that these narratives embody an attempt by the author to 'put himself outside' his own drug experience (Ebin 143). On this basis we have proposed that other works by the same writer might also be read in relation to his drug habit, a hypothesis for which we have found support in the identification of parallels of various types between *Kokain* and several other poetic and prose texts of Rheiner's authorship. Although these texts exhibit obvious variations in tone, theme and genre, as well as in the degree of explicitness of their drug references, when seen as a chronological series they dovetail into a master narrative following the development of Rheiner's relationship to cocaine, in which each text can be seen as marking a distinct stage. Indeed, the formal and thematic distinctions between these works are easily reconciled to the same master narrative progression.

In part 3 we have stressed that Trakl's cocaine use, documented only for the final months of his life (spent on active military service in Galicia and subsequently in a Kraków hospital), should be regarded as a single but important element in his long-standing and wide-ranging drug and alcohol abuse, and his fatal overdose of this drug as the culmination of the self-destructive tendency already evident in his teenage 'refuge' in substances such as chloroform. Moreover, we have argued that the prevailing view of his prodigious drug consumption as no more than an escape 'aus schmerzhaften inneren Zuständen' (Weichselbaum 48) is simplistic, as it neglects the more profound connection between his experience of intoxication and the aesthetic-metaphysical principles that both shape and find expression in his poetry. The extent and the subtlety of the parallels between Trakl's life and art are nowhere more apparent than in the poems 'Klage' and 'Grodek', written and revised in the period of his heavy cocaine use. Neither of these poems is in any way about cocaine, yet they both exhibit a radicalization of Trakl's dominant decay theme corresponding to the radicalization of the self-destructive behaviour manifest in his contemporaneous drug abuse. Further, both these poems are informed by the stylistic traits we have described as constituting Trakl's 'poetics of intoxication,' traits that contribute greatly to producing the distinctive tone of his poetic language. We have divided these into three categories: the destabilization of textual subjectivity; the dominance of colour and light imagery; and the generation of ambiguity, in particular by means of a multi-levelled semantic structure combined with radical semantic underdetermination. In combination these features create a subtextual isotope or semantic undercurrent of intoxication that periodically breaks through the surface of Trakl's verse, typically in references to wine and drunkenness, in opiate symbolism, or in the sinister image of 'dark poisons' in the poems of his last phase. Although cocaine itself never appears explicitly in Trakl's writings, we have examined the possibility (suggested by Castoldi) of reading his frequent snow images as oblique references to this drug, and have found that such readings may be considered valid, to various degrees in different poems, in relation to the prominence of the intoxication isotope in a given text.

Taking each poet's cocaine use as the point of departure, in the three main parts of this study we have in fact touched upon many other questions pertaining to these writers and their literary creations, including those recognized in specialist scholarship as most fundamental. Our approach has enabled us variously to confirm, adjust or modify established interpretive positions, and in certain instances to develop entirely new ones. We may conclude, therefore, that a consideration of the role of this drug in the lives and works of Benn, Rheiner and Trakl, when combined with close attention to the complexities of the text–drug relationship and its many hidden snags for the literary critic, may serve to enrich our response to their writings and to broaden our view of their place in literary history, as well as the place of the Expressionist movement with which they are associated. At the same time, it is hoped that the emphasis given in this discussion to defining the possibilities and limits of assimilating biographical information to the reading of literary works may act as a stimulus for applying similar considerations to the analysis of drug-related works by other writers (from perhaps entirely different eras), especially as such questions have often been treated with insufficient care in studies addressing the drug–literature association. As Benn himself recognizes in the *Genie* essays, the drug question is intimately linked with many of the most central concerns of literature as it has developed in the last two centuries, and for this reason merits careful and systematic analysis from literary scholars.

Acknowledgements

This book could not have been written without the practical and moral support of my mentor and friend Peter Russell and my wife Elena Monetti. Special thanks also go to Jeremy Macey for his enthusiastic proofreading, to Paul Vincent for his scholarly solidarity, and to Martina Räber for her highly professional editorial supervision. Important financial assistance has been provided by Victoria University of Wellington, including grants towards publication costs from the Faculty of Humanities and Social Sciences and the School of Languages and Cultures. In addition I have received scholarships arising from the generosity of Gerda Bell and J.L. Stewart. I gratefully acknowledge the permission granted by the editors of *Seminar: A Journal of Germanic Studies* and *AUMLA: Journal of the Australasian Universities Languages and Literature Association* to reuse material that was originally published in *Seminar* 40/4 (2004) and *AUMLA* 107 (2007). An earlier version of this study was presented as a doctoral thesis at Victoria University of Wellington, and thanks are due to my three thesis examiners for their constructive feedback and encouragement: Axel Vieregg, Friedrich Voit and Andrew Webber. Their comments and suggestions have been instrumental in the revision that has given this study its present form.

Bibliography

Works by Benn, Rheiner and Trakl

Benn, Gottfried. *Ausgewählte Briefe.* Wiesbaden: Limes-Verlag, 1957. (*AB*)

——*Gesammelte Werke in acht Bänden.* Ed. Dieter Wellershoff. Wiesbaden: Limes, 1960. 8 volumes. (*GW*)

Rheiner, Walter. *Kokain. Eine Novelle und andere Prosa.* Berlin/Darmstadt: Agora, 1977. (*KNP*)

——*Kokain. Lyrik, Prosa, Briefe.* Ed. Thomas Rietzschel. Leipzig: Reclam, 1985. (*KLPB*)

——*Ich bin ein Mensch – ich fürchte mich. Vergessene Verse und Prosaversuche.* Ed. Thomas Rietzschel. Assenheim: BrennGlas, 1986. (*M*)

——*Kokain.* Ed. Michael Grimm. Vienna: Tatto, 2008. (*K*)

Trakl, Georg. *Dichtungen und Briefe. Historisch-kritische Ausgabe.* Ed. Walther Killy and Hans Szklenar. Salzburg: Müller, 1969. 2 volumes. (*HkA*)

——*Sämtliche Werke und Briefwechsel. Innsbrucker Ausgabe.* Ed. Eberhard Sauermann and Hermann Zwerschina. Basel, Frankfurt a/M: Stroemfeld/Roter Stern, 1995. 4 volumes to date. (*SWB*)

Other Works Cited

Ageev, M. (Mark Levi). *Roman s kokainom.* Paris: Booking Int., 1995.

Andrews, George, and David Solomon (ed.). *The Coca Leaf and Cocaine Papers.* New York: Harcourt Brace Jovanovich, 1975.

Antonin, Dominique (ed.). *Un peu d'encre sur la neige. L'expérience de la cocaïne par les écrivains.* Paris: Lézard, 1997.

Arend, Angelika. 'Der Dichter braucht die Droge nicht.' *Neophilologus* 71.1 (1987): 102–113.

Artaud, Antonin. *Les Tarahumaras.* Paris: Gallimard, 1971.

Ashley, Richard. *Cocaine. Its History, Uses, and Effects.* New York: St. Martin's, 1975.

Atai, Jeanine. *Kokainliteratur in der Zwischenkriegszeit. Spuren des Giftes in den Texten von Walter Rheiner, Otto Rung und Pitigrilli.* Frankfurt a/M: Peter Lang, 2008.

Balser, Hans-Dieter. *Das Problem des Nihilismus im Werke Gottfried Benns.* Bonn: Bouvier, 1965.

Barthes, Roland. 'The Death of the Author.' In *Image, Music, Text.* Ed. and tr. Stephen Heath. New York: Hill, 1977.

Basil, Otto. *Georg Trakl in Selbstzeugnissen und Bilddokumenten.* Reinbeck b. Hamburg: Rowohlt, 1965.

Baudelaire, Charles. *Les Paradis artificiels.* Paris: Gallimard, 1964. (*Pa*)

——*Œuvres complètes.* Paris: Pléiade, 1961. (*Oc*)

Becher, Johannes R. *Abschied.* Berlin: Aufbau, 1965.

——*Gedichte 1911–1918.* Ed. Paul Raabe. Munich: dtv, 1973.

Becht, Evemarie. 'Die Farbe Blau in den dichterischen Texten Georg Trakls.' In Adam. J. Bisanz, Herbert A. Frenzel, and Raymond Trousson (ed.). *Elemente der Literatur. Beiträge zur Stoff-, Motiv- und Themenforschung.* Stuttgart: Kröner, 1980. 2:108–131.

Benjamin, Walter. *Illuminationen. Ausgewählte Schriften.* Frankfurt a/M: Suhrkamp, 1977.

Bendix, Konstantin. *Rauschformen und Formenrausch. Untersuchungen über den Einfluß von Drogen auf das Werk Gottfried Benns.* Frankfurt a/M: Peter Lang, 1988.

Bergsten, Gunilla. 'Georg Trakls traumatischer Kode.' In *Studia Neophilologica* 43 (1971): 333–351.

Bernhard, Thomas. *In Hora Mortis / Under the Iron of the Moon.* Tr. James Reidel. Princeton UP, 2006.

Best, Otto F. (ed.). *Theorie des Expressionismus.* Stuttgart: Reclam, 1976.

Blass, Regine. *Die Dichtung Georg Trakls. Von der Trivialsprache zum Kunstwerk.* Berlin: Schmidt, 1968.

Blunden, Allan. 'Notes on Georg Heym's Novelle *Der Irre.*' In *German Life and Letters* 28 (1974–75): 107–119.

Bolli, Erich. *Georg Trakls 'dunkler Wohllaut.' Ein Beitrag zum Verständnis seines dichterischen Sprechens.* Zürich/Munich: Artemis, 1978.

Bondy, Barbara. ' "Ein Kind wie wir anderen auch…" Unterhaltung mit dem Bruder Georg Trakls.' In *Die Neue Zeitung* 28. 2.2.1952.

Boon, Marcus. *The Road of Excess. The History of Writers on Drugs.* Cambridge (Mass.), London: Harvard UP, 2002.

Böschenstein, Bernhard. 'Hölderlin und Rimbaud. Simultane Rezeption als Quelle poetischer Innovation im Werk Georg Trakls.' In Walter Weiss and Hans Weichselbaum (ed.). *Salzburger Trakl Symposium.* Salzburg: Müller, 1978. 9–27.

Brau, Jean-Louis. *Histoire de la drogue.* Paris: Tschou, 1968.

Bridgwater, Patrick. 'Georg Trakl and the Poetry of the First World War.' In Walter Methlagl and William E. Yuill (ed.). *Londoner Trakl Symposium.* Salzburg: Müller, 1981. 96–113. (*GT*)

——*Poet of Expressionist Berlin. The Life and Work of Georg Heym.* London: Libris, 1991. (*PEB*)

Brik, Osip. 'The So-Called Formal Method.' Tr. Ann Shukman. In L.M. O'Toole and Ann Shukman (ed.). *Formalist Theory.* Oxford: Holdan, 1977. 90–91.

Buddeberg, Else. *Studien zur lyrischen Sprache Gottfried Benns.* Düsseldorf: Schwann, 1964.

Bulgakov, Mikhail. *Sobranije sočinenij v pjati tomakh.* Moscow: Khudožestvennaja literatura, 1989.

Burnett, Lynn Barkley, and Jonathan Adler. 'Toxicity, Cocaine.' 26 July 2002. *eMedicine: Instant Access to the Minds of Medicine.* <http://www.-emedicine.com/emerg/topic102.htm>. Last access 28 Sep. 2003.

Burroughs, William. *Naked Lunch.* New York: Grove, 1992.

Burroughs, William, and Allen Ginsberg. *The Yage Letters.* San Francisco: City Lights, 1975.

Canetti, Elias. *Masse und Macht.* Hamburg: Claassen, 1960.

Caran d'Ache of Switzerland. History Page. <http://www.carandache.ch/company/html/en/history.htm>. Last access 13 March 2003.

Castaneda, Carlos. *The Teachings of Don Juan. A Yaqui Way of Knowledge.* Berkeley: U of California, 1968.

Castoldi, Alberto. *Il testo drogato. Letteratura e droga tra ottocento e novecento.* Turin: Einaudi, 1994.

Coelln, Hermann von. *Sprachbildung und Bildstruktur in der Lyrik Georg Trakls.* Heidelberg, 1960.

Cooke, Michael G. 'De Quincey, Coleridge, and the Formal Uses of Intoxication.' In *Yale French Studies* 50 (1974): 26–40.

Crowley, Aleister. *Diary of a Drug Fiend.* York Beach: Weiser, 1995.

Daumal, René. 'A Fundamental Experiment.' In John Strausbaugh and Donald Blaise (ed.). *The Drug User. Documents 1840–1960*. New York: Blast, 1991.

Deleuze, Gilles, and Félix Guattari. *A Thousand Plateaus*. Tr. Brian Massumi. Minneapolis: U of Minnesota, 1987.

Denneler, Iris. *Konstruktion und Expression. Zur Strategie und Wirkung der Lyrik Georg Trakls*. Salzburg: Müller, 1984.

De Quincey, Thomas. *Confessions of an English Opium Eater*. Ed. Alethea Hayter. London: Penguin, 1971.

——'The English Mail-Coach.' In *Miscellaneous Essays*. Authorama. <http://www.authorama.com/book/miscellaneous-essays.html>. Last access 23 Feb. 2005. (*EM*)

Derrida, Jacques. 'Plato's Pharmacy.' Tr. Barbara Johnson. In *Dissemination*. London: Athlone, 1981. 61–172. (*PP*)

——'The Rhetoric of Drugs.' Tr. Michael Israel. In Anna Alexander and Mark S. Roberts (ed.). *High Culture: Reflections on Addiction and Modernity*. Albany: State U. of NY, 2003. 19–44. (*RD*)

Dick, Philip K. *A Scanner Darkly*. London: HarperCollins, 1996.

Dickhoff, Wilfried W. *Zur Hermeneutik des Schweigens. Ein Versuch über das Imaginäre bei Gottfried Benn*. Königstein/Ts.: Athenäum–Hain–Hanstein, 1984.

Diel, Marcel et al. (ed.). *Rausch. Kritische Ausgabe* 13 (2005).

Dierick, Augustinus P. *Gottfried Benn and his Critics: Major Interpretations 1912–1992*. Columbia: Camden House, 1992.

Doyle, Sir Arthur Conan. *The Penguin Complete Sherlock Holmes*. London: Penguin, 1981.

Ebin, David (ed.). *The Drug Experience*. New York: Grove, 1961.

Einstein, Carl. 'Gottfried Benns *Gesammelte Gedichte*.' In *Werke*. Ed. Marion Schmid. Berlin: Medusa, 1981. 2:369–372.

Emerson, Ralph Waldo. *Selected Essays*. Ed. Larzer Ziff. Harmondsworth: Penguin, 1984.

Esselborn, Hans. *Georg Trakl. Die Krise der Elebnislyrik*. Cologne: Böhlau, 1981.

Felman, Shoshana. 'Henry James: Madness and the Risks of Practice (Turning the Screw of Interpretation).' In *Writing and Madness (Literature / Philosophy / Psychoanalysis)*. Ithaca: Cornell UP, 1985. 141–247.

Ficker, Ludwig von. *Denkzettel und Danksagungen. Aufsätze und Reden*. Ed. Franz Seyr. Munich: 1967. (*DD*)

——'Der Abschied.' In *Erinnerung an Georg Trakl. Zeugnisse und Briefe*. Salzburg: Müller, 1966. (*A*)

Freud, Sigmund. *Gesammelte Werke*. Ed. Anna Freud. London: Imago, 1945. (*GW*)

——*Briefe 1873–1939*. Ed. Ernst and Lucie Freud. Frankfurt a/M: Fischer, 1960.(*B*)

Foi, Maria Carolina. 'La Vita.' In Georg Trakl. *Le poesie*. Milan: Garzanti, 1983. ix–xi.

Frank, Leonhard. *Links, wo das Herz ist*. Munich: Nymphenburger, 1952.

Gilbert-Lecomte, Roger. *Monsieur Morphée, empoisonneur public*. Paris: Fata Morgana, 1998.

Goethe, Johann Wolfgang von. *Goethes Werke in 14 Bänden* (Hamburger Ausgabe). Hamburg: Christian Wegner, 1955.

Goldmann, Heinrich. *Katabasis. Eine tiefenpsychologische Studie zur Symbolik der Dichtungen Georg Trakls*. Salzburg: Müller, 1957.

Gorgé, Walter. ' "Das Laub fällt rot vom alten Baum." Zum hundertsten Geburtstag des Dichters Georg Trakl am 3. Februar.' In *Neue Zürcher Zeitung* 30.1.1987. 43.

Grass, Günter. 'So bin ich weiterhin verletzbar. Ein ZEIT-Gespräch mit Günter Grass.' In *Zeitliteratur* 41.56 (Oct 2001): 63–66.

Greimas, Algirdas Julius. *Sémantique structurale. Recherche de méthode*. Paris: Larousse, 1966.

Grimm, Reinhold. 'Georg Trakls Verhältnis zu Rimbaud.' In *Germanisch-Romanische Monatsschrift* 9 (1959): 271–313.

Guattari, Félix. 'Socially Significant Drugs.' Tr. Mark S. Roberts. In Anna Alexander and Mark S. Roberts (ed.). *High Culture: Reflections on Addiction and Modernity*. Albany: State U. of NY, 2003. 199–208.

Haase, Horst. *Johannes R. Becher. Leben und Werk*. Berlin (West): Das Europäische Buch, 1981.

Harper, Douglas. *Online Etymology Dictionary*. November 2001. <http://www.etymonline.com/s8etym.htm>. Last access 7 July 2004.

Haupt, Jürgen. *Natur und Lyrik. Naturbeziehungen im 20. Jahrhundert*. Stuttgart: Metzler, 1983.

Hayter, Alethea. *Opium and the Romantic Imagination*. London: Faber & Faber, 1968.

Heidegger, Martin. 'Georg Trakl. Eine Erörterung seines Gedichtes.' In *Unterwegs zur Sprache*. Frankfurt a/M: Neske, 1985. 35–82.

Heimann, Bodo. 'Ich-Zerfall als Thema und Stil.' In *Germanisch-Romanische Monatsschrift* 14 (1964): 384–403.

Heselhaus, Clemens. 'Das metaphorische Gedicht von Georg Trakl.' In *Deutsche Lyrik der Moderne von Nietzsche bis Ivan Goll.* Düsseldorf: Bagel, 1962. 228–257.

Hesse, Hermann. *Der Steppenwolf.* Frankfurt a/M: Suhrkamp, 1974.

Heym, Georg. *Dichtungen und Schriften.* Ed. Karl-Ludwig Schneider. Ellermann: Hamburg & Munich, 1962. 4 volumes.

Horvath, Ödön von. *Jugend ohne Gott.* Frankfurt a/M: Suhrkamp, 1994.

Huder, Walter. 'Nachwort.' In Rheiner, Walter. *Kokain. Eine Novelle und andere Prosa.* Ed. Huder. Berlin/Darmstadt: Agora, 1977. 77–85.

Huxley, Aldous. *The Doors of Perception.* New York: Perennial Library, 1970.

James, Henry. *The Turn of the Screw.* Ed. Robert Kimbrough. New York: Norton, 1966.

Jakobson, Roman. *Language in Literature.* Ed. Krystyna Pomorska and Stephen Rudy. Cambridge (Mass.): Harvard UP, 1987.

Johst, Hanns. *Der Einsame. Ein Menschenuntergang.* Munich: Delphin, 1917.

Jung, Franz. 'Sophie: Der Kreuzweg der Demut.' Berlin: Die Aktion, 1916.

——*Der Weg nach unten.* Neuwied: Luchterhand, 1961.

Kafka, Franz. *Der Prozeß.* Frankfurt a/M: Fischer, 1994.

Kallmeyer, Werner, Wolfgang Klein, Reinhard Meyer-Hermann, Klaus Netzer, and Hans-Jürgen Siebert (ed.). *Lektürekolleg zur Textlinguistik.* Frankfurt a/M: Athäneum,1974.

Kaufmann, Hans. *Fallender Mensch und entgleitende Wirklichkeit bei Georg Trakl.* Zürich: Akademische Buchgenossenshaft, 1956.

Kemper, Hans-Georg. *Georg Trakls Entwürfe. Aspekte zu ihrem Verständnis.* Tübingen: Niemeyer, 1970.

Ketteler, Daniel. 'Drogengebrauch im Dienste der Neurologie? Gottfried Benns Gedichtzyklus *Der Psychiater* im Licht aktueller Debatten um Kreativität und Gehirn.' In *Kritische Ausgabe* 13 (2005): 38–41.

Kleefeld, Gunther. *Das Gedicht als Sühne. Georg Trakls Dichtung und Krankheit. Eine psychoanalytische Studie.* Tübingen: Max Niemeyer, 1985.

Kohtes, Michael. 'Der Dichter auf der Nadel. Ein Porträt des vergessenen Expressionisten Walter Rheiner.' In *Die Horen* 37.3 (1992): 119–123.

Korte, Hermann. *Krieg in der Lyrik des Expressionismus. Studien zur Evolution eines literarischen Themas.* Bonn: Bouvier, 1981.

Kügler, Hans. 'Künstler und Geschichte im Werk Gottfried Benns.' In *Weg und Weglosigkeit: Neun Essays zur Geschichte der deutschen Literatur im zwanzigsten Jahrhundert.* Heidenheim: Heidenheim, 1970. 77–104.

Kupfer, Alexander. *Die künstlichen Paradiese. Rausch und Realität seit der Romantik. Ein Handbuch.* Stuttgart, Weimar: Metzler, 1996. (*kP*)

——*Göttliche Gifte. Kleine Kulturgeschichte des Rausches seit dem Garten Eden.* Berlin: Aufbau, 2002. (*GG*)

Küpper, Heinz (ed.). *Wörterbuch der deutschen Umgangssprache.* Hamburg/Düsseldorf: Claassen, 1970.

Kurrik, Maire. *Georg Trakl.* New York: Columbia UP, 1974.

Leiß, Ingo, and Hermann Stadler. *Weg in die Moderne. 1890–1918.* Vol. 8 of *Deutsche Literaturgeschichte.* Munich: dtv, 1997.

Liedekerke, Arnould de. *La Belle Epoque de l'opium.* Paris: Différence, 1968.

Lieuwerscheidt, Dieter. *Gottfried Benns Lyrik. Eine kritische Einführung.* Munich: Oldenbourg, 1980.

Mahrholdt, Erwin. 'Der Mensch und Dichter Georg Trakl.' In *Erinnerung an Georg Trakl. Zeugnisse und Briefe.* Salzburg: Müller, 1966. 21–90.

Maier, Hans. *Der Kokainismus. Geschichte / Pathologie, Medizinische und behördliche Bekämpfung.* Leipzig: Georg Thieme, 1926.

Mantegazza, Paolo. 'Coca Experiences.' Tr. Lara Forti and Gina Alhadeff. In George Andrews and David Solomon (ed.). *The Coca Leaf and Cocaine Papers.* New York: Harcourt Brace Jovanovich, 1975. 38–42.

Matt, Peter von. 'Die Dynamik von Georg Trakls Gedicht. Ich-Dissoziation als Zerrüttung der erotischen Identität.' In Horst Meixner and Silvio Vietta (ed.). *Expressionismus, Sozialer Wandel und künstlerische Erfahrung: Mannheimer Kolloquium.* Munich: Fink, 1982. 58–72.

Mendoza Ibáñez, Francisco José Ruiz de. 'From Semantic Underdetermination via Metaphor and Metonymy to Conceptual Interaction.' In *Theoria et Historia Scientiarum. An International Journal for Interdisciplinary Studies* 6.1 (2002). Also available at <http://cogweb.ucla.edu/Abstracts/Ruiz_99.html#_edn1>. Last access 14 June 2004.

Meister, Ulrich. *Sprache und lyrisches Ich: Zur Phänomenologie des Dichterischen bei Gottfried Benn.* Berlin: Erich Schmidt, 1983.

Meyer, Theo. *Kunstproblematik und Wortkombinatorik bei Gottfried Benn.* Cologne/Vienna: Böhlau, 1971. (*KW*)

——'Gottfried Benn und der Expressionismus. Unter besonderer Berücksichtigung der Lyrik.' In Bruno Hillebrand (ed.). *Gottfried Benn.* Darmstadt: Wissenschaftliche Buchgesellschaft, 1979. (*GBE*)

Michaux, Henri. *The Major Ordeals of the Mind & the Countless Minor Ones.* Tr. Richard Howard. New York: Wolff, 1974.

Mittner, Ladislao. *L'espressionismo.* Rome: Laterza, 1997.

Modick, Klaus. 'Formenpräger der weißen Spur. Benns Konzeption des produktiven Rausches.' In *Text + Kritik* 44 (1975): 47–53.

Moreau de Tours, Jacques. *Du Haschich et de l'aliénation mentale.* Paris and Geneva: Slatkine, 1980.

Morin, Edgar. *Les sept savoirs nécessaires à l'éducation du futur.* UNESCO document for Education, Science and Culture. 1999. <http://www.-agora21.org/unesco/7savoirs/7savoirs02.html>. Last access 8 July 2004.

Nietzsche, Friedrich. *Werke in drei Bänden.* Ed. Karl Schlechta. Munich and Vienna: Carl Hanser, 1954. 3 volumes.

Normandy, Georges, and Charles Poinsot. *La Mortelle Impuissance.* Paris: Fasquelle, 1903.

Novalis (Friedrich von Hardenberg). *Schriften. Die Werke Friedrich von Hardenbergs.* Ed. Paul Kluckhohn and Richard Samuel. Stuttgart: Kohlhammer, 1960–88. 4 volumes.

Orendi-Hinze, Diana. 'Frauen um Trakl.' In Walter Methlagl, Eberhard Sauermann, and Sigurd Paul Scheichl (ed.). *Untersuchungen zum 'Brenner'. Festschrift für Ignaz Zangerle.* Salzburg: Müller, 1981. 381–388.

Østbø, Johannes. *Expressionismus und Montage. Über Gottfried Benns Gedichtstil bis 1932.* U of Oslo: 1981.

Paulsen, Wolfgang. *Deutsche Literatur des Expressionismus.* Bern: Peter Lang, 1983.

Paz, Octavio. *Alternating Current.* Tr. Helen R. Lane. London: Wildwood House, 1974.

Peschel, Enid Rhodes (ed.). *Intoxication and Literature. Yale French Studies* 50 (1974).

——'Arthur Rimbaud. The Aesthetics of Intoxication.' In *Yale French Studies* 50 (1974): 65–80. (*AR*)

Philipp, Eckhard. *Die Funktion des Wortes in den Gedichten Georg Trakls. Linguistische Aspekte ihrer Interpretation.* Tübingen: Niemeyer, 1971.

Pierrot, Jean. *Merveilleux et fantastique. Une histoire de l'imaginaire dans la prose française du romantisme à la décadence (1830–1900).* Unpublished thesis: U of Paris, 1975.

Pinthus, Kurt (ed.). *Menschheitsdämmerung. Ein Dokument des Expressionismus.* Berlin: Rowohlt, 1959.

Pitigrilli (Dino Segre). *Cocaina*. Milan: Bompiani, 1999.

Plant, Sadie. *Writing on Drugs*. London: Faber & Faber, 1999.

Pulver, Max. *Himmelpfortgasse*. Munich: Kurt Wolff, 1927.

Raabe, Paul (ed.). *Expressionismus. Aufzeichnungen und Erinnerungen der Zeitgenossen*. Olten, Freiburg: Walter, 1965.

Resch, Stephan. *Provoziertes Schreiben. Drogen in der deutschsprachigen Literatur seit 1945*. Frankfurt a/M: Peter Lang, 2007.

Rietzschel, Thomas. 'Nachwort.' In Walter Rheiner. *Kokain*. Ed. Rietzschel. Frankfurt a/M, Olten, Vienna: Gutenberg, 1985. 285–303.

Rilke, Rainer Maria. *Gesammelte Gedichte*. Frankfurt a/M: Insel, 1962.

——*Briefe aus den Jahren 1914–1921*. Leipzig: Insel, 1938. (*B*)

Rimbaud, Arthur. *Œuvres complètes*. Paris: Gallimard, 1954. (*Oc*)

——*Leben und Dichtung*. Tr. K. L. Ammer. Leipzig: Insel, 1907. (*LD*)

Röbel, Sven. 'Nacht! Kokain! Das ist Berlin!' In *Spiegel* 44 (2000): 152.

Röck, Karl. *Tagebuch 1891–1946*. Ed. Christine Kofler. Salzburg: Brenner, 1976.

Rolleston, James. 'Choric Consciousness in Expressionist Poetry: Ernst Stadler, Else Lasker-Schüler, Georg Heym, Georg Trakl, Gottfried Benn.' In Neil H. Donahue (ed.). *A Companion to the Literature of German Expressionism*. Rochester, NY: Camden House, 2005. 157–183.

Ronell, Avital. *Crack Wars: Literature, Addiction, Mania*. Lincoln and London: U of Nebraska, 1992.

Roth, Joseph. *Werke*. Ed. Hermann Kesten. Cologne: Kiepenheuer & Witsch, 1975. 4 volumes.

Rothmann, Kurt. 'Zu Gottfried Benns Drogenlyrik. Interpretation der Gedichte "Betäubung" und "Entwurzelungen".' In *Modern Language Notes* 82 (1967): 454–461.

Rübe, Werner. 'Im Irrgarten der Alkaloide.' In *Provoziertes Leben. Gottfried Benn*. Stuttgart: Klett–Cotta, 1993. 133–154. (*IdA*).

——'Dr. Rönne im Hurenspital.' In *Provoziertes Leben*. 155–167. (*RiH*).

Rumold, Rainer. *Gottfried Benn und der Expressionismus: Provokation des Lesers; absolute Dichtung*. Königstein/Ts: Scriptor, 1982.

Sahlberg, Oskar. 'Gottfried Benns Ekstasen.' In S. Brieler, W. Müller-Jensen, W. Zangemeister and J. Zippel (ed.). *Gottfried Benn zum 100. Geburtstag. Vorträge zu Werk und Persönlichkeit von Medizinern und Philologen*. Würzburg: Könighausen & Neumann, 1988. 123–134. (*GBE*)

——' "The Jewel in the Lotus": A Re-Implantation. The Healing of a Narcissist in Gottfried Benn's Berlin Novella *Der Ptolemäer*.' Tr. Jeffrey

Adams. In Jeffrey Adams and Eric Williams (ed.). *Mimetic Desire. Essays on Narcissism in German Literature from Romanticism to Post Modernism.* Columbia: Camden House, 1995. (*JL*)

Sandblom, Philip. *Creativity and Disease. How Illness Affects Literature, Art and Music.* New York, London: Byers, 1992.

Sarup, Madan. *Jacques Lacan.* Hemel Hempstead: Harvester, 1992.

Sattler, Eve. *Vergiftete Sensationen. Soziale und kulturelle Dimensionen des Rauschmittelkonsums im literarischen Expressionismus 1910–1914.* Essen: Klartext, 1910.

Schilling, Heinar. *Du Bruder Mensch. (Opus 37) Gedichte 1918.* Dresdner Verlag von 1917, 1918.

——*Mensch, Mond, Sterne: Gedicht.* Dresdner Verlag von 1917, 1918.

Schneider, Karl-Ludwig. *Der bildhafte Ausdruck in den Dichtungen Georg Heyms, Georg Trakls und Ernst Stadlers. Studien zum lyrischen Sprachstil des deutschen Expressionismus.* Heidelberg: Winter, 1954.

Schöne, Albrecht. 'Überdauernde Temporalstruktur. Gottfried Benn.' In *Säkularisation als sprachbildende Kraft. Studien zur Dichtung deutscher Pfarrersöhne.* Göttingen: Vandenhoeck & Ruprecht, 1968. 225–267.

Schultz, Myron. 'The "Strange Case" of Robert Louis Stevenson.' *Journal of the American Medical Association* 216 (1971). 90–94.

Seymour-Smith, Martin. *Guide to Modern World Literature.* London and Basingstoke: Macmillan, 1973.

Sharp, Francis Michael. *The Poet's Madness. A Reading of Georg Trakl.* Ithaca: Cornell UP, 1981. (*PM*)

——'*Menschheitsdämmerung*: The Aging of a Canon.' In Neil H. Donahue (ed.). *A Companion to the Literature of German Expressionism.* Rochester, NY: Camden House, 2005. 137–155. (*M*)

Simon, Klaus. *Traum und Orpheus. Eine Studie zu Georgs Trakls Dichtungen.* Salzburg: Müller, 1955.

Sokel, Walter. *The Writer in Extremis. Expressionism in Twentieth-Century German Literature.* Stanford UP, 1959. (*WiE*)

——'The Prose of German Expressionism.' In Neil H. Donahue (ed.). *A Companion to the Literature of German Expressionism.* Rochester, NY: Camden House, 2005. 69–88. (*PGE*)

Spoerri, Theodor. *Georg Trakl. Strukturen in Persönlichkeit und Werk. Eine psychiatrisch-anthropologische Untersuchung.* Bern: Francke, 1954.

Springer, Alfred. 'Otto Groß und J.R. Becher. Zur Narkotomanie in der Boheme des Deutschen Expressionismus: eine soziopathologische Skizze.' In *Wiener Zeitschrift für Suchtforschung* 2 (1974/4). 23–36. (*N*)

——*Kokain: Mythos und Realität. Eine kritisch dokumentierte Anthologie.* Vienna: Brandstätter, 1989. (*KMR*)

Stark, Klaus. *Die Krise Georg Trakls.* Unpublished medical dissertation: Tübingen, 1989.

Steinkamp, Hildegard. *Die Gedichte Georg Trakls. Vom Landschaftscode zur Mythopoesie.* Frankfurt a/M: Peter Lang, 1988.

Stevenson, Robert Louis. *The Strange Case of Dr Jekyll and Mr Hyde and Other Tales of Terror.* Ed. Robert Mighall. London: Penguin, 2002.

St. Saveur, Frieda. 'Einleitung zu Kokain,' 'Biographische Notiz' & 'Eine Biographie'. In Walter Rheiner. *Kokain.* Ed. Michael Grimm. Vienna: Tatto, 2008. 12–13, 129–130 & 132–143.

Strässle, Thomas and Simon Zumsteg (ed.). *Trunkenheit. Kulturen des Rausches. Amsterdamer Beiträge zur neueren Germanistik* 65 (2008).

Swales, Martin (ed.). *German Poetry. An Anthology from Klopstock to Enzensberger.* Cambridge U, 1987.

Szklenar, Hans. 'Beiträge zur Chronologie und Anordnung von Georg Trakls Gedichten auf Grund des Nachlasses von Karl Röck.' In *Euphorion* 60 (1966).

Tomashevsky, Boris. 'Literature and Biography.' Tr. Herbert Eagle. In Ladislav Matejka & Krystyna Pomorska (ed.). *Readings in Russian Poetics. Formalist and Structuralist Views.* Cambridge (Mass.): MIT, 1971. 47–55.

Trocchi, Alexander. *Cain's Book.* London: Calder, 1992.

Twain, Mark (Samuel Langhorne Clemens). 'The Turning Point of My Life.' In *What is Man and Other Essays.* Fairfield (IA): First World Library, 2004. 141–155.

Vasmer, M. (ed.). *Vasmer's Etymological Dictionary.* In Sergei Starotsin (ed.). *The Tower of Babel: An International Etymological Database Project.* 31 January 2002. Russian State U of the Humanities, Moscow Jewish U, Russian Acad. Of Sciences, Santa Fe Inst., City U of Hong Kong, Leiden U. <http://starling.rinet.ru/>. Last access 13 March 2003.

Vietta, Silvio, and Hans-Georg Kemper. *Expressionismus.* Munich: Fink, 1975.

Weichselbaum, Hans. *Georg Trakl. Eine Biographie mit Bildern, Texten und Dokumenten.* Salzburg: Müller, 1994.

Wellmann, Hans. ' "Dichtungssprache". Zur Beziehung zwischen Text, Grammatik, Wortschatz und Sprachbegriff in Trakls Lyrik.' In Walter Methlagl, Eberhard Sauermann, and Sigurd Paul Scheichl (ed.). *Untersuchungen zum 'Brenner'. Festschrift für Ignaz Zangerle zum 75. Geburtstag*. Salzburg: Müller, 1981. 315–345.

Weiß, Norbert. 'Die große Krankheit. Hommage für Walter Rheiner.' In *EDIT* 9 (1995): 49–50.

Werfel, Franz. *Barbara oder die Frömmigkeit.* Berlin: Zsolnay, 1929.

Williams, Eric B. *The Mirror & the Word. Modernism, Literary Theory, & Georg Trakl.* Lincoln & London: U of Nebraska, 1993.

Witkiewicz, Stanisław Ignacy. *Narkotyki-niewmyte dusze.* Ed. Anna Micińska. Warsaw: Państwowy Instytut Wydawniczy, 1979.

Witschel, Günther. *Rausch und Rauschgift bei Baudelaire, Huxley, Benn und Burroughs.* Bonn: Bouvier, 1968.

Wodtke, Friedrich W. 'Gottfried Benn.' In Wolfgang Rothe (ed.). *Expressionismus als Literatur: Gesammelte Studien.* Bern: Franke, 1969. 309–332.

Zinberg, Norman E. *Drug, Set and Setting: The Basis for Controlled Intoxicant Use.* New Haven and London: Yale UP, 1984.

Zuckmayer, Carl. *Als wär's ein Stück von mir.* Frankfurt a/M: Fischer, 1966.

Index of Names (and Works by Benn, Rheiner & Trakl)

Australisch-Neuseeländische Studien zur deutschen Sprache und Literatur

Bd. 1 Dushan Stankovich: Otto Julius Bierbaum – eine Werkmonographie. 236 Seiten. 1971.

Bd. 2 David Roberts: Artistic Consciousness and Political Conscience – the Novels of Heinrich Mann 1900–1938. 262 Seiten. 1971.

Bd. 3 Anthony R. Stephens: Rilkes Malte Laurids Brigge – Strukturanalyse des erzählerischen Bewusstseins. 270 Seiten. 1974.

Bd. 4 Margaret Stoljar: Athenäum: A Critical Commentary. 152 Seiten. 1973.

Bd. 5 John Milfull: From Baal to Keuner – The «Second Optimism» of Bertolt Brecht. 156 Seiten. 1974.

Bd. 6 Ernst Keller: Kritische Intelligenz: G. E. Lessing – F. Schlegel – L. Börne – Studien zu ihren literaturkritischen Werken. 232 Seiten. 1976.

Bd. 7 A. Stephens / H. L. Rogers / B. Coghlan: Festschrift for Ralph Farrell. 236 Seiten. 1977.

Bd. 8 Reinhard Alter: Gottfried Benn – The Artist and Politics (1910–1934). 149 Seiten. 1976.

Bd. 9 E. L. Marson: The Ascetic Artist – Prefigurations in Thomas Mann's «Der Tod in Venedig». 165 Seiten. 1978.

Bd. 10 Steven R. Fischer: The Dream in the Middle High German Epic – Introduction to the Study of the Dream as a Literary Device to the Younger Contemporaries of Gottfried and Wolfram. 187 Seiten. 1978.

Bd. 11 Sybil Hitchman: The World as Theatre in the Works of Franz Grillparzer. 246 Seiten. 1979.

Bd. 12 Roger Hillman: Zeitroman – The Novel and Society in Germany 1830–1900. 186 Seiten. 1983.

Bd. 13 Gregory B. Triffitt: Kafka's «Landarzt» Collection – Rhetoric and Interpretation. 236 Seiten. 1985.

Bd. 14 Peter H. Oettli: Tradition and Creativity – The Engelhard of Konrad von Würzburg. Its Structure and its Sources. 194 Seiten. 1986.

Bd. 15 G. Schulz / T. Mehigan / M. Adams: Literatur und Geschichte 1788–1988. 350 Seiten. 1990.

Bd. 16 Rachel Jakobowicz: Jews and Gentiles – Anti-Semitism and Jewish Assimilation in German Literary Life in the Early 19th Century. 164 Seiten. 1992.

Bd. 17 Rodney W. Fisher: Heinrich von Veldeke: «Eneas» – A Comparison with the «Roman d'Eneas» and a Translation into English. 201 Seiten. 1992.

Bd. 18 David Scott: Metaphor as Thought in Elias Canetti's «Masse und Macht». 206 Seiten. 1999.

Bd. 19 Geoff Wilkes: Hans Fallada's Crisis Novels 1931–1947. 165 Seiten. 2002.

Bd. 20 Richard Millington: Snow from Broken Eyes. 341 Seiten. 2012.